SFML Game Development
By Example

Create and develop exciting games from start to finish
using SFML

Raimondas Pupius

BIRMINGHAM - MUMBAI

SFML Game Development By Example

First published: December 2015

Production reference: 1181215

Published by Packt Publishing Ltd.
Livery Place
35 Livery Street
Birmingham B3 2PB, UK.

ISBN 978-1-78528-734-3

www.packtpub.com

Credits

Author
Raimondas Pupius

Reviewers
Tom Ivanyo
Vittorio Romeo
Richa Sachdeva

Commissioning Editor
Dipika Gaonkar

Acquisition Editors
Prachi Bisht
Usha Iyer

Content Development Editor
Mamata Walker

Technical Editor
Pramod Kumavat

Copy Editors
Ting Baker
Kevin McGowan

Project Coordinator
Sanjeet Rao

Proofreader
Safis Editing

Indexer
Priya Sane

Graphics
Kirk D'Penha

Production Coordinator
Aparna Bhagat

Cover Work
Aparna Bhagat

About the Author

Raimondas Pupius is a game development enthusiast from Lithuania. He is currently working towards getting a degree in software engineering as well as working on a few projects of his own. Starting his unofficial education in this field at the age of 9, and having been introduced to video games even prior to that, helped narrow down his decision regarding a career choice. His ultimate dream is, of course, starting his own company and creating professional games for a living. "It beats my previous choice of being a plumber when I was four years old!" he says jokingly.

His other interests include web development, which was his primary interest before game development, music, and linguistics.

First, I would like to express my deepest thanks to Usha Iyer for offering me the opportunity to write this book and bringing me on board. In addition to that, I would like to thank Prachi Bisht, Mamata Walkar, and Pramod Kumavat for being great to work with and handling the production duties.

Lastly, I would like to thank my mom, grandmother, my beautiful wife, as well as her entire family for showing me endless love and support throughout this entire ordeal. I wouldn't be where I am today without your kindness, understanding, and patience during my late-night binge writing. This book is dedicated to you!

About the Reviewers

Tom Ivanyo is an aspiring game and software developer. After learning Visual Basic, he picked up several other languages, from Assembly to C#. Currently, he is working as a software developer and spending his free time creating games along with his friend, Doug Madden. Together, they started their small gaming studio named S2D Games (http://s2dgames.com).

Vittorio Romeo is a computer science student at the University of Messina and a C++ enthusiast. Since childhood, he has been interested in computers, gaming, and programming. He learned to develop games and applications as an autodidact at a very young age. He started with the VB/C# and the .NET environment, and moved on to C++ and native cross-platform programming. He works on his open source general-purpose C++14 libraries in his spare time and develops open source free games using SFML2. The evolution of C++ is something that greatly interests him. He has also spoken about game development with the latest standard features at CppCon 2014.

Richa Sachdeva is an avid programmer. She believes in designing games that are high on educational content as well as entertainment and is giving her two cents towards creating and exploring different dimensions in the field of game programming. She is a physics graduate who somewhere along the line found her true calling in computers and has ever since been amazed by this strange pixilated world. When not thinking about games or deciding on which movie to watch, she finds solace in writing.

www.PacktPub.com

Support files, eBooks, discount offers, and more

For support files and downloads related to your book, please visit www.PacktPub.com.

Did you know that Packt offers eBook versions of every book published, with PDF and ePub files available? You can upgrade to the eBook version at www.PacktPub.com and as a print book customer, you are entitled to a discount on the eBook copy. Get in touch with us at service@packtpub.com for more details.

At www.PacktPub.com, you can also read a collection of free technical articles, sign up for a range of free newsletters and receive exclusive discounts and offers on Packt books and eBooks.

https://www2.packtpub.com/books/subscription/packtlib

Do you need instant solutions to your IT questions? PacktLib is Packt's online digital book library. Here, you can search, access, and read Packt's entire library of books.

Why subscribe?

- Fully searchable across every book published by Packt
- Copy and paste, print, and bookmark content
- On demand and accessible via a web browser

Free access for Packt account holders

If you have an account with Packt at www.PacktPub.com, you can use this to access PacktLib today and view 9 entirely free books. Simply use your login credentials for immediate access.

Table of Contents

Preface

Game development is one of the most interesting career choices to date. Apart from the many other fields that are incorporated in this process, it's also a realm where pure imagination comes to life. Even during the times when one may think that there's nothing new under the sun, ground-breaking ideas are still cemented in this medium, both as revolutionary milestones and exciting adventures that will make us feel child-like excitement yet again.

Getting started with game programming is easier now than ever before! Documentation and tutorials aside, there even exist enthusiasts out there who actually put together libraries of code that can be used to eliminate the redundant or difficult parts of building different types of applications. As it so happens, one of these libraries is titled "Simple and Fast Multimedia Library", and it is the focal point of this publication.

Throughout the course of this book, three projects are built from scratch, with each one having increased complexity compared to its preceding project. We will start with a basic clone of the classical arcade game — *Snake*, which introduces the basics of SFML and some of the framework that is going to persist until the very end. As difficult subjects are addressed, we will begin to cobble the second project together, turning it into a side-scrolling platformer. The remaining chapters of this book focus on building and polishing an online RPG-style game that can be played with your friends! No detail of any of these projects will remain undiscussed, as you will be guided through the entire process of planning and implementing every single aspect of these projects.

If the vast array of features that need to be worked on hasn't scared you away yet, congratulations! You are about to embark on a journey of tremendous proportions. So don't let the odds intimidate you. We hope to see you at the finish line!

What this book covers

Chapter 1, It's Alive! It's Alive! – Setup and First Program, covers the fundamentals that are necessary in order to build basic SFML applications.

Chapter 2, Give It Some Structure – Building the Game Framework, introduces a better framework for the applications that will be used throughout the book. It also covers the basics of timing in video games.

Chapter 3, Get Your Hands Dirty – What You Need to Know, helps solidify all the information from the previous chapters by finishing our first game project.

Chapter 4, Grab That Joystick – Input and Event Management, elaborates on the process of obtaining a window event and peripheral information as well as using it in an automated way.

Chapter 5, Can I Pause This? – Application States, addresses the issue of state switching and blending using a state machine.

Chapter 6, Set It in Motion! – Animating and Moving around Your World, deals with the issues of screen scrolling and resource management as well as the usage and animation of sprite sheets.

Chapter 7, Rediscovering Fire – Common Game Design Elements, wraps up the second project of the book by dealing with entity management, tile-maps, and collision.

Chapter 8, The More You Know – Common Game Programming Patterns, introduces the third project of the book by covering the fundamentals of a few common programming patterns, including the entity component system.

Chapter 9, A Breath of Fresh Air – Entity Component System Continued, focuses on building common game functionality by breaking it down to its components and systems.

Chapter 10, Can I Click This? – GUI Fundamentals, breaks down how a graphical user interface can be implemented using the fundamental data types.

Chapter 11, Don't Touch the Red Button! – Implementing the GUI, picks up where the previous chapter left off and wraps up the implementation of a GUI system. We also discuss three basic element types.

Chapter 12, Can You Hear Me Now? – Sound and Music, livens up the third project of the book by bringing entity sounds and music to the table.

Chapter 13, We Have Contact! – Networking Basics, covers all the basics that are required in order to implement networking in our final project.

Chapter 14, Come Play with Us! – Multiplayer Subtleties, transforms the final project of the book into a multiplayer RPG-style death match with the application of a client-server network model as well as a combat system.

What you need for this book

Given that this book covers the SFML library, it's necessary to have it downloaded and set up. *Chapter 1, It's Alive! It's Alive! – Setup and First Program* covers this process step by step.

Additionally, a compiler or an IDE that supports *C++11* is needed in order to compile the code that we're about to write. The code for the book has been written on and compiled with the *Microsoft Visual Studio 2013* IDE on a system that runs *Windows 7*.

Who this book is for

This book is intended for game development enthusiasts who have at least a decent knowledge of the C++ programming language and an optional background in game design.

Conventions

In this book, you will find a number of text styles that distinguish between different kinds of information. Here are some examples of these styles and an explanation of their meaning.

Code words in text, database table names, folder names, filenames, file extensions, pathnames, dummy URLs, user input, and Twitter handles are shown as follows: "We can include other contexts through the use of the `include` directive."

A block of code is set as follows:

```
#include <SFML/Graphics.hpp>

void main(int argc, char** argv[]){

}
```

When we wish to draw your attention to a particular part of a code block, the relevant lines or items are set in bold:

```
#include <SFML/Graphics.hpp>

void main(int argc, char** argv[]){

}
```

New terms and **important words** are shown in bold. Words that you see on the screen, for example, in menus or dialog boxes, appear in the text like this: "Navigate to the **VC++ Directories** underneath **Configuration Properties** by right clicking on our project and selecting **Properties**."

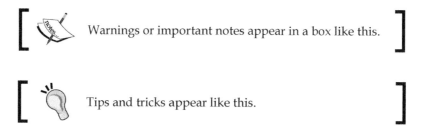

Warnings or important notes appear in a box like this.

Tips and tricks appear like this.

Reader feedback

Feedback from our readers is always welcome. Let us know what you think about this book—what you liked or disliked. Reader feedback is important for us as it helps us develop titles that you will really get the most out of.

To send us general feedback, simply e-mail feedback@packtpub.com, and mention the book's title in the subject of your message.

If there is a topic that you have expertise in and you are interested in either writing or contributing to a book, see our author guide at www.packtpub.com/authors.

Customer support

Now that you are the proud owner of a Packt book, we have a number of things to help you to get the most from your purchase.

Downloading the example code

You can download the example code files from your account at `http://www.packtpub.com` for all the Packt Publishing books you have purchased. If you purchased this book elsewhere, you can visit `http://www.packtpub.com/support` and register to have the files e-mailed directly to you.

Errata

Although we have taken every care to ensure the accuracy of our content, mistakes do happen. If you find a mistake in one of our books—maybe a mistake in the text or the code—we would be grateful if you could report this to us. By doing so, you can save other readers from frustration and help us improve subsequent versions of this book. If you find any errata, please report them by visiting `http://www.packtpub.com/submit-errata`, selecting your book, clicking on the **Errata Submission Form** link, and entering the details of your errata. Once your errata are verified, your submission will be accepted and the errata will be uploaded to our website or added to any list of existing errata under the Errata section of that title.

To view the previously submitted errata, go to `https://www.packtpub.com/books/content/support` and enter the name of the book in the search field. The required information will appear under the **Errata** section.

Piracy

Piracy of copyrighted material on the Internet is an ongoing problem across all media. At Packt, we take the protection of our copyright and licenses very seriously. If you come across any illegal copies of our works in any form on the Internet, please provide us with the location address or website name immediately so that we can pursue a remedy.

Please contact us at `copyright@packtpub.com` with a link to the suspected pirated material.

We appreciate your help in protecting our authors and our ability to bring you valuable content.

Questions

If you have a problem with any aspect of this book, you can contact us at `questions@packtpub.com`, and we will do our best to address the problem.

1
It's Alive! It's Alive! – Setup and First Program

The proud feeling of building something is a powerful one. Coupled with the thrill of exploration, it hardly makes it difficult to narrow down why most of our fellow game developers do what they do. Although creation is a major force in this process, failure governs it, much like any other subject. Sooner or later, all of us will be placed in a situation where a brick wall not only derails the development of a given project, but maybe even kills the motivation to work on it. Having a good resource to fall back on is crucial during those times, especially for new developers who are just now getting their hands dirty, and that's where we come in. Our goal is to pass on the experience in the most hands-on approach by developing real projects during the course of this book.

In this chapter, we're going to be covering:

- Setting up SFML on your machine and IDE
- Flow of an average SFML application
- Opening and managing windows
- Basics of rendering

The purpose of this chapter is to ease you into the process of developing games using **Simple and Fast Multimedia Library** (**SFML**). Let's get started by first tackling the setup process!

What is SFML?

Before we start throwing terms and code your way, it's only fair we talk a little bit about the choice library for this book. As its title clearly states, SFML is a library, which speeds up and eases the process of developing applications that rely on extensive use of media content, such as video, text, still images, audio, and animation for interactivity, and we will be focusing on a specific category of those applications, that is, video games. It provides an easy to use **application programming interface (API)**, compiles and runs out of the box on Windows, Linux, and Mac OS X, and is supported by multiple languages, such as C, .NET, C++, Java, Ruby, Python, and Go, just to name a few. Unofficial ports for certain mobile devices do exist out there, however official releases for mobile platforms are still in the works. It's also open source, so one can always go and look at the source code if one is so inclined. In this book, we will be focusing solely on development for the *Windows* platform using *C++11*.

For convenience, SFML is split into five modules, which are independent of one another and can be included on a need-to-use basis:

- **System**: A core module, which defines most basic data structures, provides access to threads, clocks, user data streams, and other essentials.

- **Window**: This module provides a means of creating and managing a window, gathering user input and events, as well as using SFML alongside OpenGL.

- **Graphics**: Everything left to be desired graphically after fully utilizing the window module falls back on the graphics module. It deals with everything concerning two-dimensional rendering.

- **Audio**: Anything to do with playing music, sounds, audio streams, or recording audio is handled by this module.

- **Network**: The last but definitely not the least interesting module that covers sending data to other computers as well as working with a few networking protocols.

Each one of these modules is compiled in a separate library (.lib) with specific postfixes that signify whether the library is being linked *statically* or *dynamically*, as well as if it's being built in *debug* or *release* mode. Linking a library statically simply means that it gets included in the executable, as opposed to dynamic linking, where .dll files are required to be present in order for the application to run. The latter situation reduces the overall size of the application by relying on the library being present on the machine that runs it. It also means that the library can be upgraded without the need to alter the application, which can be useful when fixing bugs. Static linking, on the other hand, allows your code to be executed in environments that are more limited.

It's also important to make sure that your application is being built in a mode that's suitable for the situation. Debug mode applications are bloated with additional information that is useful when you're hunting down flaws in your programs. This makes the application run considerably slower and shouldn't be used for any other purposes than testing. When building your project in release mode, tons of different optimizations are also turned on, which not only provides a smaller executable footprint, but also a much faster running speed. This should be the mode an application is compiled in, if it is to be released for any kind of use other than debugging.

Each module is named according to the format `sfml-module[-s][-d].lib`. For example, the file name of a graphics library that is being linked statically and compiled in debug mode would look like this: `sfml-graphics-s-d.lib`. When linking dynamically or compiling in release mode, the postfixes need to be omitted. SFML also requires the `SFML_STATIC` macro to be defined when linking statically, which we will cover shortly when setting up our first project.

An important thing to keep in mind about the separate libraries is that they still have dependencies. Window, graphics, audio, and network libraries are dependent on the system library, which has to be linked to for any SFML application to compile and run. The graphics library is also dependent on the window library, so all three have to be linked to if an application does any drawing. The audio and networking libraries only depend on the system library.

Since version 2.2, when linking SFML statically, its dependencies must also be linked to the project. These dependencies vary between major versions 2.2 and 2.3, so we're going to stick with the newest version, that is, 2.3. The graphics library requires `opengl32.lib`, `freetype.lib`, and `jpeg.lib` libraries. The window library depends on `opengl32.lib`, `winmm.lib`, and `gdi32.lib`. Linking to the system library only requires the `winmm.lib` library, while `sfml-network-s.lib` relies on `ws2_32.lib` in order to work. Lastly, the sound library depends on `openal32.lib`, `flac.lib`, `vorbisenc.lib`, `vorbisfile.lib`, `vorbis.lib`, and `ogg.lib`.

Each one of these five modules has a corresponding header that must be included to utilize its functionality. For example, including the graphics header would look like this:

```
#include <SFML/Graphics.hpp>
```

It is also possible to avoid including the entire module header by specifying the actual header that is desired within a module:

```
#include <SFML/Graphics/Color.hpp>
```

This gives you a chance to include only the parts that are absolutely necessary.

 It's best practice to use forward slashes when including libraries. Different operating systems do not recognize paths that have a backslash in them.

SFML licensing

Whenever you're utilizing a library of any sorts for your project, it's important to know what you can and cannot use it for. SFML is licensed under the zlib/libpng license, which is far from being restrictive. It allows anyone to use SFML for any purposes, even commercial applications, as well as alter and re-distribute it, given that the credit for writing the original software is left unchanged and the product is marked as an altered source. Giving credit for using the original software isn't required, but it would be appreciated. For more information, visit: `http://opensource.org/licenses/Zlib`.

Resources and installation

You can download the latest stable pre-built version of the library at: `http://www.sfml-dev.org/download.php`. It is also possible for you to get the latest Git revision and compile it yourself from here: `https://github.com/LaurentGomila/SFML`. The former option is easier and recommended for beginners. You have to wait for major versions to be released, however they're more stable. To build SFML yourself, you will need to use CMake, which is a tool used to generate solutions or g++ Makefiles, depending on the software that will be used to compile it. The official SFML website provides tutorials on building it yourself at: `http://www.sfml-dev.org/tutorials`.

After either obtaining the pre-built version of SFML or compiling it yourself, it's a good idea to move it somewhere more permanent, hopefully with a short path. It's not unusual to dedicate a directory somewhere on your local drive that will hold SFML and potentially other libraries, which can be linked to quickly and at all times. This becomes useful when dealing with several versions of the same library as well. For the rest of this book, we will assume the location of our SFML library and header directories to be at `C:\libs\SFML-2.3`, consequently being `C:\libs\SFML-2.3\lib` and `C:\libs\SFML-2.3\include`. These directories have to be set up correctly in your compiler of choice for the project to build. We will be using Microsoft Visual Studio 2013 throughout the course of this book, however instructions on setting up projects for Code::Blocks can be found in the tutorials section of the SFML website.

Setting up a Microsoft Visual Studio project

Create a new solution in your IDE. It can be a Win32 application or a console application, which is not really relevant, although a nice console window is often useful for debug purposes. I always go with the Empty Project option to avoid any auto-generated code. After that's done, let's prepare our project to use SFML:

1. Navigate to the **VC++ Directories** underneath **Configuration Properties** by right clicking on our project and selecting **Properties**.

2. Only two fields are of any concern to us, the **Include Directories** and **Library Directories**. Make sure the paths to the SFML library and include directories are provided for both **Debug** and **Release** configurations.

3. When linking SFML *statically*, the **Preprocessor** section underneath C/C++ is where you need to define the SFML_STATIC macro.

4. Next is the **Additional Library Directories** in **General** underneath **Linker**. Make sure that it also points to the SFML library directory in both debug and release configurations.

5. Lastly, we need to set up the project dependencies by editing the **Additional Dependencies** field in the **Input** section underneath **Linker**. It would look something like this for the debug configuration when using statically linked libraries: `sfml-graphics-s-d.lib; sfml-window-s-d.lib; sfml-system-s-d.lib; opengl32.lib; freetype.lib; jpeg.lib; winmm.lib; gdi32.lib;`

   Remember that we need to include the system library because of library dependencies. Also note the use of `-s` and `-d` postfixes. Make sure both debug and release configurations are set up and that the release configuration omits the `-d` postfix.

Opening a window

As you probably know, drawing something on screen requires a window to be present. Luckily, SFML allows us to easily open and manage our very own window! Let's start out as usual by adding a file to our project, named `Main.cpp`. This will be the entry point to our application. The bare bones of a basic application look like this:

```cpp
#include <SFML/Graphics.hpp>

void main(int argc, char** argv[]){

}
```

Note that we've already included the SFML graphics header. This will provide us with everything needed to open a window and draw to it, so without further ado, let's take a look at the code that opens our window:

```
#include <SFML/Graphics.hpp>

void main(int argc, char** argv[]){
  sf::RenderWindow window(sf::VideoMode(640,480),
    "First window!");

  while(window.isOpen()){
    sf::Event event;
    while(window.pollEvent(event)){
      if(event.type == sf::Event::Closed){
        // Close window button clicked.
        window.close();
      }
    }
    window.clear(sf::Color::Black);
    // Draw here.
    window.display();
  }
}
```

 SFML uses the sf *namespace*, so we have to prefix its data types, enumerations, and static class members with an "sf::".

The first thing we did here is declare and initialize our window instance of type RenderWindow. In this case, we used its constructor, however it is possible to leave it blank and utilize its create method later on by passing in the exact same arguments, of which it can take as little as two: an sf::videoMode and an std::string title for the window. The video mode's constructor takes two arguments: the inner window width and height. There is a third optional argument that sets color depth in bits per pixel. It defaults to 32, which is more than enough for good rendering fitting our purposes, so let's not lose sleep over that now.

After the instance of our window is created, we enter a while loop that utilizes one of our window methods to check if it's still open, isOpen. This effectively creates our game loop, which is a central piece of all of our code.

Let's take a look at a diagram of a typical game:

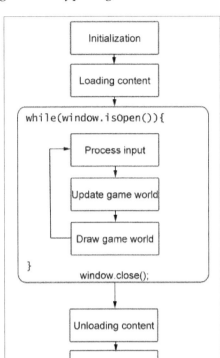

The purpose of a game loop is to check for events and input, update our game world between frames, which means moving the player, enemies, checking for changes, and so on, and finally draw everything on the screen. This process needs to be repeated many times a second until the window is closed. The amount of times varies from application to application, sometimes going as high as thousands of iterations per second. *Chapter 2, Give It Some Structure - Building the Game Framework* will cover managing and capping the frame rate of our applications as well as making the game run at constant speeds.

Most applications need to have a way to check if a window has been closed, resized, or moved. That's where event processing comes in. SFML provides an event class that we can use to store our event information. During each *iteration* of our game loop, we need to check for the events that took place by utilizing the `pollEvent` method of our window instance and process them. In this case, we're only interested in the event that gets dispatched when a mouse clicks on the close window button. We can check if the public member `type` of class `Event` matches the proper enumeration member, in this case it's `sf::Event::Closed`. If it does, we can call the `close` method of our window instance and our program will terminate.

Events must be processed in all SFML applications. Without the event loop polling events, the window will become unresponsive, since it not only provides the event information to the user, but also gives the window itself a way to handle its internal events as well, which is a necessity for it to react to being moved or resized.

After all of that is done, it's necessary to clear the window from the previous iteration. Failing to do so would result in everything we draw on it stacking and creating a mess. Imagine the screen is a whiteboard and you want to draw something new on it after someone else already scribbled all over it. Instead of grabbing the eraser, however, we need to call the `clear` method of our window instance, which takes a `sf::Color` data type as an argument and defaults to the color black if an argument isn't provided. The screen can be cleared to any of its enumerated colors that the `sf::Color` class provides as static members or we can pass an instance of `sf::Color`, which has a constructor that takes *unsigned integer* values for individual color channels: red, green, blue, and optionally alpha. The latter gives us a way to explicitly specify the color of our desired range, like so:

```
window.clear(sf::Color(0,0,0,255));
```

Finally, we call the `window.display()` method to show everything that was drawn. This utilizes a technique known as double buffering, which is standard in games nowadays. Basically, anything that is drawn isn't drawn on the screen instantly, but instead to a hidden buffer which then gets copied to our window once `display` is called. Double buffering is used to prevent graphical artifacts, such as tearing, which occurs due to video card drivers pulling from the frame buffer while it's still being written to, resulting in a partially drawn image being displayed. Calling the `display` method is mandatory and cannot be avoided, otherwise the window will show up as a static square with no changes taking place.

Remember to include SFML library `.dll` files in the same directory as your executable relies, provided the application has been dynamically linked.

Upon compilation and execution of the code, we will find ourselves with a blank console window and a black *640x480 px* window sitting over it, fewer than 20 lines of code, and an open window. Not very exciting, but it's still better than *E.T.* for *Atari 2600*. Let's draw something on the screen!

Basics of SFML drawing

Much like in kindergarten, we will start with basic shapes and make our way up to more complex types. Let's work on rendering a rectangle shape by first declaring it and setting it up:

```
sf::RectangleShape rectangle(sf::Vector2f(128.0f,128.0f));
rectangle.setFillColor(sf::Color::Red);
rectangle.setPosition(320,240);
```

`sf::RectangleShape` is a derived class of `sf::Shape` that inherits from `sf::Drawable`, which is an abstract base class that all entities must inherit from and implement its virtual methods in order to be able to be drawn on screen. It also inherits from `sf::Transformable`, which provides all the necessary functionality in order to move, scale, and rotate an entity. This relationship allows our rectangle to be transformed, as well as rendered to the screen. In its constructor, we've introduced a new data type: `sf::Vector2f`. It's essentially just a struct of two *floats*, x and y, that represent a point in a two-dimensional universe, not to be confused with the `std::vector`, which is a data container.

> SFML provides a few other vector types for integers and unsigned integers: `sf::Vector2i` and `sf::Vector2u`. The actual `sf::Vector2` class is templated, so any primitive data type can be used with it like so:
>
> ```
> sf::Vector2<long> m_vector;
> ```

The rectangle constructor takes a single argument of `sf::Vector2f` which represents the size of the rectangle in pixels and is optional. On the second line, we set the fill color of the rectangle by providing one of SFML's predefined colors this time. Lastly, we set the position of our shape by calling the `setPosition` method and passing its position in pixels alongside the *x* and *y* axis, which in this case is the centre of our window. There is only one more thing missing until we can draw the rectangle:

```
window.draw(rectangle); // Render our shape.
```

This line goes right before we call `window.display();` and is responsible for bringing our shape to the screen. Let's run our revised application and take a look at the result:

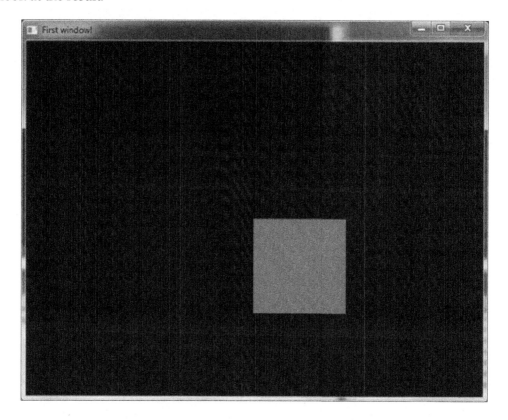

Now we have a red square drawn on the screen, but it's not quite centered. This is because the default origin of any `sf::Transformable`, which is just a 2D point that represents the global position of the object, is at the local coordinates *(0,0)*, which is the top left corner. In this case, it means that the top left corner of this rectangle is set to the position of the screen centre. That can easily be resolved by calling the `setOrigin` method and passing in the desired local coordinates of our shape that will represent the new origin, which we want to be right in the middle:

```
rectangle.setOrigin(64.0f,64.0f);
```

If the size of a shape is unknown for whatever reason, the rectangle class provides a nice method `getSize`, which returns a *float vector* containing the size:

```
rectangle.setOrigin(rectangle.getSize().x / 2, rectangle.getSize().y /
2);
```

Now our shape is sitting happily in the very middle of the black screen. The entire segment of code that makes this possible looks a little something like this:

```
#include <SFML/Graphics.hpp>

void main(int argc, char** argv[]){
  sf::RenderWindow window(sf::VideoMode(640,480),
    "Rendering the rectangle.");

  // Creating our shape.
  sf::RectangleShape rectangle(sf::Vector2f(128.0f,128.0f));
  rectangle.setFillColor(sf::Color::Red);
  rectangle.setPosition(320,240);
  rectangle.setOrigin(rectangle.getSize().x / 2,
    rectangle.getSize().y / 2);

  while(window.isOpen()){
    sf::Event event;
    while(window.pollEvent(event)){
      if(event.type == sf::Event::Closed){
        // Close window button clicked.
        window.close();
      }
    }
    window.clear(sf::Color::Black);
    window.draw(rectangle); // Drawing our shape.
    window.display();
  }
}
```

Drawing images in SFML

In order to draw an image on screen, we need to become familiar with two classes: `sf::Texture` and `sf::Sprite`. A texture is essentially just an image that lives on the graphics card for the purpose of making it fast to draw. Any given picture on your hard drive can be turned into a texture by loading it:

```
sf::Texture texture;
if(!texture.loadFromFile("filename.png")){
    // Handle an error.
}
```

The `loadFromFile` method returns a Boolean value, which serves as a simple way of handling loading errors, such as the file not being found. If you have a console window open along with your SFML window, you will notice some information being printed out in case the texture loading did fail:

Failed to load image "filename.png". Reason : Unable to open file

Unless a full path is specified in the `loadFromFile` method, it will be interpreted as relative to the working directory. It's important to note that while the working directory is usually the same as the executable's when launching it by itself, compiling and running your application in an IDE (Microsoft Visual Studio in our case) will often set it to the project directory instead of the debug or release folders. Make sure to put the resources you're trying to load in the same directory where your `.vcxproj` project file is located if you've provided a relative path.

It's also possible to load your textures from memory, custom input streams, or `sf::Image` utility classes, which help store and manipulate image data as raw pixels, which will be covered more broadly in later chapters.

What is a sprite?

A sprite, much like the `sf::Shape` derivatives we've worked with so far, is a `sf::Drawable` object, which in this case represents a `sf::Texture` and also supports a list of transformations, both physical and graphical. Think of it as a simple rectangle with a texture applied to it:

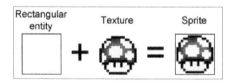

`sf::Sprite` provides the means of rendering a texture, or a part of it, on screen, as well as means of transforming it, which makes the sprite dependent on the use of textures. Since `sf::Texture` isn't a lightweight object, `sf::Sprite` comes in for performance reasons to use the pixel data of a texture it's bound to, which means that as long as a sprite is using the texture it's bound to, the texture has to be alive in memory and can only be de-allocated once it's no longer being used. After we have our texture set up, it's really easy to set up the sprite and draw it:

```
sf::Sprite sprite(texture);
...
window.draw(sprite);
```

It's optional to pass the texture by reference to the sprite constructor. The texture it's bound to can be changed at any time by using the `setTexture` method:

```
sprite.setTexture(texture);
```

Since `sf::Sprite`, just like `sf::Shape`, inherits from `sf::Transformable`, we have access to the same methods of manipulating and obtaining origin, position, scale, and rotation.

It's time to apply all the knowledge we've gained so far and write a basic application that utilizes it:

```
void main(int argc, char** argv[]){
    sf::RenderWindow window(sf::VideoMode(640,480),
        "Bouncing mushroom.");

    sf::Texture mushroomTexture;
    mushroomTexture.loadFromFile("Mushroom.png");
    sf::Sprite mushroom(mushroomTexture);
    sf::Vector2u size = mushroomTexture.getSize();
    mushroom.setOrigin(size.x / 2, size.y / 2);
    sf::Vector2f increment(0.4f, 0.4f);

    while(window.isOpen()){
        sf::Event event;
        while(window.pollEvent(event)){
            if(event.type == sf::Event::Closed){
                window.close();
            }
        }

        if((mushroom.getPosition().x + (size.x / 2) >
            window.getSize().x && increment.x > 0) ||
            (mushroom.getPosition().x - (size.x / 2) < 0 &&
            increment.x < 0))
        {
            // Reverse the direction on X axis.
            increment.x = -increment.x;
        }

        if((mushroom.getPosition().y + (size.y / 2) >
            window.getSize().y && increment.y > 0) ||
            (mushroom.getPosition().y - (size.y / 2) < 0 &&
            increment.y < 0))
        {
```

```
            // Reverse the direction on Y axis.
            increment.y = -increment.y;
        }

        mushroom.setPosition(mushroom.getPosition() + increment);

        window.clear(sf::Color(16,16,16,255)); // Dark gray.
        window.draw(mushroom); // Drawing our sprite.
        window.display();
    }
}
```

The code above will produce a sprite bouncing around the window, reversing in direction every time it hits the window boundaries. Error checking for loading the texture is omitted in this case in order to keep the code shorter. The two `if` statements after the event handling portion in the main loop are responsible for checking the current position of our sprite and updating the direction of the increment value represented by a plus or minus sign, since you can only go towards the positive or negative end on a single axis. Remember that the origin of a shape by default is its top-left corner, as shown here:

Because of this, we must either compensate for the entire width and height of a shape when checking if it's out-of-bounds on the bottom or the right side, or make sure its origin is in the middle. In this case, we do the latter and either add or subtract half of the texture's size from the mushroom's position to check if it is still within our desired space. If it's not, simply invert the sign of the increment float vector on the axis that is outside the screen and voila! We have bouncing!

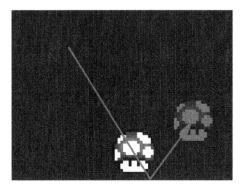

For extra credit, feel free to play around with the `sf::Sprite`'s `setColor` method, which can be used to tint a sprite with a desired color, as well as make it transparent, by adjusting the fourth argument of the `sf::Color` type, which corresponds to the alpha channel:

```
mushroom.setColor(sf::Color(255, 0, 0, 255)); // Red tint.
```

Common mistakes

Oftentimes, new users of SFML attempt to do something like this:

```
sf::Sprite CreateSprite(std::string l_path){
    sf::Texture texture;
    texture.loadFromFile(l_path);
    . . .
    return sf::Sprite(texture);
}
```

When attempting to draw the returned sprite, a white square pops out where the sprite is supposed to be located. What happened? Well, take a look back at the section where we covered textures. The texture needs to be within scope as long as it's being used by a sprite because it stores a pointer to the texture instance. From the example above, we can see that it is *statically allocated*, so when the function returns, the texture that got allocated on the stack is now out of scope and gets popped. Poof. Gone. Now the sprite is pointing to an invalid resource that it cannot use and instead draws a white rectangle. Now this is not to say that you can't just allocate memory on the heap instead by making a new call, but that's not the point of this example. The point to take away from this is that proper resource management is paramount when it comes to any application, so pay attention to the life span of your resources. In *Chapter 6, Set It in Motion! – Animating and Moving around Your World*, we will cover designing your own resource manager and automatically dealing with situations like this.

Another common mistake is keeping too many texture instances around. A single texture can be used by as many sprites as one's heart desires. `sf::Texture` is not a lightweight object at all, where it's possible to keep tons of `sf::Sprite` instances using the same texture and still achieve great performance. Reloading textures is also expensive for the graphics card, so keeping as few textures as possible is one of the things you really need to remember if you want your application to run fast. That's the idea behind using tile sheets, which are just large textures with small images packed within them. This grants better performance, since instead of keeping around hundreds of texture instances and loading files one by one, we get to simply load a single texture and access any desired tile by specifying the area to read from. That will also receive more attention in later chapters.

Using unsupported image formats or format options is another fairly common issue. It's always best to consult the official website for the most up to date information on file format support. A short list can be found here: `http://www.sfml-dev.org/documentation/2.2/classsf_1_1Image.php#a9e4f2aa8e36d0cabde5ed5a4ef80290b`

Finally, the `LNK2019` errors deserve a mention. It doesn't matter how many times a guide, tutorial, or book mentions how to properly set up and link your project to any given library. Nothing is perfect in this world, especially not a human being. Your IDE output may get flooded by messages that look something like this when trying to compile your project:

```
error LNK2019: unresolved external symbol. . .
```

Do not panic, and please, don't make a new forum post somewhere posting hundreds of lines of code. You simply forgot to include all the required additional dependencies in the linker input. Revisit the part where we covered setting up the project for use with SFML and make sure that everything is correct there. Also, remember that you need to include libraries that other libraries are dependent on. For example, the system library always has to be included, the window library has to be included if the graphics module is being used, and so on. Statically linked libraries require their dependencies to be linked as well.

Summary

A lot of ground has been covered in this chapter. Some of it may be a little bit difficult to grasp at first if you're just starting, but don't be discouraged just yet. Applying this knowledge practically is the key to understanding it better. It's important that you are competent with everything that has been introduced so far before proceeding onto the next chapter.

If you can truly look throughout this chapter and say with utmost confidence that you're ready to move forward, we would like to congratulate you on taking your first major step towards becoming a successful SFML game developer! Why stop there? In the next chapter, we will be covering a better way to structure code for our first game project. On top of that, time management will be introduced and we'll practically apply everything covered so far by building a major chunk of your first, fully functional game. There's a lot of work ahead of us, so get the lead out! Your software isn't going to write itself.

2

Give It Some Structure – Building the Game Framework

Working on a project with poor structure is much like building a house with no foundation: it's difficult to maintain, extremely unstable, and will probably cause you to abandon it shortly. While the code we worked on in *Chapter 1, It's Alive! It's Alive! – Setup and First Program*, is functional and can be managed on a very small scale, expanding it without first building a solid framework would most likely result in tons of *spaghetti code* (not to be confused with ravioli code or lasagna code) being present. Although it sounds delicious, this pejorative term describes the pain of a new feature being exponentially more difficult to implement within the source code that is unstructured and executes in a "tangled" manner, which is something we'll be focusing on avoiding.

In this chapter we will cover:

- Designing a window class, along with a main game class
- Code restructuring and proper architecture
- The importance of proper time management in applications
- Using `sf::Clock` and `sf::Time` classes
- Fixed and variable time-steps

Graduating to ravioli

Let's start small. Every game needs to have a window, and as you already know from *Chapter 1, It's Alive! It's Alive! – Setup and First Program*, it needs to be created, destroyed, and its events need to be processed. It also needs to be able to clear the screen and update itself to show anything drawn after the screen was cleared. Additionally, keeping track of whether the window is being closed and if it's in full-screen mode, as well as having a method to toggle the latter would be quite useful. Lastly, we will, of course, need to draw to the window. Knowing all of that, the header of our window class will predictably look something like this:

```cpp
class Window{
public:
    Window();
    Window(const std::string& l_title,const sf::Vector2u& l_size);
    ~Window();

    void BeginDraw(); // Clear the window.
    void EndDraw(); // Display the changes.

    void Update();

    bool IsDone();
    bool IsFullscreen();
    sf::Vector2u GetWindowSize();

    void ToggleFullscreen();

    void Draw(sf::Drawable& l_drawable);
private:
    void Setup(const std::string& l_title,
      const sf::Vector2u& l_size);
    void Destroy();
    void Create();

    sf::RenderWindow m_window;
    sf::Vector2u m_windowSize;
    std::string m_windowTitle;
    bool m_isDone;
    bool m_isFullscreen;
};
```

Because we want to handle setting up our window internally, the setup method is made private, as well as the destroy and create methods. Think of these as just helper methods that the user of this class doesn't need to know about. It's a good idea to keep certain information around after the setup is done, such as the window size or the title that's being displayed above it. Lastly, we keep around two Boolean variables to keep track of the window being closed and its state regarding full screen.

> The naming convention that's being employed in our window class is referred to as the **Hungarian notation**. Using it is, of course, not required, but it can prove useful when dealing with lots of code, trying to track down bugs, and working in larger groups of people. We'll be utilizing it throughout this book. More information about it can be found here: http://en.wikipedia.org/wiki/Hungarian_notation

Implementing the window class

Now that we have our blueprint, let's begin actually building our window class. The entry and exit points seem as good a place as any to start with:

```
Window::Window(){ Setup("Window", sf::Vector2u(640,480)); }

Window::Window(const std::string& l_title,
  const sf::Vector2u& l_size)
{
    Setup(l_title,l_size);
}


Window::~Window(){ Destroy(); }
```

Both implementations of the constructor and destructor simply utilize the helper methods which we'll be implementing shortly. There's also a default constructor that takes no arguments and initializes some pre-set default values, which is not necessary, but it's convenient. With that said, let's take a look at the setup method:

```
void Window::Setup(const std::string l_title,
  const sf::Vector2u& l_size)
{
    m_windowTitle = l_title;
    m_windowSize = l_size;
    m_isFullscreen = false;
    m_isDone = false;
    Create();
}
```

Once again, this is quite simple. As mentioned before, it initializes and keeps track of some of the window properties that will be passed to the constructor. Aside from that, it calls another method named `Create` to break up the code even more, which is what we'll be implementing next in addition to the `Destroy` method:

```
void Window::Create(){
    auto style = (m_isFullscreen ? sf::Style::Fullscreen
        : sf::Style::Default);
    m_window.create({ m_windowSize.x, m_windowSize.y, 32 },
        m_windowTitle, style);
}

void Window::Destroy(){
    m_window.close();
}
```

Here, we introduce a new data type that SFML offers: `sf::Uint32`. It gets stored inside the `style` local variable, which is automatically deduced to said type by using the `auto` keyword. It's simply an unsigned, fixed size integer type. In this particular case, we're using the *32-bit* integer, although SFML offers both signed and unsigned types of *8*, *16*, and *32* bits. We use this value to hold the current style for a window using a *ternary operator* and assigning it to either the default or full screen styles of the window style enumeration. This is the full list of all possible window styles within SFML:

Enumerator	Description	Mutually exclusive
None	No border or title bar. The most minimalistic style.	Yes
Fullscreen	Full screen mode.	Yes
Titlebar	Title bar and a fixed border.	No
Close	Title bar and a close button.	No
Resize	Title bar, resizable border and a maximize button.	No
Default	Title bar, resizable border, maximize and close buttons.	No

The mutually exclusive column simply denotes whether the style in question can be used with other styles in tandem. For example, it is possible to have a window with a title bar, resizable border, the maximize button, and a close button by combining two styles together using the bitwise *or* operator in C++:

```
auto style = sf::Style::Resize | sf::Style::Close;
```

If, however, a style is mutually exclusive, it cannot be used with any other styles in this way.

Once we have our style, we can simply pass it to the `create` method of our window, in addition to the `sf::VideoMode` type that gets constructed, using uniform initialization. It's that simple.

The `destroy` method of our `Window` class will simply close the window by invoking its `close` method. It's important to note here that the closed window will have all of its attached resources destroyed, but you can still call its `create` method again to re-create the window. Polling events and calling the `display` method will still work if a window is closed. It will just have no effect.

Let's proceed in breaking up our once solid chunk of code by processing the events of the window in the appropriate `update` method:

```
void Window::Update(){
    sf::Event event;
    while(m_window.pollEvent(event)){
        if(event.type == sf::Event::Closed){
            m_isDone = true;
        } else if(event.type == sf::Event::KeyPressed &&
            event.key.code == sf::Keyboard::F5)
        {
            ToggleFullscreen();
        }
    }
}
```

It's the same drill as before, we're simply handling events. Instead of closing the window right off the bat, however, we simply flip the Boolean flag we keep around for checking if the window has been closed or not: `m_isDone`. Since we're also interested in toggling between full screen and normal states of our window, we need to keep an eye out for another type of event: `sf::Event::KeyPressed`. This event gets dispatched whenever a keyboard key is pressed down and it includes information about that key stored in the `event.key` struct. For now, we're only interested in the code of the key being pressed, which we can then check against the `sf::Keyboard` enumeration table. Upon receiving an event of an *F5* key being pressed, we call the `ToggleFullscreen` method, which is fairly simple to implement now that we have broken up the code into manageable sections:

```
void Window::ToggleFullscreen(){
    m_isFullscreen = !m_isFullscreen;
    Destroy();
    Create();
}
```

As you can see, the only thing we do here is invert the value of our *Boolean* class member, m_isFullscreen, that keeps track of the window state. Afterwards, we need to destroy and re-create the window in order to make it honor our changes. Let's take a look at the drawing methods:

```
void Window::BeginDraw(){ m_window.clear(sf::Color::Black); }
void Window::EndDraw(){ m_window.display(); }
```

Nothing new gets introduced here. We're simply wrapping the functionality of clearing and displaying in BeginDraw and EndDraw methods. All that's left now are the simple helper methods:

```
bool Window::IsDone(){ return m_isDone; }
bool Window::IsFullscreen(){ return m_isFullscreen; }
sf::Vector2u Window::GetWindowSize(){ return m_windowSize; }

void Window::Draw(sf::Drawable&l_drawable){
    m_window.draw(l_drawable);
}
```

These basic methods provide the means for retrieving information about the window without giving too much control to anything outside the window class. For now, our window class is more than sufficient.

Building the game class

We've done a good job at wrapping up the basic functionality of our window class, but that's not the only chunk of code in need of refactoring. In *Chapter 1, It's Alive! It's Alive! – Setup and First Program*, we've discussed the main game loop and its contents, mainly processing input, updating the game world and the player, and finally, rendering everything on screen. Cramming all of that functionality into the game loop alone is generally known to produce spaghetti code, and since we want to move away from that, let's consider a better structure that would allow this kind of behavior:

```
#include "Game.h"

void main(int argc, void** argv[]){
    // Program entry point.
    Game game; // Creating our game object.
    while(!game.GetWindow()->IsDone()){
        // Game loop.
        game.HandleInput();
```

```
        game.Update();
        game.Render();
    }
}
```

The code above represents the *entire* content of our `main.cpp` file and perfectly illustrates the use of a properly structured game class, which doesn't go beyond calling the proper methods in the right order in an endless loop until the window is closed. Just for the sake of clarity, let's take a look at a simplified version of the game class header:

```
class Game{
public:
    Game();
    ~Game();

    void HandleInput();
    void Update();
    void Render();
    Window* GetWindow();
    ...
private:
    void MoveMushroom();
    Window m_window;
    ...
};
```

Note that the game class holds an instance of our window. It can be done differently, but for our current needs this will more than suffice.

Putting our code to work

We're now ready to re-implement the bouncing mushroom demo from *Chapter 1, It's Alive! It's Alive! – Setup and First Program*. Given how simple it is, we'll walk you through the entire process of adapting our previously written code to our new structure. Let's begin by setting up our window and graphics we'll be using:

```
Game::Game(): m_window("Chapter 2", sf::Vector2u(800,600)){
    // Setting up class members.
    m_mushroomTexture.loadFromFile("Mushroom.png");
    m_mushroom.setTexture(m_mushroomTexture);
    m_increment = sf::Vector2i(4,4);
}
```

Because we have nothing to clean up, our game destructor will remain empty for now:

```
Game::~Game(){}
```

We have no need to check for input for this example, so let's leave that method alone for now. What we will be doing, however, is updating the position of our sprite each frame:

```
void Game::Update(){
    m_window.Update(); // Update window events.
    MoveMushroom();
}
void Game::MoveMushroom(){
    sf::Vector2u l_windSize = m_window.GetWindowSize();
    sf::Vector2u l_textSize = m_mushroomTexture.getSize();

    if((m_mushroom.getPosition().x >
       l_windSize.x - l_textSize.x&&m_increment.x> 0) ||
       (m_mushroom.getPosition().x < 0 &&m_increment.x< 0)){
           m_increment.x = -m_increment.x;
    }

    if((m_mushroom.getPosition().y >
       l_windSize.y - l_textSize.y&&m_increment.y> 0) ||
       (m_mushroom.getPosition().y < 0 &&m_increment.y< 0)){
           m_increment.y = -m_increment.y;
    }

    m_mushroom.setPosition(
       m_mushroom.getPosition().x + m_increment.x,
       m_mushroom.getPosition().y + m_increment.y);
}
```

Literally the first thing you'll probably notice is the update method call of our window class. We've already covered the importance of *event processing* in SFML, but it's still worthy to note that one more time. The rest of the code is pretty much the same, except we now have a separate method that is responsible for updating the position of the mushroom sprite. We used two local variables to hold the window and texture sizes in order to increase readability, but that's about it. Time to draw our sprite to the screen:

```
void Game::Render(){
    m_window.BeginDraw(); // Clear.
```

```
    m_window.Draw(m_mushroom);
    m_window.EndDraw(); // Display.
}
```

Once again, the code is fairly straight forward. Our window class does all the work, and all we have to do is call the `Draw` method and pass in our `sf::Drawable` right in between the wrapper methods for clearing the screen and displaying the changes.

Putting everything together and running it should produce the exact same bouncing mushroom we had back in *Chapter 1, It's Alive! It's Alive! – Setup and First Program*. However, you may have noticed that the sprite moves differently based on how busy your computer is. In this observation lies an important lesson about game development.

Hardware and execution time

Let's travel back in time to May 5, 1992. Apogee Software begins publishing the now known cult classic *Wolfenstein 3D* developed by *id Software*:

The man with the vision, *John Carmack*, took massive strides forward and not only popularized, but also revolutionized the first person shooter genre on the PC. Its massive success cannot be overstated, as even now it's difficult to accurately predict how many times it has been downloaded. Having grown up at right around that time, one can't help but feel nostalgic sometimes and attempt to play this game again. Ever since its original release for the *DOS* operating system on the PC, it has been ported to many other operating systems and consoles. While it's still possible to play it, we've come a long way since the days of using DOS. The environment our software runs in has fundamentally changed, ergo the software from the past is no longer compatible, hence the need for emulation.

An **emulator** is either software, hardware, or the combination of both, that simulates the functionality of a certain system, usually referred to as a guest, on a primary system, referred to as the host.

Every emulator used for this purpose not only has to imitate the software of a system that would be compatible with a title you're attempting to play, but also the hardware. Why is that important? Most games in the days of DOS counted on the hardware being roughly similar. In the case of Wolfenstein 3D, it assumed it was running on a *4.77 MHz* system, which allowed the developers to save some clock cycles for the sake of efficiency by not writing internal timing loops. A game like Wolfenstein 3D consumed all of the processing power, which was a fine strategy for the time, until more powerful and faster processors came about. Today, the puny 4.77 MHz speed is dwarfed by comparison, even when looking at all of the cheapest consumer-grade processors, so proper emulation of a specific system also requires the reduction of CPU clock cycles, otherwise these games will run too fast, which is exactly what happens when an emulator is set up in the wrong way and doesn't throttle the speed enough.

While this is the most extreme example, speed management is an important component of any piece of software today that has to run at a constant speed. Different choices of hardware and architecture aside, your software might run faster or slower simply based on how busy your system is at the time or the different tasks your code needs to accomplish every iteration before the image is rendered. Consider the following illustration:

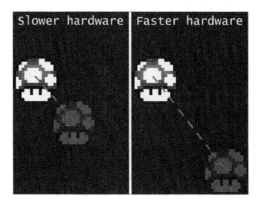

The changes on the left side as well as the right side both take place over a 1 second interval. The code is exactly the same in both cases. The only difference is the number of iterations the main loop manages to complete during that interval. Predictably, the slower hardware will take longer to execute your code and therefore will yield fewer iterations, resulting in the sprite being moved fewer times during our 1 second time interval and end up looking like the left side. As a game developer, it is important to ensure that your product runs the same on all systems within the designated specification guidelines. This is where SFML time management comes in.

Controlling the frame-rate

SFML provides a means of setting a frame-rate cap for your applications. It's a method in the `sf::RenderWindow` class, appropriately called `setFramerateLimit`:

```
m_window.setFramerateLimit(60); // 60 FPS cap.
```

Although this feature is not absolutely reliable, it ensures that the application's frame-rate is capped at the provided maximum value with reasonable precision, as long as the provided cap isn't too high. Keep in mind that capping the frame-rate reduces the overall CPU consumption of the program as well, since it doesn't need to update and re-draw the same scene as many times anymore. It does, however, raise a problem for slower hardware. If the frame-rate is lower than the provided value, the simulation will run slower too. Setting the limit solves only half of our problem. Let's take a look at something more practical. Enter `sf::Clock`!

Using the SFML clock

The `sf::Clock` class is very simple and lightweight, so it has only two methods: `getElapsedTime()` and `restart()`. Its sole purpose is to measure elapsed time since the last instance of the clock being restarted, or since its creation, in the most precise manner the operating system can provide. When retrieving the elapsed time using the `getElapsedTime` method, it returns a type `sf::Time`. The main reasoning behind that is an additional layer of abstraction to provide flexibility and avoid imposing any fixed data types. The `sf::Time` class is also lightweight and provides three useful methods for conversion of elapsed time to seconds which returns a *floating point* value, milliseconds, which returns a *32-bit integer* value and microseconds, which returns a *64-bit integer* value, as represented here:

```
sf::Clock clock;
...
sf::Time time = clock.getElapsedTime();
```

```
float seconds = time.asSeconds();
sf::Int32 milliseconds = time.asMilliseconds();
sf::Int64 microseconds = time.asMicroseconds();
...
time = clock.restart();
```

As you can see, the `restart` method also returns an `sf::Time` value. This is provided in order to avoid calling `getElapsedTime` right before calling the `restart` method and having some time pass between those two calls that would otherwise be unaccounted for. How is this useful for us? Well, the problem we were dealing with was the same code running differently on other platforms because we couldn't account for their speed. We moved our sprite across the screen using this line of code:

```
m_mushroom.setPosition(
    m_mushroom.getPosition().x + m_increment.x,
    m_mushroom.getPosition().y + m_increment.y);
```

The `m_increment` vector here is used with an assumption that the time between iterations is constant, but that's obviously not true. Recall the magic triangle for the speed, time, and distance formula:

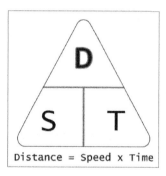

Distance = Speed x Time

Finding the distance a sprite should travel in between updates can be done by first defining a set speed at which it moves. The time value here is simply how long it takes for an entire cycle of the program to finish. In order to accurately measure that, we're going to be adjusting the `Game` class to utilize the `sf::Clock`:

```
class Game{
public:
...
    sf::Time GetElapsed();
    void RestartClock();
private:
...
```

```
    sf::Clock m_clock;
    sf::Time m_elapsed;
...
};
```

The two new public methods we've added can be implemented like so:

```
sf::Time Game::GetElapsed(){ return m_elapsed; }
void Game::RestartClock(){ m_elapsed = m_clock.restart(); }
```

Once that is done, it's important to actually utilize this functionality and restart the game clock after each iteration. That can be achieved in the main game loop by simply calling the `RestartClock` method after all the work is done:

```
while(!game.GetWindow()->IsDone()){
    // Game loop.
    game.HandleInput();
    game.Update();
    game.Render();
    game.RestartClock(); // Restarting our clock.
}
```

The last line in the loop will make sure that the `m_elapsed` member of the game class will always have a value of the time passed during the previous iteration, so let's use that time and determine how far our sprite should have moved:

```
float fElapsed = m_elapsed.asSeconds();

m_mushroom.setPosition(
    m_mushroom.getPosition().x + (m_increment.x * fElapsed),
    m_mushroom.getPosition().y + (m_increment.y * fElapsed));
```

We're now using `m_increment` as a variable of speed, not distance. By looking at our previous code in the constructor, we've set both x and y values of the `m_increment` vector to a value of 4. Since we're expressing our elapsed time as seconds, this is essentially like saying that the sprite needs to move 4 pixels a second. That's really slow, so let's change it to something a little bit more stimulating:

```
Game::Game(){
...
    m_increment = sf::Vector2i(400,400); // 400px a second.
}
```

Upon compiling and running the project, you should see our sprite happily bouncing across the screen. It will now be moved the same distance on every single machine it's executed on, no matter how choppy the frame-rate is. For extra points, try it out yourself by artificially slowing down the game loop with the `sf::sleep` function that SFML provides, like so:

```
while(!game.GetWindow()->IsDone()){
    // Game loop.
    game.HandleInput();
    game.Update();
    game.Render();
    sf::sleep(sf::seconds(0.2)); // Sleep for 0.2 seconds.
    game.RestartClock();
}
```

Feel free to adjust the argument passed to the sleep function. You will notice that it moves the sprite across exactly the same distance, no matter how long each iteration takes to finish.

Fixed time-step

In some cases, the code for time management that we've written doesn't really apply correctly. Let's say we only want to call certain methods at a fixed rate of 60 times per second. It could be a physics system that requires updating only a certain amount of times, or it can be useful if the game is grid-based. Whatever the case is, when an update rate is really important, a fixed time-step is your friend. Unlike the variable time-step, where the next update and draw happens as soon as the previous one is done, the fixed time-step approach will ensure that certain game logic is only happening at a provided rate. It's fairly simple to implement a fixed time-step. First, we must make sure that instead of overwriting the elapsed time value of the previous iteration, we add to it like so:

```
void Game::RestartClock(){
    m_elapsed += m_clock.restart();
}
```

The basic expression for calculating the amount of time for an individual update throughout a 1 second interval is illustrated here:

$$FrameTime = \frac{1.0f}{Updates/s}$$

Let's say we want our game to update *60* times a second. To find the frame time, we would divide *1* by *60* and check if the elapsed time has exceeded that value, as shown here:

```
float frametime = 1.0f / 60.0f;

if(m_elapsed.asSeconds() >= frametime){
    // Do something 60 times a second.
    ...
    m_elapsed -= sf::seconds(frametime); // Subtracting.
}
```

Notice the subtraction at the end. This is how we reset the cycle and keep the simulation running at a *constant* speed. Depending on your application, you might want to put it to *sleep* in between updates in order to relieve the CPU. Aside from that detail, these are the bare bones of the fixed time-step. This is the exact technique that will be used in the game that we will finish building in the next chapter.

Common mistakes

Often, when using clocks, newbies to SFML tend to stick them in the wrong places and restart them at the wrong times. Things like that can result in "funky" behavior at best.

Keep in mind that every line of code that isn't empty or commented out takes time to execute. Depending on how a function that is being called, or a class that is being constructed, is implemented, the time value might range from miniscule to infinite.

Things like updating all of the game entities in the world, performing calculations, and rendering are fairly computationally expensive, so make sure to not somehow exclude these calls from the span of your time measurement. Always make sure that restarting the clock and grabbing the elapsed time is the *last* thing you're doing before the main game loop ends.

Another mistake is having your clock object within the wrong scope. Consider this example:

```
void Game::SomeMethod(){
    sf::Clock clock;
    ...
    sf::Time time = clock.getElapsedTime();
}
```

Assuming that the intention of this code was to measure anything else other than the time since the sf::Clock object was initiated, this code will produce faulty results. Creating an instance of a clock simply measures the time it has been alive within its scope, not anything else. This is the reason why the clock in the game class was declared as the class member. Since the clock is *created on the stack*, as soon as the method above concludes, the clock will be destroyed again.

Keeping an elapsed time in a float data type, or any other data type that isn't sf::Time for that matter, is also something that's generally frowned upon. Something like this would not be a great example of proper use of SFML:

```
class Game{
...
private:
...
    float m_elapsed;
...
};
```

Although it works, this isn't exactly type-safe. It also requires more type conversions along the way, since you have to call one of the three conversion methods each time the clock gets restarted. One more nail to seal the coffin would be code readability. SFML provides its own time class for a reason and convenience, so unless there's a good reason not to use it, do avoid any other data types.

One last thing that deserves a mention since we're talking about time is the console output in C++. While it's just fine to print something out every now and then, even for just debugging purposes, constant console spam will slow your application down. The console output itself is quite slow and cannot be expected to execute at exactly the same speed as the rest of your program. Printing something on every iteration of the main game loop, for example, would throttle your application speed horribly.

Summary

Congratulations on finishing the second chapter of this book! As mentioned previously, it is imperative that you understand everything covered in this chapter, since everything that follows will rely heavily on what we covered here.

Smooth and consistent results on different platforms and under different conditions are just as important as a good structure of an application, which is yet another layer of lasagna, if you will. Upon successful completion of this chapter, you are left yet again with sufficient knowledge to produce applications that can utilize both fixed and variable time-steps in order to create simulations that run identically and independently of the underlying architecture.

Finally, we will leave you with a piece of good advice. The first few chapters are something most readers follow relatively closely and literally. While that's an acceptable way of doing things, we'd prefer you to use this more like a guide instead of a recipe. The most amazing thing about human knowledge is that it isn't simply absorbed through endless memorization. Experimentation and gaining actual experience is the other half of the key to successfully mastering this, so go ahead and write code. Write it good or bad, compile it, or get a bunch of errors, run it or crash it, it's good either way. Try out new things and fail miserably in order to one day succeed spectacularly. You are well on your way to getting your hands dirty, as we will actually begin implementing our first game project for this book in the next chapter. See you there!

Get Your Hands Dirty – What You Need to Know

3

Game development can often be a tedious process to bear. In many instances, the amount of time spent on writing a specific chunk of code, implementing a certain set of features, or revising an old code that you or someone else had written shows very few results that can be immediately appreciated; which is why you may at some point see a game developer's face light up in instant joy when a flashier segment of their project sees the light of day. Seeing your game actually come to life and begin changing before your very eyes is the reason most of our fellow game developers do what they do. Those moments make writing tons of code that show little stimulating results possible.

So, now that we have our game structure ready, it's time to focus on the fun, flashy parts!

In this chapter, we will cover:

- The game of choice for our first project and its history
- Building the game we've chosen
- Common game programming elements
- Additional SFML elements needed to complete our project
- Building helper elements for all our game projects
- Effective debugging and common problem solving in games

Introducing snake

If right now you're imagining building a game with *Solid Snake* wearing his trademark bandana, we're not quite there yet, although the eagerness to do so is understandable. However, if you pictured something like the following, you're right on point:

First published by *Gremlin* in 1976 under the name "Blockade", the snake concept is one of the most famous game types of all time. Countless ports have been written for this type of mechanic, such as *Surround* by *Atari* in 1978 and *Worm* by *Peter Trefonas*. Pretty much any platform that crosses one's mind has a port of snake on it, even including the early monochrome *Nokia* phones, such as the *3310* and *6110*. The graphics changed from port to port and improved with time. However, the main idea and the rules remained the same ever since its humble beginnings:

- The snake can move in four total directions: up, down, left, and right
- Eating an apple makes the snake grow in length
- You cannot touch the walls or your own body, otherwise the game is over

Other things may vary depending on which version of the game you play, such as the score you receive for eating an apple, the amount of lives you have, the speed at which the snake moves, the size of the playing field, obstacles, and so on.

Game design decisions

Certain versions of snake run differently; however, for the sake of paying homage to the classical approach, we will be implementing a snake that moves based on a **grid**, as illustrated next:

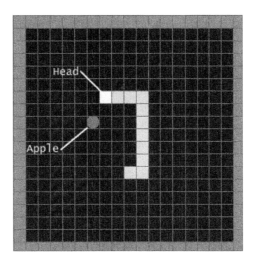

Taking this approach makes it easier to later check for collision between the snake segments and the apple. Grid movement basically means updating at a static rate. This can be achieved by utilizing a fixed time-step, which we covered back in *Chapter 2, Give It Some Structure – Building the Game Framework*.

The outside area symbolizes the boundaries of the game, which in the case of a grid-based movement would be in the range of *[1;Width-1]* and *[1;Height-1]*. If the snake head isn't within that range, it's safe to say that the player has crashed into a wall. All the grid segments here are 16px by 16px big; however, that can be adjusted at any time.

Unless the player runs out of lives, we want to cut the snake at the point of intersection if its head collides with its body and decrease the amount of lives left. This adds a little variety to the game without being too unbalanced.

Lastly, you've probably already picked up on the fact that we're using very simplistic graphical representations of what a snake is in this game. This is done mainly to keep things simple for now, as well as to add the charm of a classic to the mix. It wouldn't be terribly complicated to use sprites for this, however, let's not worry about that just yet.

Implementing the snake structure

Let's now create the two files we'll be working with: `Snake.h` and `Snake.cpp`. Prior to actually developing the snake class, a definition of some data types and structures is in order. We can begin by actually defining the structure that our apple eating serpent will be made out of, right in the snake header file:

```
struct SnakeSegment{
    SnakeSegment(int x, int y) : position(x,y){}
    sf::Vector2i position;
};
```

As you can tell, it's a very simple structure that contains a single member, which is an *integer vector* representing the position of the segment on the grid. The constructor here is utilized to set the position of the segment through an *initializer list*.

 Before moving past this point, make sure you're competent with the **Standard Template Library** and the data containers it provides. We will specifically be using `std::vector` for our needs.

We now have the segment type defined, so let's get started on actually storing the snake somewhere. For beginner purposes, `std::vector` will do nicely! Before going too far with that, here's a neat little trick for curing our code of "long-line-itus":

```
using SnakeContainer = std::vector<SnakeSegment>;
```

As you should already know from your *C/C++* background, `using` is a neat little keyword that allows the user to define aliases for the known data types. By using our clean new definitions together with the `auto` keyword, we're preventing a scenario like the following from ever happening:

```
std::vector<SnakeSegment>::iterator someIterator = ...
```

It's a simple matter of convenience and is completely optional to use, however, we will be equipping this useful tool all the way through this book.

One last type we need to define before beginning to really work on the snake class, is the direction enumeration:

```
enum class Direction{ None, Up, Down, Left, Right };
```

Once again, it's nothing too fancy. The snake has four directions it can move in. We also have a possibility of it standing still, in which case we can just set the direction to NONE.

The snake class

Before designing any object, one must ask oneself what it needs. In our case, the snake needs to have a direction to move towards. It also needs to have lives, keep track of the score, its speed, whether it lost or not, and whether it lost or not. Lastly, we're going to store a rectangle shape that will represent every segment of the snake. When all these are addressed, the header of the snake class would look something like the following:

```cpp
class Snake{
public:
    Snake(int l_blockSize);
    ~Snake();

    // Helper methods.
    void SetDirection(Direction l_dir);
    Direction GetDirection();
    int GetSpeed();
    sf::Vector2i GetPosition();
    int GetLives();
    int GetScore();
    void IncreaseScore();
    bool HasLost();

    void Lose(); // Handle losing here.
    void ToggleLost();

    void Extend(); // Grow the snake.
    void Reset(); // Reset to starting position.

    void Move(); // Movement method.
    void Tick(); // Update method.
    void Cut(int l_segments); // Method for cutting snake.
    void Render(sf::RenderWindow& l_window);
private:
    void CheckCollision(); // Checking for collisions.

    SnakeContainer m_snakeBody; // Segment vector.
    int m_size; // Size of the graphics.
    Direction m_dir; // Current direction.
    int m_speed; // Speed of the snake.
    int m_lives; // Lives.
    int m_score; // Score.
    bool m_lost; // Losing state.
    sf::RectangleShape m_bodyRect; // Shape used in rendering.
};
```

Note that we're using our new type alias for the snake segment vector. This doesn't look that helpful just yet, but it's about to be, really soon.

As you can see, our class has a few methods defined that are designed to split up the functionality, such as Lose(), Extend(), Reset(), and CheckCollision(). This will increase code re-usability as well as readability. Let's begin actually implementing these methods:

```
Snake::Snake(int l_blockSize){
    m_size = l_blockSize;
    m_bodyRect.setSize(sf::Vector2f(m_size - 1, m_size - 1));
    Reset();
}
Snake::~Snake(){}
```

The constructor is pretty straightforward. It takes one argument, which is the size of our graphics. This value gets stored for later use and the member of type sf::RectangleShape gets its size adjusted based on it. The subtraction of one pixel from the size is a very simple way of maintaining that the snake segments appear visually slightly separated, as illustrated here:

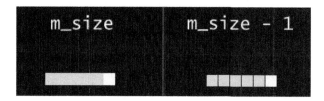

The constructor also calls the Reset() method on the last line. A comment in the header file states that this method is responsible for moving the snake into its starting position. Let's make that happen:

```
void Snake::Reset(){
    m_snakeBody.clear();

    m_snakeBody.push_back(SnakeSegment(5,7));
    m_snakeBody.push_back(SnakeSegment(5,6));
    m_snakeBody.push_back(SnakeSegment(5,5));

    SetDirection(Direction::None); // Start off still.
    m_speed = 15;
    m_lives = 3;
    m_score = 0;
    m_lost = false;
}
```

This chunk of code will be called every time a new game begins. First, it will clear the snake segment vector from the previous game. After that, some snake segments will get added. Because of our implementation, the first element in the vector is always going to be the head. The coordinates for the snake pieces are hardcoded for now, just to keep it simple.

Now we have a three-piece snake. The first thing we do now is set its direction to None. We want no movement to happen until a player presses a key to move the snake. Next, we set up some arbitrary values for the speed, the lives, and the starting score. These can be adjusted to your liking later. We also set the `m_lost` flag to `false` in order to signify a new round taking place.

Before moving on to more difficult to implement methods, let's quickly cover all the helper ones:

```
void Snake::SetDirection(Direction l_dir){ m_dir = l_dir; }
Direction Snake::GetDirection(){ return m_dir; }
int Snake::GetSpeed(){ return m_speed; }

sf::Vector2i Snake::GetPosition(){
    return (!m_snakeBody.empty() ?
        m_snakeBody.front().position : sf::Vector2i(1,1));
}

int Snake::GetLives(){ return m_lives; }
int Snake::GetScore(){ return m_score; }

void Snake::IncreaseScore(){ m_score += 10; }
bool Snake::HasLost(){ return m_lost; }
void Snake::Lose(){ m_lost = true; }
void Snake::ToggleLost(){ m_lost = !m_lost; }
```

These methods are fairly simple. Having descriptive names helps a lot. Let's take a look at the `Extend` method now:

```
void Snake::Extend(){
  if (m_snakeBody.empty()){ return; }
  SnakeSegment& tail_head =
    m_snakeBody[m_snakeBody.size() - 1];

  if(m_snakeBody.size() > 1){
    SnakeSegment& tail_bone =
      m_snakeBody[m_snakeBody.size() - 2];
```

```
      if(tail_head.position.x == tail_bone.position.x){
        if(tail_head.position.y > tail_bone.position.y){
          m_snakeBody.push_back(SnakeSegment(
            tail_head.position.x, tail_head.position.y + 1));
        } else {
          m_snakeBody.push_back(SnakeSegment(
            tail_head.position.x, tail_head.position.y - 1));
        }
      } else if(tail_head.position.y == tail_bone.position.y){
        if(tail_head.position.x > tail_bone.position.x){
          m_snakeBody.push_back(SnakeSegment(
            tail_head.position.x + 1, tail_head.position.y));
        } else {
          m_snakeBody.push_back(SnakeSegment(
            tail_head.position.x - 1, tail_head.position.y));
        }
      }
    } else {
      if(m_dir == Direction::Up){
        m_snakeBody.push_back(SnakeSegment(
          tail_head.position.x, tail_head.position.y + 1));
      } else if (m_dir == Direction::Down){
        m_snakeBody.push_back(SnakeSegment(
          tail_head.position.x, tail_head.position.y - 1));
      } else if (m_dir == Direction::Left){
        m_snakeBody.push_back(SnakeSegment(
          tail_head.position.x + 1, tail_head.position.y));
      } else if (m_dir == Direction::Right){
        m_snakeBody.push_back(SnakeSegment(
          tail_head.position.x - 1, tail_head.position.y));
      }
    }
  }
```

This preceding method is the one responsible for actually growing out our snake when it touches an apple. The first thing we did was create a reference to the *last* element in the segment vector, called `tail_head`. We have a fairly large *if-else statement* chunk of code next, and both cases of it require access to the last element, so it's a good idea to create the reference now in order to prevent duplicated code.

The `std::vector` container overloads the **bracket operator** in order to support random access via a numeric index. It being similar to an array enables us to reference the last element by simply using an index of `size() - 1`. The random access speed is also constant, regardless of the number of elements in this container, which is what makes the `std::vector` a good choice for this project.

Essentially, it comes down to two cases: either the snake is longer than one segment or it's not. If it does have more than one piece, we create another reference, called `tail_bone`, which points to the *next to last* element. This is needed in order to determine where a new piece of the snake should be placed upon extending it, and the way we check for that is by comparing the `position.x` and `position.y` values of the `tail_head` and `tail_bone` segments. If the x values are the same, it's safe to say that the difference between the two pieces is on the y axis and vice versa. Consider the following illustration, where the orange rectangle is `tail_bone` and the red rectangle is `tail_head`:

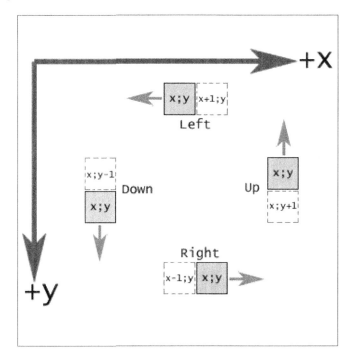

Let's take the example that's facing left and analyze it: `tail_bone` and `tail_head` have the same *y* coordinate, and the *x* coordinate of `tail_head` is greater than that of `tail_bone`, so the next segment will be added at the same coordinates as `tail_head`, except the x value will be increased by one. Because the `SnakeSegment` constructor is conveniently overloaded to accept coordinates, it's easy to perform this simple math at the same time as pushing the segment onto the back of our vector.

In the case of there only being one segment in the vector, we simply check the direction of our snake and perform the same math as we did before, except that this time it's based on which way the head is facing. The preceding illustration applies to this as well, where the orange rectangle is the head and the red rectangle is the piece that's about to be added. If it's facing left, we increase the *x* coordinate by one while leaving *y* the same. Subtracting from x happens if it's facing right, and so on. Take your time to analyze this picture and associate it with the previous code.

Of course, none of this would matter if our snake didn't move. That's exactly what is being handled in the update method, which in our case of a *fixed time-step* is referred to as a "tick":

```
void Snake::Tick(){
    if (m_snakeBody.empty()){ return; }
    if (m_dir == Direction::None){ return; }
    Move();
    CheckCollision();
}
```

The first two lines in the method are used to check if the snake should be moved or not, based on its size and direction. As mentioned earlier, the `Direction::None` value is used specifically for the purpose of keeping it still. The snake movement is contained entirely within the `Move` method:

```
void Snake::Move(){
    for (int i = m_snakeBody.size() - 1; i > 0; --i){
        m_snakeBody[i].position = m_snakeBody[i - 1].position;
    }
    if (m_dir == Direction::Left){
        --m_snakeBody[0].position.x;
    } else if (m_dir == Direction::Right){
        ++m_snakeBody[0].position.x;
    } else if (m_dir == Direction::Up){
        --m_snakeBody[0].position.y;
    } else if (m_dir == Direction::Down){
        ++m_snakeBody[0].position.y;
    }
}
```

We start by iterating over the vector *backwards*. This is done in order to achieve an *inchworm* effect of sorts. It is possible to do it without iterating over the vector in reverse as well, however, this serves the purpose of simplicity and makes it easier to understand how the game works. We're also utilizing the *random access operator* again to use numeric indices instead of the vector *iterators* for the same reasons. Consider the following illustration:

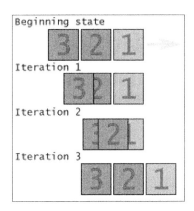

We have a set of segments in their positions before we call the `tick` method, which can be referred to as the "beginning state". As we begin iterating over our vector backwards, we start with the segment #3. In our `for` loop, we check if the index is equal to `0` or not in order to determine if the current segment is the front of the snake. In this case, it's not, so we set the position of segment #3 to be the *same* as the segment #2. The preceding illustration shows the piece to be, sort of, in between the two positions, which is only done for the purpose of being able to see both of them. In reality, segment #3 is sitting right on top of segment #2.

After the same process is applied again to the second part of the snake, we move on to its head. At this point, we simply move it across one space in the axis that corresponds to its facing direction. The same idea applies here as it did in the illustration before this one, but the sign is reversed. Since in our example, the snake is facing right, it gets moved to the coordinates *(x+1;y)*. Once that is done, we have successfully moved our snake by one space.

One last thing our tick does is call the `CheckCollision()` method. Let's take a look at its implementation:

```
void Snake::CheckCollision(){
    if (m_snakeBody.size() < 5){ return; }
    SnakeSegment& head = m_snakeBody.front();
    for(auto itr = m_snakeBody.begin() + 1;
        itr != m_snakeBody.end(); ++itr)
```

```
    {
        if(itr->position == head.position){
            int segments = m_snakeBody.end() - itr;
            Cut(segments);
            break;
        }
    }
}
```

First, there's no need to check for a collision unless we have over four segments. Understanding certain scenarios of your game and putting in checks to not waste resources is an important part of game development. If we have over four segments of our snake, we create a reference to the head again, because in any case of collision, that's the first part that would hit another segment. There is no need to check for a collision between all of its parts twice. We also skip an iteration for the head of the snake, since there's obviously no need to check if it's colliding with itself.

The basic way we check for a collision in this grid-based game is essentially by comparing the position of the head to the position of the current segment represented by our iterator. If both positions are the same, the head is intersecting with the body. The way we resolve this was briefly covered in the *Game design decisions* section of this chapter. The snake has to be cut at the point of collision until the player runs out of lives. We do this by first obtaining an integer value of the segment count between the end and the segment being hit. STL is fairly flexible with its iterators, and since the memory in the case of using a vector is all laid out contiguously, we can simply subtract our current iterator from the last element in the vector to obtain this value. This is done in order to know how many elements to remove from the back of the snake up until the point of intersection. We then invoke the method that is responsible for cutting the snake. Also, since there can only be one collision at a time, we break out of the `for` loop to not waste any more clock cycles.

Let's take a look at the `Cut` method:

```
void Snake::Cut(int l_segments){
    for (int i = 0; i < l_segments; ++i){
        m_snakeBody.pop_back();
    }
    --m_lives;
    if (!m_lives){ Lose(); return; }
}
```

At this point, it's as simple as looping a certain amount of times based on the `l_segments` value and popping the elements from the back of the vector. This effectively slices through the snake.

The rest of the code simply decreases the amount of lives left, checks if it's at zero, and calls the `Lose()` method if there are no more lives.

Phew! That's quite a bit of code. One thing still remains, however, and that is rendering our square serpent to the screen:

```
void Snake::Render(sf::RenderWindow& l_window){
    if (m_snakeBody.empty()){ return; }

    auto head = m_snakeBody.begin();
    m_bodyRect.setFillColor(sf::Color::Yellow);
    m_bodyRect.setPosition(head->position.x * m_size,
        head->position.y * m_size);
    l_window.draw(m_bodyRect);

    m_bodyRect.setFillColor(sf::Color::Green);
    for(auto itr = m_snakeBody.begin() + 1;
        itr != m_snakeBody.end(); ++itr)
    {
        m_bodyRect.setPosition(itr->position.x * m_size,
            itr->position.y * m_size);
        l_window.draw(m_bodyRect);
    }
}
```

Quite similarly to a lot of the methods we've implemented here, there's a need to iterate over each segment. The head itself is drawn outside of the loop in order to avoid unnecessary checks. We set the position of our `sf::RectangleShape` that graphically represents a snake segment to its grid position multiplied by the `m_size` value in order to obtain the pixel coordinates on the screen. Drawing the rectangle is the last step of implementing the snake class in its entirety!

The World class

Our snake can now move and collide with itself. While functional, this doesn't make a really exciting game. Let's give it some boundaries and something to munch on to increase the score by introducing the `World` class.

While it's possible to just make separate objects for everything we talk about in here, this project is simple enough to allow certain aspects of itself to be nicely contained within a single class that can manage them without too much trouble. This class takes care of everything to do with keeping the game boundaries, as well as maintaining the apple the player will be trying to grab.

Let's take a look at the class header:

```
class World{
public:
    World(sf::Vector2u l_windSize);
    ~World();

    int GetBlockSize();

    void RespawnApple();

    void Update(Snake& l_player);
    void Render(sf::RenderWindow& l_window);
private:
    sf::Vector2u m_windowSize;
    sf::Vector2i m_item;
    int m_blockSize;

    sf::CircleShape m_appleShape;
    sf::RectangleShape m_bounds[4];
};
```

As you can see from the preceding code, this class also keeps track of how big the objects in the game are. Aside from that, it simply retains four rectangles for the boundary graphics, a circle for drawing the apple, and an integer vector to keep track of the apple's coordinates, which is named `m_item`. Let's start implementing the constructor:

```
World::World(sf::Vector2u l_windSize){
  m_blockSize = 16;

  m_windowSize = l_windSize;
  RespawnApple();
  m_appleShape.setFillColor(sf::Color::Red);
  m_appleShape.setRadius(m_blockSize / 2);

  for(int i = 0; i < 4; ++i){
    m_bounds[i].setFillColor(sf::Color(150,0,0));
    if(!((i + 1) % 2)){
      m_bounds[i].setSize(sf::Vector2f(m_windowSize.x,
        m_blockSize));
    } else {
      m_bounds[i].setSize(sf::Vector2f(m_blockSize,
        m_windowSize.y));
    }
```

```
      if(i < 2){
        m_bounds[i].setPosition(0,0);
      } else {
        m_bounds[i].setOrigin(m_bounds[i].getSize());
        m_bounds[i].setPosition(sf::Vector2f(m_windowSize));
      }
    }
  }

  World::~World(){}
```

Up until the complex looking `for` loops, we simply initialize some member values from the local constructor variables, set the color and radius of the apple circle, and call the `RespawnApple()` method in order to place it somewhere on the grid.

The first `for` loop just iterates four times for each of the four sides of the game screen in order to set up a red rectangle wall on each side. It sets a dark red color for the rectangle fill and proceeds with checking the index value. First, we determine if the index is an even or an odd value by checking it with the following expression: `if(!((i + 1) % 2)){`.... This is done in order to know how big each wall has to be on a specific axis. Because it has to be as large as one of the screen dimensions, we simply make the other one as large as all the other graphics on the screen, which is represented by the `m_blockSize` value.

The last `if` statement checks if the index is below two. If it is, we're working with the top-left corner, so we simply set the position of the rectangle to (0,0). Since the origin of all the rectangle-based drawables in SFML is always the top-left corner, we don't need to worry about that in this case. However, if the index is 2 or higher, we set the origin to the size of the rectangle, which effectively makes it the bottom right corner. Afterwards, we set the position of the rectangle to be the same as the size of the screen, which puts the shape all the way down to the bottom right corner. You can simply set all the coordinates and origins by hand, but this approach makes the initialization of the basic features more automated. It may be hard to see the use for it now, but in more complicated projects this kind of thinking will come in handy, so why not start now?

Since we have our walls, let's take a look at how one might go about re-spawning the apple:

```
void World::RespawnApple(){
    int maxX = (m_windowSize.x / m_blockSize) - 2;
    int maxY = (m_windowSize.y / m_blockSize) - 2;
    m_item = sf::Vector2i(
        rand() % maxX + 1, rand() % maxY + 1);
    m_appleShape.setPosition(
```

```
        m_item.x * m_blockSize,
        m_item.y * m_blockSize);
}
```

The first thing we must do is determine the boundaries within which the apple can be spawned. We do so by defining two values: maxX and maxY. These are set to the window size divided by the block size, which gives us the number of spaces in the grid, from which we must then subtract 2. This is due to the fact that the grid indices begin with 0, not 1, and because we don't want to spawn the apple within the right or bottom walls.

The next step is to actually generate the random values for the apple coordinates. We use our pre-calculated values here and set the *lowest* possible random value to 1, because we don't want anything spawning in the top wall or the left wall. Since the coordinates of the apple are now available, we can set the m_appleShape graphic's position in pixel coordinates by multiplying the grid coordinates by the size of all our graphics.

Let's actually make all these features come to life by implementing the update method:

```
void World::Update(Snake& l_player){
    if(l_player.GetPosition() == m_item){
        l_player.Extend();
        l_player.IncreaseScore();
        RespawnApple();
    }

    int gridSize_x = m_windowSize.x / m_blockSize;
    int gridSize_y = m_windowSize.y / m_blockSize;

    if(l_player.GetPosition().x <= 0 ||
        l_player.GetPosition().y <= 0 ||
        l_player.GetPosition().x >= gridSize_x - 1 ||
        l_player.GetPosition().y >= gridSize_y - 1)
    {
            l_player.Lose();
    }
}
```

First, we check if the player's position is the same as that of the apple. If it is, we have a collision and the snake gets extended, the score increases, and the apple gets re-spawned. Next, we determine our grid size and check if the player coordinates are anywhere outside of the designated boundaries. If that's the case, we call the Lose() method to illustrate the collision with the wall and give the player a "game over".

In order to not keep the player blind, we must display the boundaries of the game, as well as the main point of interest - the apple. Let's draw everything on screen:

```
void World::Render(sf::RenderWindow& l_window){
    for(int i = 0; i < 4; ++i){
        l_window.draw(m_bounds[i]);
    }
    l_window.draw(m_appleShape);
}
```

All we have to do is iterate four times and draw each of the four respective boundaries. Then we draw the apple, which concludes our interest in this method.

One more thing to point out is that the other classes might need to know how big the graphics need to be, and for this reason, let's implement a simple method for obtaining that value:

```
int World::GetBlockSize(){ return m_blockSize; }
```

This concludes the `World` class.

Time to integrate

Much like how a hammer is useless without someone using it, so are our two classes without being properly adopted by the `Game` class. Since we didn't write all that code just to practise typing, let's work on putting all the pieces together. First, we need to actually add two new members to the `Game` class, and you might already have guessed what they are:

```
class Game{
...
private:
...
    World m_world;
    Snake m_snake;
};
```

Next, let's initialize these members. Since both of them have constructors that take arguments, it's the time for *initializer list*:

```
Game::Game(): m_window("Snake", sf::Vector2u(800, 600)),
  m_snake(m_world.GetBlockSize()),m_world(sf::Vector2u(800,600))
{
    ...
}
```

Next, we need to process some input. As you may recall from the previous chapters, utilizing events for live input is really delayed and should never be used for anything else but checking for key presses that aren't time sensitive. Luckily, SFML provides means of obtaining the real-time state of the keyboard through the `sf::Keyboard` class. It only contains the static functions and is never meant to be initialized. One of those functions is exactly what we need here: `isKeyPressed(sf::Keyboard::Key)`. The sole argument that it takes is the actual key you want to check the state of, which can be obtained through the use of the `sf::Keyboard::Key` enumeration, as follows:

```
if(sf::Keyboard::isKeyPressed(sf::Keyboard::Up)
    && m_snake.GetDirection() != Direction::Down)
{
    m_snake.SetDirection(Direction::Up);
} else if(sf::Keyboard::isKeyPressed(sf::Keyboard::Down)
    && m_snake.GetDirection() != Direction::Up)
{
    m_snake.SetDirection(Direction::Down);
} else if(sf::Keyboard::isKeyPressed(sf::Keyboard::Left)
    && m_snake.GetDirection() != Direction::Right)
{
    m_snake.SetDirection(Direction::Left);
} else if(sf::Keyboard::isKeyPressed(sf::Keyboard::Right)
    && m_snake.GetDirection() != Direction::Left)
{
    m_snake.SetDirection(Direction::Right);
}
```

Something we don't want the snake to do is to go in the direction that is opposite to its current one. At any given time, there should only be three directions it can go in, and the use of the `GetDirection()` method ensures that we don't send the snake in reverse, essentially eating itself. If we have the proper combination of input and its current direction, it's safe to adjust its direction through the use of the `SetDirection()` method.

Let's get things moving by updating both our classes:

```
void Game::Update(){
...
    float timestep = 1.0f / m_snake.GetSpeed();

    if(m_elapsed >= timestep){
        m_snake.Tick();
        m_world.Update(m_snake);
        m_elapsed -= timestep;
        if(m_snake.HasLost()){
```

```
            m_snake.Reset();
        }
    }
    ...
}
```

As mentioned previously, we're using *fixed time-step* here, which incorporates the snake speed in order to update the appropriate amount of times per second. This is also where we check if the player has lost the game and reset the snake if he has.

We're really close now. Time to draw everything on screen:

```
void Game::Render(){
    m_window.BeginDraw();
    // Render here.
    m_world.Render(*m_window.GetRenderWindow());
    m_snake.Render(*m_window.GetRenderWindow());

    m_window.EndDraw();
}
```

Much like before, we simply invoke the Render methods of both our classes and pass in a reference to sf::RenderWindow. With that, our game is actually playable! Upon successful compilation and execution of our project, we should end up with something looking like this following image:

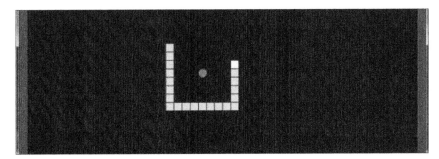

The snake will be still at first, until one of the four arrow keys is pressed. Once it does start moving, it will be able to eat the apple and grow by one segment, collide with its own tail and lose it twice before it dies, and end the game if the player crashes into a wall. The core version of our game is complete! Pat yourself on the back, as you just created your first game.

Hunting bugs

As proud and satisfied as you may be with your first project, nothing is ever perfect. If you've spent some time actually playing the game, you may have noticed an odd event when quickly mashing the buttons, looking something like this:

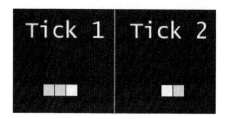

The image represents the difference between two sequential updates. It seems that earlier it was facing the right direction and then it's facing left and missing its tail. What happened? Try to figure it out on your own before continuing, as it perfectly illustrates the experience of fixing game flaws.

Playing around with it some more reveals certain details that narrow down our problem. Let's break down what happens when a player starts mashing keys quickly:

- The snake is facing right.
- Any arrow key other than the left or right is pressed.
- The direction of the snake gets set to something else, let's say up.
- The right key is pressed before the game has a chance to update.
- Since the snake's direction is no longer set to right or left, `if` statement in the input handler is satisfied and sets the direction to left.
- The game updates the snake and moves it left by one space. The head collides with its tail and it gets cut off.

Yes, it seems that our direction checking is flawed and causes this bug. Once again, spend some time trying to think of a way to fix this before moving on.

Fixing bugs

Let's discuss the several approaches that might be used in a situation like this. First, the programmer might think about putting a flag somewhere that remembers if the direction has already been set for the current iteration and gets reset afterwards. This would prevent the bug we're experiencing, but would also lock down the number of times a player can interact with the snake. Let's say it moves once a second. That would mean that if you press a key at the beginning of that second, you wouldn't be able to change your mind and hit another key quickly to rectify your wrong decision before the snake moves. That's no good. Let's move on to a new idea.

Another approach may be to keep track of the original direction before any changes were made to that *iteration*. Then, once the update method gets called, we could check if the original direction, before any changes were made, is the opposite of the newest direction that we've received. If it is, we could simply ignore it and move the snake in the direction before any changes were made. This would fix the bug and not present us with a new one, but it comes with keeping track of one more variable and might get confusing. Imagine that in the future you're presented with a similar bug or a request for a feature that needs you to keep track of another variable on top of this one. Imagine that happens one more time, then another. Very soon, your checking statement might look a little something like this:

```
if(var1 != something && var2 == something && var3 == true && var4 ==
!var3 ...)
```

Now that is what we call a mess. On top of that, imagine you have to check the same variables four times for four different conditions. It quickly becomes apparent that this is a bad design and it shouldn't be used by anyone with intentions of ever showing their code to another person.

You may ask how we can rectify our problem then. Well, we could simply not rely on the use of a variable in the snake class to determine its direction, and instead implement a method that looks at its structure and spits out the direction it's facing, as shown next:

```
Direction Snake::GetPhysicalDirection(){
    if(m_snakeBody.size() <= 1){
        return Direction::None;
    }

    SnakeSegment& head = m_snakeBody[0];
    SnakeSegment& neck = m_snakeBody[1];

    if(head.position.x == neck.position.x){
        return (head.position.y > neck.position.y
```

```
            ? Direction::Down : Direction::Up);
    } else if(head.position.y == neck.position.y){
        return (head.position.x > neck.position.x
            ? Direction::Right : Direction::Left);
    }

    return Direction::None;
}
```

First, we check if the snake is *1* segment long or less; in this case, it doesn't matter which direction it's facing as it wouldn't eat itself if it only had a head, and it wouldn't even have a direction if there are no segments in the vector at all. Assuming it's longer than one segment, we obtain two references: the head and the neck, which is the second piece of the snake right after the head. Then, we simply check the positions of both of them and determine the direction the snake is facing using the same logic as before, while implementing the snake class, as illustrated in the following image:

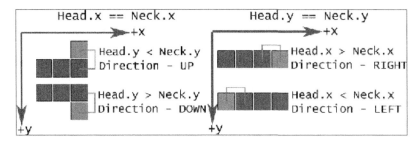

This will return a proper direction that won't be altered unless the snake moves, so let's adjust our input handling code to cater to these changes:

```
if(sf::Keyboard::isKeyPressed(sf::Keyboard::Up)
  && m_snake.GetPhysicalDirection() != Direction::Down)
{
    m_snake.SetDirection(Direction::Up);
} else if(sf::Keyboard::isKeyPressed(sf::Keyboard::Down)
  && m_snake.GetPhysicalDirection() != Direction::Up)
{
    m_snake.SetDirection(Direction::Down);
} else if(sf::Keyboard::isKeyPressed(sf::Keyboard::Left)
  && m_snake.GetPhysicalDirection() != Direction::Right)
{
    m_snake.SetDirection(Direction::Left);
} else if(sf::Keyboard::isKeyPressed(sf::Keyboard::Right)
  && m_snake.GetPhysicalDirection() != Direction::Left)
```

```
    {
        m_snake.SetDirection(Direction::Right);
    }
```

Voila! No more of our snake turning inside out.

There's one more fault with the game that didn't get addressed here on purpose. Try to find it and fix it in order to practise resolving problems like this in the future.

 Hint: It has to do with how many segments the snake has when the game starts.

If you want to do this one fairly, do your best not to reference the code of the finished project that came with this book, as that has it fixed already.

Going the extra mile

A functional game is far from a fully finished product. Sure, we have everything we wanted in the beginning, but it still leaves things to be desired, such as keeping track of the score and showing how many lives we have. At first, your main instinct might be to just add a bit of text somewhere on the screen that simply prints the number of lives you have left. You may even be tempted to do as little as simply printing it out in the console window. If that's the case, the purpose of this part is to change your way of thinking by introducing something that we will be using and improving over the course of this book: the textbox.

If that name doesn't really mean anything to you, simply imagine a chat window on any given communication application, such as *MSN Messenger* or *Skype*. Whenever a new message is added, it's added to the bottom as the older messages are moved up. The window holds a certain number of messages that are visible at one time. That's not only useful for the purpose of the game printing a casual message, but can also be used for debugging. Let's start by writing our header, as usual:

```
using MessageContainer = std::vector<std::string>;

class Textbox{
public:
    Textbox();
    Textbox(int l_visible, int l_charSize,
        int l_width, sf::Vector2f l_screenPos);
    ~Textbox();

    void Setup(int l_visible, int l_charSize,
        int l_width, sf::Vector2f l_screenPos);
```

```
        void Add(std::string l_message);
        void Clear();

        void Render(sf::RenderWindow& l_wind);
private:
        MessageContainer m_messages;
        int m_numVisible;

        sf::RectangleShape m_backdrop;
        sf::Font m_font;
        sf::Text m_content;
};
```

We begin by defining the data type for the container of all the messages. In this case, we went with `std::vector` again, simply because that's the more familiar choice at this point. Just to make it look better and more readable, we've added a rectangle shape as one of the members of the class that will be used as a backdrop. On top of that, we have introduced a new data type: `sf::Text`. This is a drawable type that represents any typed characters or strings of characters, and can be adjusted in size, font, and color, as well as transformed, much like any other drawable in SFML.

Let's start implementing our fancy new feature:

```
Textbox::Textbox(){
        Setup(5,9,200,sf::Vector2f(0,0));
}

Textbox::Textbox(int l_visible, int l_charSize,
int l_width, sf::Vector2f l_screenPos){
        Setup(l_visible, l_charSize, l_width, l_screenPos);
}

Textbox::~Textbox(){ Clear(); }
```

As you can see, it has two constructors, one of which can be used to initialize some default values and the other that allows customization by passing in some values as arguments. The first argument is the number of lines that are visible in the textbox. It is followed by the character size in pixels, the width of the entire textbox in pixels, and float vector that represents the position on the screen where it should be drawn at. All that these constructors do is invoke the `Setup` method and pass all these arguments to it, so let's take a look at it:

```
void Textbox::Setup(int l_visible, int l_charSize,
  int l_width, sf::Vector2f l_screenPos)
  {
```

```
        m_numVisible = l_visible;

        sf::Vector2f l_offset(2.0f, 2.0f);

        m_font.loadFromFile("arial.ttf");
        m_content.setFont(m_font);
        m_content.setString("");
        m_content.setCharacterSize(l_charSize);
        m_content.setColor(sf::Color::White);
        m_content.setPosition(l_screenPos + l_offset);

        m_backdrop.setSize(sf::Vector2f(
            l_width, (l_visible * (l_charSize * 1.2f))));
        m_backdrop.setFillColor(sf::Color(90,90,90,90));
        m_backdrop.setPosition(l_screenPos);
    }
```

Aside from initializing its member values, this method defines an offset float vector that will be used to space the text appropriately and provide some padding from the top-left corner. It also sets up our sf::Text member by first creating a font to which it's bound, setting the initial string to nothing, setting up the character size and color, and setting its position on the screen to the provided position argument with the proper offset factored in. Additionally, it sets up the size of the backdrop by using the width that was provided and multiplying the number of visible lines by the result of the multiplication of the character size and a constant floating point value of 1.2, in order to account for spacing between the lines.

From time to time, it does simply come down to playing with code to seeing what really works. Finding certain numeric constants that work in all cases is one of the situations where it's just a matter of testing in order to determine the correct value. Don't be afraid to try out new things and see what works.

Since we're utilizing a vector to store our messages, adding a new one or removing them all is as simple as using the push_back and clear methods:

```
void Textbox::Add(std::string l_message){
    m_messages.push_back(l_message);
    if(m_messages.size() < 6){ return; }
    m_messages.erase(m_messages.begin());
}

void Textbox::Clear(){ m_messages.clear(); }
```

In the case of adding a new message, checking whether we have more of them than we can see would be a good idea. Having something around that we're not going to see or need ever again is wasteful, so the very first message that is definitely out of sight at that time is removed from the message container.

We're very close to actually finishing this neat feature. The only thing left now is drawing it, which, as always, is taken care of by the `Render` method:

```
void Textbox::Render(sf::RenderWindow& l_wind){
  std::string l_content;

  for(auto &itr : m_messages){
    l_content.append(itr+"\n");
  }

  if(l_content != ""){
    m_content.setString(l_content);
    l_wind.draw(m_backdrop);
    l_wind.draw(m_content);
  }
}
```

The code begins with `std::string` being set up to hold all the visible messages on the screen. Afterwards, it's as simple as looping over the message vector and appending the text of each message to our local `std::string` variable with a new line symbol at the end. Lastly, after checking the local variable and making sure it isn't empty, we must set our `m_content` member of type `sf::Text` to hold the string we've been pushing our messages to and draw both the background and the text on the screen. That's all there is to the `Textbox` class.

After adding an instance of `Textbox` as a member to our game class, we can start setting it up:

```
Game::Game() ... {
...
    m_textbox.Setup(5,14,350,sf::Vector2f(225,0));
...
    m_textbox.Add("Seeded random number generator with: " + std::to_
string(time(NULL)));
}
```

After passing some constant values to the `Setup` method of our `m_textbox` member, we immediately start using it right there in the constructor by actually outputting our first message. Let's finish integrating it fully by making one last adjustment to the `Game::Render()` method:

```
void Game::Render(){
    m_window.BeginDraw();
    // Render here.
    m_world.Render(*m_window.GetRenderWindow());
    m_snake.Render(*m_window.GetRenderWindow());
    m_textbox.Render(*m_window.GetRenderWindow());

    m_window.EndDraw();
}
```

It's the same as both the classes we've implemented before this, except that the text box is now the last thing we draw, which means it will be displayed over everything else. After adding more messages to the game to be printed and compiling our project, we should end up with something like this:

This text box, in its most basic form, is the last addition to our snake game that we will be covering in this book. Feel free to play around with it and see what else you can come up with to spice up the game!

Common mistakes

A fairly common thing people often forget is the following line:

```
srand(time(nullptr));
```

If you notice, the numbers being generated are exactly the same each time you launch the game-chances are that you haven't seeded the random number generator or you haven't provided a proper seed. It's recommended to always use a unix timestamp, as shown.

The use of this particular random function should be restricted to something that isn't related to security and cryptography. Using it in combination with the modulus operator can produce incredibly non-uniform results due to the introduced bias.

Another fairly common problem is the programmers' choice of the data container to hold their structures. Let's take the following for example:

```
using SnakeContainer = std::vector<SnakeSegment>;
```

This defines the type of our `SnakeContainer`. If you've compiled the code we've written, you will notice that it runs fairly smoothly. Now consider this next line of code:

```
Using SnakeContainer = std::deque<SnakeSegment>;
```

Because of the way these two containers are implemented in STL, nothing else changes in our code, so feel free to try to change the data type of your `SnakeContainer` from `std::vector` to `std::deque`. After compiling and running the project, you will definitely pick up on the hit on performance. Why is that happening? Well, even though `std::vector` and `std::deque` can be used basically in the same way, they're fundamentally different under the hood. The vector offers the certainty of its elements being contiguous in memory, while the double ended queue does not. There are also differences in performances, depending on where the most inserts and removals are done. If you're unsure about which container to use, make sure to either look it up or benchmark it yourself. Never just blindly assume, unless performance isn't the main concern to you.

Lastly, on a more open-ended note, don't be afraid to play with, modify, change, hack, or otherwise alter any piece of code that you see. The biggest mistake you can make is the mistake of not learning by breaking and fixing things. Consider the code we've written as only a push in the right direction and not a specific recipe. If understanding something better means you have to break it first, so be it.

Summary

Game development is a great journey to embark on. You had taken your first and second steps earlier, but now you have boarded the plane with your first, fully functional game in the bag. You are now officially a game developer! Where will this plane of opportunity take you and how long will it be there for? All of that is entirely up to you. While you're still not in the air, however, we will do our best to inspire you and show you all the different places to go to and the wonderful experiences to be had there. One thing is definitely for sure, however, and that is that this is not the end. If your enthusiasm has led you this far, there's only one direction to head to, and that's forward.

A lot was covered in this chapter, and now it's impossible to say that you haven't gotten your hands dirty while paying homage to one of the all time arcade classics. In the next chapter, we will take on input handling and event management in order to provide flexibility and fluent means of interaction between you and your application, all while introducing our brand new project for the next few chapters. There's still a lot to learn and many lines of code to write, so don't spend too much time hesitating to proceed onto the next chapter. A brand new adventure is waiting to unfold. See you there!

4
Grab That Joystick – Input and Event Management

Arguably, the most important aspect of any game ever made is actually being able to play it. Regardless of the purpose of input, ranging from simply hitting keys to navigating through menus to controlling when your character jumps and which direction he or she walks to, the lack of an application presenting a way for you to interact with it might as well leave you with a very fancy screensaver. We have very briefly looked at the primitive way of grabbing and using the keyboard input, however our motivation for this chapter is quite different than simply being content with a large nest of if/else statements that handle every single key being pressed. Instead, we want to look at a more robust way of handling not just the keyboard, but also the mouse and any events that happen between the frames, along with adding potential for processing input of additional peripherals, such as joysticks. With that in mind, let's take a look at what we will be covering in this chapter:

- Basic means of checking the states of keyboard and mouse buttons
- Understanding and processing different types of events
- Understanding and utilizing callbacks
- Designing and implementing an event manager

Let's not sit still like the character of your game without input and get on coding!

Retrieving peripheral input

A few of the previous chapters have already touched on this subject of retrieving peripheral output a little bit, and, ironically enough, the entire scope of the class was covered. Just to recap, `sf::Keyboard` is a class that provides a single static method `isKeyPressed(sf::Keyboard::Key)` to determine the real-time state of a certain keyboard key, which gets passed in as an argument to the method, represented by the `sf::Keyboard::Key` enumeration table. Because this method is static, `sf::Keyboard` doesn't need to be instantiated and can be used as follows:

```
if(sf::Keyboard::isKeyPressed(sf::Keyboard::W)){
    // Do something if the W key is pressed.
}
```

This is the way we checked for input in the previous chapters, however, it does lend itself to quite a bit of a mess of `if/else` statements if we want to check for more keystrokes.

Checking for mouse input

Predictably enough, SFML also provides a class similar to `sf::Keyboard` with the same idea of obtaining real-time status of a mouse: `sf::Mouse`. Much like its partner in crime, the keyboard, it provides a way to check for the mouse buttons being pressed, as shown next:

```
if(sf::Mouse::isButtonPressed(sf::Mouse::Left)){
    // Do something if the left mouse button is pressed.
}
```

The `sf::Mouse` class provides its own enumeration of possible buttons on any given mice, of which we have a grand total of five:

`sf::Mouse::Left`	The left mouse button
`sf::Mouse::Right`	The right mouse button
`sf::Mouse::Middle`	Mouse wheel being clicked
`sf::Mouse::XButton1`	First extra mouse button
`sf::Mouse::XButton2`	Second extra mouse button

In addition to that, the `sf::Mouse` class provides a way to get and set the current mouse position:

```
// Getting the mouse position.
sf::Vector2i mousePos = sf::Mouse::getPosition(); // 1
sf::Vector2i mousePos = sf::Mouse::getPosition(m_window); // 2
```

```
// Setting the mouse position.
sf::Mouse::setPosition(sf::Vector2i(0,0)); // 3
sf::Mouse::setPosition(sf::Vector2i(0,0),m_window); // 4
```

Both these methods have an overloaded version that takes in a reference to a window in order to determine whether to look at the mouse coordinates relative to the window or relative to the desktop. Consider the following illustration:

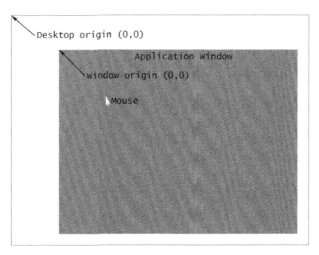

If the reference to a window isn't provided, like on line #1 of the previous example, the mouse position that gets returned is the distance from the desktop origin to the point the mouse is at. If, however, the reference to a window is provided, the position is simply the distance between the window origin and the mouse location. In other words, the mouse position in the example #2 is relative to the window. The same logic is true for lines #3 and #4, except the position of the mouse gets set to the provided int vector argument.

Plug in your controller

Yes, as the title states, SFML supports input not only from your keyboard and mouse, but also from additional peripherals that you may have hooked up to your computer. By utilizing the class `sf::Joystick`, which only contains static methods, just like the previous two classes, it is possible to check if a controller is connected, check for its button states, and even determine the positions along certain axes, if the controller supports that.

SFML supports up to eight different controllers being connected at the same time, which are identified by a numerical index in the range of [0;7]. Because of that, every method that `sf::Joystick` provides has to have at least one argument, which is the controller ID. First, let's take a look at a way to determine if a controller is connected:

```
if (sf::Joystick::isConnected(0))
{
    // We have a controller with an id 0.
}
```

If we have a controller with an ID of 0, we can check how many buttons it actually supports, as follows:

```
unsigned int n_buttons = sf::Joystick::getButtonCount(0);
```

Because there is no other way to abstractly define the buttons for every controller on the planet, they're simply referred to by numeric indices between 0 and 31. Checking for a button push can be done by calling the `isButtonPressed()` method, as shown next:

```
if(sf::Joystick::isButtonPressed(0,1)){
    // Button 1 on controller 0 is pressed.
}
```

In order to check if a controller supports a specific axis, we can use the `hasAxis()` method:

```
if(sf::Joystick::hasAxis(0,sf::Joystick::X)){
    // Controller 0 supports movement on X axis.
}
```

The `sf::Joystick::Axis` enumeration encapsulates all the possible axes that a controller could support, so one can check for that as shown in the preceding code. Assuming the controller supports it, obtaining its current position along an axis can be done as follows:

```
float p_x = sf::Joystick::getAxisPosition(0, sf::Joystick::X);
float p_y = sf::Joystick::getAxisPosition(0, sf::Joystick::Y);
// Do something with p_x and p_y.
```

The preceding methods will return the current position of the X and Y axes on the controller 0.

Because the `sf::Joystick` states are updated when checking for events, it might present some problems when using any of these methods before the events have had a chance to be polled. If that's the case, it is best to manually call the `sf::Joystick:Update()` method in order to make sure you have the latest state of your peripherals.

Understanding the sf::Event

Once again, `sf::Event` is something we briefly touched on, however, it's imperative to expand on it and understand it better before proceeding, if we want to build a system that can seamlessly handle all types of events without any hiccups. First, let's reiterate what an event is. `sf::Event` is a union, which in C++ terms means that it's a special class which can hold only one of its non-static data members at a time, of which it has several, such as `KeyEvent`, which holds the information about a keyboard event, `SizeEvent`, which holds information about the size of our window that got resized, and many others. Because of this nature of `sf::Event`, it can be a trap for newcomers if they handle the event in a wrong way, such as accessing the `KeyEvent` struct inside `sf::Event`, when that is not the active data member. Since all the members of a union share the *same memory space*, this results in undefined behavior and will crash your application, unless you know what you're doing.

Let's take a look at the most basic way of processing events:

```
sf::Event event;

while(m_window.pollEvent(event)){
    switch(event.type){
    case sf::Event::Closed:
        m_window.close();
        break;

    case sf::Event::KeyPressed:
        if(event.key.code == sf::Keyboard::W){
            // Do something when W key gets pressed once.
        }
        break;
    }
}
```

Nothing we haven't seen before, although it's important we fill in the blanks of what exactly is going on. First, the `sf::Event` instance named `event` gets filled out by the `pollEvent()` method. Based on its type, it will choose one of the structures in the union to be the active one to carry the data relevant to the event. Afterwards, we can check for the type of the event, which is defined by the `sf::Event::Type` enumeration table and make sure we're using the correct data member to obtain the information we need. As mentioned before, trying to access `event.key.code` if the event type is `sf::Event::Closed`, for example, would result in an undefined behavior.

Remember, using the `sf::Event::KeyPressed` event for something like real-time character movement is a bad idea. This event gets dispatched only once before a small delay is applied and then it gets dispatched again. Think of a document editor here. When you press down on a key and hold it, at first it only shows a single character before it writes more. This is exactly the same way this event works. Using it for any action that needs to be continuous as long as the key is being held down is not even close to optimal and should be replaced with `sf::Keyboard::isKeyPressed()` in order to check the actual state of the key. The same idea applies to the mouse and controller input. Using these events is ideal for things that only need to happen once per keystroke, but not much else.

While this approach is manageable in cases of small projects, pretty much the same as the input example was before, it can get out of hand quickly on a larger scale. Let's face it, handling all the events, keystrokes, and states of every input device the way we did in the previous project is a nightmare. Still not convinced? Imagine having an application where you want to check for multiple keys being pressed at the same time and call some function when they are. Not too bad? Well, let's include events in that scenario. You want to check for two keys being pressed and a certain event taking place at the same time, in order to call a function. That adds another layer of complexity, but nothing you can't handle, right? Throwing in some Boolean flags in there to keep track of the event states or maybe the keystrokes shouldn't be too hard.

Some time passes and the application now needs support for loading key combinations from a file in order to make your approach more dynamic and customizable. You have a mess on your hands. You can build it, but it's going to be so awkward to add new functionality or expand that mountain of nonsense that you are likely to just throw your arms in the air and give up. Why put yourself through all of that when with just some effort and white-boarding you can come up with an automated approach that will need no flags, is flexible, can load any combination of keys and events from a file, and still keep your code just as neat and clean as it was before, if not more so? Let's solve this problem intelligently by working on a system that will handle all of these headaches for us.

Introducing the event manager

Figuring out what we want from our application is the first and the most crucial part of the design process. Sometimes it's difficult to cover all your bases, but forgetting about a feature that might alter the way all the code is structured and trying to implement it later can wreak some serious havoc on all the work you put into your software. Having said that, let's make a list of what features we want our event manager to have:

- The ability to couple any mix of keys, buttons, or events (from now on referred to as bindings) with desired functionality identified by a string
- Binding of the said functionalities to methods that get called if all the conditions (such as a key being pressed, the left mouse button being clicked, or the window losing focus, for example) for the binding are satisfied
- A way through which the event manager can deal with actual SFML events being polled
- Loading the bindings from a configuration file

We have our specifications, now let's start designing! We'll be using the EventManager.h file to include all the little bits and pieces that make this possible on top of having the definition of the class. The first thing that we need to define is all the types of events we'll be dealing with. This can be extended later on, but as this will more than suit our purposes for now, we don't need to worry about that just yet. Let's write the enumeration table:

```
enum class EventType{
    KeyDown = sf::Event::KeyPressed,
    KeyUp = sf::Event::KeyReleased,
    MButtonDown = sf::Event::MouseButtonPressed,
    MButtonUp = sf::Event::MouseButtonReleased,
    MouseWheel = sf::Event::MouseWheelMoved,
    WindowResized = sf::Event::Resized,
    GainedFocus = sf::Event::GainedFocus,
    LostFocus = sf::Event::LostFocus,
    MouseEntered = sf::Event::MouseEntered,
    MouseLeft = sf::Event::MouseLeft,
    Closed = sf::Event::Closed,
    TextEntered = sf::Event::TextEntered,
    Keyboard = sf::Event::Count + 1, Mouse, Joystick
};
```

The majority of these are actual events; however, note the last row before the enumeration is terminated. We're setting up our own event, called `Keyboard` to the value of `sf::Event::Count + 1`. Because all the enumerations are essentially keywords pointing to integer values, the last row prevents any kind of identifier clashing and makes sure that anything added past this point is higher than the absolute maximum `sf::Event::EventType` enumeration value. As long as anything added before the last row is a valid event type, there should be no clashes.

 The `sf::Event` enumeration values can be different, depending on which version of SFML you are using!

Next, let's make it possible to store these groups of events for each binding. We know that in order to bind to a key, we need both the event type and the code for the key that we're interested in. Some events we'll be working with only need to have a type stored, in which cases we can simply store an integer value of 0 with the type. Knowing that, let's define a new structure that will help us store this information:

```
struct EventInfo{
    EventInfo(){ m_code = 0; }
    EventInfo(int l_event){ m_code = l_event; }
    union{
        int m_code;
    };
};
```

In order to leave room for expansions, we're already using a **union** to store the event code. Next, we can set up the data type that we're going to be using to hold the event information:

```
using Events = std::vector<std::pair<EventType, EventInfo>>;
```

Since we're going to need to share the event information with the code that uses this class, now is as good a time as any to set up a data type that will help us do that:

```
struct EventDetails{
    EventDetails(const std::string& l_bindName)
        : m_name(l_bindName)
    {
        Clear();
    }
    std::string m_name;

    sf::Vector2i m_size;
    sf::Uint32 m_textEntered;
```

```
    sf::Vector2i m_mouse;
    int m_mouseWheelDelta;
    int m_keyCode; // Single key code.

    void Clear(){
        m_size = sf::Vector2i(0, 0);
        m_textEntered = 0;
        m_mouse = sf::Vector2i(0, 0);
        m_mouseWheelDelta = 0;
        m_keyCode = -1;
    }
};
```

Now it's time to design the binding structure, which is going to hold all the event information. Seems quite simple, so let's implement it:

```
struct Binding{
    Binding(const std::string& l_name)
        : m_name(l_name), m_details(l_name), c(0){}
    void BindEvent(EventType l_type,
        EventInfo l_info = EventInfo())
    {
        m_events.emplace_back(l_type, l_info);
    }

    Events m_events;
    std::string m_name;
    int c; // Count of events that are "happening".

    EventDetails m_details;
};
```

The constructor takes the name of the action we want to bind the events to and uses the initializer list to set up the class data members. We also have a `BindEvent()` method, which simply takes in an event type and an event information structure in order to add it to the event vector. One additional data member that we haven't mentioned before is the integer with the name `c`. As the comment suggests, this keeps track of how many events are actually taking place, which will be useful later on in order to determine if all the keys and events in the binding are "on". Lastly, this is the structure where the event detail data member that gets shared around resides.

These bindings will also have to be stored somehow, so let's define the data type for the container that will take care of it:

```
using Bindings = std::unordered_map<std::string, Binding*>;
```

Using `std::unordered_map` for our bindings guarantees that there will only be one binding per action, since it's an associative container and the action name string is the key for that container.

We're doing great so far, however, without a way to actually tie these actions to valid methods that will get called, this system is fairly useless. Let's talk about how we could implement this. In the world of computer science, every now and then you've probably heard the term "callback" being thrown around. In simplest terms, a callback is some chunk of code that gets passed as an argument to another piece of code, which *will* execute it at a convenient time. In the case of our event manager, the convenient time is whenever all the events that are bound to a specific action are happening, and the callback is a method that represents the action being performed. Let's say, we want the character to jump when the spacebar is hit. We would create a binding with a name "Jump", which is our action name, and add a single event of type `KeyDown` and code `sf::Keyboard::Space` to it. For argument sake, let's say the character has a method called `Jump()`. That's our callback. We want to bind that method to the name "Jump" and have the event manager call the character's `Jump()` method when the space key is pressed. That, in a nutshell, is how we're going to be handling input with this new system.

By now, your C++ background is probably driving you towards the term "function pointers". While that's not necessarily a bad option, it can get a little messy if you're quite new to the scene. The main problem with that approach is the scenario of adding a method of a class as a callback. Pointers to the class members aren't exactly the same as regular functions, unless it's a static method. Following is a basic definition of a member function pointer:

```
void(SomeClass::*_callback)();
```

Already this shows a few major limitations. For one, we can only have pointers to methods of the class "SomeClass". Secondly, without having an instance to the class that has the method we're pointing to, it's quite useless. A thought has probably popped into your mind of just storing the instance together with the function pointer in some callback structure. Let's take a look:

```
struct Callback{
    std::string m_name;
    SomeClass* CallbackInstance; // Pointer to instance.
    void(SomeClass::*_callback)();
```

```
    void Call(){
    CallbackInstance->*_callback();
    }
};
```

That's a little better. At least we can call the method now, although we're still limited to only one class. We could just wrap every other class method call in the methods of the "SomeClass" class, but that's tedious and more importantly, it's a bad practice. Maybe now you're thinking that some template magic might solve this problem. While it is possible, you have to also take into account the compatibility and the mess that it might create. Consider the most minimum amount of effort this could possibly take:

```
template<class T>
struct Callback{
    ...
    T* CallbackInstance; // Pointer to instance.
    void(T::*_callback)();
    ...
};
```

This by itself doesn't solve anything, but instead it only brings more problems. For one, you now have to define that template in your event manager class, which is problematic because we need a container for all these callbacks and that means having to template the entire event manager class, which locks it down to one class type. We're right back to where we started. Using typedef would be a clever idea, except that it's not supported in most of the Visual Studio compilers in this form:

```
template <class T>
using Function = void (T::*)();
```

There are some hackish workarounds for non C++11 compilers, like wrapping typedef in struct after defining the template. However, that doesn't solve our problem either. There have been instances of the Visual Studio 2010 compiler even crashing when using "templated" member function pointer type definitions. This is quite a mess, and at this point you're probably thinking about simply going back to regular function pointers and wrapping every single member function call in a different function. Fear not, C++11 introduces a much better approach than that.

Standard function wrapper

The C++ utilities library provides us with just what we need in order to solve this pickle elegantly: `std::function` and `std::bind`. The `std::function` type is a general purpose polymorphic function wrapper. Amongst many other things it supports, it can store the member function pointers and call them. Let's take a look at a minimal example of using it:

```
#include <functional> // Defines std::function & std::bind.
...
std::function<void(void)> foo = std::bind(&Bar::method1, this);
```

In this case, we're instantiating a function wrapper called "`foo`", which holds a function with the signature `void(void)`. On the right side of the equals sign, we use `std::bind` to bind the member function "`method1`" of the class "`Bar`" to the `foo` object. The second argument, because this is a member function pointer, is the instance of the class that is having its method registered as a callback. In this case, it has to be an instance of the `Bar` class, so let's imagine this line of code is written somewhere in the implementation of it and just pass in "`this`". Now our `foo` object is bound to the method `method1` of class `Bar`. Because `std::function` overloads the parenthesis operator, calling it is as easy as this:

```
foo(); // Equivalent to barInstance->method1();
```

Now we can finally define the type of the callback container:

```
using Callbacks = std::unordered_map<std::string,
    std::function<void(EventDetails*)>>;
```

Once again, using `std::unordered_map` ensures that there's only one callback per action. This can be changed later if needed.

Building the event manager

At this time, we have everything we need to actually write the header of our event manager class. Given all the design decisions we made previously, it should come out looking something like the following:

```
class EventManager{
public:
    EventManager();
    ~EventManager();

    bool AddBinding(Binding *l_binding);
    bool RemoveBinding(std::string l_name);
```

```cpp
    void SetFocus(const bool& l_focus);

    // Needs to be defined in the header!
    template<class T>
    bool AddCallback(const std::string& l_name,
      void(T::*l_func)(EventDetails*), T* l_instance)
    {
        auto temp = std::bind(l_func,l_instance,
          std::placeholders::_1);
        return m_callbacks.emplace(l_name, temp).second;
    }

    void RemoveCallback(const std::string& l_name){
        m_callbacks.erase(l_name);
    }

    void HandleEvent(sf::Event& l_event);
    void Update();

    sf::Vector2i GetMousePos(sf::RenderWindow* l_wind = nullptr){
        return (l_wind ? sf::Mouse::getPosition(*l_wind)
            : sf::Mouse::getPosition());
    }
private:
    void LoadBindings();

    Bindings m_bindings;
    Callbacks m_callbacks;
    bool m_hasFocus;
};
```

As you can gather from looking at the class definition, we still needed to use a templated member function pointer argument for the `AddCallback()` method. The use of `std::function`, however, isolates this to a single method, meaning we don't have to template the entire class, and that is an improvement. After the pointers to the method and the instance of the class, as well as a single placeholder that will be replaced by an argument in the future, are bound to a temporary function, we insert it into the callback container. Because of the way the compiler deals with the templated classes, we need to implement our template `AddCallback()` method in the header file, instead of the .cpp file. Just for the sake of consistency, and because it's a really simple method, we define `RemoveCallback()` in the header file too.

The other thing worthy of pointing out about the header is the implementation of the method that will be used to obtain the position of the mouse: `GetMousePos()`. It takes a pointer to a type of `sf::RenderWindow`, in case we want the coordinates returned to be relative to a specific window. The same window can also have or lose focus, so a flag `m_hasFocus` is kept around to keep track of that.

Implementing the event manager

Let's get started with actually implementing all the event manager class methods, starting, as always, with the constructor and destructor:

```
EventManager::EventManager(): m_hasFocus(true){ LoadBindings(); }
EventManager::~EventManager(){
    for (auto &itr : m_bindings){
        delete itr.second;
        itr.second = nullptr;
    }
}
```

The constructor's job in this case is really simple. All it has to do is call a private method `LoadBindings()`, which is used to load the information about our bindings from a file. We will cover that shortly.

The destructor's job is also fairly run-of-the-mill for this type of class. If you recall, we store the bindings on the heap, so this dynamic memory has to be de-allocated.

Let's take a gander at the `AddBinding` method implementation:

```
bool EventManager::AddBinding(Binding *l_binding){
    if (m_bindings.find(l_binding->m_name) != m_bindings.end())
        return false;

    return m_bindings.emplace(l_binding->m_name,
        l_binding).second;
}
```

As you can see, it takes in a pointer to a binding. It then checks if the binding container already has a binding with the same name. If it does, the method returns `false`, which is useful for error-checking. If there are no name clashes, the new binding gets inserted into the container.

We have a way to add the bindings, but what about removing them? That's where the `RemoveBinding` method comes in:

```
bool EventManager::RemoveBinding(std::string l_name){
    auto itr = m_bindings.find(l_name);
    if (itr == m_bindings.end()){ return false; }
    delete itr->second;
    m_bindings.erase(itr);
    return true;
}
```

It takes in a string argument and searches the container for a match to store into an iterator. If a match is found, it first frees up the memory by deleting the second element in the key-value pair, which is the dynamic memory allocated for the binding object, and then erases the entry from the container shortly before returning `true` for success. Easy.

As mentioned in the specifications for designing this class, we need a way to process the SFML events that are being polled in each iteration in order to look at them and see if there's anything in there we're interested in. This is where `HandleEvent` comes in:

```
void EventManager::HandleEvent(sf::Event& l_event){
  // Handling SFML events.
  for (auto &b_itr : m_bindings){
    Binding* bind = b_itr.second;
    for (auto &e_itr : bind->m_events){
      EventType sfmlEvent = (EventType)l_event.type;
      if (e_itr.first != sfmlEvent){ continue; }
      if (sfmlEvent == EventType::KeyDown ||
        sfmlEvent == EventType::KeyUp)
      {
        if (e_itr.second.m_code == l_event.key.code){
          // Matching event/keystroke.
          // Increase count.
          if (bind->m_details.m_keyCode != -1){
            bind->m_details.m_keyCode = e_itr.second.m_code;
          }
          ++(bind->c);
          break;
        }
      } else if (sfmlEvent == EventType::MButtonDown ||
        sfmlEvent == EventType::MButtonUp)
      {
```

```
            if (e_itr.second.m_code == l_event.mouseButton.button){
              // Matching event/keystroke.
              // Increase count.
              bind->m_details.m_mouse.x = l_event.mouseButton.x;
              bind->m_details.m_mouse.y = l_event.mouseButton.y;
              if (bind->m_details.m_keyCode != -1){
                bind->m_details.m_keyCode = e_itr.second.m_code;
              }
              ++(bind->c);
              break;
            }
          } else {
            // No need for additional checking.
            if (sfmlEvent == EventType::MouseWheel){
              bind->m_details.m_mouseWheelDelta =
                  l_event.mouseWheel.delta;
            } else if (sfmlEvent == EventType::WindowResized){
              bind->m_details.m_size.x = l_event.size.width;
              bind->m_details.m_size.y = l_event.size.height;
            } else if (sfmlEvent == EventType::TextEntered){
              bind->m_details.m_textEntered = l_event.text.unicode;
            }
            ++(bind->c);
          }
        }
      }
    }
  }
```

It takes in, appropriately enough, an argument of type sf::Event. This method then has to iterate over all the bindings and through each event inside the binding to check if the type of the l_event argument matches the type of the binding event that's currently being processed. If it does, we check if it's a keyboard event or a mouse event, because that involves further checking for the keyboard keys or the mouse buttons matching our desired bindings. If it is either one of them, the last step is to check if either the keyboard key code or the mouse button code, which are respectively stored in the l_event.key and l_event.mouseButton structs, match the code of our binding event. With that being the case, or if it's a different type of event that doesn't require further processing, as demonstrated a few lines down, we increment the member c of the binding instance to signify a match shortly after relevant event information is stored in the event details structure of the binding.

Lastly, for input processing, we need to have an update method, which can handle real-time input checking as well as the validating and resetting of the states of the bindings. Let's write it:

```
void EventManager::Update(){
  if (!m_hasFocus){ return; }
  for (auto &b_itr : m_bindings){
    Binding* bind = b_itr.second;
    for (auto &e_itr : bind->m_events){
      switch (e_itr.first){
      case(EventType::Keyboard) :
        if (sf::Keyboard::isKeyPressed(
          sf::Keyboard::Key(e_itr.second.m_code)))
        {
          if (bind->m_details.m_keyCode != -1){
            bind->m_details.m_keyCode = e_itr.second.m_code;
          }
          ++(bind->c);
        }
      break;
      case(EventType::Mouse) :
        if (sf::Mouse::isButtonPressed(
          sf::Mouse::Button(e_itr.second.m_code)))
        {
          if (bind->m_details.m_keyCode != -1){
            bind->m_details.m_keyCode = e_itr.second.m_code;
          }
          ++(bind->c);
        }
      break;
      case(EventType::Joystick) :
        // Up for expansion.
        break;
      }
    }

    if (bind->m_events.size() == bind->c){
      auto callItr = m_callbacks.find(bind->m_name);
      if(callItr != m_callbacks.end()){
        callItr->second(&bind->m_details);
      }
    }
    bind->c = 0;
    bind->m_details.Clear();
  }
}
```

Once again, we iterate over all the bindings and their events. In this case, however, we're only interested in `Keyboard`, `Mouse`, and `Joystick`, as those are the only devices we can check the real-time input of. Much like before, we check for the type of event we're dealing with, and use the appropriate class to check for the input. Incrementing the `c` member of the binding class, as usual, is our way of registering a match.

The final step is checking if the number of events in the event container matches the number of events that are "on". If that's the case, we locate our callback in the `m_callbacks` container and invoke the `second` data member with the parenthesis operator, because it is an `std::function` method wrapper, in turn officially implementing the callbacks. To it, we pass the address of the `EventDetails` structure that contains all the event information. Afterwards, it's important to reset the active event counter `c` to `0` for the next iteration because the state of any of the events checked previously could've changed and they all need to be re-evaluated.

Lastly, if you looked at the code top to bottom, you probably noticed that the case for controller input isn't doing anything. As a matter of fact, we don't even handle any events related to the controller. This is something that can be expanded later on and isn't vital to any of our projects. If you are eager to add support for joysticks and have access to one, consider it to be homework after this chapter.

Now that we have all this functionality, why not actually read in some binding information from a file? Let's take a look at the example configuration, named `keys.cfg`, that we will be loading in:

```
Window_close 0:0
Fullscreen_toggle 5:89
Move 9:0 24:38
```

This can be formatted in any way you want, however, for the sake of simplicity, the layout for it will remain pretty basic here. Each line is a new binding. It starts with the binding name, which is followed by the numerical representation of the event type enumeration and the code for the event separated by a colon. Every different event key:value pair is separated by spaces, as well as the binding name and the beginning of the events. Let's read this in:

```
void EventManager::LoadBindings(){
  std::string delimiter = ":";

  std::ifstream bindings;
  bindings.open("keys.cfg");
  if (!bindings.is_open()){
    std::cout << "! Failed loading keys.cfg." << std::endl;
    return;
```

```
        }
        std::string line;
        while (std::getline(bindings, line)){
            std::stringstream keystream(line);
            std::string callbackName;
            keystream >> callbackName;
            Binding* bind = new Binding(callbackName);
            while (!keystream.eof()){
                std::string keyval;
                keystream >> keyval;
                int start = 0;
                int end = keyval.find(delimiter);
                if (end == std::string::npos){
                    delete bind;
                    bind = nullptr;
                    break;
                }
                EventType type = EventType(
                    stoi(keyval.substr(start, end - start)));
                int code = stoi(keyval.substr(end + delimiter.length(),
                    keyval.find(delimiter, end + delimiter.length())));
                    EventInfo eventInfo;
                eventInfo.m_code = code;

                bind->BindEvent(type, eventInfo);
            }

            if (!AddBinding(bind)){ delete bind; }
            bind = nullptr;
        }
        bindings.close();
    }
```

We start by attempting to open the `keys.cfg` file. If it fails, this method spits out
a console message notifying us about it. Next, we proceed into a `while` loop in
order to read every single line in the file. We define an `std::stringstream` object,
which allows us to nicely "stream" our string piece by piece, using the `>>` operator.
It uses the default delimiter of a space, which is why we made that decision for the
configuration file. After obtaining the name of our binding, we create a new `Binding`
instance and pass the name in the constructor. Afterwards, by proceeding into a
`while` loop and using `!keystream.eof()` as an argument, we make sure that it loops
until the `std::stringstream` object reaches the end of the line it was reading. This
loop runs once for each key:value pair, once again thanks to `std::stringstream`
and its overloaded `>>` operator using whitespaces as delimiters by default.

After streaming in the type and code of an event, we have to make sure that we convert it from a string into two integer values, which are then stored in their respective local variables. It takes in parts of the string that got read in earlier in order to separate the key:value pair by splitting it at the delimiter character, which in this case was defined at the very top of this method as ":". If that character is not found within the string, the binding instance gets deleted and the line gets skipped, because it is most likely not formatted properly. If that's not the case, then the event gets successfully bound and the code moves on to the next pair.

Once all the values are read in and the end of the line is reached, we attempt to add the binding to the event manager. It is done in the if-statement in order to catch the error we talked about earlier relating to binding name clashes. If there is a clash, the binding instance gets deleted.

As you probably already know, it's also important to close the file after using it, so that's the last thing we do before this method concludes. With that done, our event manager is finally complete and it's time to actually put it to work.

Integrating the Event Manager class

Because the event manager needs to check all the events that get processed, it makes sense to keep it in our `Window` class, where we actually do the event polling. After all, the events that we're processing all originate from the window that's open, so it only makes sense to keep an instance of the event manager here. Let's make a slight adjustment to the `Window` class by adding a data member to it:

```
class Window{
public:
    ...
    bool IsFocused();
    EventManager* GetEventManager();
    void ToggleFullscreen(EventDetails* l_details);
    void Close(EventDetails* l_details = nullptr);
    ...
private:
    ...
    EventManager m_eventManager;
    bool m_isFocused;
};
```

In addition to adding an extra method for obtaining the event manager, the full screen toggle method has been modified to take in the `EventDetails` structure as an argument. A `Close` method is also added to our `Window` class, as well as a flag to keep track of whether the window is in focus or not. The method for closing the window itself is as simple as setting a single flag to `true`:

```
void Window::Close(){ m_isDone = true; }
```

Now it's time to adjust the `Window::Update` method and pass in all the events being polled to the event manager:

```
void Window::Update(){
    sf::Event event;
    while(m_window.pollEvent(event)){
        if (event.type == sf::Event::LostFocus){
            m_isFocused = false;
            m_eventManager.SetFocus(false);
        }
        else if (event.type == sf::Event::GainedFocus){
            m_isFocused = true;
            m_eventManager.SetFocus(true);
        }
        m_eventManager.HandleEvent(event);
    }
    m_eventManager.Update();
}
```

This ensures that every single event that ever gets dispatched in the window will be properly handled. It also notifies the event manager if the focus of the window changes.

Time to actually use the event manager! Let's do that in `Window::Setup` by registering two callbacks to some member functions, right after creating a new instance of the event manager:

```
void Window::Setup(...){
    ...
    m_isFocused = true; // Default value for focused flag.
    m_eventManager->AddCallback("Fullscreen_toggle",
      &Window::ToggleFullscreen,this);
    m_eventManager->AddCallback("Window_close",
      &Window::Close,this);
    ...
}
```

Let's refer back to the `keys.cfg` file. We define the `Fullscreen_toggle` action and set up a key:value pair of 5:89, which essentially gets broken down to the event type of `KeyDown` (the number 5) and the code for the *F5* key on the keyboard (number 89). Both of these values are integer representations of the enumerations that we used.

The other callback that gets set up is for the action `Window_close`, which in the configuration file is bound to 0:0. The event type 0 corresponds to `Closed` in the enumeration table, and the code is irrelevant, so we just set that to 0 as well.

Both these actions get bound to methods of the `Window` class. Note the last argument in the `AddCallback` method, which is a `this` pointer referring to the current instance of the window. After successful compilation and launch, you should discover that hitting the *F5* key on your keyboard toggles the full screen mode of the window and clicking on the close button actually closes it. It works! Let's do something a little bit more fun with this now.

Moving a sprite revisited

Now that we have a fancy event manager, let's test it fully by moving a sprite to the location of the mouse when the left shift key is held down and the left mouse button is pressed. Add two new data members to your `Game` class: `m_texture` and `m_sprite`. Set them up as discussed in the previous chapters. For our purposes, we'll just be re-using the mushroom graphic from the first few chapters. Now add and implement a new method in your game class called `MoveSprite`:

```
void Game::MoveSprite(EventDetails* l_details){
    sf::Vector2i mousepos =
      m_window->GetEventManager()->GetMousePos(
      m_window->GetRenderWindow());
    m_sprite.setPosition(mousepos.x, mousepos.y);
    std::cout << "Moving sprite to: "
      << mousepos.x << ":"
      << mousepos.y << std::endl;
}
```

What we do here is grab the mouse position relative to the current window from the event manager and store it in a local integer vector called `mousepos`. We then set the position of our sprite to the current mouse position and print out a little sentence in the console window. Very basic, but it will serve nicely as a test. Let's set up our callback:

```
Game::Game(){
    ...
    // Texture and sprite setup.
```

```
    ...
    m_window->GetEventManager()->AddCallback("Move",
        &Game::MoveSprite,this);
}
```

We tie the action name Move to the MoveSprite method of the Game class and pass in a pointer to the current instance, just like before. Before running this, let's take a peek at the way the move action is defined in the keys.cfg file:

```
Move 9:0 24:38
```

The first event type corresponds to MButtonDown, which is the event of the left mouse button being pressed down. The second event type corresponds to the Keyboard event, which checks for real-time input through the sf::Keyboard class. The number 38 is the left shift key code, corresponding to sf::Keyboard::LShift.

Upon compilation and execution of our application, we should end up with a sprite being rendered on the screen. If we hold the left shift key and left click anywhere on the screen, it will magically move to that position!

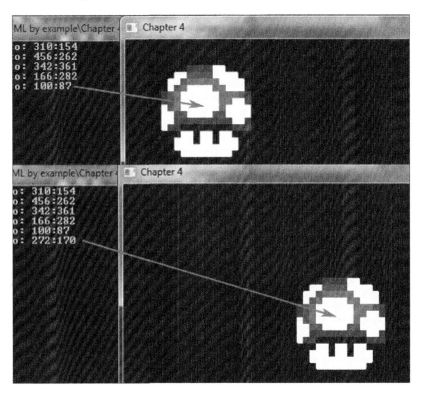

Principles of use

Knowing when to use which types of events is important even in this design. Let's say, for example, that you only want a callback to be called once for a binding that involves the left shift and the *R* key. You wouldn't define both the event types as `Keyboard`, because that would keep invoking the callback method as long as these keys are down. You also don't want to define both of them as `KeyDown` events, because that would mean that both of these events would have to be registered at the same time, which, when holding down multiple keys, is likely not going to happen because of the screen refresh rate. The correct way to use this is mixing the `Keyboard` and `KeyDown` events so that the very last key to be pressed is the `KeyDown` type and the rest of the keys will be `Keyboard` types. In our example, it means that we would have the left shift key being checked through the `sf::Keyboard` class, while the *R* key would default to an event being dispatched. That might sound odd at first, however, consider the famous example of the key combination *Ctrl + Alt + Del* on your computer. It works that way, but if you hold the keys in reverse order, it would do nothing. If we were implementing this functionality, we'd most likely make sure that the *Ctrl* and *Alt* keys are always checked through the `sf::Keyboard` class, while the *Del* key is registered through the event polling.

One last thing to note as far as the use of this class goes, is that some events aren't yet supported, such as the `sf::Event::TextEntered` event because additional information is required in order to fully utilize them, which is obtained from the `sf::Event` class. Proper expansion of the event manager to support these features will be covered in the later chapters, once we're dealing with problems that require the said events.

Common mistakes

One of the most common mistakes the newcomers make when it comes to SFML input is using certain methods of checking the user input for the wrong tasks, such as using the window events for real time character movement or capturing text input. Understanding the limitations of anything you use is the key to cultivating any kind of decent performance. Make sure to stick to the intended uses of all the different mechanisms we've discussed in order to achieve optimal results.

Another fairly common mistake people make is defining templates in the .cpp file instead of the header. If you are getting linking errors pertaining to a method that just so happens to utilize templates, such as the `EventManager::AddCallback()` method, make sure to move the implementation of the method and the definition of the template right to the header of your class, otherwise the compiler cannot instantiate the template and the method becomes inaccessible during the linking process.

Lastly, a rather simple yet extremely popular mistake lots of new users of SFML are guilty of is not knowing how to correctly obtain the mouse coordinates that are relative to the window. It ranges from simply using the wrong coordinates and experiencing weird behavior to grabbing the coordinates relative to the desktop as well as the position of the window and subtracting one from another to obtain the local mouse position. While the latter works, it's a bit excessive, especially since SFML already provides you with a way to do it without reinventing the wheel. Simply pass in a reference of your window to the `sf::Mouse::getPosition()` method. That's all you need.

Summary

Much like proper code organization, robust input management is one of the many things that can mean the difference between you happily developing an application and the same application drowning in the sea of other failed projects. With proper and flexible design comes great code reusability, so congratulations on taking yet another step towards building an application that will not bite the dust simply because it was painful to work with due to its myopic construction.

There is no design in this world that's inarguably perfect, however, with this chapter coming to fruition we are now yet another step closer to the goal that we set for ourselves at the very beginning of this experience. This goal varies between individuals. Maybe it has grown since we started; it may have even manifested itself into something completely different than it was before. None of that is certain to the rest of us, but it doesn't really matter. What matters is that we are in full control of where we take those goals, even if we have no control of where they take us. And while this journey towards our goals continues, and even as the new ones begin to emerge, we can now say that we have stronger means of taking control over the entire process, much like we built our own stronger means of taking control of our applications. So, move yourself forward to the next chapter and resume your journey, by learning about application states. We'll see you there!

5
Can I Pause This?
– Application States

A piece of software like a video game is rarely as simple as the term suggests. Most of the time, it's not just the game mechanics and rendering one has to deal with in such an application. Nowadays, an industry-standard product also includes a nice introduction animation before the game begins. It also has a menu for the player to tinker with in order to start playing the game, manage the different settings it offers, view the credits or quit the application. On top of that, the title of this chapter also suggests the possibility of putting your game on pause for a moment or two. In hindsight, it's simple conveniences like this that draw the line in the sand between a game in its early stages, that's awkward to navigate and possibly confusing, and a product that offers the same level of control as most games on the market. To supply the backbone to such an idea, in this chapter we will be covering:

- Implementing the state manager
- Upgrading the event manager to handle different states
- Creating different states for the introduction, main menu and game-play sections of our game
- Providing the means to pause the game
- Implementing state blending
- Stringing the states together to create cohesive application flow

What is a state?

Before we get into any kind of implementation, it's necessary to understand what we're dealing with. If you've been reading up on any kind of game development material before, you probably came across the term **state**. It can mean different things, depending on its context. In this case, a state is any one of the many different layers of your game, like the main menu, the intro that plays before the menu is shown, or the actual game-play. Naturally, each one of these layers has its own way of updating itself and rendering its contents onto the screen. The game developer's job when utilizing this system is to break down a given problem into separate, manageable states and transitions between them. This essentially means that if you are presented with the problem of having a menu in the game, the solution would be creating two states, one for the menu and one for your game-play, and transitioning between the two at appropriate times.

The most simplistic approach

Let's begin by illustrating the most common approach newcomers take in order to solve this problem. It starts by enumerating all the possible states a game could have:

```
enum class StateType{
    Intro = 1, MainMenu, Game, Paused, GameOver, Credits
};
```

Good start. Now let's put it to work by simply using a `switch` statement:

```
void Game::Update(){
  switch(m_state){
    case(StateType::Intro):
      UpdateIntro();
      break;
    case(StateType::Game):
      UpdateGame();
      break;
    case(StateType::MainMenu):
      UpdateMenu();
      break;
    ...
  }
}
```

The same goes for drawing it on screen:

```
void Game::Render(){
  switch(m_state){
    case(StateType::Intro):
      DrawIntro();
      break;
    case(StateType::Game):
      DrawGame();
      break;
    case(StateType::MainMenu):
      DrawMenu();
      break;
    ...
  }
}
```

While this approach is okay for really small games, scalability here is completely out of the question. First of all, the switch statements are going to continue to grow when more states are added. Assuming we keep the functionality for updating and rendering a specific state localized to just one method, the number of these methods will also continue to grow by at least two methods per state, one of them being used for updating and another for rendering. Keep in mind, that's the *minimal* amount of expansion needed in order to support an extra state. If we also process events for each state individually or perform some kind of additional logic like *late updating*, that's four switch statements, one extra switch branch for each state and four extra methods that have to be implemented and added to the branches.

Next, consider state transitions. If, for whatever reason, you want to render two states at the same time for a short while, this entire approach collapses. It is possible to still somehow string that functionality together by tying up a bunch of flags or creating combination states as follows:

```
enum StateType{
    Intro = 1, Intro_MainMenu, MainMenu, Game, MainMenu_Game
    Paused, GameOver, MainMenu_GameOver, Credits, MainMenu_Credits
    ...
    // Crying in the corner.
};
```

This just keeps getting messier by the minute, and we haven't even got to expand our already large switch statements yet, let alone implement all the states we want!

If you still aren't thinking about migrating to a different tactic by now, consider this one final point: resources. If you're keeping all of the data from all of the possible states a game might have loaded at the same time, you may have quite a bit of a problem on your hands from the point of efficiency. You may dynamically allocate classes that represent certain states and check for when they're not in use anymore somehow to de-allocate them, however that's additional clutter in your already mostly unreadable code-base, and since you're already thinking of using classes, why not do it better?

Introducing the state pattern

All of the problems mentioned previously can be avoided after some careful white-boarding and consideration. The possibility was brought up earlier of different game states simply being localized to their own classes. All of these classes will share the same methods for being updated and rendered, which makes **inheritance** the word of the hour. Let's take a look at our base state header:

```
class StateManager;

class BaseState{
   friend class StateManager;
public:
   BaseState(StateManager* l_stateManager)
     :m_stateMgr(l_stateManager),m_transparent(false),
     m_transcendent(false){}
   virtual ~BaseState(){}

   virtual void OnCreate() = 0;
   virtual void OnDestroy() = 0;

   virtual void Activate() = 0;
   virtual void Deactivate() = 0;

   virtual void Update(const sf::Time& l_time) = 0;
   virtual void Draw() = 0;

   void SetTransparent(const bool& l_transparent){
     m_transparent = l_transparent;
   }
   bool IsTransparent()const{ return m_transparent; }
   void SetTranscendent(const bool& l_transcendence){
     m_transcendent = l_transcendence;
   }
```

```
    bool IsTranscendent()const{ return m_transcendent; }
    StateManager* GetStateManager(){ return m_stateMgr; }
  protected:
    StateManager* m_stateMgr;
    bool m_transparent;
    bool m_transcendent;
};
```

First, you'll notice we're using a *forward declaration* of the StateManager class. The base class doesn't really need to know anything about the way our state manager will be implemented, only that it needs to keep a pointer to it. This is also done in order to avoid *recursive definitions*, because the StateManager class header needs to include the BaseState class header.

Since we want to enforce the use of the same methods throughout all states, we make them *purely virtual*, which means that the class inheriting from BaseState has to implement each and every one of them in order for the project to compile. The methods that any derived class has to implement consist of OnCreate and OnDestroy, which get invoked when the state is created and pushed on the stack, and later removed from the stack, Activate and Deactivate, which are called once a state is moved to the top of the stack as well as when it gets removed from the top position, and lastly, Update and Draw, which are used for updating the state and drawing its contents.

One last thing to note about this class is that it has a pair of flags: m_transparent and m_transcendent. These flags indicate if this state also needs to render or update a state that came before it. This eliminates the need for countless enumerations of different transitions between states and can be done automatically without any additional expansion.

Defining common types

One thing that we're definitely going to keep from the previous example is the enumeration table of the state types:

```
enum class StateType{
    Intro = 1, MainMenu, Game, Paused, GameOver, Credits
};
```

Having the state types enumerated is convenient and it helps with automating the state creation, as you will see later on.

Another common type we need to keep around is the device context we'll be using with our states. Don't be confused by the name, it simply means having a pointer to some of our most commonly used classes or "devices." Because there's more than one, it's quite useful to define a simple structure that will keep around pointers to the main window class and the event manager:

```
struct SharedContext{
    SharedContext():m_wind(nullptr),m_eventManager(nullptr){}
    Window* m_wind;
    EventManager* m_eventManager;
};
```

This can and will be expanded later when needed, in order to hold information about the player and other assistant classes that deal with resource allocation, sound and networking.

The state manager class

Now that we have our helper structures set up, let's actually define the types that will be used to hold information in our state manager class. As always, we will be using type definitions, the beauty of which is the fact that they reduce the amount of code you have to change in a case of modifying something about the type definition. Let's take a look at the state container type first:

```
using StateContainer = std::vector<
    std::pair<StateType, BaseState*>>;
```

Once again, we're using a vector. The element type is a pair of our state type and a pointer to a `BaseState` type object. You might be wondering why a map isn't a better choice, and the answer depends on your idea of implementation, however, one major factor is that a map doesn't keep a stack-like order in the container, which is important if we want our state manager to work correctly.

One of the design decisions in the state manager class also requires a container of state types, so let's define that:

```
using TypeContainer = std::vector<StateType>;
```

As you can see, it's simply a vector of the `StateType` enumeration types.

The last type we need to define is a container for custom functions that will serve as a way of automatically producing objects of different types derived from the `BaseState` class:

```
using StateFactory = std::unordered_map<
    StateType, std::function<BaseState*(void)>>;
```

We're using an unordered map here in order to map a specific state type to a specific function that will generate that type. If that sounds confusing now, be patient. It will be covered more thoroughly when we actually use it.

Defining the state manager class

All the individual bits and pieces we needed to actually bang out a header for the state manager class are now present, so let's write it:

```
class StateManager{
public:
    StateManager(SharedContext* l_shared);
    ~StateManager();

    void Update(const sf::Time& l_time);
    void Draw();

    void ProcessRequests();

    SharedContext* GetContext();
    bool HasState(const StateType& l_type);

    void SwitchTo(const StateType& l_type);
    void Remove(const StateType& l_type);
private:
    // Methods.
    void CreateState(const StateType& l_type);
    void RemoveState(const StateType& l_type);

    template<class T>
    void RegisterState(const StateType& l_type){...}

    // Members.
    SharedContext* m_shared;
    StateContainer m_states;
    TypeContainer m_toRemove;
    StateFactory m_stateFactory;
};
```

The constructor takes in a pointer to the SharedContext type we talked about earlier, which will be created in our main Game class. Predictably enough, the state manager also employs the use of Update and Draw methods, because it will be operated by the Game class, and it's nice to keep the interface familiar. For convenience sake, it offers helper methods for obtaining the context as well as determining if it currently has a certain state on the stack.

Concluding the public methods, we have `SwitchTo`, which takes in a state type and changes the current state to one that corresponds to said type, and `Remove`, for removing a state from the state stack by its type.

If you looked at the class definition from top to bottom, you may have noticed that we have a `TypeContainer` member called `m_toRemove`. In order to ensure smooth and error-free transitions, we cannot simply delete any state we want from the state container at any time. A simple solution here is keeping track of the state types we want to remove and only removing them when they're no longer being used, which is what the `ProcessRequests` method does. It is called last in the game loop, which ensures that the states in the `m_toRemove` container are no longer in use.

Let's continue with the more advanced private methods and implementation of our state manager class in the next section.

Implementing the state manager

In order to maintain the automated approach of creating our states on the heap, we must have some way of defining how they're created. The `m_stateFactory` member is a map that links a state type to a `std::function` type, which we can be set to hold a body of a function through use of the lambda expression:

```
template<class T>
void RegisterState(const StateType& l_type){
    m_stateFactory[l_type] = [this]() -> BaseState*
    {
        return new T(this);
    };
}
```

The code above maps the type `l_type` in the `m_stateFactory` map to a function that simply returns a pointer to newly allocated memory. We're using templates here in order to reduce the amount of code. Because each state requires a pointer to the `StateManager` class in its constructor, we pass the *this pointer* in. We can now register different states like so:

```
StateManager::StateManager(SharedContext* l_shared)
  : m_shared(l_shared)
{
    RegisterState<State_Intro>(StateType::Intro);
    RegisterState<State_MainMenu>(StateType::MainMenu);
    RegisterState<State_Game>(StateType::Game);
    RegisterState<State_Paused>(StateType::Paused);
}
```

It's time to begin implementing the rest of the class now. Let's take a look at the destructor:

```
StateManager::~StateManager(){
    for (auto &itr : m_states){
        itr.second->OnDestroy();
        delete itr.second;
    }
}
```

Because we localize all the dynamic memory allocation of any states to this class, it's imperative that we also free the memory appropriately. Iterating over all the states and deleting the second value of the pair which makes up the element does just that.

Next, let's take a look at how to implement the draw method:

```
void StateManager::Draw(){
  if (m_states.empty()){ return; }
  if (m_states.back().second->IsTransparent()
    && m_states.size() > 1)
  {
    auto itr = m_states.end();
    while (itr != m_states.begin()){
      if (itr != m_states.end()){
        if (!itr->second->IsTransparent()){
          break;
        }
      }
      --itr;
    }
    for (; itr != m_states.end(); ++itr){
      itr->second->Draw();
    }
  } else {
    m_states.back().second->Draw();
  }
}
```

First, just like the Update method, we check if the state container has *at least one* state. If it does, we check the most recently added one's **transparency flag**, as well as if there's more than one state on the stack, otherwise the transparency would be useless. If there's only one state on the stack or if the current state isn't transparent, we simply invoke its Draw method. Otherwise, things get a little bit more interesting.

In order to correctly render transparent states, we must call their respective `Draw` methods in a correct order, where the latest state on the stack is drawn on screen last. To do that, it's necessary to iterate through the state vector *backwards* until a state is found that is either not transparent or is the first state on the stack, which is what the `while` loop does. After such state is found, the `Draw` calls of all states from and including the one found, up to the very last one are invoked in the `for` loop. This effectively renders multiple states at once in correct order.

A fairly similar procedure is followed when updating states:

```
void StateManager::Update(const sf::Time& l_time){
  if (m_states.empty()){ return; }
  if (m_states.back().second->IsTranscendent()
    && m_states.size() > 1)
  {
    auto itr = m_states.end();
    while (itr != m_states.begin()){
      if (itr != m_states.end()){
        if (!itr->second->IsTranscendent()){
          break;
        }
      }
      --itr;
    }
    for (; itr != m_states.end(); ++itr){
      itr->second->Update(l_time);
    }
  } else {
    m_states.back().second->Update(l_time);
  }
}
```

The state's *transcendence* flag is checked first, in order to determine whether the top state allows others to be updated. The state or states that need to get updated then have their `Update` methods invoked with the elapsed time passed in as the argument, more commonly known as **delta time**.

As always, we need to define some helper methods for a class to be truly flexible and useful:

```
SharedContext* StateManager::GetContext(){ return m_shared; }

bool StateManager::HasState(const StateType& l_type){
  for (auto itr = m_states.begin();
    itr != m_states.end(); ++itr)
```

```
    {
    if (itr->first == l_type){
        auto removed = std::find(m_toRemove.begin(),
          m_toRemove.end(), l_type);
        if (removed == m_toRemove.end()){ return true; }
        return false;
      }
    }
    return false;
  }
```

The first method of obtaining the context is pretty straightforward. All it does is return a pointer to the `m_shared` member. The second method simply iterates over the `m_states` container until it finds a state with the type `l_type` and returns `true`. If it doesn't find such state, or if the state is found but it's about to be removed, it returns `false`. This gives us a way to check if a certain state is on the stack.

Having a way to remove a state is just as necessary as having a way of adding one. Let's implement the public method `Remove`:

```
void StateManager::Remove(const StateType& l_type){
    m_toRemove.push_back(l_type);
}
```

This method pushes back a state type into the `m_toRemove` vector for later removal, which is then processed by this method:

```
void StateManager::ProcessRequests(){
    while (m_toRemove.begin() != m_toRemove.end()){
        RemoveState(*m_toRemove.begin());
        m_toRemove.erase(m_toRemove.begin());
    }
}
```

The last method of this class that ever gets called, `ProcessRequests`, simply iterates over the `m_toRemove` vector and invokes a private method `RemoveState` which takes care of actual resource de-allocation. It then removes the element, ensuring the container is cleared.

Being able to change the current state is of paramount importance, which is what the `SwitchTo` method takes care of:

```
void StateManager::SwitchTo(const StateType& l_type){
    m_shared->m_eventManager->SetCurrentState(l_type);
    for (auto itr = m_states.begin();
        itr != m_states.end(); ++itr)
```

```
{
    if (itr->first == l_type){
        m_states.back().second->Deactivate();
        StateType tmp_type = itr->first;
        BaseState* tmp_state = itr->second;
        m_states.erase(itr);
        m_states.emplace_back(tmp_type, tmp_state);
        tmp_state->Activate();
        return;
    }
}

// State with l_type wasn't found.
if (!m_states.empty()){ m_states.back().second->Deactivate(); }
CreateState(l_type);
m_states.back().second->Activate();
}
```

First, you will notice that we access the event manager through our shared context and call a method `SetCurrentState`. We haven't yet gotten around to adding it, however it will be covered shortly. What it does is it simply modifies an internal data member of the event manager class, which keeps track of which state the game is in.

Next, we must find the state with the type we want to switch to, so we iterate over the state vector. If we have a match, the current state that's about to be pushed back has its `Deactivate` method called to perform whatever functionality it has to, in case the state cares about when it gets moved down. Then, we create two temporary variables to hold the state type and the pointer to a state object, so we don't lose that information when the element we're interested in is removed from the vector by calling `erase`. After doing that, all the *iterators* to the state container are invalidated, but it doesn't matter in our case, because we no longer need any. Moving the desired state is now as simple as pushing back another element onto the vector and passing in our temporary variables. Then, we call the `Activate` method of the state that just got moved in case it has any logic that is needed to be performed at that time.

If the state with `l_type` isn't found, creating one is necessary. First, however, it's important to check if there's at least one state for which to call the `Deactivate` method, and call it, if there is one. After invoking a private method `CreateState` and passing in the state type, we grab the element from the state vector that was added most recently by `CreateState`, and call `Activate`.

It's time to see what exactly goes into creating a state:

```
void StateManager::CreateState(const StateType& l_type){
    auto newState = m_stateFactory.find(l_type);
    if (newState == m_stateFactory.end()){ return; }
    BaseState* state = newState->second();
    m_states.emplace_back(l_type, state);
    state->OnCreate();
}
```

A state factory iterator gets created and checked for matching the iterator returned by the `end()` method of `std::unordered_map`, allowing us to make sure a state with such type can be created. If it can, a pointer of type `BaseState`, called `state` is created. It catches the return result of our iterator's second value getting invoked as a function, which if you remember was the `std::function` type and returns a pointer to a newly created state class. This is how we put the previously mentioned "factory" to work. After retrieving a pointer to the newly allocated memory for a state, we simply push it back onto the state vector and call `OnCreate` for the state to do its internal logic regarding being freshly created.

How do we go about removing a state? Let's take a look:

```
void StateManager::RemoveState(const StateType& l_type){
  for (auto itr = m_states.begin();
    itr != m_states.end(); ++itr)
  {
    if (itr->first == l_type){
      itr->second->OnDestroy();
      delete itr->second;
      m_states.erase(itr);
      return;
    }
  }
}
```

As always when dealing with `std::vector` types, we iterate over it until a match is found. Removing the actual state begins by calling the `OnDestroy` method of said state, again, just so it can perform whatever logic it needs in order to be ready for removal. Then we simply de-allocate the memory by using the `delete` keyword. Finally, we erase the element from the state vector and return from the method.

Improving the Event Manager class

Having different states in a game will, without a shadow of a doubt, create situations where the same key or event will be needed by at least two of the states. Let's say we have a menu, where navigation is done by pressing the arrow keys. That's all fine, but what if the game-play state also registers the use of arrow keys and sets up its own callbacks? The very best case scenario is that callbacks from all states will be invoked at the same time and create weird behavior. Things get worse, however, when you have function pointers to methods that are no longer in memory, especially since nobody likes application crashes. A simple way of dealing with this problem is grouping the callbacks together by state and only invoking them if the current state is that of a callback. This obviously means some re-definition of the types being dealt with:

```
using CallbackContainer = std::unordered_map<
  std::string, std::function<void(EventDetails*)>>;
enum class StateType;
using Callbacks = std::unordered_map<
  StateType, CallbackContainer>;
```

Things are getting a little bit more complicated now. What used to be the `Callback` definition is now renamed `CallbackContainer`. We only want one of those per state, so it means having to use another map, which is where the new `Callback` definition comes in. It maps a state type to a `CallbackContainer` type, so that we can have only one `CallbackContainer` per state in addition to only one callback function per name.

Despite these changes, the declaration for `m_callbacks` in the event manager header remains the same:

```
Callbacks m_callbacks;
```

There is one minor addition to the class data member list, and that is the current state:

```
StateType m_currentState;
```

What does change, however, are the methods for adding, removing and utilizing callbacks. Let's adapt the `AddCallback` method to these changes:

```
template<class T>
bool AddCallback(StateType l_state, const std::string& l_name,
  void(T::*l_func)(EventDetails*), T* l_instance)
{
    auto itr = m_callbacks.emplace(
      l_state, CallbackContainer()).first;
```

```
        auto temp = std::bind(l_func, l_instance,
          std::placeholders::_1);
        return itr->second.emplace(l_name, temp).second;
    }
```

The first thing to note is that we have a new argument l_state in the method's footprint. Next, we attempt to insert a new element to the m_callbacks map, pairing together the state argument and a new CallbackContainer. Since a map can only have one element with a specific index, in this case it's the state type, the emplace method always returns a pair of elements, the first of which is an iterator. If the insertion succeeded, the iterator points to the element that was newly created. On the other hand, if an element with a specified index already existed, the iterator points to that element instead. This is a good strategy to use, because we need that iterator no matter what, and if there is no element with the index we specified, we're going to want to insert one.

After the function binding, which remains unchanged, we need to insert the actual callback into the CallbackContainer type, which is the second value in the pair that makes up the m_callbacks elements. The second value of a pair that gets returned by the insert method of a map is a Boolean that represents the success of an insertion, and that's what gets returned for error checking.

Now let's take a look at revising the removal of callbacks:

```
    bool RemoveCallback(StateType l_state, const std::string& l_name){
        auto itr = m_callbacks.find(l_state);
        if (itr == m_callbacks.end()){ return false; }
        auto itr2 = itr->second.find(l_name);
        if (itr2 == itr->second.end()){ return false; }
        itr->second.erase(l_name);
        return true;
    }
```

This one's fairly simple. All we do is use the find method twice instead of once. First, we find the state pair in the first map, then we erase the actual callback by its name in the second map, just like before.

The last part of making this work just the way we want is fixing the way callback functions are actually called. Due to the type definitions that got changed, the way we invoke callbacks is also slightly different:

```
    void EventManager::Update(){
      ...
      if (bind->m_events.size() == bind->c){
        auto stateCallbacks = m_callbacks.find(m_currentState);
```

```
    auto otherCallbacks = m_callbacks.find(StateType(0));

    if (stateCallbacks != m_callbacks.end()){
      auto callItr = stateCallbacks->second.find(bind->m_name);
      if (callItr != stateCallbacks->second.end()){
        // Pass in information about events.
        callItr->second(&bind->m_details);
      }
    }

    if (otherCallbacks != m_callbacks.end()){
      auto callItr = otherCallbacks->second.find(bind->m_name);
      if (callItr != otherCallbacks->second.end()){
        // Pass in information about events.
        callItr->second(&bind->m_details);
      }
    }
  }
  ...
}
```

The main difference here is that we have two states for which callbacks get checked now, not just one: `stateCallbacks` and `otherCallbacks`. The former is quite obvious, we're simply using `find` to obtain the map of all callbacks for the current state. The latter, however, passes in a state type value of `0`, which isn't a valid state type, since the enumeration starts at `1`. This is done because even in the case of having multiple states in a game, we still want to process global callbacks for the `Window` class, as well as other classes that extend beyond the scope of simple states and persist all the way throughout the life of an application. Anything with the state type `0` will be invoked regardless of which state we're in.

The rest is fairly straightforward. Just like before, we're using the find method of the second value in the iterator that gets returned from the first search, which is our actual callback map. If a match is found, the function gets invoked.

One last thing we want to do here is modify the `keys.cfg` file to hold some extra keys for us in order to use them later:

```
Window_close 0:0
Fullscreen_toggle 5:89
Intro_Continue 5:57
Mouse_Left 9:0
Key_Escape 5:36
Key_P 5:15
```

The `Intro_Continue` binding represents a Spacebar "key down" event, `Mouse_Left` is the mouse left click event, `Key_Escape` is bound to the *ESC* "key down" event, and lastly, `Key_P` represents the letter *P* "key down" event.

Incorporating the state manager

While it's not quite time for fanfare, excitement is definitely in order because we can finally put our brand new `StateManager` class to work! The `Game` class header modification is a good start:

```
...
#include "StateManager.h"
...
class Game{
public:
    ...
    void LateUpdate();
private:
    ...
    StateManager m_stateManager;
};
```

Sticking a new data member to the `Game` class and adding a new method for late updating are all the adjustments that need to be made in the header. Let's adjust the `Game` constructor to initialize the state manager:

```
Game::Game(): m_window("Chapter 5", sf::Vector2u(800, 600)),
  m_stateManager(&m_context)
{
    ...
    m_context.m_wind = &m_window;
    m_context.m_eventManager = m_window.GetEventManager();
    m_stateManager.SwitchTo(StateType::Intro);
}
```

Naturally, the first thing we do is create the context that will be used by all of the states and pass it into the constructor of the state manager. We then begin the "domino effect" by switching to the introduction state, which will in due time switch to other states and force the flow of the application.

Lastly, let's adjust the three most important methods of the Game class:

```
void Game::Update(){
    m_window.Update();
    m_stateManager.Update(m_elapsed);
}
void Game::Render(){
    m_window.BeginDraw();
    m_stateManager.Draw();
    m_window.EndDraw();
}
void Game::LateUpdate(){
    m_stateManager.ProcessRequests();
    RestartClock();
}
```

That's about as straightforward as it can be. One thing to note is that the RestartClock method is now called by the LateUpdate, which means we have to adjust the main.cpp file as follows:

```
#include "Game.h"

void main(int argc, void** argv[]){
    // Program entry point.
    Game game;
    while(!game.GetWindow()->IsDone()){
        game.Update();
        game.Render();
        game.LateUpdate();
    }
}
```

Everything seems to be in order now. Compiling and launching the application should give you a very impressive black screen. Hoorah! Let's actually create some states for the game in order to honor the work that was put into this.

Creating the intro state

It seems rather fitting to start with the intro state, in turn giving the state manager a bit of an introduction at the same time. As always, a good place to start is with the header file, so let's get going:

```
class State_Intro : public BaseState{
public:
    ...
```

```
    void Continue(EventDetails* l_details);
private:
    sf::Texture m_introTexture;
    sf::Sprite m_introSprite;
    sf::Text m_text;
    float m_timePassed;
};
```

The `State_Intro` class, just like all the other state classes we'll build, inherits from the `BaseState` class. All of the purely virtual methods of the base class have to be implemented here. In addition to that, we have a unique method named `Continue` and some private data members that will be used in this state. Predictably enough, we will be rendering a sprite on screen, as well as some text. The floating point data member on the very bottom will be used to keep track of how much time we have spent in this state, in order to present the user with the ability to hit the Spacebar key after a certain interval to proceed into the main menu. The `Continue` method is responsible for handling that transition.

Implementing the intro state

We are getting close to finishing our first functional state! All that needs to be finished now is the actual implementation of the methods declared in the header file, and we're golden. Let's begin by including the header file of our class in `State_Intro.cpp`:

```
#include "State_Intro.h"
#include "StateManager.h"
```

Note the second line. Because the `StateManager` class is forwardly declared in the `BaseState` header, we *must* include the state manager header in the implementation file. This is true for any state we build in the future, including this one.

We will never use constructors and destructors of our states to initialize or allocate anything and instead rely on the `OnCreate` and `OnDestroy` methods in order to retain maximum control of when the resource allocation and de-allocation actually happens:

```
void State_Intro::OnCreate(){
  m_timePassed = 0.0f;

  sf::Vector2u windowSize = m_stateMgr->GetContext()->
    m_wind->GetRenderWindow()->getSize();

  m_introTexture.loadFromFile("intro.png");
  m_introSprite.setTexture(m_introTexture);
```

```
m_introSprite.setOrigin(m_introTexture.getSize().x / 2.0f,
    m_introTexture.getSize().y / 2.0f);

m_introSprite.setPosition(windowSize.x / 2.0f, 0);

m_font.loadFromFile("arial.ttf");
m_text.setFont(m_font);
m_text.setString({ "Press SPACE to continue" });
m_text.setCharacterSize(15);
sf::FloatRect textRect = m_text.getLocalBounds();
m_text.setOrigin(textRect.left + textRect.width / 2.0f,
    textRect.top + textRect.height / 2.0f);
m_text.setPosition(windowSize.x / 2.0f, windowSize.y / 2.0f);

EventManager* evMgr = m_stateMgr->
    GetContext()->m_eventManager;
evMgr->AddCallback(StateType::Intro,"Intro_Continue",
    &State_Intro::Continue,this);
}
```

There's quite a bit of code, however, only a tiny portion of it is new to us at this point. First, we must initialize our data member m_timePassed to zero. Next, we obtain the shared context through the use of the state manager pointer from the base class, and use it to obtain the current window size.

In order to position the m_text right in the middle of the screen, we set its origin to be the absolute center first, which is done by first obtaining a sf::FloatRect data type by calling the getLocalBounds method of our sf::text object. The left and top values of the sf::FloatRect represent the top left corner of the text, which can be used to calculate the center by adding half of the rectangle size to it.

If any changes are made to the character size, the string or to the font that the sf::text object is using, the origin has to be re-calculated, because the physical dimensions of the local boundary rectangle are changed too.

The basic idea of this intro state is to have a sprite come down from the top of the screen to the middle. After five seconds have passed, some text will appear underneath the sprite notifying the user that they can hit the Spacebar in order to proceed to the main menu. This is the texture we will be using for the descending sprite:

The last thing we need to do is to bind the Spacebar key to the `Continue` method of our intro class. We do that by obtaining the event manager instance through the shared context and setting up the callback, pretty much as we did in the previous chapter, except this time we need an additional argument: the state type.

Even though this class doesn't allocate any memory, it's still important it removes its callback when removed, which can be done here:

```
void State_Intro::OnDestroy(){
    EventManager* evMgr = m_stateMgr->
      GetContext()->m_eventManager;
    evMgr->RemoveCallback(StateType::Intro,"Intro_Continue");
}
```

Just like the `AddCallback` method, removal of callbacks also requires a state type as its first argument.

Because we're dealing with time and movement here, updating this state will be necessary:

```
void State_Intro::Update(const sf::Time& l_time){
  if(m_timePassed < 5.0f){ // Less than five seconds.
    m_timePassed += l_time.asSeconds();
    m_introSprite.setPosition(m_introSprite.getPosition().x,
      m_introSprite.getPosition().y + (48 * l_time.asSeconds())));
  }
}
```

Seeing how it's only desired for the sprite to be moving until it reaches the middle, a five second window is defined. If the total time passed is less than that, we add the delta time argument to it for the next iteration and move the sprite by a set number of pixels per second in the y direction, while keeping x the same. This guarantees vertical movement, which is, of course, completely useless, unless we draw everything:

```
void State_Intro::Draw(){
    sf::RenderWindow* window = m_stateMgr->
      GetContext()->m_wind->GetRenderWindow();
```

```
window->draw(m_introSprite);
if(m_timePassed >= 5.0f){
    window->draw(m_text);
}
}
```

After obtaining a pointer to a window through the shared context, we draw the sprite on screen. If more than five seconds have passed, we also draw the text, which notifies the player about the possibility of continuing past the intro state, the final piece of the puzzle:

```
void State_Intro::Continue(){
    if(m_timePassed >= 5.0f){
        m_stateMgr->SwitchTo(StateType::MainMenu);
        m_stateMgr->Remove(StateType::Intro);
    }
}
```

Once again, we check if enough time has passed to continue past this state. The actual switching happens when the `SwitchTo` method is called. Because we won't need the introduction state on the stack anymore, it removes itself in the next line.

Although we won't be needing the last two methods, we still need to implement empty versions of them, like so:

```
void State_Intro::Activate(){}
void State_Intro::Deactivate(){}
```

Now it's time to sound the fanfares! Our first state's done and is ready for use. Building and launching your application should leave you with something like this:

As illustrated above, the sprite descends all the way to the middle of the screen and displays the message about continuing underneath after five seconds. Upon hitting Spacebar you will find yourself in a black window because we haven't implemented the main menu state yet.

From this point on, all the repetitive code will be left out. For complete source code, please take a look at the source files of this chapter.

The main menu state

The main menu of any game out there is a major vein in terms of application flow, even though it's mostly overlooked. It's time we took a stab at building one, albeit a very simplistic version, starting as always with the header file:

```
class State_MainMenu : public BaseState{
public:
    ...
    void MouseClick(EventDetails* l_details);
private:
    sf::Text m_text;

    sf::Vector2f m_buttonSize;
    sf::Vector2f m_buttonPos;
    unsigned int m_buttonPadding;

    sf::RectangleShape m_rects[3];
    sf::Text m_labels[3];
};
```

The unique method to this class is the `MouseClick`. Since we're dealing with a menu here, predictably enough it will be used to process mouse input. For private data members, we have a text variable for the title, size, position and padding size variables for buttons, drawable rectangles for buttons and text variables for button labels. Let's throw it all together:

```
void State_MainMenu::OnCreate(){
  m_font.loadFromFile("arial.ttf");
  m_text.setFont(m_font);
  m_text.setString(sf::String("MAIN MENU:"));
  m_text.setCharacterSize(18);

  sf::FloatRect textRect = m_text.getLocalBounds();
  m_text.setOrigin(textRect.left + textRect.width / 2.0f,
    textRect.top + textRect.height / 2.0f);
```

```
m_text.setPosition(400,100);

m_buttonSize = sf::Vector2f(300.0f,32.0f);
m_buttonPos = sf::Vector2f(400,200);
m_buttonPadding = 4; // 4px.

std::string str[3];
str[0] = "PLAY";
str[1] = "CREDITS";
str[2] = "EXIT";

for(int i = 0; i < 3; ++i){
  sf::Vector2f buttonPosition(m_buttonPos.x,m_buttonPos.y +
    (i * (m_buttonSize.y + m_buttonPadding)));
  m_rects[i].setSize(m_buttonSize);
  m_rects[i].setFillColor(sf::Color::Red);

  m_rects[i].setOrigin(m_buttonSize.x / 2.0f,
    m_buttonSize.y / 2.0f);
  m_rects[i].setPosition(buttonPosition);

  m_labels[i].setFont(m_font);
  m_labels[i].setString(sf::String(str[i]));
  m_labels[i].setCharacterSize(12);

  sf::FloatRect rect = m_labels[i].getLocalBounds();
  m_labels[i].setOrigin(rect.left + rect.width / 2.0f,
    rect.top + rect.height / 2.0f);

  m_labels[i].setPosition(buttonPosition);
}

EventManager* evMgr = m_stateMgr->
  GetContext()->m_eventManager;
evMgr->AddCallback(StateType::MainMenu, "Mouse_Left",
  &State_MainMenu::MouseClick,this);
}
```

In the method above, all of the graphical elements get set up. The text data members get defined, origins are set up, and the labels for individual buttons get named. Lastly, the callback for the mouse left click gets set up. This is by no means a sophisticated GUI system. A more robust way of actually designing one will be covered in later chapters, however, this will suit our needs for now.

When the state gets destroyed, we need to remove its callbacks, as mentioned before:

```
void State_MainMenu::OnDestroy(){
    EventManager* evMgr = m_stateMgr->
      GetContext()->m_eventManager;
    evMgr->RemoveCallback(StateType::MainMenu,"Mouse_Left");
}
```

Upon the state getting activated, we need to check if the main game-play state exists on the state stack in order to adjust the "play" button to instead say "resume":

```
void State_MainMenu::Activate(){
    if(m_stateMgr->HasState(StateType::Game)
      && m_labels[0].getString() == "PLAY")
    {
        m_labels[0].setString(sf::String("RESUME"));
        sf::FloatRect rect = m_labels[0].getLocalBounds();
        m_labels[0].setOrigin(rect.left + rect.width / 2.0f,
          rect.top + rect.height / 2.0f);
    }
}
```

 The text origin has to be recalculated again because the dimensions of the `sf::drawable` object are now different.

The `MouseClick` method can be implemented as follows:

```
void State_MainMenu::MouseClick(EventDetails* l_details){
  sf::Vector2i mousePos = l_details->m_mouse;

  float halfX = m_buttonSize.x / 2.0f;
  float halfY = m_buttonSize.y / 2.0f;
  for(int i = 0; i < 3; ++i){
    if(mousePos.x >= m_rects[i].getPosition().x - halfX &&
      mousePos.x <= m_rects[i].getPosition().x + halfX &&
      mousePos.y >= m_rects[i].getPosition().y - halfY &&
      mousePos.y <= m_rects[i].getPosition().y + halfY)
    {
      if(i == 0){
        m_stateMgr->SwitchTo(StateType::Game);
      } else if(i == 1){
        // Credits state.
      } else if(i == 2){
```

```
        m_stateMgr->GetContext()->m_wind->Close();
      }
    }
  }
}
```

First, we obtain the mouse position from the event information structure, which gets passed in as the argument. Then we set up some local floating point type variables that will be used to check the boundaries of the buttons and begin looping over all the buttons. Because the origins of every button are set to the absolute middle, we must adjust the position according to that when checking if the mouse position is within the rectangle. If we have a mouse to button collision, an if-else statement checks which ID has collided and performs an action accordingly. In the case of the "play" button being pressed, we switch to the game state. If the exit button is pressed, we invoke the `Window::Close` method through the shared context.

Finally, let's draw the main menu:

```
void State_MainMenu::Draw(){
    sf::RenderWindow* window = m_stateMgr->GetContext()->
      m_wind->GetRenderWindow();
    window->draw(m_text);
    for(int i = 0; i < 3; ++i){
        window->draw(m_rects[i]);
        window->draw(m_labels[i]);
    }
}
```

After obtaining the render window pointer through the shared context, drawing the entire menu is as easy as iterating a few times to draw a button and a label.

Upon successful compilation and execution, we're again presented with the intro screen. When hitting spacebar, a main menu opens, looking something like this:

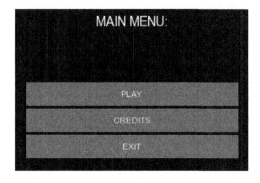

It's not the prettiest sight in the world, but it gets the job done. Clicking the **PLAY** button once again leaves us with a black screen, while hitting **EXIT** closes the application. Neat!

A sample game state

Just to demonstrate the full use of our system, let's get something bouncing on the screen that will demonstrate switching between the menu, game, and paused states. For testing purposes, a bouncing mushroom from previous chapters will more than suffice. We also need methods for switching to the menu state, as well as the paused state. Knowing that, let's bang out the header for the game-play state:

```
class State_Game : public BaseState{
public:
    ...
    void MainMenu(EventDetails* l_details);
    void Pause(EventDetails* l_details);
private:
    sf::Texture m_texture;
    sf::Sprite m_sprite;
    sf::Vector2f m_increment;
};
```

We begin, like many other times, with resource allocation and set up of data members in the OnCreate method:

```
void State_Game::OnCreate(){
    m_texture.loadFromFile("Mushroom.png");
    m_sprite.setTexture(m_texture);
    m_sprite.setPosition(0,0);
    m_increment = sf::Vector2f(400.0f,400.0f);

    EventManager* evMgr = m_stateMgr->
      GetContext()->m_eventManager;
    evMgr->AddCallback(StateType::Game,"Key_Escape",
      &State_Game::MainMenu,this);
    evMgr->AddCallback(StateType::Game,"Key_P",
      &State_Game::Pause,this);
}
```

After loading the texture and binding the sprite to it, we set up its position, define the increment vector, much like before, and add callbacks to our extra two methods for switching to different states. Of course, we need to remove them upon destruction of the state, like so:

```
void State_Game::OnDestroy(){
    EventManager* evMgr = m_stateMgr->
      GetContext()->m_eventManager;
    evMgr->RemoveCallback(StateType::GAME,"Key_Escape");
    evMgr->RemoveCallback(StateType::GAME,"Key_P");
}
```

The update method will hold the same code we've used previously:

```
void State_Game::Update(const sf::Time& l_time){
  sf::Vector2u l_windSize = m_stateMgr->GetContext()->
    m_wind->GetWindowSize();
  sf::Vector2u l_textSize = m_texture.getSize();

  if((m_sprite.getPosition().x > l_windSize.x -
    l_textSize.x && m_increment.x > 0) ||
    (m_sprite.getPosition().x < 0 && m_increment.x < 0))
  {
      m_increment.x = -m_increment.x;
  }

  if((m_sprite.getPosition().y > l_windSize.y -
    l_textSize.y && m_increment.y > 0) ||
    (m_sprite.getPosition().y < 0 && m_increment.y < 0))
  {
      m_increment.y = -m_increment.y;
  }

  m_sprite.setPosition(m_sprite.getPosition().x +
    (m_increment.x * l_time.asSeconds()),
    m_sprite.getPosition().y +
    (m_increment.y * l_time.asSeconds()));
}
```

The sprite position gets checked, and if it is outside of the window boundaries, the increment vector on the appropriate axis gets inverted. Then, the sprite position is updated, taking into account the time passed between frames. It's as regular as clockwork. Let's draw the sprite on the screen:

```
void State_Game::Draw(){
    m_stateMgr->GetContext()->m_wind->
      GetRenderWindow()->draw(m_sprite);
}
```

Now let's implement the methods for switching states:

```
void State_Game::MainMenu(EventDetails* l_details){
    m_stateMgr->SwitchTo(StateType::MAIN_MENU);
}

void State_Game::Pause(EventDetails* l_details){
    m_stateMgr->SwitchTo(StateType::PAUSED);
}
```

Notice that the game state does not remove itself here, just like the main menu state. This means that it's still alive in memory and is waiting to be pushed back to the front of the vector to be updated and rendered again. This allows the user to pop back to the main menu and resume the game state at any time without losing progress.

Running the application now will transition us through the intro state into the main menu. Hitting the **PLAY** button will leave us with a bouncing mushroom, just like before:

Hitting the escape key now will bring you back to the main menu, at which point you can choose to click the **RESUME** button to pop back into the game state, or the **EXIT** button to quit the application. There's just one more state left to implement to fully showcase the abilities of this system!

The means to pause

One might simply consider navigating to the main menu from the game state as a way of putting the game on pause. While that's technically true, why not explore a second option, which looks much trendier than simply popping the main menu open? After writing so much code, we deserve a nice looking paused state:

```
class State_Paused : public BaseState{
public:
    ...
    void Unpause(EventDetails* l_details);
private:
```

```
    sf::Text m_text;
    sf::RectangleShape m_rect;
};
```

This one is quite simple. Once more, we define an additional method, in this case Unpause, to switch to a different state. There's also only two data members used in order to draw the text "PAUSED" on screen, as well as a nice semi-transparent backdrop, represented by the sf::RectangleShape. Let's implement the OnCreate method for the last time in this chapter:

```cpp
void State_Paused::OnCreate(){
    SetTransparent(true); // Set our transparency flag.
    m_font.loadFromFile("arial.ttf");
    m_text.setFont(m_font);
    m_text.setString(sf::String("PAUSED"));
    m_text.setCharacterSize(14);
    m_text.setStyle(sf::Text::Bold);

    sf::Vector2u windowSize = m_stateMgr->
        GetContext()->m_wind->GetRenderWindow()->getSize();

    sf::FloatRect textRect = m_text.getLocalBounds();
    m_text.setOrigin(textRect.left + textRect.width / 2.0f,
        textRect.top + textRect.height / 2.0f);
    m_text.setPosition(windowSize.x / 2.0f, windowSize.y / 2.0f);

    m_rect.setSize(sf::Vector2f(windowSize));
    m_rect.setPosition(0,0);
    m_rect.setFillColor(sf::Color(0,0,0,150));

    EventManager* evMgr = m_stateMgr->
        GetContext()->m_eventManager;
    evMgr->AddCallback(StateType::Paused, "Key_P",
        &State_Paused::Unpause, this);
}
```

A distinct difference here is the use of m_transparent flag, which is a protected data member of the BaseState class. Setting it to true means we're allowing the state manager to render the state directly behind this one on the state stack.

Besides that, we create a rectangle the size of the entire window and set its fill color to black with the alpha channel value of 150 out of the maximum 255. This makes it nice and translucent while darkening everything that's behind it.

The final part of the method above, quite like all the other ones, is adding the callback to the `Unpause` method. Upon destruction of this state, it needs to be removed like so:

```
void State_Paused::OnDestroy(){
    EventManager* evMgr = m_stateMgr->
      GetContext()->m_eventManager;
    evMgr->RemoveCallback(StateType::Paused,"Key_P");
}
```

Now let's draw the rectangle and text we created:

```
void State_Paused::Draw(){
    sf::RenderWindow* wind = m_stateMgr->
      GetContext()->m_wind->GetRenderWindow();
    wind->draw(m_rect);
    wind->draw(m_text);
}
```

Also, let's implement the `Unpause` method by simply switching to the game-play state:

```
void State_Paused::Unpause(EventDetails* l_details){
    m_stateMgr->SwitchTo(StateType::Game);
}
```

Because the main game state is the only state that can be paused so far, simply switching back to it is sufficient.

Now, take a deep breath and compile the application again. Getting past the intro state, hitting the **PLAY** button in the main menu, and hitting the **P** key on your keyboard will effectively pause the game-play state and darken the screen subtly, while displaying the text **PAUSED** right in the middle, as shown here:

If you have come this far, congratulations! While this is by no means a finished product, it has come a long way from being a static, immovable class that can barely be controlled.

Common mistakes

A likely mistake that might be made when using this system is the absence of registration of newly added states. If you have built a state and it simply draws a black screen when you switch to it, chances are it was never registered in the constructor of `StateManager`.

The window not responding to the *F5* key being pressed or the close button being hit is a sign of the global callbacks not being set up right. In order to make sure a callback is invoked no matter which state you're in, it must be set up with the state type of 0, like so:

```
m_eventManager->AddCallback(StateType(0),"Fullscreen_toggle",
    &Window::ToggleFullscreen,this);
m_eventManager->AddCallback(StateType(0),"Window_close",
    &Window::Close,this);
```

Finally, remember that when the mouse position is retrieved in the main menu state, the coordinates stored inside the event are automatically relative to the window. Obtaining coordinates through `sf::Mouse::GetPosition` is not going to do the same, unless a reference to a `sf::Window` class is provided as an argument.

Summary

Upon this chapter concluding, you should have everything you need in your tool belt to fashion states that can be transparent, updated in groups, and supported by the rest of our codebase. There's no reason to stop there. Build it again, make it better, faster and implement different features that didn't get covered in this chapter. Expand it, crash it, fix it and learn from it. Nothing is ever good enough, so build onto the knowledge you've gained here.

> *A famous Chinese proverb states: "Life is like a game of chess, changing with each move".*

While that analogy holds true, life can also be like a game with states. Breaking it down into smaller and more manageable parts makes it a whole lot easier to handle. Whether it is life imitating code or code imitating life is irrelevant. Great ideas come from different backgrounds coming together. Hopefully, by the end of this chapter you are taking off with not only the knowledge of simply how to build yet another manager, but also the wisdom to seek inspiration from every resource and idea available. There is no exclusive knowledge, only inclusive thinking. See you in the next chapter!

6
Set It in Motion! – Animating and Moving around Your World

Our first game, while functional, certainly wasn't that visually appealing, at least not for this century. First of all, the graphics barely represented what they were supposed to. Referring to a chain of blocks as a snake was the only thing that gave the player an idea of what they were in control of. The second staple of an older design was the static camera position. While it is a design choice in a game like *Snake*, more complex genres would be crippled by such a limitation. Titles like *Super Mario Bros* rely on the fact that the game world extends beyond the boundaries of your screen, not only because of visual appeal, but also because of the ability to build a larger game world that doesn't have to fit within a certain pre-designated rectangle. A simple decision to represent game characters with images instead of basic shapes, as well as providing the means for the screen to be moved opens up a lot of doors.

In this chapter, we will be covering:

- SFML views and screen scrolling
- Automated resource management and handling
- Creation and application of sprite-sheets
- Sprite-sheet animation

There's a lot to learn, so let's not waste any time and dive right in!

Use of copyrighted resources

Before proceeding any further, we would like to give credit where credit's due to the artists who created the textures, sprites, and other art we're going to be using for our game. These assets include:

- *Lemcraft* by richtaur under CC0 1.0 license: `http://opengameart.org/content/lemcraft`

- *Prototyping 2D Pixelart Tilesets* by `http://www.robotality.com` under CC-BY-SA 3.0 license: `http://opengameart.org/content/prototyping-2d-pixelart-tilesets`

- *Generic Platformer Tileset (16x16) + Background* by etqws3 under CC0 1.0 license: `http://opengameart.org/content/generic-platformer-tileset-16x16-background`

- *Knight* and *Rat* sprites by backyardninja: `http://www.dumbmanex.com/bynd_freestuff.html`

The licensing of all the resources listed above allows for any use of the material, even commercial. For more information on the two specific licenses, please visit the following links:

- `http://creativecommons.org/publicdomain/zero/1.0/`

- `http://creativecommons.org/licenses/by-sa/3.0/`

Finding and using the current directory

There's no doubt that after programming for a while, the inconveniences of reading or writing to files start to quickly build up. It may not be so bad when running programs outside of your compiler, but using a relative path can be a pain while debugging, because it is no longer relative to the directory where the executable is, but instead where the `.obj` files are located. For the rest of this book, we will be using a function to obtain the full path to your executable, regardless of where it is or how it's being launched. Let's take a look at a new header file that will contain this function, called `Utilities.h`:

```
#pragma once
#define RUNNING_WINDOWS
#include <iostream>
#include <string>
#include <algorithm>

namespace Utils{
  #ifdef RUNNING_WINDOWS
```

```
#define WIN32_LEAN_AND_MEAN
#include <windows.h>
#include <Shlwapi.h>
inline std::string GetWorkingDirectory(){
  HMODULE hModule = GetModuleHandle(nullptr);
  if(hModule){
    char path[256];
    GetModuleFileName(hModule,path,sizeof(path));
    PathRemoveFileSpec(path);
    strcat_s(path,"\\"); // new
    return std::string(path); // new
  }
  return "";
}
#elif defined RUNNING_LINUX
#include <unistd.h>
inline std::string GetWorkingDirectory(){
  char cwd[1024];
  if(getcwd(cwd, sizeof(cwd)) != nullptr){
    return std::string(cwd) + std::string("/");
  }
  return "";
}
#endif
}
```

#pragma once is widely supported, but is non-standard. It can be replaced by a typical inclusion guard if the code is being processed in an older compiler.

If a RUNNING_WINDOWS macro is set, it defines a method that first obtains the full path including the executable and its extension, then obtains only the name and extension of the executable and finally strips the full path of it before returning the string, that now contains the full "address" of the directory the executable resides in. These functions are specific to Windows and won't work on other operating systems, so this header needs to define the same method differently for each of them.

Using these functions to obtain the current directory requires the Shlwapi.h header file to be included, as well as the shlwapi.lib file being listed in the linker's additional dependencies in *all* configurations. Forgetting to fulfill these requirements will cause linker errors.

As you can see, we have Windows and Linux operating systems covered here. It is up to you to implement versions of the same function for other platforms if you want your application to run properly.

Using the SFML views

Up until this point, we have only dealt with code that renders things within the boundaries of the window that's open. There hasn't been an instance where we needed the screen to move yet, which would be fine if we lived in the early days of the 80s, but games even a decade after that time were a lot more advanced. Take, for example, *Super Mario Brothers*, a classic *side-scroller*. Its genre alone pinpoints what our first game didn't have: scrolling. If the scrolling effect or any kind of movement, resizing or rotation of the screen is desirable, using the `sf::View` is necessary.

What is `sf::View`? It's a rectangle. That's it. If you have ever held your fingers in a rectangle shape to "frame" the world you're observing, you have created a view with your hands. By moving it, you are essentially moving through the scene beyond the cut-off point of the window. If you're still not "getting the picture," here's an illustration to lead you in the right direction:

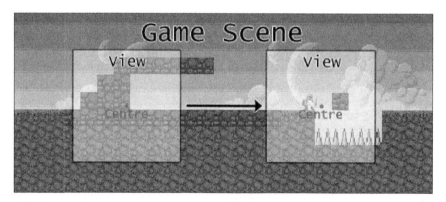

The `sf::View` is a very lightweight object that essentially holds a few floating point variables and a number of methods to retrieve its values. Its constructor can take in a `sf::FloatRect` type, which defines a rectangular area of the screen, or it can take two `sf::Vector2f` types, the first one being the centre of the view and the second one being the size:

```
// Top-left corner at 500:500, bottom-right at 1000:1000.
sf::View first(sf::FloatRect(500,500,1000,1000));
// Center at 250:250, size is 800:600.
sf::View second(sf::Vector2f(250,250), sf::Vector2f(800,600));
```

As you can see, views are mostly manipulated by their centre instead of their top-left corner, unlike most of the other shapes.

Moving the view can be done by manipulating its centre, like so:

```
// Top-left corner at 0:0, bottom-right at 800:600.
sf::View view(sf::FloatRect(0,0,800,600));
view.setCenter(100,100); // Move center to 100:100.
```

It can also be moved by an offset, via the move method:

```
view.move(100,100); // Move by 100x100 offset.
```

Resizing the view can be accomplished by either using the setSize method or zooming by a factor, using the zoom method:

```
view.setSize(640, 480); // Creates a smaller view space.
view.zoom(0.5f); // Also creates a smaller view space.
```

In the first case, it resizes a view of 800x600 px down to 640x480 px. The second case applies a factor of 0.5f to its current size, which cuts it down in half, making everything on screen larger.

In order to use a specific view, you must call the setView method of the window instance you're using:

```
window.setView(view); // Applies view to window.
```

> The setView method does *not* take values in by reference. It simply copies the values from the view and stores them in the window object. If the view is altered at any point in your code, you must call the setView method *again* in order to apply those changes and make them reflect.

One last thing worthy of mentioning is that two views can be obtained from the window object as well. The first kind of view is the current one being used, and the second view is the default a window starts with. It's the same size as the window and its left corner is positioned at coordinates (0;0). Retrieving these views can be done like so:

```
sf::View view = window.getView();
sf::View defaultView = window.getDefaultView();
```

Preparing application states for views

In order to add support for panning around our world, we must adjust the state system. The main idea here is that each state has its own view. Something like the main menu will most likely never need to move past the default view the window provides, unlike the game state, which will be focusing on the character every frame. A simple and elegant approach would be to store a view with each state, so it can adjust the screen view space if it needs to. Let's start by modifying the `BaseState.h` file:

```
class BaseState{
public:
    ...
    sf::View& GetView(){ return m_view; }
protected:
    ...
    sf::View m_view;
};
```

Like most of the classes we're going to be modifying, we're only showing the relevant parts here, which are fairly conservative size wise in this case. All we've added is a view data member and a method for obtaining it. Let's move on to putting this view to work in our state manager:

```
void StateManager::CreateState(const StateType& l_type){
    ...
    BaseState* state = newState->second();
    state->m_view = m_shared->m_wind->
        GetRenderWindow()->getDefaultView();
    ...
}
```

Because we don't want the default constructor of `sf::View` to initialize our view member to its own default values, it's necessary to set the view up when creating the state. Most of the states we have so far rely on the fact that the view never moves, which is why it's set to default first. If a state wishes to define its own view, it can always do so in the `OnCreate` method, as you will see shortly. Let's move on to state switching:

```
void StateManager::SwitchTo(const StateType& l_type){
    ...
    for(...)
    {
        if(itr->first == l_type){
            ...
```

```
        m_shared->m_wind->GetRenderWindow()->
          setView(tmp_state->GetView());
        return;
      }
    }
    ...
    m_states.back().second->Activate();
    m_shared->m_wind->GetRenderWindow()->setView(
      m_states.back().second->GetView());
  }
```

This is fairly straightforward. When switching to a different state, we want to change the view space of the window to match the state we're switching to. If that's not accomplished and the game state moves the view, switching to another state will simply leave you with a blank screen, because the new state's contents are rendered outside the window's view space.

Drawing multiple states at once can raise some problems, now that different views are introduced. This can be a little bit difficult to understand, so let's illustrate the problem with an example. Let's say the game is paused. Because the paused state is transparent, it needs to draw the state before it first, in order to blend them together. Instantly there's a problem, because the paused state positions its elements in window coordinates and it never needs the view to move. If the view of the window does move, whatever the state on top draws is going to be outside its view space and will therefore be either partially visible or not there at all. We could translate window coordinates to world coordinates and update positions of these elements each frame to "follow" the screen, but that's not an elegant or efficient solution. Therefore, we must set the window view to the state view before it gets rendered, like so:

```
void StateManager::Draw(){
  ...
  for(; itr != m_states.end(); ++itr){
    m_shared->m_wind->GetRenderWindow()->
      setView(itr->second->GetView());
    itr->second->Draw();
  }
  ...
}
```

Because of the way views and rendering works, the problem above is resolved. Consider the following illustration:

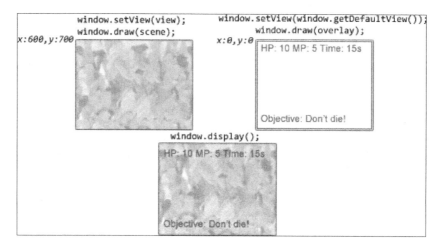

First, the window view is set to the view of the game in order to render the scene. Let's say it's top-left corner is at position (600;700). The default view of the window is then applied. This moves the window view space's top-left corner back to (0;0), which matches the local window coordinates. Because the elements that are about to be drawn are positioned based on these coordinates, they are now in the window's view space again and are drawn on top of the frame buffer. The transparent parts are blended, while opaque pixels are overwritten. Finally, `window.display();` gets called and the frame buffer is drawn on screen. The result is both the scene and the elements being blended together.

The last thing we want to add to our existing code-base before moving on is a new method in the Window class for obtaining a `sf::FloatRect` type that defines the window view space:

```
sf::FloatRect Window::GetViewSpace(){
    sf::Vector2f viewCenter = m_window.getView().getCenter();
    sf::Vector2f viewSize = m_window.getView().getSize();
    sf::Vector2f viewSizeHalf(viewSize.x / 2, viewSize.y / 2);
    sf::FloatRect viewSpace(viewCenter - viewSizeHalf, viewSize);
    return viewSpace;
}
```

First, this method obtains the centre and the size of the current view. Then it calculates what half of the size is and subtracts it from the coordinates of the view's centre, in order to obtain its top-left corner. Lastly, it constructs the rectangle of the view space by passing in the top-left corner of the view and its size. This will be useful later on.

Automated resource management

Let's talk about textures and the way we've been using them so far. A texture in SFML is something you want to only have one of, since it's not cheap memory wise. Our approach so far was simply storing the textures as data members of relevant classes. A scenario that illustrates how horrendous this strategy is would be as follows: you need the same texture somewhere else. That's it. It really doesn't seem like the type of thing that you could just brush off your shoulders, as it only happens once in a blue moon. Creating multiple textures that all hold the same data is a huge waste of resources, and adding methods for obtaining textures from the classes that use them is a disaster. Not only does it clutter the class footprint, it would also mean that other classes would have to have access to the one that holds this texture. Nobody should subject themselves to such torture.

How do we remedy this situation then? By creating a class that holds all of our textures in the same place and keeps track of how many times they're used in order to manage its resources in a smart way. We also want to give them unique identifiers in order to refer to them quickly, which can be done by loading them from a file that maps a name to a path. We can name it `Textures.cfg` and it would look something like this:

```
Intro media/Textures/intro.png
PlayerSprite media/Textures/PlayerSheet.png
RatSprite media/Textures/RatSheet.png
TileSheet media/Textures/tilesheet.png
Bg1 media/Textures/bg1.png
Bg2 media/Textures/bg2.png
Bg3 media/Textures/bg3.png
```

This approach, of course, can be used for other types of resources, not just textures. Later on, we'll be working with fonts and sound files as well, so let's design an abstract base class that will take care of all the common tasks first, before delving into handling textures specifically.

Designing a resource manager

All of the resources we're going to be working with are going to be counted and accounted for, so to speak. Whenever we want to use a texture, for example, it needs to be requested. If it's no longer needed, the resource is released. It sounds simple enough, so let's write it:

```
template<typename Derived, typename T>
class ResourceManager{
public:
```

```cpp
        ResourceManager(const std::string& l_pathsFile){
            LoadPaths(l_pathsFile);
        }

        virtual ~ResourceManager(){ PurgeResources(); }
        ...
    private:
        std::unordered_map<std::string,
            std::pair<T*, unsigned int>> m_resources;
        std::unordered_map<std::string, std::string> m_paths;
    };
```

When dealing with classes that use templates, it's necessary for the implementation of the methods to be in the header file, because the compiler needs to have access to the implementation in order to instantiate the methods with the template arguments. With that being said, let's talk about the `m_resources` data member. It's using a map, which is going to tie a string handle to a pair of elements, the first of which is the template parameter of a resource and the second is an unsigned integer type that will be used as a counter for how many places are currently using this particular resource.

Another data member we have is a map of two strings for the resource paths. The constructor calls an internal method in order to load the paths from a specific location, while the destructor invokes another internal method to purge and de-allocate all of its resources.

Let's begin implementing other methods we're going to need to use this class, starting with the public ones:

```cpp
    T* GetResource(const std::string& l_id){
        auto res = Find(l_id);
        return(res ? res->first : nullptr);
    }
```

This is a method for acquiring a resource that's being kept in the manager. It uses the string argument as a handle and looks for it in the map, using the internal `Find` method that we'll define later. It returns a pointer to the pair element of the map if something is found, or `nullptr` if nothing is found.

We also might be interested in retrieving one of the paths to a particular resource:

```cpp
    std::string GetPath(const std::string& l_id){
        auto path = m_paths.find(l_id);
        return(path != m_paths.end() ? path->second : "");
    }
```

This system would be useless without some way to guarantee that a resource doesn't get de-allocated while it's still being used. In order to prevent that, let's implement a method that will register the use of a resource:

```
bool RequireResource(const std::string& l_id){
  auto res = Find(l_id);
  if(res){
    ++res->second;
    return true;
  }
  auto path = m_paths.find(l_id);
  if (path == m_paths.end()){ return false; }
  T* resource = Load(path->second);
  if (!resource){ return false; }
  m_resources.emplace(l_id, std::make_pair(resource, 1));
  return true;
}
```

This method serves two purposes. One is simply incrementing the counter of instances a resource is being used when it's required. The second purpose of it is to create a resource, if the handle is not found in the resource container. It first looks as if the resource handle is valid, by checking the path container. If a match is found, it tries to acquire a pointer to newly allocated memory, which gets returned by the Load method. If it hasn't returned a `nullptr` value, the resource gets inserted with a counter set to 1.

Just like for every yin there must be a yang, for every resource required, there must be a point where it's no longer needed:

```
bool ReleaseResource(const std::string& l_id){
    auto res = Find(l_id);
    if (!res){ return false; }
    --res->second;
    if (!res->second){ Unload(l_id); }
    return true;
}
```

This method tries to find a resource in the container using the string handle. If one is found, its use counter is decremented. If the counter is now at 0, this resource is no longer needed and the memory for it can be de-allocated by calling the `Unload` method.

At some point, everything must go. This is the purge method:

```
void PurgeResources(){
  while(m_resources.begin() != m_resources.end()){
    delete m_resources.begin()->second.first;
    m_resources.erase(m_resources.begin());
  }
}
```

This is a fairly straightforward method. It loops until there are no more elements in the container. Each time it deletes the resource memory and erases the container entry by passing in an iterator.

Because of the unique nature of some resources, certain methods aren't universal. For the purposes of expanding this base class to support any resource we want, a Load method is going to be used in each derived manager. In order to avoid run-time polymorphism, a **Curiously Recurring Template Pattern** can be used like so:

```
T* Load(const std::string& l_path){
  return static_cast<Derived*>(this)->Load(l_path);
}
```

Derived classes will implement their own versions of Load, but will not rely on resolving virtual pointers to functions during run-time.

Now that the scratching of the surface is done, let's dive deep into the private methods that make this functionality possible, beginning with Find:

```
std::pair<T*,unsigned int>* Find(const std::string& l_id){
  auto itr = m_resources.find(l_id);
  return (itr != m_resources.end() ? &itr->second : nullptr);
}
```

This method returns a pointer to a pair structure that includes the actual resource and the number of instances using it. If the string handle provided as an argument isn't located in the resource container, nullptr is returned instead.

Unloading a resource doesn't bring anything new to the table:

```
bool Unload(const std::string& l_id){
  auto itr = m_resources.find(l_id);
  if (itr == m_resources.end()){ return false; }
  delete itr->second.first;
  m_resources.erase(itr);
  return true;
}
```

As always, we first look for the element in the container by the string handle. If it is found, we free the allocated memory, erase the element from the container and return from the method.

Lastly, we can't use those string handles without having paths that they map to. Let's load them in:

```
void LoadPaths(const std::string& l_pathFile){
  std::ifstream paths;
  paths.open(Utils::GetWorkingDirectory() + l_pathFile);
  if(paths.is_open()){
    std::string line;
    while(std::getline(paths,line)){
      std::stringstream keystream(line);
      std::string pathName;
      std::string path;
      keystream >> pathName;
      keystream >> path;
      m_paths.emplace(pathName,path);
    }
    paths.close();
    return;
  }
  std::cerr <<
    "! Failed loading the path file: "
    << l_pathFile << std::endl;
}
```

If you know anything about loading in files in C++, this should raise no eyebrows. All it does is set up an input stream called `paths`. It then tries to open it, by passing in the full path to the file, thanks to our `GetWorkingDirectory` function that was mentioned earlier. If the file is open, it means it was found and can be read. A string type is defined for use as a way of holding the current line of the file as it reads them one by one sequentially. The method loops while there's still a new line in the file we're parsing and passes in that new line to the `line` variable. A `stringstream` variable is then set up, which is designed for operations with strings. Two `string` variables are defined, one for the path identifier and one for the actual path. They get filled from the `keystream` variable by using its overloaded `>>` operator, which essentially just grabs everything in the line until it encounters a space delimiter. We then insert this information into the path container and close the file after the loop is over.

Implementing the texture manager

With the resource management part done, we can now implement the actual texture loading in its own class. Because there's only one method that we want to implement, it might as well be done in the header file:

```
class TextureManager:
  public ResourceManager<TextureManager, sf::Texture>
{
public:
  TextureManager(): ResourceManager("textures.cfg"){}

  sf::Texture* Load(const std::string& l_path){
    sf::Texture* texture = new sf::Texture();
    if(!texture->loadFromFile(
      Utils::GetWorkingDirectory() + l_path))
    {
      delete texture;
      texture = nullptr;
      std::cerr << "! Failed to load texture: "
        << l_path << std::endl;
    }
    return texture;
  }
};
```

We create the `TextureManager` class and inherit from `ResourceManager` in addition to specifying the data types of this manager class and the resource it deals with for the template, which is, of course, a `sf::Texture`. The constructor of the texture manager is only used to call the base class constructor in the initializer list to pass in the file name that contains the bindings of handles and paths.

In the `Load` method, we allocate new memory for the texture and attempt to load it from the path provided as an argument. If the loading fails, we delete the allocated memory and print out a console message to notify the user of the failure. That is literally all there is to the texture manager class. Time to put it to work!

Introducing sprite sheets

First, let's whet your appetite by looking into the future of using sprite sheets, which allow you to create animations that look like this:

From our previous experience with SFML, we know that a sprite is essentially an image that can be moved around, cropped, scaled, and rotated just to mention a few options. A sprite sheet, on the other hand, is a texture that contains multiple sprites. From the image above, you can see the player is moving left and his animation is progressing. Each frame of the player's animation is stored in a sprite sheet, which is being accessed and cropped in order to represent a single sprite. This is what a small part of it looks like as a texture:

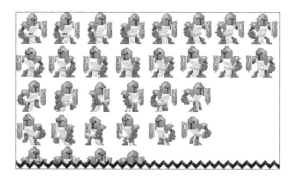

The way sprites are laid out can differ from game to game. It depends on the size constraints of a particular project, as well as the specifics of game-play. The format of the sprite sheet above is just what works the best here and is by no means the "perfect design."

Why would we want to use a sprite sheet? Well, the biggest advantage is that it makes accessing sprites easier and faster, not to mention less memory-consuming. Animation is also easier to pull off on a sprite sheet. Loading multiple textures of different sprites is more expensive than loading a single texture that can be cropped. In certain cases, careful packing of a sprite sheet can save a lot of resources. If efficiency is what you're after, use of sprite sheets over different textures for each sprite definitely takes the cake.

Implementing a sprite sheet class

Because we want to be able to modify anything related to sprite sheets on the fly, loading them from a file makes the most sense. Let's start by taking a look at what the sprite sheet for a player might look like by making a `Player.sheet` file:

```
Texture PlayerSprite
Size 32 32
Scale 1.0 1.0
|Type|Name|StartFrame|EndFrame|Row|FrameTime|FrameActionStart|End|
AnimationType Directional
Animation Idle 0 7 0 0.2 -1 -1
Animation Walk 0 5 2 0.1 -1 -1
Animation Jump 0 3 4 0.2 -1 -1
Animation Attack 0 4 6 0.08 2 3
Animation Hurt 0 2 8 0.2 -1 -1
Animation Death 0 8 10 0.15 -1 -1
```

It starts by specifying a handle of the texture that will be used. Some additional data about the sprite itself is also defined, such as the individual sprite size and scale. We then jump to a row that's commented out. It describes the order and meaning of values for the rest of the file, which is designated for defining sequences of animations in the sprite sheet. After defining the animation type, it proceeds in defining all of these different parameters about the animation. There's no need to focus on this part for now, as it will be covered in depth later.

With the file format out of the way, let's get started with the sprite sheet class! First, a container type is defined to hold the animations. An unordered map is used because it offers faster lookups than its ordered counter-part:

```
using Animations = std::unordered_map<std::string,Anim_Base*>;
```

Once again, try not to dwell on this too much, as it will be explained in more depth later. Let's write the header for the sprite sheet class:

```
class SpriteSheet{
public:
  SpriteSheet(TextureManager* l_textMgr);
  ~SpriteSheet();

  void CropSprite(const sf::IntRect& l_rect);
  ... // Basic setters/getters.
  bool LoadSheet(const std::string& l_file);
  void ReleaseSheet();

  Anim_Base* GetCurrentAnim();
  bool SetAnimation(const std::string& l_name,
    const bool& l_play = false,
    const bool& l_loop = false);

  void Update(const float& l_dT);
  void Draw(sf::RenderWindow* l_wnd);
private:
  std::string m_texture;
  sf::Sprite m_sprite;
  sf::Vector2i m_spriteSize;
  sf::Vector2f m_spriteScale;
  Direction m_direction;
  std::string m_animType;
  Animations m_animations;
  Anim_Base* m_animationCurrent;
  TextureManager* m_textureManager;
};
```

As you can see, it offers methods for cropping the texture and updating and drawing the sprite sheet. The class holds on to a pointer to a texture manager in order to obtain and free up resources. One last thing about this class is that it holds a data member of type `Direction`. It's simply just an enumeration, defined in the `Directions.h` file:

```
enum class Direction{ Right = 0, Left };
```

It's barely even worth its own header. However, quite a few classes actually rely on this, so a separate header is where it needs to be.

Let's begin implementing the actual methods of the sprite sheet class, starting, as always, with the constructor and destructor:

```
SpriteSheet::SpriteSheet(TextureManager* l_textMgr)
  :m_textureManager(l_textMgr), m_animationCurrent(nullptr),
   m_spriteScale(1.f, 1.f), m_direction(Direction::Right){}
```

Apart from initializing its data members to default values, there's nothing else of interest here. The destructor simply calls another method to clean up, much like a lot of other classes:

```
SpriteSheet::~SpriteSheet(){ ReleaseSheet(); }

void SpriteSheet::ReleaseSheet(){
    m_textureManager->ReleaseResource(m_texture);
    m_animationCurrent = nullptr;
    while(m_animations.begin() != m_animations.end()){
        delete m_animations.begin()->second;
        m_animations.erase(m_animations.begin());
    }
}
```

The `ReleaseSheet` method uses the texture manager to release the resource it was using, as well as delete all of the animations it has currently allocated.

When setting the sprite size, it's important to also reset the origin, so it's always in the middle of the sprite on the *x* axis and down all the way on the *y* axis:

```
void SpriteSheet::SetSpriteSize(const sf::Vector2i& l_size){
    m_spriteSize = l_size;
    m_sprite.setOrigin(m_spriteSize.x / 2, m_spriteSize.y);
}
```

Naturally, we also need a method for setting the position of the sprite:

```
void SpriteSheet::SetSpritePosition(const sf::Vector2f& l_pos){
    m_sprite.setPosition(l_pos);
}
```

Setting a different direction of a sprite will change its sprite, so we need to re-crop it afterwards:

```
void SpriteSheet::SetDirection(const Direction& l_dir){
    if (l_dir == m_direction){ return; }
    m_direction = l_dir;
    m_animationCurrent->CropSprite();
}
```

The actual cropping is done through the `setTextureRect` method of a sprite class:

```
void SpriteSheet::CropSprite(const sf::IntRect& l_rect){
    m_sprite.setTextureRect(l_rect);
}
```

It takes in a `sf::IntRect` type, which defines its top-left corner, as well as the size of the rectangle. The top-left corner coordinates are local to the texture that's being cropped. Let's say we want to obtain the first sprite in the sprite sheet. If we know that each sprite is 32px by 32px in size, all we need to do is pass in the position (0;0) for the top-left corner and then the size (32;32) in order to obtain the sprite.

Although we haven't covered animations yet, let's get the `SetAnimation` method out of the way, since it's not too difficult to understand, even without knowing every specific detail about our soon-to-be animation class:

```
bool SpriteSheet::SetAnimation(const std::string& l_name,
    const bool& l_play, const bool& l_loop)
{
    auto itr = m_animations.find(l_name);
    if (itr == m_animations.end()){ return false; }
    if (itr->second == m_animationCurrent){ return false; }
    if (m_animationCurrent){ m_animationCurrent->Stop(); }
    m_animationCurrent = itr->second;
    m_animationCurrent->SetLooping(l_loop);
    if(l_play){ m_animationCurrent->Play(); }
    m_animationCurrent->CropSprite();
    return true;
}
```

It takes in three arguments: a string handle and two Boolean flags for playing the animation instantly and whether it's looped or not. The method itself looks through the animation container for an animation that matches the string handle. If one is found, it checks if any current animation is set because it needs to be stopped. Once that is done, it simply changes the pointer to the current animation to the animation that was found in the container, as well as calls the respective methods in order to loop and play the animation. Nothing too complicated.

We then top off this class with the most run of the mill update and draw methods:

```
void SpriteSheet::Update(const float& l_dT){
    m_animationCurrent->Update(l_dT);
}

void SpriteSheet::Draw(sf::RenderWindow* l_wnd){
    l_wnd->draw(m_sprite);
}
```

This is about as simple as it gets. However, it does leave us with one method unaccounted for: `LoadSheet`. Before we can implement that, we need to know more about the animation classes we'll be working with.

The base animation class

Much like with the resource manager, we want to off-load any and all functionality that isn't unique to more specific classes and put it in a base class. This is where the base animation class comes in. Let's take a look at the `Anim_Base.h` header file:

```
class SpriteSheet;
using Frame = unsigned int;

class Anim_Base{
  friend class SpriteSheet;
public:
  Anim_Base();
  virtual ~Anim_Base();
  ... // Setters/getters.
  void Play();
  void Pause();
  void Stop();
  void Reset();

  virtual void Update(const float& l_dT);

  friend std::stringstream& operator >>(
    std::stringstream& l_stream, Anim_Base& a)
  {
    a.ReadIn(l_stream);
    return l_stream;
  }
protected:
  virtual void FrameStep() = 0;
  virtual void CropSprite() = 0;
  virtual void ReadIn(std::stringstream& l_stream) = 0;

  Frame m_frameCurrent;
  Frame m_frameStart;
  Frame m_frameEnd;
  Frame m_frameRow;
  int m_frameActionStart; // Frame when a specific "action" begins
  int m_frameActionEnd; // Frame when a specific "action" ends
  float m_frameTime;
```

```
    float m_elapsedTime;
    bool m_loop;
    bool m_playing;
    std::string m_name;
    SpriteSheet* m_spriteSheet;
};
```

First, notice the forward declaration of class `SpriteSheet`. Because this class needs to include `SpriteSheet` and `SpriteSheet` needs to include this class, forward declarations are necessary to prevent cross-inclusions. We're also going to be using an alias for the unsigned integer type, simply named `Frame`.

Most of the data member as well as method names are fairly self-explanatory. A few terms might be confusing, such as frame time and action. Frame time is the amount of time each frame takes to finish. Action defines a range of frames during which a behavior which is specific to that animation can be performed. If it's set to negative one, this behavior can be performed throughout the entire animation. These are some things that we want to keep track of in order to make the game more interactive and responsive. Note that we're overloading the `>>` operator in order to ease animation loading from files. More on that later.

The last thing to point out is the three purely virtual methods: `FrameStep`, `CropSprite`, and `ReadIn`. `FrameStep` is the update portion that's unique to different types of animations. `CropSprite` is a unique way different types of animations would obtain sprites from a sprite sheet. Lastly, `ReadIn` is the method that defines how exactly the stringstream object is used when data is being loaded from files. These three methods will only be defined in derived classes.

Implementing the base animation class

Due to forward declarations, we need to include the actual header files of classes that were declared in the `.cpp` file:

```
#include "Anim_Base.h"
#include "SpriteSheet.h"
```

Now we have no more cross-inclusions and we get to use the `SpriteSheet` class. Time to implement the actual class:

```
Anim_Base::Anim_Base(): m_frameCurrent(0), m_frameStart(0),
    m_frameEnd(0), m_frameRow(0), m_frameTime(0.f),
    m_elapsedTime(0.f), m_frameActionStart(-1),
    m_frameActionEnd(-1), m_loop(false), m_playing(false){}
Anim_Base::~Anim_Base(){}
```

The constructor is doing its intended job of initializing default values, while the destructor isn't going to be used at all in this class.

Of course, we need a method for setting our sprite sheet data member to something:

```
void Anim_Base::SetSpriteSheet(SpriteSheet* l_sheet){
    m_spriteSheet = l_sheet;
}
```

The same thing is true for setting the animation frame, although this method is slightly more intricate:

```
void Anim_Base::SetFrame(const unsigned int& l_frame){
    if((l_frame >= m_frameStart && l_frame <= m_frameEnd) ||
      (l_frame >= m_frameEnd && l_frame <= m_frameStart))
    {
        m_frameCurrent = l_frame;
    }
}
```

The argument that is passed to this method is checked for being in two specific ranges, which is done in order to add support for types of animation that can play backwards in the future.

Here's a method for checking if this animation is currently able to perform its custom behavior:

```
bool Anim_Base::IsInAction(){
    if(m_frameActionStart == -1 || m_frameActionEnd == -1){
        return true;
    }

    return (m_frameCurrent >= m_frameActionStart
      && m_frameCurrent <= m_frameActionEnd);
}
```

If any of the values are -1, the "action" is always performed. Otherwise, the current frame is checked for being within the designated range that will be loaded from the sprite sheet file.

We can't go far without controlling these animations in one way or another. It's a good idea to provide a simple interface to do that:

```
void Anim_Base::Play(){ m_playing = true; }
void Anim_Base::Pause(){ m_playing = false; }
void Anim_Base::Stop(){ m_playing = false; Reset(); }
```

The `Play` and `Pause` methods simply manipulate a Boolean flag, while the `Stop` method also resets the animation:

```
void Anim_Base::Reset(){
    m_frameCurrent = m_frameStart;
    m_elapsedTime = 0.0f;
    CropSprite();
}
```

After moving the frame back to the beginning and resetting the timer, it crops the sprite because of the frame change. We are almost done with this class. All that's missing now is a way to update it:

```
void Anim_Base::Update(const float& l_dT){
    if (!m_playing){ return; }
    m_elapsedTime += l_dT;
    if (m_elapsedTime < m_frameTime){ return; }
    FrameStep();
    CropSprite();
    m_elapsedTime = 0;
}
```

The `Update` method, as per usual, takes in an argument that represents the elapsed time between frames. It then simply adds it to the elapsed time of the animation if it's playing and checks if it has exceeded the frame time. If it did, our two virtual methods are called and the timer is reset back to `0`.

Directional animation

There's not always a clear dichotomy present between different types of animation depending on implementation details. For the purposes of this chapter not dragging on with specific subjects, only one type of animation will be implemented, which is the directional animation. This type of animation is usually used with any kind of moving entities that have a specific animation for each direction. Unlike other types of animation, where an increased frame can lead to a jump in rows, directional animation will always remain on the row that represents the proper type of animation in the proper direction. Consider the following illustration:

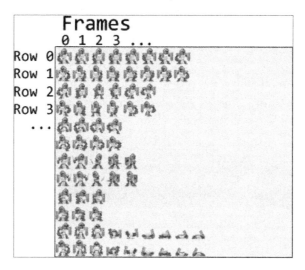

In our case, each row contains either the left or the right facing version of a specific animation. Knowing that, let's create the header of the directional animation class:

```
class Anim_Directional : public Anim_Base{
protected:
    void FrameStep();
    void CropSprite();
    void ReadIn(std::stringstream& l_stream);
};
```

This class doesn't even require a constructor or a destructor, only the three methods from the base class that need to be implemented. Once again, note the inclusion of the SpriteSheet.h file due to its forward declaration in the header of the Anim_Base class:

```
#include "Anim_Directional.h"
#include "SpriteSheet.h"
```

Now let's slice through that texture to fashion our sprite:

```
void Anim_Directional::CropSprite(){
  sf::IntRect rect(
    m_spriteSheet->GetSpriteSize().x * m_frameCurrent,
    m_spriteSheet->GetSpriteSize().y *
    (m_frameRow + (short)m_spriteSheet->GetDirection()),
    m_spriteSheet->GetSpriteSize().x,
    m_spriteSheet->GetSpriteSize().y);
  m_spriteSheet->CropSprite(rect);
}
```

First, we construct a rectangle. Its top-left corner position is the sprite size multiplied by the current frame on the *x* axis and the sprite size multiplied by the sum of the current animation row and the sprite sheet direction on the *y* axis. Because the direction enumeration maps the directions to numerical values of either 0 or 1, it makes obtaining the row for the correct direction really easy, as shown above. After the top-left corner is set up, we pass in the sprite size in pixels and crop the sprite sheet based on the rectangle that was constructed. This yields us a sprite!

The final piece of the puzzle in the animation department is implementing the `FrameStep` method:

```
void Anim_Directional::FrameStep(){
  if (m_frameStart < m_frameEnd){ ++m_frameCurrent; }
  else { --m_frameCurrent; }

  if ((m_frameStart < m_frameEnd && m_frameCurrent > m_frameEnd)||
    (m_frameStart > m_frameEnd && m_frameCurrent < m_frameEnd))
  {
    if (m_loop){ m_frameCurrent = m_frameStart; return; }
    m_frameCurrent = m_frameEnd;
    Pause();
  }
}
```

First, we check which direction we should roll the frames in, since it could be necessary in the future to define backwards-moving animations. If the starting frame number is lower than the ending frame number, we're moving in the positive direction. We then check if the frame is out of bounds, and based on whether it is looping or not, we either reset the current frame to start, or set it to the end of the animation and then pause it. The same logic applies if the animation is playing backwards, except the direction is reversed.

Lastly, the method responsible for reading in data from files:

```
void Anim_Directional::ReadIn(std::stringstream& l_stream){
  l_stream >> m_frameStart >> m_frameEnd >> m_frameRow
    >> m_frameTime >> m_frameActionStart >> m_frameActionEnd;
}
```

With that final bit of code, the animation portion is finished! Everything we need in order to implement loading the sprite sheet file is now available.

Loading the sprite sheet files

The loading method begins, as per usual, by setting up the file, reading it, and obtaining the current line. The first identifier from the line is loaded into the type variable. The rest is fairly typical:

```
bool SpriteSheet::LoadSheet(const std::string& l_file){
  std::ifstream sheet;
  sheet.open(Utils::GetWorkingDirectory() + l_file);
  if(sheet.is_open()){
    ReleaseSheet(); // Release current sheet resources.
    std::string line;
    while(std::getline(sheet,line)){
      if (line[0] == '|'){ continue; }
      std::stringstream keystream(line);
      std::string type;
      keystream >> type;
      ...
    }
    sheet.close();
    return true;
  }
  std::cerr << "! Failed loading spritesheet: "
    << l_file << std::endl;
  return false;
}
```

In order to avoid confusion, the parsing of different types of entries in this file has been split up into separate sections. Let's begin with the texture loading:

```
if(type == "Texture"){
  if (m_texture != ""){
    std::cerr << "! Duplicate texture entries in: "
      << l_file << std::endl;
    continue;
```

```
    }
    std::string texture;
    keystream >> texture;
    if (!m_textureManager->RequireResource(texture)){
      std::cerr << "! Could not set up the texture: "
        << texture << std::endl;
      continue;
    }
    m_texture = texture;
    m_sprite.setTexture(*m_textureManager->GetResource(m_texture));
  } else if ...
```

First, we check if the texture hasn't been initialized already in order to avoid duplicate entries. If it hasn't, the `keystream` variable spits out the texture handle, which gets passed into the texture manager in an `if` statement. This is done to catch errors of invalid handles. If the handle is valid, the texture name is kept around for later freeing of resources and the sprite we'll be using for drawing is set to point to the texture.

Time to read the smaller bits of information in:

```
  } else if(type == "Size"){
      keystream >> m_spriteSize.x >> m_spriteSize.y;
      SetSpriteSize(m_spriteSize);
  } else if(type == "Scale"){
      keystream >> m_spriteScale.x >> m_spriteScale.y;
      m_sprite.setScale(m_spriteScale);
  } else if(type == "AnimationType"){
      keystream >> m_animType;
  } else if ...
```

The most dramatic entry has been saved for last. At this moment, we parse the animations:

```
  } else if(type == "Animation"){
    std::string name;
    keystream >> name;
    if (m_animations.find(name) != m_animations.end()){
      std::cerr << "! Duplicate animation(" << name
        << ") in: " << l_file << std::endl;
      continue;
    }
    Anim_Base* anim  = nullptr;
    if(m_animType == "Directional"){
      anim = new Anim_Directional();
    } else {
```

```
        std::cerr << "! Unknown animation type: "
            << m_animType << std::endl;
        continue;
    }

    keystream >> *anim;
    anim->SetSpriteSheet(this);
    anim->SetName(name);
    anim->Reset();
    m_animations.emplace(name,anim);

    if (m_animationCurrent){ continue; }
    m_animationCurrent = anim;
    m_animationCurrent->Play();
}
```

First, the animation name gets loaded and the animation container is checked in order to avoid duplicates. The type of animation that was loaded previously is then checked in order to construct a correct animation type. We could use a factory method for this, but since we only have one type of animation so far, it seems pointless at this time. The animation structure then gets data streamed into it from our `stringstream` object, initializing it. Furthermore, the animation is reset in order to zero-out its values. Once it gets inserted into the animation container, the last thing we check for is whether the current animation member has been assigned a value yet. If it hasn't, this is the first animation in the sprite sheet file, which we're assuming is the default. It gets assigned to the current animation member and set to play.

Summary

While having good graphics isn't the most important aspect of a game, going from basic shapes to actual sprites being animated on screen can make a world of difference in the eyes of a player. Granted, prettifying a product doesn't fix whatever flaws it may have, which seems like a popular mentality nowadays. Immersing the player into the game world, however, as well as bringing to life what seemed like a bunch of squares, is the effect we're after, which, with the completion of this chapter, you are now able to achieve with a few basic techniques.

In the next chapter, we will be covering common game development elements that will unify all of the graphical bits and pieces we built into a fully functional game with platforming elements, enemies, and multiple levels. See you there!

7
Rediscovering Fire – Common Game Design Elements

Video games are getting more and more intricate every day. It seems that innovative ideas are on the rise, especially with the increasing popularity of indie games, such as *Minecraft* and *Super Meat Boy*. While the game ideas themselves are getting more and more abstract, at least on the outside, the rigid skeleton behind the pretty skin that keeps it standing and helps it retain shape is still taking the place of the lowest common denominator in the eyes of game developers. Even if the focus of the game centers around two unicorns who spend their free time smoking fairy dust and helping Dracula make muffins so that Neptune doesn't blow up, that concept coming to life is going to depend greatly on the underlying logic of the game before anything else. If there are no entities in the game, there are no unicorns. If the entities are simply bouncing around a black screen, the game is not engaging. These are the most common game design elements that any project must be able to fall back on, otherwise it is doomed to fail.

In this chapter, we will be covering the following:

- Designing and implementing the game map class
- Populating the map by creating and managing entities
- Checking for and handling collisions
- Meshing all of our code together into a finished game

The game map

The actual environment and surroundings a player explores are just as important as the rest of the game. Without the world being present, the player is simply left spinning in an empty void of the screen clear color. Designing a good interface to bring out various parts of the game, ranging from the level backdrop to numerous hazards our player has to face can be tricky. Let's build a solid foundation for that right now, starting with defining what our map format is going to be like, as we take a look ahead to determine what we want to accomplish:

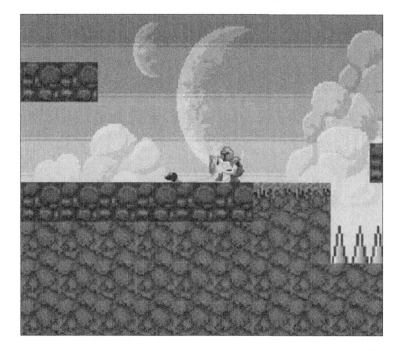

First, we want to specify a texture handle as the background. Then, we want to clearly define the map size and set up the gravity, which determines how fast entities fall to the ground. Additionally, we need to store the default friction, which determines how slippery the average tile is. The last property we want to store is the name of the next map that gets loaded when the end of the current map is reached. Here is a snippet from one of the maps that we will be working with, `Map1.map`:

```
|type|~id|x|y|
BACKGROUND Bg1
SIZE 63 32
GRAVITY 512
DEFAULT_FRICTION 0.8 0
NEXTMAP map2.map
```

```
|PLAYER 0 512
|ENEMY Rat 128 512
TILE 0 0 25
TILE 1 0 26 WARP
...
```

As you can tell, in addition to defining all of the things discussed, the map file also stores the player position, as well as different enemies and their spawn positions. The last but definitely not the least important part of it is tile storage and the indication of which tile is going to "warp" the player to the next stage when touched.

What is a tile?

The term "tile" keeps getting thrown around, but it hasn't been defined yet. To put it simply, a tile is one of the many segments that make up the world. Tiles are blocks that create the game environment, whether it's the grass you're standing on or the spikes you're falling onto. The map uses a tile sheet, which is fairly similar to a sprite sheet, in that it holds many different sprites at once. The main difference is how those sprites are obtained from the tile sheet. This is what the texture that is going to be used as a tile sheet looks like in our case:

Each tile also has unique properties, which we will want to load from the `Tiles.cfg` file:

```
|id|name|friction x|friction y|deadly
0 Grass 0.8 0 0
1 Dirt 0.8 0 0
2 Stone 0.8 0 0
3 Brick 0.8 0 0
4 Brick_Red 0.8 0 0
5 Rock 0.8 0 0
6 Icy_Rock 0.6 0 0
7 Spikes 1.0 0 1
8 Ice 0.25 0 0
```

It is quite simple and only contains the tile ID, name, both axes of friction, and a binary flag for the tile being deadly to touch.

Building the game world

Since tiles are going to play such a huge role in our game design, it would be greatly helpful to have a separate data structure that all tile information can be localized to. A good place to start is by defining some constants of the tile size, as well as dimensions of the tile sheets that are going to be used. A simple enumeration can be quite helpful when storing this information:

```
enum Sheet{Tile_Size = 32, Sheet_Width = 256, Sheet_Height = 256};
```

Here, we make it so all tiles are going to be 32 px wide and 32 px tall and every single tile sheet is going to be 256 px wide and 256 px tall. These constants, obviously, can be changed, but the idea here is to keep them the same during runtime.

To keep our code a little shorter, we can also benefit from a type alias for tile IDs:

```
using TileID = unsigned int;
```

The flyweight pattern

Each tile, obviously, has to have a sprite that represents its type graphically speaking. In order to draw a grass tile, we want to adjust the sprite to be cropped to only the grass tile in the tile sheet. Then, we set its position on the screen and draw it. Seems simple enough, but consider the following situation: you have a map that's 1000x1000 tiles in size, and perhaps 25% of that map's size is actual tiles that aren't just air, which leaves you with the total amount of 62,500 tiles to draw. Now imagine you're storing a sprite with each tile. Granted, sprites are lightweight objects, but that's still a huge waste of resources. This is where the flyweight pattern comes in.

Storing huge chunks of redundant data is obviously a waste, so why not just store one instance of each type and simply store a pointer to the type in the tile? That, in a nutshell, is the flyweight pattern. Let's see it in action, by implementing a tile information structure:

```
struct TileInfo{
  TileInfo(SharedContext* l_context,
    const std::string& l_texture = "", TileID l_id = 0)
    : m_context(l_context), m_id(0), m_deadly(false)
  {
    TextureManager* tmgr = l_context->m_textureManager;
    if (l_texture == ""){ m_id = l_id; return; }
    if (!tmgr->RequireResource(l_texture)){ return; }
    m_texture = l_texture;
    m_id = l_id;
    m_sprite.setTexture(*tmgr->GetResource(m_texture));
    sf::IntRect tileBoundaries(m_id %
```

```
      (Sheet::Sheet_Width / Sheet::Tile_Size) * Sheet::Tile_Size,
        m_id/(Sheet::Sheet_Height/Sheet::Tile_Size)*Sheet::Tile_Size,
        Sheet::Tile_Size,Sheet::Tile_Size);
      m_sprite.setTextureRect(tileBoundaries);
  }

  ~TileInfo(){
    if (m_texture == ""){ return; }
    m_context->m_textureManager->ReleaseResource(m_texture);
  }

  sf::Sprite m_sprite;

  TileID m_id;
  std::string m_name;
  sf::Vector2f m_friction;
  bool m_deadly;

  SharedContext* m_context;
  std::string m_texture;
};
```

This struct essentially holds everything about every tile type that isn't unique. It
stores the texture that it's using, as well as the sprite that will represent the tile. As
you can see, in the constructor of this structure, we set the sprite to point to the tile
sheet texture and then crop it based on its tile ID. This type of cropping is a little
different than the one in the sprite sheet class, because now we only have the tile
ID to work with, and we don't know which row the sprite is on. Using some basic
math allows us to first figure out how many columns and rows the tile sheet has,
by dividing our sheet dimensions by the tile size. In this case, a 256x256 px sized
sprite sheet with tiles of 32x32 px in size would have eight tiles per row and column.
Obtaining the coordinate of a tile ID on an *x* axis can be done by using the modulus
operator %. In a case of eight tiles per row, it would return values from 0 to 7, based
on the ID. Figuring out the *y* coordinate is done simply by dividing the ID by the
number of tiles per column. This gives us the top-left coordinate of the tile sprite in
the tile sheet, so we finish the cropping by passing in the Sheet::Tile_Size.

The TileInfo destructor simply frees the texture used for the tile sheet. The rest of
the values stored in this structure will be initialized when the map is loaded. Now
let's define our tile structure:

```
struct Tile{
    TileInfo* m_properties;
    bool m_warp; // Is the tile a warp.
    // Other flags unique to each tile.
};
```

This is the reason why the flyweight pattern is so powerful. The tile objects are incredibly lightweight, if they only store information that can be unique to each tile and not the tile type. The only flag we're interested in so far is if the tile is a warp, which means it loads the next level when the player is standing on it.

Designing the map class

With tiles out of the way, we can move on to higher-level structures, such as the game map. Let's begin by creating a few suitable types of containers that will hold the map information, as well as the tile type information:

```
using TileMap = std::unordered_map<TileID,Tile*>;
using TileSet = std::unordered_map<TileID,TileInfo*>;
```

The `TileMap` type is an `unordered_map` container, which holds pointers to `Tile` objects that are addressed by an unsigned integer.

 In cases where tile counts are known in advance, it would be prudent to use a container that will not change in size (such as `std::array` or a pre-allocated `std::vector`) in order to achieve continuous storage, and in turn, much faster access.

But wait a minute! Aren't we working in two dimensions? How are we mapping the tiles to only one integer, if the coordinates are represented by two numbers? Well, with a little bit of mathematics, it's entirely possible to manipulate indices of two dimensions to be represented as a single number. This will be covered shortly.

The `TileSet` data type represents the container of all different types of tiles, which are tied to a tile ID that's represented by the unsigned integer. This brings us everything we need in order to write the map header file, which might look a little something like this:

```
class Map{
public:
  Map(SharedContext* l_context, BaseState* l_currentState);
  ~Map();
  Tile* GetTile(unsigned int l_x, unsigned int l_y);
  TileInfo* GetDefaultTile();
  float GetGravity()const;
  unsigned int GetTileSize()const;
  const sf::Vector2u& GetMapSize()const;
  const sf::Vector2f& GetPlayerStart()const;
  void LoadMap(const std::string& l_path);
  void LoadNext();
  void Update(float l_dT);
  void Draw();
```

```
private:
    // Method for converting 2D coordinates to 1D ints.
    unsigned int ConvertCoords(unsigned int l_x, unsigned int l_y);
    void LoadTiles(const std::string& l_path);
    void PurgeMap();
    void PurgeTileSet();

    TileSet m_tileSet;
    TileMap m_tileMap;
    sf::Sprite m_background;
    TileInfo m_defaultTile;
    sf::Vector2u m_maxMapSize;
    sf::Vector2f m_playerStart;
    unsigned int m_tileCount;
    unsigned int m_tileSetCount;
    float m_mapGravity;
    std::string m_nextMap;
    bool m_loadNextMap;
    std::string m_backgroundTexture;
    BaseState* m_currentState;
    SharedContext* m_context;
};
```

First, we define all the predictable methods, such as obtaining a tile at specific coordinates, getting various information from the class, and, of course, methods for updating and drawing the map. Let's move on to the implementation of these methods, in order to talk about them more in depth:

```
Map::Map(SharedContext* l_context, BaseState* l_currentState)
    :m_context(l_context), m_defaultTile(l_context),
      m_maxMapSize(32, 32), m_tileCount(0), m_tileSetCount(0),
      m_mapGravity(512.f), m_loadNextMap(false),
      m_currentState(l_currentState)
{
    m_context->m_gameMap = this;
    LoadTiles("tiles.cfg");
}
```

The map constructor initializes its data members to some default values and calls a private method in order to load different types of tiles from the `tiles.cfg` file. Fairly standard. Predictably enough, the destructor of this class does nothing out of the ordinary either:

```
Map::~Map(){
    PurgeMap();
```

```
    PurgeTileSet();
    m_context->m_gameMap = nullptr;
}
```

Obtaining tiles from the map is done by first converting the 2D coordinates provided as arguments to this method into a single number, and then locating the specific tile in an unordered map:

```
Tile* Map::GetTile(unsigned int l_x, unsigned int l_y){
  auto itr = m_tileMap.find(ConvertCoords(l_x,l_y));
  return(itr != m_tileMap.end() ? itr->second : nullptr);
}
```

The conversion of coordinates looks like this:

```
unsigned int Map::ConvertCoords(const unsigned int& l_x,
  const unsigned int& l_y)
{
    return (l_x * m_maxMapSize.x) + l_y; // Row-major.
}
```

In order for this to work, we must have the maximum size of the map defined, otherwise it will produce wrong results.

Updating the map is another crucial part:

```
void Map::Update(float l_dT){
  if(m_loadNextMap){
    PurgeMap();
    m_loadNextMap = false;
    if(m_nextMap != ""){
      LoadMap("media/maps/"+m_nextMap);
    } else {
      m_currentState->GetStateManager()->
        SwitchTo(StateType::GameOver);
    }
    m_nextMap = "";
  }
  sf::FloatRect viewSpace = m_context->m_wind->GetViewSpace();
  m_background.setPosition(viewSpace.left, viewSpace.top);
}
```

Here, it checks the `m_loadNextMap` flag. If it's set to `true`, the map information gets purged and the next map is loaded, if the data member that holds its handle is set. If it isn't, the application state is set to `GameOver`, which will be created later. This will simulate the player beating the game. Finally, we obtain the view space of the window and set our map background's top-left corner to the view space's left corner in order for the background to follow the camera. Let's draw these changes on the screen:

```
void Map::Draw(){
    sf::RenderWindow* l_wind = m_context->m_wind->GetRenderWindow();
    l_wind->draw(m_background);
    sf::FloatRect viewSpace = m_context->m_wind->GetViewSpace();

    sf::Vector2i tileBegin(
      floor(viewSpace.left / Sheet::Tile_Size),
      floor(viewSpace.top / Sheet::Tile_Size));
    sf::Vector2i tileEnd(
      ceil((viewSpace.left + viewSpace.width) / Sheet::Tile_Size),
      ceil((viewSpace.top + viewSpace.height) / Sheet::Tile_Size));

    unsigned int count = 0;
    for(int x = tileBegin.x; x <= tileEnd.x; ++x){
      for(int y = tileBegin.y; y <= tileEnd.y; ++y){
        if(x < 0 || y < 0){ continue; }
        Tile* tile = GetTile(x,y);
        if (!tile){ continue; }
        sf::Sprite& sprite = tile->m_properties->m_sprite;
        sprite.setPosition(x * Sheet::Tile_Size,
          y * Sheet::Tile_Size);
        l_wind->draw(sprite);
        ++count;
      }
    }
}
```

A pointer to the render window is obtained through the share context and the background is drawn in the first two lines here. The next three lines serve a purpose, simply known by a name of culling. It is a technique that any good game programmer should utilize, where anything that's not currently within the view space of the screen should be left undrawn. Once again, consider the situation where you have a massive map of size 1000x1000. Although modern hardware nowadays could draw that really fast, there's still no need to waste those clock-cycles when they could instead be used to perform a much better task, instead of bringing something to the screen that isn't even visible. If you are not culling anything in your game, it will eventually start taking serious performance hits.

The tile coordinates all the way from the top-left corner of the view space to its bottom-right corner are fed into a loop. First, they get evaluated to be positive. If they're negative, the way we calculate our 1D index for the map container will produce some mirroring artifacts, where the same map you see will be repeated over and over again if you go up or left far enough.

A pointer to a tile is obtained by passing in the *x* and *y* coordinates from the loop. If it is a valid tile, we obtain its sprite from the pointer to the `TileInfo` structure. The position of the sprite is set to match the coordinates of the tile and the sprite is drawn on screen.

Now for a way to erase the entire map:

```
void Map::PurgeMap(){
  m_tileCount = 0;
  for (auto &itr : m_tileMap){
    delete itr.second;
  }
  m_tileMap.clear();
  m_context->m_entityManager->Purge();

  if (m_backgroundTexture == ""){ return; }
  m_context->m_textureManager->
    ReleaseResource(m_backgroundTexture);
  m_backgroundTexture = "";
}
```

In addition to clearing the map container, you will notice that we're calling the `Purge` method of an entity manager. For now, ignore that line. Entities will be covered shortly. We must also not forget to free up the background texture when erasing the map.

Emptying the container of different tile types is also a necessary part:

```
void Map::PurgeTileSet(){
  for (auto &itr : m_tileSet){
    delete itr.second;
  }
  m_tileSet.clear();
  m_tileSetCount = 0;
}
```

This will most likely only be called in the destructor, but it's still nice to have a separate method. Speaking of different tile types, we need to load them in from a file:

```
void Map::LoadTiles(const std::string& l_path){
  std::ifstream file;
  file.open(Utils::GetWorkingDirectory() + l_path);
  if (!file.is_open()){
    std::cout << "! Failed loading tile set file: "
      << l_path << std::endl;
    return;
  }
  std::string line;
  while(std::getline(file,line)){
    if (line[0] == '|'){ continue; }
    std::stringstream keystream(line);
    int tileId;
    keystream >> tileId;
    if (tileId < 0){ continue; }
    TileInfo* tile = new TileInfo(m_context,"TileSheet",tileId);
    keystream >> tile->m_name >> tile->m_friction.x
      >> tile->m_friction.y >> tile->m_deadly;
    if(!m_tileSet.emplace(tileId,tile).second){
      // Duplicate tile detected!
      std::cout << "! Duplicate tile type: "
        << tile->m_name << std::endl;
      delete tile;
    }
  }
  file.close();
}
```

The tile ID gets loaded first, as the `tiles.cfg` format suggests. It gets checked for being out of bounds, and if it isn't, dynamic memory is allocated for the tile type, at which point all of its internal data members are initialized to the values from the string stream. If the tile information object cannot be inserted into the tile set container, there must be a duplicate entry, and the dynamic memory is de-allocated.

Now for the grand finale of the map – the loading method. Since the actual file loading code remains pretty much the same, let's jump right to reading the contents of the map file, starting with tile entries:

```
if(type == "TILE"){
  int tileId = 0;
  keystream >> tileId;
  if (tileId < 0){ std::cout << "! Bad tile id: "
    << tileId << std::endl;
```

```
        continue;
    }
    auto itr = m_tileSet.find(tileId);
    if (itr == m_tileSet.end()){
        std::cout << "! Tile id(" << tileId
            << ") was not found in tileset." << std::endl;
        continue;
    }
    sf::Vector2i tileCoords;
    keystream >> tileCoords.x >> tileCoords.y;
    if (tileCoords.x>m_maxMapSize.x || tileCoords.y>m_maxMapSize.y)
    {
        std::cout << "! Tile is out of range: " <<
            tileCoords.x << " " << tileCoords.y << std::endl;
        continue;
    }
    Tile* tile = new Tile();
    // Bind properties of a tile from a set.
    tile->m_properties = itr->second;
    if(!m_tileMap.emplace(ConvertCoords(
        tileCoords.x,tileCoords.y),tile).second)
    {
        // Duplicate tile detected!
        std::cout << "! Duplicate tile! : " << tileCoords.x
            << "" << tileCoords.y << std::endl;
        delete tile;
        tile = nullptr;
        continue;
    }
    std::string warp;
    keystream >> warp;
    tile->m_warp = false;
    if(warp == "WARP"){ tile->m_warp = true; }
} else if ...
```

The first segment of the TILE line is loaded in, which is the tile ID. It is checked, as per usual, to be within the boundaries of positive numbers and *0*. If it is, the tile information of that specific tile ID is looked up in the tile set. Because we don't want empty tiles around our map, we only proceed if the tile information of the specific ID is located. Next, the tile coordinates are read in and checked for being within the boundaries of the map size. If they are, the memory for the tile is allocated and its tile information data member is set to point to the one located in the tile set. Lastly, we attempt to read in a string at the end of the TILE line and check if it says "WARP". That's the indication that touching a specific tile should load the next level.

Now for the background of the map:

```
} else if(type == "BACKGROUND"){
  if (m_backgroundTexture != ""){ continue; }
  keystream >> m_backgroundTexture;
  if (!m_context->m_textureManager->
    RequireResource(m_backgroundTexture))
  {
    m_backgroundTexture = "";
    continue;
  }
  sf::Texture* texture = m_context->m_textureManager->
    GetResource(m_backgroundTexture);
  m_background.setTexture(*texture);
  sf::Vector2f viewSize = m_currentState->GetView().getSize();
  sf::Vector2u textureSize = texture->getSize();
  sf::Vector2f scaleFactors;
  scaleFactors.x = viewSize.x / textureSize.x;
  scaleFactors.y = viewSize.y / textureSize.y;
  m_background.setScale(scaleFactors);
} else if ...
```

This one is quite straightforward. A texture handle gets loaded from the BACKGROUND
line. If the handle is valid, the background sprite gets tied to the texture. There is a
catch though. Let's say that the view of our window is larger than the texture of the
background. That would result in empty areas all around the background, which looks
horrendous. Repeating the texture might remedy the empty areas, but the specific
backgrounds we're going to be working with don't tile well, so the best solution is to
scale the sprite enough to fit the view space fully, whether it's larger or smaller. The
factors of the scaling can be obtained by multiplying the size of the view by the size of
the texture. If, for example, we have a view that's 800x600 px large and a texture of a
size 400x300 px, the scale factor for both axes would be 2 and the background is scaled
up to twice its size.

Next is the easy part of simply reading in some data members from a file:

```
} else if(type == "SIZE"){
    keystream >> m_maxMapSize.x >> m_maxMapSize.y;
} else if(type == "GRAVITY"){
    keystream >> m_mapGravity;
} else if(type == "DEFAULT_FRICTION"){
    keystream >> m_defaultTile->m_friction.x
      >> m_defaultTile->m_friction.y;
} else if(type == "NEXTMAP"){
    keystream >> m_nextMap;
}
```

Let's wrap this class up with a little helper method that will help us keep track of when the next map should be loaded:

```
void Map::LoadNext(){ m_loadNextMap = true; }
```

This concludes the map class implementation. The world now exists, but nobody is there to occupy it. Outrageous! Let's not insult our work and create some entities to explore the environments we conjure up.

The parent of all world objects

An entity is essentially just another word for a game object. It's an abstract class that acts as a parent to all of its derivatives, which include the player, enemies, and perhaps even items, depending on how you want to implement that. Having these entirely different concepts share the same roots allows the programmer to define types of behavior that are common to all of them. Moreover, it lets the game engine act upon them in the same manner, as they all share the same interface. For example, the enemy can be pushed, and so can the player. All enemies, items, and the player have to be affected by gravity as well. Having that common ancestry between these different types allows us to offload a lot of redundant code and focus on the aspects that are unique to each entity, instead of re-writing the same code over and over again.

Let's begin by defining what entity types we're going to be dealing with:

```
enum class EntityType{ Base, Enemy, Player };
```

The base entity type is just the abstract class, which will not actually be instantiated. That leaves us with enemies and a player. Now to set up all the possible states an entity can have:

```
enum class EntityState{
    Idle, Walking, Jumping, Attacking, Hurt, Dying
};
```

You have probably noticed that these states vaguely match the animations from the player sprite sheet. All character entities will be modeled this way.

Creating the base entity class

In cases where entities are built using inheritance, writing a basic parent class like this is fairly common. It has to provide any and all functionality that any given entity within the game should have.

With all of the setting up out of the way, we can finally start shaping it like so:

```
class EntityManager;
class EntityBase{
friend class EntityManager;
public:
  EntityBase(EntityManager* l_entityMgr);
  virtual ~EntityBase();
  ... // Getters and setters.
  void Move(float l_x, float l_y);
  void AddVelocity(float l_x, float l_y);
  void Accelerate(float l_x, float l_y);
  void SetAcceleration(float l_x, float l_y);
  void ApplyFriction(float l_x, float l_y);
  virtual void Update(float l_dT);
  virtual void Draw(sf::RenderWindow* l_wind) = 0;
protected:
  // Methods.
  void UpdateAABB();
  void CheckCollisions();
  void ResolveCollisions();
  // Method for what THIS entity does TO the l_collider entity.
  virtual void OnEntityCollision(EntityBase* l_collider,
    bool l_attack) = 0;
  // Data members.
  std::string m_name;
  EntityType m_type;
  unsigned int m_id; // Entity id in the entity manager.
  sf::Vector2f m_position; // Current position.
  sf::Vector2f m_positionOld; // Position before entity moved.
  sf::Vector2f m_velocity; // Current velocity.
  sf::Vector2f m_maxVelocity; // Maximum velocity.
  sf::Vector2f m_speed; // Value of acceleration.
  sf::Vector2f m_acceleration; // Current acceleration.
  sf::Vector2f m_friction; // Default friction value.
  TileInfo* m_referenceTile; // Tile underneath entity.
  sf::Vector2f m_size; // Size of the collision box.
  sf::FloatRect m_AABB; // The bounding box for collisions.
  EntityState m_state; // Current entity state.
  // Flags for remembering axis collisions.
  bool m_collidingOnX;
  bool m_collidingOnY;

  Collisions m_collisions;
  EntityManager* m_entityManager;
};
```

Right off the bat, we set up the `EntityManager` class that we haven't written yet to be a friend class of the base entities. Because the code might be a little confusing, a barrage of comments was added to explain every data member of the class, so we're not going to touch on those too much until we encounter them during the implementation of the class.

The three major properties of an entity include its position, velocity, and acceleration. The position of an entity is self explanatory. Its velocity represents how fast an entity is moving. Because all of the update methods in our application take in the delta time in seconds, the velocity is going to represent the number of pixels that an entity moves across per second. The last element of the major three is acceleration, which is responsible for how fast the entity's velocity increases. It, too, is defined as the number of pixels per second that get added to the entity's velocity. The sequence of events here is as follows:

1. The entity is accelerated and its acceleration adjusts its velocity.
2. The entity's position is re-calculated based on its velocity.
3. The velocity of an entity is damped by the friction coefficient.

Collisions and bounding boxes

Before jumping into implementations, let's talk about one of the most commonly used elements in all games – collisions. Detecting and resolving a collision is what keeps the player from falling through the map or going outside the screen. It's also what determines if a player gets hurt if they get touched by the enemy. In a round-about way, we used a basic form of collision detection in order to determine which tiles we should render in the map class. How does one detect and resolve collisions? There are many ways to do so, but for our purposes, the most basic form of a bounding box collision will do just fine. Other types of collisions that incorporate different shapes, such as circles, can also be used, but may not be the most efficient or appropriate depending on the kind of game that's being built.

A bounding box, much like it sounds, is a box or a rectangle which represents the solid portion of an entity. Here's a good example of a bounding box:

It isn't visible like that, unless we create an actual `sf::RectangleShape` with the same position and size as the bounding box and render that, which is a useful way to debug your applications. In our base entity class, the bounding box named `m_AABB` is simply a `sf::FloatRect` type. The name "AABB" represents two pairs of different values it holds: the position and the size. Bounding box collision, also referred to as an AABB collision, is simply a situation where two bounding boxes intersect with one another. The rectangle data types in SFML provide us with a method that checks for intersections:

```
if(m_AABB.intersects(SomeRectangle){...}
```

The term collision resolution simply means performing some sequence of actions in order to notify and move the colliding entities. In a case of collision with tiles, for example, the collision resolution means pushing the entity back just far enough so it isn't intersecting with the tile any more.

The code files of this project contain an additional class that allows debug information rendering to take place, as well as all of these bits of information already set up. Hitting the *O* key will toggle its visibility.

Implementing the base entity class

With all of that information out of the way, we can finally return to implementing the base entity class. As always, what better place is there to start than the constructor? Let's take a look:

```
EntityBase::EntityBase(EntityManager* l_entityMgr)
    :m_entityManager(l_entityMgr), m_name("BaseEntity"),
    m_type(EntityType::Base), m_referenceTile(nullptr),
    m_state(EntityState::Idle), m_id(0),
    m_collidingOnX(false), m_collidingOnY(false){}
```

It simply initializes all of its data members to default values. Notice that out of all the members it sets to zero, the friction actually gets set up for the *x* axis to be 0.8. This is because we don't want the default behavior of the entity to be equal to that of a cow on ice, to put it frankly. Friction defines how much of the entity's velocity is lost to the environment. If it doesn't make too much sense now, don't worry. We're about to cover it in greater detail.

Here we have all of the methods for modifying data members of the entity base class:

```
void EntityBase::SetPosition(const float& l_x, const float& l_y){
    m_position = sf::Vector2f(l_x,l_y);
    UpdateAABB();
}
void EntityBase::SetPosition(const sf::Vector2f& l_pos){
    m_position = l_pos;
    UpdateAABB();
}
void EntityBase::SetSize(const float& l_x, const float& l_y){
    m_size = sf::Vector2f(l_x,l_y);
    UpdateAABB();
}
void EntityBase::SetState(const EntityState& l_state){
    if(m_state == EntityState::Dying){ return; }
    m_state = l_state;
}
```

As you can see, modifying either the position or size of an entity results in a call of the internal method UpdateAABB. Simply put, it's responsible for updating the position of the bounding box. More information on that is coming soon.

One interesting thing to note is in the SetState method. It does not allow the state to change if the current state is Dying. This is done in order to prevent some other event in the game to snap an entity out of death magically.

Now we have a more interesting chunk of code, responsible for moving an entity:

```
void EntityBase::Move(float l_x, float l_y){
  m_positionOld = m_position;
  m_position += sf::Vector2f(l_x,l_y);
  sf::Vector2u mapSize = m_entityManager->
    GetContext()->m_gameMap->GetMapSize();
  if(m_position.x < 0){
    m_position.x = 0;
  } else if(m_position.x > (mapSize.x + 1) * Sheet::Tile_Size){
    m_position.x = (mapSize.x + 1) * Sheet::Tile_Size;
  }

  if(m_position.y < 0){
    m_position.y = 0;
  } else if(m_position.y > (mapSize.y + 1) * Sheet::Tile_Size){
    m_position.y = (mapSize.y + 1) * Sheet::Tile_Size;
    SetState(EntityState::Dying);
  }

  UpdateAABB();
}
```

First, we copy the current position to another data member: m_positionOld. It's always good to keep track of this information, in case we need it later. Then, the position is adjusted by the offset provided through the arguments. The size of the map is obtained afterwards, in order to check the current position for being outside of the map. If it is on either axis, we simply reset its position to something that's at the very edge of the out-of-bounds area. In the case of the entity being outside of the map on the *y* axis, its state is set to Dying. After all of that, the bounding box is updated in order to reflect the changes to the position of the entity sprite.

Now let's work on adding to and managing the entity's velocity:

```
void EntityBase::AddVelocity(float l_x, float l_y){
  m_velocity += sf::Vector2f(l_x,l_y);
  if(abs(m_velocity.x) > m_maxVelocity.x){
    if(m_velocity.x < 0){ m_velocity.x = -m_maxVelocity.x; }
    else { m_velocity.x = m_maxVelocity.x; }
  }

  if(abs(m_velocity.y) > m_maxVelocity.y){
    if(m_velocity.y < 0){ m_velocity.y = -m_maxVelocity.y; }
    else { m_velocity.y = m_maxVelocity.y; }
  }
}
```

As you can see, it's fairly simple stuff. The velocity member is added to and then checked for being outside of the bounds of allowed maximum velocity. In the first check we're using absolute values, because velocity can be both positive and negative, which indicates the direction the entity's moving in. If the velocity is out of bounds, it gets reset to the maximum allowed value it can have.

Accelerating an entity, you could say, is as simple as adding one vector to another:

```
void EntityBase::Accelerate(float l_x, float l_y){
    m_acceleration += sf::Vector2f(l_x,l_y);
}
```

Applying friction is no more complex than managing our velocity:

```
void EntityBase::ApplyFriction(float l_x, float l_y){
  if(m_velocity.x != 0){
    if(abs(m_velocity.x) - abs(l_x) < 0){ m_velocity.x = 0; }
    else {
      if(m_velocity.x < 0){ m_velocity.x += l_x; }
      else { m_velocity.x -= l_x; }
    }
  }

  if(m_velocity.y != 0){
    if (abs(m_velocity.y) - abs(l_y) < 0){ m_velocity.y = 0; }
    else {
      if(m_velocity.y < 0){ m_velocity.y += l_y; }
      else { m_velocity.y -= l_y; }
    }
  }
}
```

It needs to check if the difference between the absolute values of both the velocity and the friction coefficient on that axis isn't less than zero, in order to prevent changing the direction of the entity's movement through friction, which would simply be weird. If it is less than zero, the velocity gets set back to zero. If it isn't, the velocity's sign is checked and friction in the proper direction is applied.

In order for an entity to not be a static part of the backdrop, it needs to be updated:

```
void EntityBase::Update(float l_dT){
  Map* map = m_entityManager->GetContext()->m_gameMap;
  float gravity = map->GetGravity();
  Accelerate(0,gravity);
  AddVelocity(m_acceleration.x * l_dT, m_acceleration.y * l_dT);
  SetAcceleration(0.0f, 0.0f);
```

```
        sf::Vector2f frictionValue;
        if(m_referenceTile){
          frictionValue = m_referenceTile->m_friction;
          if(m_referenceTile->m_deadly){ SetState(EntityState::Dying); }
        } else if(map->GetDefaultTile()){
          frictionValue = map->GetDefaultTile()->m_friction;
        } else {
          frictionValue = m_friction;
        }

        float friction_x = (m_speed.x * frictionValue.x) * l_dT;
        float friction_y = (m_speed.y * frictionValue.y) * l_dT;
        ApplyFriction(friction_x, friction_y);
        sf::Vector2f deltaPos = m_velocity * l_dT;
        Move(deltaPos.x, deltaPos.y);
        m_collidingOnX = false;
        m_collidingOnY = false;
        CheckCollisions();
        ResolveCollisions();
    }
```

Quite a bit is happening here. Let's take it step by step. First, an instance of the game map is obtained through the shared context. It is then used to obtain the gravity of the map, which was loaded from the map file. The entity's acceleration is then increased by the gravity on the *y* axis. By using the `AddVelocity` method and passing in the acceleration multiplied by delta time, the velocity is adjusted and the acceleration is set back to zero. Next, we must obtain the friction coefficient that the velocity will be damped by. The `m_referenceTile` data member, if it's not set to `nullptr`, is used first, in order to obtain the friction from a tile the entity's standing on. If it is set to `nullptr`, the entity must be in mid-air, so the default tile from the map is obtained to grab the friction values that were loaded from the map file. If that, for whatever reason, is also not set up, we default to the value set in the `EntityBase`'s constructor.

Before we get to calculating friction, it's important to clarify that the `m_speed` data member is not set up or initialized in this class, aside from being set to a default value. The speed is how much an entity is accelerated when it's moving and it will be implemented in one of the derived classes of `EntityBase`.

If you recall from the constructor of this class, we set up the default friction to be 0.8f. That is not just an incredibly small value. We're using friction as a factor in order to determine how much of the entity's speed should be lost. Having said that, multiplying the speed by a friction coefficient and multiplying that by delta time yields us the velocity that is lost during this frame, which is then passed into the `ApplyFriction` method in order to manipulate the velocity.

Finally, the change in position, called `deltaPos` is calculated by multiplying the velocity by delta time, and is passed into the `Move` method to adjust the entity's position in the world. The flags for collisions on both axes get reset to false and the entity calls its own private members for first obtaining and then resolving collisions.

Let's take a look at the method responsible for updating the bounding box:

```
void EntityBase::UpdateAABB(){
  m_AABB = sf::FloatRect(m_position.x - (m_size.x / 2),
    m_position.y - m_size.y, m_size.x, m_size.y);
}
```

Because the origin of the bounding box is left at the top-left corner and the entity's position is set to (width / 2, height), accounting for that is necessary if we want to have accurate collisions. The rectangle that represents the bounding box is reset to match the new position of the sprite.

Entity-on-tile collisions

Before jumping into collision detection and resolution, let's revisit the method SFML provides to check if two rectangles are intersecting:

```
sf::FloatRect r1;
sf::FloatRect r2;
if(r1.intersects(r2)){ ... }
```

It doesn't matter which rectangle we check, the intersecting method will still return true if they are intersecting. However, this method does take in an optional second argument, which is a reference of a rectangle class that will be filled with the information about the intersection itself. Consider the following illustration:

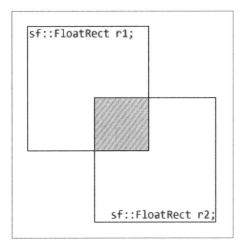

We have two rectangles that are intersecting. The diagonal striped area represents the rectangle of intersection, which can be obtained by doing this:

```
...
sf::FloatRect intersection;
if(r1.intersects(r2,intersection)){ ... }
```

This is important to us, because an entity could be colliding with more than one tile at a time. Knowing the depth of a collision is also a crucial part of resolving it. With that in mind, let's define a structure to temporarily hold the collision information before it gets resolved:

```
struct CollisionElement{
  CollisionElement(float l_area, TileInfo* l_info,
    const sf::FloatRect& l_bounds):m_area(l_area),
    m_tile(l_info), m_tileBounds(l_bounds){}
  float m_area;
  TileInfo* m_tile;
  sf::FloatRect m_tileBounds;
};

using Collisions = std::vector<CollisionElement>;
```

First, we're creating a structure that holds a floating point number representing the area of collision, a rectangle that holds the boundary information of a tile the entity's colliding with, and a pointer to a `TileInfo` instance. You always want to resolve the biggest collisions first, and this information is going to help us do just that. The collision elements themselves are going to be stored in a vector this time.

Next, we need a function that can compare two elements of our custom container in order to sort it, the blueprint of which in the header file of the `EntityBase` class looks like this:

```
bool SortCollisions(const CollisionElement& l_1,
  const CollisionElement& l_2);
```

Implementing this function is incredibly easy. The vector container simply uses a Boolean check to determine which one of the two elements it's comparing is larger. We simply return true or false, based on which element is bigger. Because we're sorting our container by the area size, the comparison is done between the first elements of the first pairs:

```
bool SortCollisions(const CollisionElement& l_1,
  const CollisionElement& l_2)
{ return l_1.m_area > l_2.m_area; }
```

Now onto the interesting part, detecting the collisions:

```
void EntityBase::CheckCollisions(){
  Map* gameMap = m_entityManager->GetContext()->m_gameMap;
  unsigned int tileSize = gameMap->GetTileSize();
  int fromX = floor(m_AABB.left / tileSize);
  int toX = floor((m_AABB.left + m_AABB.width) / tileSize);
  int fromY = floor(m_AABB.top / tileSize);
  int toY = floor((m_AABB.top + m_AABB.height) / tileSize);

  for(int x = fromX; x <= toX; ++x){
    for(int y = fromY; y <= toY; ++y){
      Tile* tile = gameMap->GetTile(x,y);
      if (!tile){ continue; }
      sf::FloatRect tileBounds(x * tileSize, y * tileSize,
        tileSize,tileSize);
      sf::FloatRect intersection;
      m_AABB.intersects(tileBounds,intersection);
      float area = intersection.width * intersection.height;

      CollisionElement e(area, tile->m_properties, tileBounds);
      m_collisions.emplace_back(e);
      if(tile->m_warp && m_type == EntityType::Player){
        gameMap->LoadNext();
      }
    }
  }
}
```

We begin by using the coordinates and size of the bounding box to obtain the coordinates of tiles it is potentially intersecting. This is illustrated better in the following image:

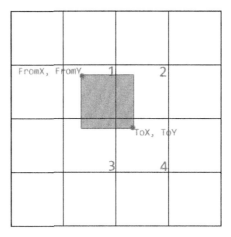

The range of tile coordinates represented by the four integers is then fed into a double loop which checks if there is a tile occupying the space we're interested in. If a tile is returned from the `GetTile` method, the bounding box of the entity is definitely intersecting a tile, so a float rectangle that represents the bounding box of a tile is created. We also prepare another float rectangle to hold the data of the intersection and call the `intersects` method in order to obtain this information. The area of the intersection is calculated by multiplying its width and height, and the information about the collision is pushed into the collision container, along with a pointer to the `TileInfo` object that represents the type of tile the entity is colliding with.

The last thing we do before wrapping up this method is check if the current tile the entity is colliding with is a warp tile and if the entity is a player. If both of these conditions are met, the next map is loaded.

Now that a list of collisions for an entity has been obtained, resolving them is the next step:

```
void EntityBase::ResolveCollisions(){
  if(!m_collisions.empty()){
    std::sort(m_collisions.begin(),
      m_collisions.end(), SortCollisions);
    Map* gameMap = m_entityManager->GetContext()->m_gameMap;
    unsigned int tileSize = gameMap->GetTileSize();
    for (auto &itr : m_collisions){
      if (!m_AABB.intersects(itr.m_tileBounds)){ continue; }
```

```
float xDiff = (m_AABB.left + (m_AABB.width / 2)) -
    (itr.m_tileBounds.left + (itr.m_tileBounds.width / 2));
float yDiff = (m_AABB.top + (m_AABB.height / 2)) -
    (itr.m_tileBounds.top + (itr.m_tileBounds.height / 2));
float resolve = 0;
if(abs(xDiff) > abs(yDiff)){
  if(xDiff > 0){
    resolve = (itr.m_tileBounds.left + tileSize) -
      m_AABB.left;
  } else {
    resolve = -((m_AABB.left + m_AABB.width) -
      itr.m_tileBounds.left);
  }
  Move(resolve, 0);
  m_velocity.x = 0;
  m_collidingOnX = true;
} else {
  if(yDiff > 0){
    resolve = (itr.m_tileBounds.top + tileSize) -
      m_AABB.top;
  } else {
    resolve = - ((m_AABB.top + m_AABB.height) -
      itr.m_tileBounds.top);
  }
  Move(0,resolve);
  m_velocity.y = 0;
  if (m_collidingOnY){ continue; }
  m_referenceTile = itr.m_tile;
  m_collidingOnY = true;
}
  }
}
m_collisions.clear();
}
if(!m_collidingOnY){ m_referenceTile = nullptr; }
}
```

First, we check if there are any collisions in the container. Sorting of all the elements happens next. The std::sort function is called and iterators to the beginning and end of the container are passed in, along with the name of the function that will do the comparisons between the elements.

The code proceeds to loop over all of the collisions stored in the container. There is another intersection check here between the bounding box of the entity and the tile. This is done because resolving a previous collision could have moved an entity in such a way that it is no longer colliding with the next tile in the container. If there still is a collision, distances from the center of the entity's bounding box to the center of the tile's bounding box are calculated. The first purpose these distances serve is illustrated in the next line, where their absolute values get compared. If the distance on the x axis is bigger than on the y axis, the resolution takes place on the x axis. Otherwise, it's resolved on the y axis.

The second purpose of the distance calculation is determining which side of the tile the entity is on. If the distance is positive, the entity is on the right side of the tile, so it gets moved in the positive x direction. Otherwise, it gets moved in the negative x direction. The *resolve* variable takes in the amount of penetration between the tile and the entity, which is different based on the axis and the side of the collision.

In the case of both axes, the entity is moved by calling its `Move` method and passing in the depth of penetration. Killing the entity's velocity on that axis is also important, in order to simulate the entity hitting a solid. Lastly, the flag for a collision on a specific axis is set to true.

If a collision is resolved on the y axis, in addition to all the same steps that are taken in a case of x axis collision resolution, we also check if the flag is set for a y axis collision. If it hasn't been set yet, we change the `m_referenceTile` data member to point to the tile type of the current tile the entity is colliding with, which is followed by that flag getting set to true in order to keep the reference unchanged until the next time collisions are checked. This little snippet of code gives any entity the ability to behave differently based on which tile it's standing on. For example, the entity can slide a lot more on ice tiles than on simple grass tiles, as illustrated here:

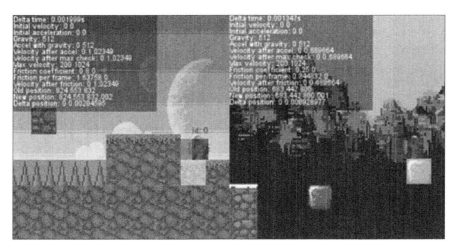

As the arrow points out, the friction coefficient of these tiles is different, which means we are in fact obtaining the information from the tiles directly below.

Entity storage and management

Without proper management, these entities are just random classes scattered about in your memory with no rhyme or reason. In order to produce a robust way to create interactions between entities, they need to be babysat by a manager class. Before we begin designing it, let's define some data types to contain the information we're going to be working with:

```
using EntityContainer = std::unordered_map<
   unsigned int,EntityBase*>;
using EntityFactory = std::unordered_map<
   EntityType, std::function<EntityBase*(void)>>;
using EnemyTypes = std::unordered_map<std::string,std::string>;
```

The `EntityContainer` type is, as the name suggests, a container of entities. It is once again powered by an `unordered_map`, which ties instances of entities to unsigned integers that serve as identifiers. The next type is a container of lambda functions that links entity types to code that can allocate memory and return instances of classes that inherit from the base entity class and serves as a factory. This behavior isn't new to us, so let's move on to defining the entity manager class:

```
class EntityManager{
public:
   EntityManager(SharedContext* l_context,
      unsigned int l_maxEntities);
   ~EntityManager();

   int Add(const EntityType& l_type,
      const std::string& l_name = "");
   EntityBase* Find(unsigned int l_id);
   EntityBase* Find(const std::string& l_name);
   void Remove(unsigned int l_id);

   void Update(float l_dT);
   void Draw();

   void Purge();

   SharedContext* GetContext();
private:
   template<class T>
```

```
    void RegisterEntity(const EntityType& l_type){
      m_entityFactory[l_type] = [this]() -> EntityBase*
      {
        return new T(this);
      };
    }

    void ProcessRemovals();
    void LoadEnemyTypes(const std::string& l_name);
    void EntityCollisionCheck();

    EntityContainer m_entities;
    EnemyTypes m_enemyTypes;
    EntityFactory m_entityFactory;
    SharedContext* m_context;
    unsigned int m_idCounter;
    unsigned int m_maxEntities;

    std::vector<unsigned int> m_entitiesToRemove;
};
```

Aside from the private template method for inserting lambda functions into the entity factory container, this looks like a relatively typical class. We have methods for updating and drawing entities, adding, finding and removing them and purging all of the data, as we tend to do. The presence of the private method called ProcessRemovals insists that we're using delayed removals of entities, much like we did in our state manager class. Let's take a closer look at how this class will operate by implementing it.

Implementing the entity manager

As always, a good place to start is the constructor:

```
EntityManager::EntityManager(SharedContext* l_context,
  unsigned int l_maxEntities):m_context(l_context),
  m_maxEntities(l_maxEntities), m_idCounter(0)
{
    LoadEnemyTypes("EnemyList.list");
    RegisterEntity<Player>(EntityType::Player);
    RegisterEntity<Enemy>(EntityType::Enemy);
}
EntityManager::~EntityManager(){ Purge(); }
```

Some of its data members are initialized through an initializer list. The m_idCounter variable will be used to keep track of the highest ID that was given to an entity. Next, a private method is invoked for loading pairs of enemy names and their character definition files, which will be explained a little later.

Lastly, two entity types are registered: player and enemy. We don't have their classes set up yet, but it's coming soon, so we may as well just register them now.

The destructor of an entity manager simply invokes the Purge method.

Adding a new entity to the game is done by passing in an entity type along with its name to the Add method of the entity manager:

```cpp
int EntityManager::Add(const EntityType& l_type,
  const std::string& l_name)
{
  auto itr = m_entityFactory.find(l_type);
  if (itr == m_entityFactory.end()){ return -1; }
  EntityBase* entity = itr->second();
  entity->m_id = m_idCounter;
  if (l_name != ""){ entity->m_name = l_name; }
  m_entities.emplace(m_idCounter,entity);
  if(l_type == EntityType::Enemy){
    auto itr = m_enemyTypes.find(l_name);
    if(itr != m_enemyTypes.end()){
      Enemy* enemy = (Enemy*)entity;
      enemy->Load(itr->second);
    }
  }

  ++m_idCounter;
  return m_idCounter - 1;
}
```

The entity factory container is searched for the type that was provided as an argument. If that type is registered, the lambda function is invoked to allocate dynamic memory for the entity and the memory address is caught by a pointer variable to the EntityBase class – entity. The newly created entity is then inserted into the entity container and its ID is set up by using the m_idCounter data member. If the user provides an argument for the entity name, it gets set up as well.

The entity type then gets checked. If it's an enemy, the enemy type container is searched in order to locate the path to a character definition file. If it's found, the entity is type-cast into an enemy instance and a Load method is called, to which the character file path is passed.

Lastly, the ID counter is incremented and the entity ID that was just used gets returned to signify success. If the method failed at any point, it will instead return *-1,* signifying a failure.

Having an entity manager is pointless if you can't obtain the entities. That's where the `Find` method comes in:

```
EntityBase* EntityManager::Find(const std::string& l_name){
  for(auto &itr : m_entities){
    if(itr.second->GetName() == l_name){
      return itr.second;
    }
  }
  return nullptr;
}
```

Our entity manager provides two versions of this method. The first version takes in an entity name and searches the container until an entity is found with that name, at which point it gets returned. The second version looks up entities based on a numerical identifier:

```
EntityBase* EntityManager::Find(unsigned int l_id){
  auto itr = m_entities.find(l_id);
  if (itr == m_entities.end()){ return nullptr; }
  return itr->second;
}
```

Because we map instances of entities to numerical values, this is easier, as we can simply call the `Find` method of our container in order to find the element we're looking for.

Now let's work on removing entities:

```
void EntityManager::Remove(unsigned int l_id){
    m_entitiesToRemove.emplace_back(l_id);
}
```

This is the public method that takes in an entity ID and inserts it into a container, which will be used later to remove entities.

Updating all entities can be achieved as follows:

```
void EntityManager::Update(float l_dT){
  for(auto &itr : m_entities){
    itr.second->Update(l_dT);
  }
```

```
        EntityCollisionCheck();
        ProcessRemovals();
    }
```

The manager iterates through all of its elements and invokes their respective `Update` methods by passing in the delta time it receives as an argument. After all of the entities are updated, a private method `EntityCollisionCheck` is invoked in order to check for and resolve collisions between entities. Then, we process the entity removals that were added by the `Remove` method implemented previously.

Let's take a look at how we can draw all of these entities:

```
    void EntityManager::Draw(){
        sf::RenderWindow* wnd = m_context->m_wind->GetRenderWindow();
        sf::FloatRect viewSpace = m_context->m_wind->GetViewSpace();

        for(auto &itr : m_entities){
            if (!viewSpace.intersects(itr.second->m_AABB)){ continue; }
            itr.second->Draw(wnd);
        }
    }
```

After obtaining a pointer to the render window, we also get the view space of it in order to cull entities for efficiency reasons. Because both the view space and the bounding box of an entity are rectangles, we can simply check if they're intersecting in order to determine if an entity is within the view space, and if it is, it gets drawn.

The entity manager needs to have a way to dispatch of all of its resources. This is where the `Purge` method comes in:

```
    void EntityManager::Purge(){
        for (auto &itr : m_entities){
            delete itr.second;
        }
        m_entities.clear();
        m_idCounter = 0;
    }
```

Entities get iterated over and their dynamic memory is de-allocated – regular as clockwork. Now to process the entities that need to be removed:

```
    void EntityManager::ProcessRemovals(){
        while(m_entitiesToRemove.begin() != m_entitiesToRemove.end()){
            unsigned int id = m_entitiesToRemove.back();
            auto itr = m_entities.find(id);
            if(itr != m_entities.end()){
```

```
        std::cout << "Discarding entity: "
          << itr->second->GetId() << std::endl;
        delete itr->second;
        m_entities.erase(itr);
      }
      m_entitiesToRemove.pop_back();
    }
  }
```

As we're iterating over the container that holds the IDs of entities that need to be removed, the entity container is checked for the existence of every ID that was added. If an entity with the ID does in fact exist, its memory is de-allocated and the element is popped from the entity container.

Now for the interesting part – detecting entity-to-entity collisions:

```
void EntityManager::EntityCollisionCheck(){
  if (m_entities.empty()){ return; }
  for(auto itr = m_entities.begin();
    std::next(itr) != m_entities.end(); ++itr)
  {
    for(auto itr2 = std::next(itr);
      itr2 != m_entities.end(); ++itr2)
    {
      if(itr->first == itr2->first){ continue; }

      // Regular AABB bounding box collision.
      if(itr->second->m_AABB.intersects(itr2->second->m_AABB)){
        itr->second->OnEntityCollision(itr2->second, false);
        itr2->second->OnEntityCollision(itr->second, false);
      }

      EntityType t1 = itr->second->GetType();
      EntityType t2 = itr2->second->GetType();
      if (t1 == EntityType::Player || t1 == EntityType::Enemy){
        Character* c1 = (Character*)itr->second;
        if (c1->m_attackAABB.intersects(itr2->second->m_AABB)){
          c1->OnEntityCollision(itr2->second, true);
        }
      }

      if (t2 == EntityType::Player || t2 == EntityType::Enemy){
        Character* c2 = (Character*)itr2->second;
        if (c2->m_attackAABB.intersects(itr->second->m_AABB)){
```

```
            c2->OnEntityCollision(itr->second, true);
        }
      }
    }
  }
}
```

First, the way we're checking every entity against every other entity needs to be addressed. There are, of course, much better and more efficient ways to determine which entities to check without simply iterating over all of them, such as binary space partitioning. However, given the scope of our project, that would be overkill:

> *"Premature optimization is the root of all evil (or at least most of it) in programming."*
>
> – *Donald Knuth*

Having said that, we are going to be a bit smarter and not simply iterate over all of the entities twice. Because checking entity 0 against entity 1 is the same as checking entity 1 against 0, we can implement a much more efficient algorithm by using `std::next`, which creates an iterator that is one space ahead of the one fed to it, and use it in the second loop. This creates a check pattern that looks something like this:

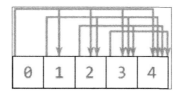

That is about as much optimization as we need in the early stages of making a game.

When iterating over entities, the collision check method first makes sure that both iterators do not share the same entity ID, for some odd reason. Then, it's simply a matter of checking for intersections between the bounding boxes of the two entities we're interested in. If there is a collision, the methods for handling it are called in both instances, passing in the entity being collided with as an argument, along with false as the second argument, to let the entity know it's a simple AABB collision. What does that mean? Well, generally, there are going to be two types of collisions between entities: regular bounding box collisions and attack collisions. Children of the `EntityBase` class, mainly the `Character` instances, will have to keep another bounding box in order to perform attacks, as illustrated here:

Because this isn't terribly complicated to implement, we can continue implementing the entity manger until we implement the Character class shortly.

Since only the Character class and any class that inherits from it is going to have an attack bounding box, it's necessary to first check if we're dealing with a Character instance by verifying the entity type. If an entity is of the type Enemy or Player, the OnEntityCollision method of the Character instance is invoked and receives the entity it's colliding with, as well as a Boolean constant of true this time, as arguments, to indicate an attack collision.

We're mostly done. Let's write the method for loading different enemy types that can parse files like this:

```
|Name|CharFile|
Rat Rat.char
```

It's quite a simple format. Let's read it in:

```
void EntityManager::LoadEnemyTypes(const std::string& l_name){
  std::ifstream file;
  ... // Opening the file.
  while(std::getline(file,line)){
    if (line[0] == '|'){ continue; }
    std::stringstream keystream(line);
    std::string name;
    std::string charFile;
    keystream >> name >> charFile;
    m_enemyTypes.emplace(name,charFile);
  }
  file.close();
}
```

There is nothing here you haven't seen before. The two string values get read in and stored in the enemy type container. This simple bit of code concludes our interest in the entity manager class.

Using entities to build characters

So far, we only have entities that define some abstract methods and provide the means of manipulating them, but nothing that can appear in the game world, be rendered, and walk around. At the same time, we don't want to re-implement all of that functionality all over again in the player or enemy classes, which means we need an intermediate-level abstract class: Character. This class will provide all of the functionality that is shared between all entities that need to move around the world and be rendered. Let's get on with designing:

```
class Character : public EntityBase{
friend class EntityManager;
public:
  Character(EntityManager* l_entityMgr);
  virtual ~Character();
  void Move(const Direction& l_dir);
  void Jump();
  void Attack();
  void GetHurt(const int& l_damage);
  void Load(const std::string& l_path);
  virtual void OnEntityCollision(
    EntityBase* l_collider, bool l_attack) = 0;
  virtual void Update(float l_dT);
  void Draw(sf::RenderWindow* l_wind);
```

```
protected:
  void UpdateAttackAABB();
  void Animate();
  SpriteSheet m_spriteSheet;
  float m_jumpVelocity;
  int m_hitpoints;
  sf::FloatRect m_attackAABB;
  sf::Vector2f m_attackAABBoffset;
};
```

First, let's talk about the public methods. Moving, jumping, attacking, and receiving damage are the common actions of every character-entity in the game. The character also has to be loaded in order to provide it with the correct graphics and properties that differ between each enemy type and the player. All classes derived from it have to implement their own version of handling collisions with other entities. Also, the Update method of the character class is made to be virtual, which allows any class inheriting from this one to either define its own update method or extend the existing one.

All characters will be using the sprite sheet class that we designed previously in order to support animations.

Implementing the character class

You know the drill by now. Here's the constructor:

```
Character::Character(EntityManager* l_entityMgr)
  :EntityBase(l_entityMgr),
  m_spriteSheet(m_entityManager->GetContext()->m_textureManager),
  m_jumpVelocity(250), m_hitpoints(5)
{ m_name = "Character"; }
```

The sprite sheet is created and set up by passing a pointer to the texture manager in its constructor. We also have a data member called m_jumpVelocity, which specifies how far the player can jump. Lastly, we set some arbitrary value to the m_hitpoints variable, which represents how many times an entity can be hit before it dies.

Let's move on to the Move method:

```
void Character::Move(const Direction& l_dir){
  if (GetState() == EntityState::Dying){ return; }
  m_spriteSheet.SetDirection(l_dir);
  if (l_dir == Direction::Left){ Accelerate(-m_speed.x, 0); }
  else { Accelerate(m_speed.x, 0); }
```

```
    if (GetState() == EntityState::Idle){
      SetState(EntityState::Walking);
    }
  }
```

Regardless of the entity's direction, the state of the entity is checked in order to make sure the entity isn't dying. If it isn't, the direction of the sprite sheet is set up and the character begins to accelerate on a relevant axis. Lastly, if the entity is currently in an idle state, it gets set to walking simply to play the walking animation:

```
void Character::Jump(){
  if (GetState() == EntityState::Dying ||
    GetState() == EntityState::Jumping ||
    GetState() == EntityState::Hurt)
  {
    return;
  }
  SetState(EntityState::Jumping);
  AddVelocity(0, -m_jumpVelocity);
}
```

A character should only be able to jump if it isn't dying, taking damage, or jumping already. When those conditions are met and the character is instructed to jump, its state is set to Jumping and it receives negative velocity on the y axis that makes it combat the gravity force and go up. The velocity has to be high enough in order to break the gravitational force of the level.

Attacking is fairly straightforward. Because the entity manager already does the collision checking for us, all that's left to do is set the state if an entity isn't dying, jumping, taking damage, or already attacking:

```
void Character::Attack(){
  if (GetState() == EntityState::Dying ||
    GetState() == EntityState::Jumping ||
    GetState() == EntityState::Hurt ||
    GetState() == EntityState::Attacking)
  {
    return;
  }
  SetState(EntityState::Attacking);
}
```

In order to bestow mortality onto our entities, they need to have a way to be hurt:

```cpp
void Character::GetHurt(const int& l_damage){
  if (GetState() == EntityState::Dying ||
    GetState() == EntityState::Hurt)
  {
    return;
  }
  m_hitpoints = (m_hitpoints - l_damage > 0 ?
    m_hitpoints - l_damage : 0);
  if (m_hitpoints){ SetState(EntityState::Hurt); }
  else { SetState(EntityState::Dying); }
}
```

This method inflicts damage to the character if it isn't already taking damage or dying. The damage value is either subtracted from the hit-points or the hitpoints variable is set to *0* in order to keep it from reaching the negatives. If the entity still has lives after the subtraction, its state is set to HURT in order to play the proper animation. Otherwise, the entity is sentenced to death by the programmer.

As previously mentioned, we want to be able to load our characters in from files like this one (Player.char):

```
Name Player
Spritesheet Player.sheet
Hitpoints 5
BoundingBox 20 26
DamageBox -5 0 26 26
Speed 1024 128
JumpVelocity 250
MaxVelocity 200 1024
```

It contains all the basic bits and pieces of what makes up a character, like the sprite sheet handle and all of the other information discussed in earlier sections. The loading method for this type of file will not differ much from the ones we've already implemented:

```cpp
void Character::Load(const std::string& l_path){
  std::ifstream file;
  ...
  while(std::getline(file,line)){
    ...
    std::string type;
    keystream >> type;
    if(type == "Name"){
```

```
        keystream >> m_name;
    } else if(type == "Spritesheet"){
        std::string path;
        keystream >> path;
        m_spriteSheet.LoadSheet("media/SpriteSheets/" + path);
    } else if(type == "Hitpoints"){
        keystream >> m_hitpoints;
    } else if(type == "BoundingBox"){
        sf::Vector2f boundingSize;
        keystream >> boundingSize.x >> boundingSize.y;
        SetSize(boundingSize.x, boundingSize.y);
    } else if(type == "DamageBox"){
        keystream >> m_attackAABBoffset.x >> m_attackAABBoffset.y
            >> m_attackAABB.width >> m_attackAABB.height;
    } else if(type == "Speed"){
        keystream >> m_speed.x >> m_speed.y;
    } else if(type == "JumpVelocity"){
        keystream >> m_jumpVelocity;
    } else if(type == "MaxVelocity"){
        keystream >> m_maxVelocity.x >> m_maxVelocity.y;
    } else {
        std::cout << "! Unknown type in character file: "
            << type << std::endl;
    }
    }
    file.close();
}
```

Aside from the sprite sheet having to call a load method, the rest is simply loading in data members from a string stream.

Just like the base entity and its bounding box, the character has to have a way to update the position of its attack area:

```
void Character::UpdateAttackAABB(){
    m_attackAABB.left =
        (m_spriteSheet.GetDirection() == Direction::Left ?
        (m_AABB.left - m_attackAABB.width) - m_attackAABBoffset.x
        : (m_AABB.left + m_AABB.width) + m_attackAABBoffset.x);
    m_attackAABB.top = m_AABB.top + m_attackAABBoffset.y;
}
```

One subtle difference here is that the attack bounding box uses the position of the entity's bounding box, not its sprite position. Also, the way it's positioned is different based on the direction an entity is facing, due to the fact that the bounding box's position represents its top-left corner.

Now for the method that will make the biggest difference, visually speaking:

```
void Character::Animate(){
  EntityState state = GetState();

  if(state == EntityState::Walking && m_spriteSheet.
    GetCurrentAnim()->GetName() != "Walk")
  {
    m_spriteSheet.SetAnimation("Walk",true,true);
  }
  else if(state == EntityState::Jumping && m_spriteSheet.
    GetCurrentAnim()->GetName() != "Jump")
  {
    m_spriteSheet.SetAnimation("Jump",true,false);
  }
  else if(state == EntityState::Attacking && m_spriteSheet.
    GetCurrentAnim()->GetName() != "Attack")
  {
    m_spriteSheet.SetAnimation("Attack",true,false);
  } else if(state == EntityState::Hurt && m_spriteSheet.
    GetCurrentAnim()->GetName() != "Hurt")
  {
    m_spriteSheet.SetAnimation("Hurt",true,false);
  }
  else if(state == EntityState::Dying && m_spriteSheet.
    GetCurrentAnim()->GetName() != "Death")
  {
    m_spriteSheet.SetAnimation("Death",true,false);
  }
  else if(state == EntityState::Idle && m_spriteSheet.
    GetCurrentAnim()->GetName() != "Idle")
  {
    m_spriteSheet.SetAnimation("Idle",true,true);
  }
}
```

All it does is simply check the current state and the current animation. If the current animation does not match the current state, it gets set to something else. Note the use of the third argument in the `SetAnimation` method, which is a Boolean constant and represents animation looping. Certain animations do not need to loop, like the attack or hurt animation. The fact that they do not loop and are stopped when they reach the end frame gives us a hook to manipulate what happens in the game, simply based on the progress of a certain animation. Case in point – the `Update` method:

```
void Character::Update(float l_dT){
  EntityBase::Update(l_dT);
  if(m_attackAABB.width != 0 && m_attackAABB.height != 0){
```

```
      UpdateAttackAABB();
    }
    if(GetState() != EntityState::Dying && GetState() !=
      EntityState::Attacking && GetState() != EntityState::Hurt)
    {
      if(abs(m_velocity.y) >= 0.001f){
        SetState(EntityState::Jumping);
      } else if(abs(m_velocity.x) >= 0.1f){
        SetState(EntityState::Walking);
      } else {
        SetState(EntityState::Idle);
      }
    } else if(GetState() == EntityState::Attacking ||
      GetState() == EntityState::Hurt)
    {
      if(!m_spriteSheet.GetCurrentAnim()->IsPlaying()){
        SetState(EntityState::Idle);
      }
    } else if(GetState() == EntityState::Dying){
      if(!m_spriteSheet.GetCurrentAnim()->IsPlaying()){
        m_entityManager->Remove(m_id);
      }
    }
    Animate();
    m_spriteSheet.Update(l_dT);
    m_spriteSheet.SetSpritePosition(m_position);
  }
```

First, we invoke the update method of the entity's base class, because the character's state depends on it. Then, we check if the width and height of the attack bounding box aren't still at 0, which are the default values for them. If they aren't, it means the attack bounding box has been set up and can be updated. The rest of the update method pretty much just handles state transitions. If the entity isn't dying, attacking something, or taking damage, its current state is going to be determined by its velocity. In order to accurately depict an entity falling, we have to make the velocity on y axis take precedence over everything else. If the entity has no vertical velocity, it's checked for horizontal velocity instead and sets the state to Walking if the velocity is higher than the specified minimum. Using small values instead of absolute zero takes care of problems with animations being jittery sometimes.

Because the attacking and taking damage states are not set to loop, the sprite sheet animation is checked in order to see if it is still playing. If it isn't, the state is switched back to idle. Lastly, if the entity is dying and the dying animation is finished playing, we call the Remove method of our entity manager in order to remove this entity from the world.

The `Animate` method is called near the end of the update in order to reflect the state changes that may have taken place. Also, this is where the sprite sheet gets updated and has its position set to match the position of the entity.

After all of that code, let's end on something really simple – the `Draw` method:

```
void Character::Draw(sf::RenderWindow* l_wind){
    m_spriteSheet.Draw(l_wind);
}
```

Since our sprite-sheet class takes care of drawing, all we need to do is pass a pointer of a render window to its `Draw` method.

Creating the player

Now we have a solid base for creating entities that are visually represented on screen. Let's put that to good use and finally build our player class by starting with the header:

```
class Player : public Character{
public:
  Player(EntityManager* l_entityMgr);
  ~Player();

  void OnEntityCollision(EntityBase* l_collider, bool l_attack);
  void React(EventDetails* l_details);
};
```

This is where things get easy. Because we essentially "outsourced" most of the common functionality to the base classes, all we're left with now is player-specific logic. Notice the `React` method. Judging by its argument list, it's obvious that we're going to be using it as a callback for handling player input. Before we do that, however, we must register this method as one:

```
Player::Player(EntityManager* l_entityMgr)
  : Character(l_entityMgr)
{
  Load("Player.char");
  m_type = EntityType::Player;

  EventManager* events = m_entityManager->
    GetContext()->m_eventManager;
  events->AddCallback<Player>(StateType::Game,
    "Player_MoveLeft", &Player::React, this);
  events->AddCallback<Player>(StateType::Game,
```

```
      "Player_MoveRight", &Player::React, this);
    events->AddCallback<Player>(StateType::Game,
      "Player_Jump", &Player::React, this);
    events->AddCallback<Player>(StateType::Game,
      "Player_Attack", &Player::React, this);
}
```

All we're doing here is calling the `Load` method in order to set up the character values for our player and adding multiple callbacks to the same `React` method that will be used to process keyboard input. The type of the entity is also set to `Player`:

```
Player::~Player(){
    EventManager* events =
      m_entityManager->GetContext()->m_eventManager;
    events->RemoveCallback(GAME,"Player_MoveLeft");
    events->RemoveCallback(GAME,"Player_MoveRight");
    events->RemoveCallback(GAME,"Player_Jump");
    events->RemoveCallback(GAME,"Player_Attack");
}
```

The destructor, predictably enough, simply removes callbacks that we were using to move the player around.

The last method we are required to implement by the `Character` class is responsible for entity-on-entity collision:

```
void Player::OnEntityCollision(EntityBase* l_collider,
  bool l_attack)
{
  if (m_state == EntityState::Dying){ return; }
  if(l_attack){
    if (m_state != EntityState::Attacking){ return; }
    if (!m_spriteSheet.GetCurrentAnim()->IsInAction()){ return; }
    if (l_collider->GetType() != EntityType::Enemy &&
      l_collider->GetType() != EntityType::Player)
    {
      return;
    }
    Character* opponent = (Character*)l_collider;
    opponent->GetHurt(1);
    if(m_position.x > opponent->GetPosition().x){
      opponent->AddVelocity(-32,0);
    } else {
      opponent->AddVelocity(32,0);
    }
```

```
    } else {
      // Other behavior.
    }
  }
```

This method, as you remember from the entity manager portion of this chapter, is invoked when something is colliding with this particular entity. In a case of collision, the other colliding entity is passed in as an argument to this method together with a flag to determine if the entity is colliding with your bounding box or your attack region.

First, we make sure the player entity isn't dying. Afterwards, we check if it's the attack region that is colliding with another entity. If it is and the player is in the attack state, we check if the attack animation in the sprite sheet is currently "in action." If the current frame is within range of the beginning and end frames when the action is supposed to happen, the last check is made to determine if the entity is either a player or an enemy. Finally, if it is one or the other, the opponent gets hit with a pre-determined damage value, and based on its position will have some velocity added to it for a knock-back effect. That's about as basic a game design as it gets.

Adding enemies

In order to keep our player from walking the world lonely and un-attacked, we must add enemies to the game. Once again, let's begin with the header file:

```
#pragma once
#include "Character.h"

class Enemy : public Character{
public:
    Enemy(EntityManager* l_entityMgr);
    ~Enemy();

    void OnEntityCollision(
      EntityBase* l_collider, bool l_attack);
    void Update(float l_dT);
private:
    sf::Vector2f m_destination;
    bool m_hasDestination;
};
```

It's the same basic idea here as it was in the player class. This time, however, the enemy class needs to specify its own version of the Update method. It also has two private data members, one of which is a destination vector. It is a very simple attempt at adding basic artificial intelligence to the game. All it will do is keep track of a destination position, which the Update method will randomize every now and then to simulate wandering entities. Let's implement this:

```
Enemy::Enemy(EntityManager* l_entityMgr)
  :Character(l_entityMgr), m_hasDestination(false)
{
  m_type = EntityType::Enemy;
}
Enemy::~Enemy(){}
```

The constructor simply initializes a few data members to their default values, while the destructor remains unused. So far, so good!

```
void Enemy::OnEntityCollision(EntityBase* l_collider,
  bool l_attack)
{
  if (m_state == EntityState::Dying){ return; }
  if (l_attack){ return; }
  if (l_collider->GetType() != EntityType::Player){ return; }
  Character* player = (Character*)l_collider;
  SetState(EntityState::Attacking);
  player->GetHurt(1);
  if(m_position.x > player->GetPosition().x){
    player->AddVelocity(-m_speed.x,0);
    m_spriteSheet.SetDirection(Direction::Left);
  } else {
    player->AddVelocity(m_speed.y,0);
    m_spriteSheet.SetDirection(Direction::Right);
  }
}
```

The entity collision method is fairly similar as well, except this time we make sure to act if the enemy's bounding box is colliding with another entity, not its attack region. Also, we ignore every single collision, unless it's colliding with a player entity, in which case the enemy's state is set to Attacking in order to display the attack animation. It inflicts damage of *1* point to the player and knocks them back just a little bit based on where the entity is. The sprite-sheet direction is also set based on the position of the enemy entity relative to what it's attacking.

Now, to update our enemy:

```
void Enemy::Update(float l_dT){
  Character::Update(l_dT);

  if (m_hasDestination){
    if (abs(m_destination.x - m_position.x) < 16){
      m_hasDestination = false;
      return;
    }
    if (m_destination.x - m_position.x > 0){
      Move(Direction::Right);
    } else { Move(Direction::Left); }
    if (m_collidingOnX){ m_hasDestination = false; }
    return;
  }
  int random = rand() % 1000 + 1;
  if (random != 1000){ return; }
  int newX = rand() % 65 + 0;
  if (rand() % 2){ newX = -newX; }
  m_destination.x = m_position.x + newX;
  if (m_destination.x < 0){ m_destination.x = 0; }
  m_hasDestination = true;
}
```

Because this depends on the functionality of the Character class, we invoke its update method first before doing anything. Then the most basic simulation of A.I. begins by first checking if the entity has a destination. If it does not, a random number is generated between 1 and 1000. It has a 1/1000 chance to have its destination set to be anywhere within 128 pixels of its current position. The direction is decided by another random number generation, except much smaller this time. The destination finally is set and gets checked for being outside the world boundaries.

If, on the other hand, the entity does have a destination, the distance between it and its current position is checked. If it is above 16, the appropriate method for moving in a specific direction is called, based on which direction the destination point is in. We must also check for horizontal collisions, because an enemy entity could easily be assigned a destination that's beyond a tile it cannot cross. If that happens, the destination is simply taken away.

With that done, we now have wandering entities and a player that can be moved around the world! The only thing left to do in order to actually bring these entities into the game now is to load them.

Loading entities from the map file

If you recall from the section of this chapter that dealt with the issue of creating a map class, we haven't finished implementing the loading method fully, because we had no entities yet. With that no longer being the case, let's take a look at extending it:

```
} else if(type == "PLAYER"){
    if (playerId != -1){ continue; }
    // Set up the player position here.
    playerId = entityMgr->Add(EntityType::Player);
    if (playerId < 0){ continue; }
    float playerX = 0; float playerY = 0;
    keystream >> playerX >> playerY;
    entityMgr->Find(playerId)->SetPosition(playerX,playerY);
    m_playerStart = sf::Vector2f(playerX, playerY);
} else if(type == "ENEMY"){
    std::string enemyName;
    keystream >> enemyName;
    int enemyId = entityMgr->Add(EntityType::Enemy, enemyName);
    if (enemyId < 0){ continue; }
    float enemyX = 0; float enemyY = 0;
    keystream >> enemyX >> enemyY;
    entityMgr->Find(enemyId)->SetPosition(enemyX, enemyY);
} ...
```

If the map encounters a PLAYER line, it simply attempts to add an entity of type Player and grabs its ID. If it's above or equal to 0, the entity creation was successful, meaning that we can read in the rest of the data from the map file, which happens to be the player position. After obtaining it, we set the player's position and make sure we keep track of the starting position in the map class itself too.

All of the above is true for the ENEMY line as well, except it also loads in the name of the entity, which is needed in order to load its character information from the file.

Now our game is capable of loading entities from the map files and thus putting them into the game world like so:

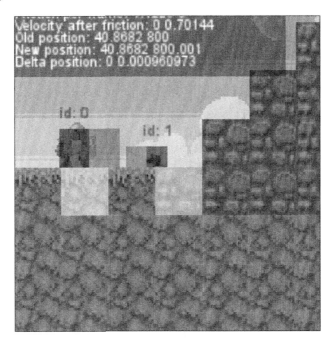

Final editions to our code base

In this last portion of the chapter, we will be covering small changes and additions/editions that have been made all over the code written in the previous chapters in order to make this possible, starting with the shared context, which is now moved into its own header file.

Changes to the shared context

Out of all of the extra classes we defined, some of them need to be accessible to the rest of the code-base. This is what the shared context structure looks like now:

```
class Map;
struct SharedContext{
  SharedContext():
    m_wind(nullptr),
    m_eventManager(nullptr),
    m_textureManager(nullptr),
    m_entityManager(nullptr),
```

```
        m_gameMap(nullptr){}

    Window* m_wind;
    EventManager* m_eventManager;
    TextureManager* m_textureManager;
    EntityManager* m_entityManager;
    Map* m_gameMap;
    DebugOverlay m_debugOverlay;
};
```

The last object in it is the debug overlay we briefly discussed while working on the base entity class, which helps us see what's going on in our game by providing overlay graphics for tiles that entities collide with, warp tiles, and spike tiles, giving us the visual representations of entity bounding boxes and so on. Because the debug code was not essential to this chapter, snippets of it did not get included here, but they're present in the code that comes with it.

Putting all the pieces together

Next, we need to put instances of the code we worked so hard on in the right places, starting with the entity manager class, which goes straight into the game class as a data member:

```
class Game{
public:
    ...
private:
    ...
    EntityManager m_entityManager;
};
```

The map class instance is kept around in the game state class:

```
class State_Game : public BaseState{
public:
    ...
private:
    ...
    Map* m_gameMap;
};
```

The main game state is also responsible for setting up its own view and zooming in just enough to make the game look more appealing and less prone to cause squinting, not to mention initializing and loading the map:

```
void State_Game::OnCreate(){
    ...
    sf::Vector2u size = m_stateMgr->GetContext()->
        m_wind->GetWindowSize();
    m_view.setSize(size.x,size.y);
    m_view.setCenter(size.x/2,size.y/2);
    m_view.zoom(0.6f);
    m_stateMgr->GetContext()->m_wind->
        GetRenderWindow()->setView(m_view);

    m_gameMap = new Map(m_stateMgr->GetContext(), this);
    m_gameMap->LoadMap("media/Maps/map1.map");
}
```

Because the map is dynamically allocated, it must be deleted in the `OnDestroy` method of the game state:

```
void State_Game::OnDestroy(){
    ...
    delete m_gameMap;
    m_gameMap = nullptr;
}
```

Now onto the final piece of this puzzle – the game state update method:

```
void State_Game::Update(const sf::Time& l_time){
    SharedContext* context = m_stateMgr->GetContext();
    EntityBase* player = context->m_entityManager->Find("Player");
    if(!player){
        std::cout << "Respawning player..." << std::endl;
        context->m_entityManager->Add(EntityType::Player,"Player");
        player = context->m_entityManager->Find("Player");
        player->SetPosition(m_gameMap->GetPlayerStart());
    } else {
        m_view.setCenter(player->GetPosition());
        context->m_wind->GetRenderWindow()->setView(m_view);
    }

    sf::FloatRect viewSpace = context->m_wind->GetViewSpace();
    if(viewSpace.left <= 0){
```

```
      m_view.setCenter(viewSpace.width / 2,m_view.getCenter().y);
      context->m_wind->GetRenderWindow()->setView(m_view);
    } else if (viewSpace.left + viewSpace.width >
      (m_gameMap->GetMapSize().x + 1) * Sheet::Tile_Size)
    {
      m_view.setCenter(((m_gameMap->GetMapSize().x + 1) *
        Sheet::Tile_Size) - (viewSpace.width / 2),
        m_view.getCenter().y);
      context->m_wind->GetRenderWindow()->setView(m_view);
    }

    m_gameMap->Update(l_time.asSeconds());
    m_stateMgr->GetContext()->
      m_entityManager->Update(l_time.asSeconds());
  }
```

First, we determine if the player is still alive in the game by searching for them by name. If the player isn't found, they must've died, so a re-spawn is in order. A new player entity is created and the starting coordinates of the map are passed to its SetPosition method.

Now comes the part where we manage how the view is scrolling. If the player entity exists, we set the view's centre to match the exact player position and use the shared context to obtain the render window, which will be using the updated view. Now, we have an issue of the screen leaving the boundaries of the map, which can be resolved by checking the top-left corner of the view space. If it's below or equal to zero, we set the view's centre on the x axis to a position that would put its top-left corner at the very edge of the screen, in order to prevent scrolling infinitely to the left. If, however, the view is outside of the map in the opposite direction, the view centre's x coordinate is set up so that the right side of it is also at the very edge of the map's boundaries.

Finally, the game map, along with the entity manager, is updated right here, because we don't want the map updating or entities moving around if the current state is different.

Summary

Congratulations on making it past the halfway point of this book! All of the code that was written, the design decisions, accounting for efficiency, and trial and error has brought you to this point. While the game we built is fairly basic, its architecture is also quite robust and expandable, and that is no small feat. Although some things in it may not be perfect, you have also followed the golden rule of getting it working first, before refining it, and now you have quite a few game design patterns under your belt to start building more complex game applications, as well as a solid code-base to expand and improve.

With the conclusion of this chapter, the second project of the book is officially finished. We have solved some quite tricky problems, written thousands of lines of code, and broadened our understanding of the game development process beyond the stages of myopic, callow naïveté, but the real adventure is still ahead of us. We may not know where it will ultimately lead us, but one thing is for sure: now is not a time to stop. See you in the next chapter.

8
The More You Know
– Common Game
Programming Patterns

As we move past the halfway point of this book, the bells and whistles in our games are going to get more and more advanced. To showcase them properly, the genre of our final project will be a classical 2D **Role Playing Game** with orthographic projection. With our code-base growing at a rapid rate, poor design quickly becomes tedious to maintain, or even unmanageable. As new features get added, we want expansion of code to be easy and not slow down the overall process. This is the area where game programming patterns shine the brightest.

In this chapter, we will be covering:

- The design and implementation of the entity component system
- Inter-system communication using the observer pattern
- Render ordering
- Implementation of map layers

Let's not waste any time and jump right into making our code base more robust!

Use of copyrighted resources

Once again, before beginning this chapter, we'd like to give credit where credit's due. The graphics used for the third project of this book consist of but are not limited to:

[LPC] Medieval fantasy character sprites by *wulax* under CC-BY-SA 3.0 and GPL 3.0 licenses:

```
http://opengameart.org/content/lpc-medieval-fantasy-character-sprites
```

Lots of free 2D tiles and sprites by *Hyptosis* under the CC-BY 3.0 license:

```
http://opengameart.org/content/lots-of-free-2d-tiles-and-sprites-by-
hyptosis
```

All of the licenses that apply to the use of these resources can be found here:

- `http://creativecommons.org/licenses/by/3.0/`
- `http://creativecommons.org/licenses/by-sa/3.0/`
- `http://www.gnu.org/licenses/gpl-3.0.html`

What is a programming pattern?

Programming patterns, or design patterns, at they're more commonly referred to, are reusable and widely-implemented solutions to a given problem. That is not to say that these patterns exist as some sort of libraries out there, although there are libraries based on them. Instead, a programming pattern is more of an idea or a strategy. It is a well laid out plan on tackling a certain problem, the best possible answer to a given problematic situation, proven by time and experience, which is one of the the best reasons they should be used.

There are quite a few design patterns out there, as well as books, tutorials and even classes dedicated solely to understanding and implementing them. For our purposes, we're going to be covering four: the entity component system, event queue, observer and factory patterns. We'll be talking about each one separately, as they're non overlapping in function, even though they can be working together.

The entity component system

The **entity component system** is a programming pattern, which allows entities to possess properties and functionality through the means of composition, as opposed to inheritance. The biggest benefits of using this pattern include stronger decoupling of logic, easier serialization and de-serialization of entities, better reusability of code and ease of creating new entities. It does, however, add a fair bit of complexity to your code base.

The typical implementation of this pattern consists of three parts:

- **Entities**: In most cases, entities are barely anything more than identifiers, slapped on a collection of components

- **Components**: These are the building blocks of entities, that are nothing more than collections of data

- **Systems**: These are specialized classes that deal with a very specific task and are responsible for holding all of the logic in this paradigm

In addition to working with these three distinct types of elements, our entity component system is also going to need an entity manager to keep and manage all of the entity and component data, as well as the system manager, which will be responsible for updating each system, in addition to some other functionality we'll be covering soon.

In order to differentiate between different types of components and systems, we're going to create a new header file, ECS_Types.h, which will be used to store this information:

```
using ComponentType = unsigned int;
#define N_COMPONENT_TYPES 32

enum class Component{
 Position = 0, SpriteSheet, State, Movable, Controller, Collidable
};

enum class System{
 Renderer = 0, Movement, Collision, Control, State, SheetAnimation
};
```

In addition to component and system enumerations, we're also aliasing an unsigned integer to act as the component type and defining a macro N_COMPONENT_TYPES, which represents the maximum number of component types we can have.

What is a component?

Within the entity component system paradigm, a **component** is the smallest, non-overlapping aspect of an entity, such as its position, velocity or a sprite. From the programming point of view, however, it is nothing more than a simple data structure, which has no real logic in it. Its only job is storing information about the feature of an entity it represents, as illustrated below:

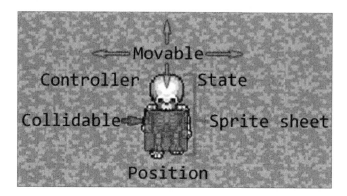

In order to store components easily, they have to rely on principles of inheritance. Let's take a look at a base component class definition:

```
class C_Base{
public:
  C_Base(const Component& l_type): m_type(l_type){}
  virtual ~C_Base(){}

  Component GetType(){ return m_type; }

  friend std::stringstream& operator >>(
    std::stringstream& l_stream, C_Base& b)
  {
    b.ReadIn(l_stream);
    return l_stream;
  }

  virtual void ReadIn(std::stringstream& l_stream) = 0;
protected:
  Component m_type;
};
```

The constructor of our component base class will take in the type of the component it represents. One thing to note is the overloaded >> operator, which calls a purely virtual function `ReadIn`. This serves as a quick way to read component data in from a file. Because each component is unique, it defines its own version of the `ReadIn` method in order to load its data correctly.

The position component

A good example of putting the base component class to work is actually implementing the first and arguably most common type of component: **position**.

```
class C_Position : public C_Base{
public:
  C_Position(): C_Base(Component::Position), m_elevation(0){}
  ~C_Position(){}

  void ReadIn(std::stringstream& l_stream){
    l_stream >> m_position.x >> m_position.y >> m_elevation;
  }

  const sf::Vector2f& GetPosition(){ return m_position; }
  const sf::Vector2f& GetOldPosition(){ return m_positionOld; }
  unsigned int GetElevation(){ return m_elevation; }

  void SetPosition(float l_x, float l_y){
    m_positionOld = m_position;
    m_position = sf::Vector2f(l_x,l_y);
  }

  void SetPosition(const sf::Vector2f& l_vec){
    m_positionOld = m_position;
    m_position = l_vec;
  }

  void SetElevation(unsigned int l_elevation){
    m_elevation = l_elevation;
  }

  void MoveBy(float l_x, float l_y){
    m_positionOld = m_position;
    m_position += sf::Vector2f(l_x,l_y);
  }
```

```
    void MoveBy(const sf::Vector2f& l_vec){
      m_positionOld = m_position;
      m_position += l_vec;
    }

private:
  sf::Vector2f m_position;
  sf::Vector2f m_positionOld;
  unsigned int m_elevation;
};
```

The constructor of our component base class is invoked in the initializer list, with the component type being passed in as the only argument. Although there are better ways of assigning individual component types their own unique identifiers, it's better to start simple for clarity's sake.

This component keeps track of three pieces of data: its current position, the position it was at during the previous cycle, and the current elevation of an entity, which is simply a value that represents how high the entity is in relation to the map.

Much like any other component we will be covering later in the chapter, it offers a number of methods for modifying and obtaining its data members. While making its data members publically available is perfectly valid, offering helper methods reduces code redundancy and offers a familiar interface.

Lastly, note the implementation of the `ReadIn` method. It uses a `stringstream` object as an argument and loads the relevant pieces of data from it.

The bitmask

Having a lightweight, easy-to-use as well as easy-to-expend data structure, representing the makeup of any given entity, as well as a set of requirements imposed by a system saves a lot of headaches. For us, that data structure is a **bitmask**.

> The standard template library provides its own version of a bitmask: the `std::bitset`. For educational purposes, we're going to be implementing our own version of this class.

As you probably know already, in binary, any and all numbers can be represented as a combination of zeroes and ones. However, who's to say that those two values have to be used only to represent a number? With some quick bitwise operator magic, any simple integer can be turned into a string of continuous flags that represent different aspects of an entity, such as which components it has, or types of components it needs to have in order to belong to a system.

Consider the following illustration:

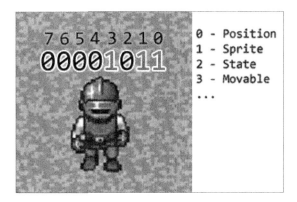

The only real difference in practice would be a lot more than eight flags available. Let's get coding:

```cpp
#include <stdint.h>

using Bitset = uint32_t;
class Bitmask{
public:
  Bitmask() : bits(0){}
  Bitmask(const Bitset& l_bits) : bits(l_bits){}

  Bitset GetMask() const{ return bits; }
  void SetMask(const Bitset& l_value){ bits = l_value; }

  bool Matches(const Bitmask& l_bits,
    const Bitset& l_relevant = 0)const
  {
    return(l_relevant ?
      ((l_bits.GetMask() & l_relevant) == (bits & l_relevant))
      :(l_bits.GetMask() == bits));
  }

  bool GetBit(const unsigned int& l_pos)const{
    return ((bits&(1 << l_pos)) != 0);
  }
  void TurnOnBit(const unsigned int& l_pos){
    bits |= 1 << l_pos;
  }
  void TurnOnBits(const Bitset& l_bits){
    bits |= l_bits;
```

```
  }
  void ClearBit(const unsigned int& l_pos){
    bits &= ~(1 << l_pos);
  }
  void ToggleBit(const unsigned int& l_pos){
    bits ^= 1 << l_pos;
  }

  void Clear(){ bits = 0; }
private:
  Bitset bits;
};
```

We begin by defining the data type for our bitset, kindly provided by the stdint.h header. As the name implies, the uint32_t type is exactly 32 bits wide. Using this type, and not, let's say, a typical integer, eliminates the possibility of cross-platform differences. A regular integer could take up less or more memory, depending on the platform our code is executed on. Using specialized types from the stdint.h header ensures the exact same results, regardless of platform differences.

The majority of the Bitmask class consists of nothing but bitwise operations, which are an essential part of the C/C++ background. If you are not yet familiar with them, it's not the end of the world, however, it would be more beneficial to at least understand how they work before moving forward.

Managing entities

Now that we have the building blocks of entities defined, it's time to talk about storing and managing them. As mentioned previously, all an entity is at this point is a single identifier. Knowing that, we can begin shaping the way this data is going to be stored, beginning, as always, with the definition of data types to be used:

```
using EntityId = unsigned int;

using ComponentContainer = std::vector<C_Base*>;
using EntityData = std::pair<Bitmask,ComponentContainer>;
using EntityContainer = std::unordered_map<EntityId,EntityData>;
using ComponentFactory = std::unordered_map<
  Component,std::function<C_Base*(void)>>;
```

The first data type we'll be working with is the entity identifier, once again represented by an unsigned integer. Next, a container is needed to hold all of the components for an entity. A vector works just fine for this purpose. Following that, we define a pair, a bitmask and the component container, which will hold all of the information about the entity. The bitmask is used here in order to alleviate the need to iterate over containers searching for components, when it can be quickly queried for the same purpose. The last piece of the entity puzzle is mapping an entity identifier to all of its data, for which we'll be using the `unordered_map`.

In order to generate different component types with as little code as possible, we'll be using our trusty lambda-expression factory method here as well. The last four lines of type definitions here make that possible.

Having all of the data types defined allows us to finally take a look at the entity manager class declaration:

```
class SystemManager;
class EntityManager{
public:
  EntityManager(SystemManager* l_sysMgr,
    TextureManager* l_textureMgr);
  ~EntityManager();

  int AddEntity(const Bitmask& l_mask);
  int AddEntity(const std::string& l_entityFile);
  bool RemoveEntity(const EntityId& l_id);

  bool AddComponent(const EntityId& l_entity,
    const Component& l_component);

  template<class T>
  T* GetComponent(const EntityId& l_entity,
    const Component& l_component){ ... }

  bool RemoveComponent(const EntityId& l_entity,
    const Component& l_component);
  bool HasComponent(const EntityId& l_entity,
    const Component& l_component);

  void Purge();
private:
  template<class T>
  void AddComponentType(const Component& l_id){
    m_cFactory[l_id] = []()->C_Base* { return new T(); };
  }
```

```
  // Data members
  unsigned int m_idCounter;
  EntityContainer m_entities;
  ComponentFactory m_cFactory;

  SystemManager* m_systems;
  TextureManager* m_textureManager;
};
```

In a fairly predictable fashion, we have all of the methods that would exist in any other class that serves as a container. Two different versions of adding entities are provided, one based on a bitmask passed in as an argument, and the other for loading an entity configuration from a file. The method for obtaining a component from a specific entity is templated, reducing the amount of code that has to be written outside of this class in order to obtain the type of component that is desired. Let's take a look at how it's implemented:

```
template<class T>
T* GetComponent(const EntityId& l_entity,
  const Component& l_component)
{
  auto itr = m_entities.find(l_entity);
  if (itr == m_entities.end()){ return nullptr; }
  // Found the entity.
  if (!itr->second.first.GetBit((unsigned int)l_component))
  {
    return nullptr;
  }
  // Component exists.
  auto& container = itr->second.second;
  auto component = std::find_if(container.begin(),container.end(),
    [&l_component](C_Base* c){
      return c->GetType() == l_component;
    });
  return (component != container.end() ?
    dynamic_cast<T*>(*component) : nullptr);
}
```

The entity argument passed into the method is evaluated first, in order to determine if one with the provided identifier exists. If it does, the bitmask of that entity is checked to verify that a component with the requested type is part of it. The component is then located in the vector and returned as the dynamically-cast type of the template.

Implementing the entity manager

With the class definition out of the way, we can start implementing its methods.
As per usual, let's address the constructor and destructor of the entity manager
class first:

```
EntityManager::EntityManager(SystemManager* l_sysMgr,
  TextureManager* l_textureMgr): m_idCounter(0),
  m_systems(l_sysMgr), m_textureManager(l_textureMgr)
{
  AddComponentType<C_Position>(Component::Position);
  AddComponentType<C_SpriteSheet>(Component::SpriteSheet);
  AddComponentType<C_State>(Component::State);
  AddComponentType<C_Movable>(Component::Movable);
  AddComponentType<C_Controller>(Component::Controller);
  AddComponentType<C_Collidable>(Component::Collidable);
}


EntityManager::~EntityManager(){ Purge(); }
```

The constructor takes in a pointer to the SystemManager class, which we will be
implementing shortly, as well as a pointer the TextureManager. In its initializer list,
the idCounter data member is set to zero. This is simply a variable that will be used
to keep track of the last identifier that was given to an entity. Additionally, both the
system manager and the texture manager pointers are stored for later reference. The
last purpose of the constructor is adding all of the different types of components to
the component factory.

The destructor simply invokes a Purge method, which will be used to clean up all of
the dynamically allocated memory and clear all possible containers in this class.

```
int EntityManager::AddEntity(const Bitmask& l_mask){
  unsigned int entity = m_idCounter;
  if (!m_entities.emplace(entity,
    EntityData(0,ComponentContainer())).second)
  { return -1; }
  ++m_idCounter;
  for(unsigned int i = 0; i < N_COMPONENT_TYPES; ++i){
    if(l_mask.GetBit(i)){ AddComponent(entity,(Component)i); }
  }
  // Notifying the system manager of a modified entity.
  m_systems->EntityModified(entity,l_mask);
  m_systems->AddEvent(entity,(EventID)EntityEvent::Spawned);
  return entity;
}
```

In the case of adding an entity based on the provided bitmask, a new entity pair is inserted into the entity container first. If the insertion was successful, a `for` loop iterates over all possible types of components and checks the mask for that type. The `AddComponent` method is then invoked, if the bitmask has the said type enabled.

After the component insertion, the system manager is notified of an entity being modified, or, in this case, inserted. The entity identifier, along with the bitmask of the said entity is passed into the `EntityModified` method of the system manager. An event is also created to alert the systems that this entity just spawned.

The identifier of the newly created entity is then returned. If the method failed to add an entity, -1 is returned instead, to signify an error.

Removing an entity is every bit as easy, if not more so:

```
bool EntityManager::RemoveEntity(const EntityId& l_id){
  auto itr = m_entities.find(l_id);
  if (itr == m_entities.end()){ return false; }
  // Removing all components.
  while(itr->second.second.begin() != itr->second.second.end()){
    delete itr->second.second.back();
    itr->second.second.pop_back();
  }
  m_entities.erase(itr);
  m_systems->RemoveEntity(l_id);
  return true;
}
```

After the entity is successfully located in the entity container, the dynamically allocated memory of every single component it has is first freed, and the component is then removed from the vector. The entity itself is then erased from the entity container and the system manager is notified of its removal.

```
bool EntityManager::AddComponent(const EntityId& l_entity,
  const Component& l_component)
{
  auto itr = m_entities.find(l_entity);
  if (itr == m_entities.end()){ return false; }
  if (itr->second.first.GetBit((unsigned int)l_component))
  {
    return false;
  }
  // Component doesn't exist.
  auto itr2 = m_cFactory.find(l_component);
  if (itr2 == m_cFactory.end()){ return false; }
  // Component type does exist.
```

```
    C_Base* component = itr2->second();
    itr->second.second.emplace_back(component);
    itr->second.first.TurnOnBit((unsigned int)l_component);
    // Notifying the system manager of a modified entity.
    m_systems->EntityModified(l_entity,itr->second.first);
    return true;
}
```

Adding a component to an entity begins by verifying an entity with the provided identifier exists. If it does, and if there isn't already a component of that type added to the entity, the lambda-function container is queried for the desired type. Once the memory for the component is allocated, it's pushed into the component vector. The bitmask is then modified to reflect the changes made to the entity. The system manager is notified of those changes as well.

Predictably, a very similar process takes place when removing the component from an entity:

```
bool EntityManager::RemoveComponent(const EntityId& l_entity,
  const Component& l_component)
{
  auto itr = m_entities.find(l_entity);
  if (itr == m_entities.end()){ return false; }
  // Found the entity.
  if (!itr->second.first.GetBit((unsigned int)l_component))
  {
    return false;
  }
  // Component exists.
  auto& container = itr->second.second;
  auto component = std::find_if(container.begin(),container.end(),
    [&l_component](C_Base* c){
      return c->GetType() == l_component;
    });
  if (component == container.end()){ return false; }
  delete (*component);
  container.erase(component);
  itr->second.first.ClearBit((unsigned int)l_component);

  m_systems->EntityModified(l_entity, itr->second.first);
  return true;
}
```

After confirming that both the entity and component exist, the memory allocated for the component is freed and the component itself is erased. The bitmask also gets modified to reflect these changes. Much like before, the system manager needs to know if an entity was altered, so the `EntityModified` method is invoked.

A fairly useful method to have for outside classes is one that checks if an entity has a certain type of component:

```
bool EntityManager::HasComponent(const EntityId& l_entity,
  const Component& l_component)
{
  auto itr = m_entities.find(l_entity);
  if (itr == m_entities.end()){ return false; }
  return itr->second.first.GetBit((unsigned int)l_component);
}
```

This follows the same pattern as before by checking if an entity exists first, then checking its bitmask for a certain component type.

It's cleanup time. Correctly disposing of all allocated resources is left up to the `Purge` method:

```
void EntityManager::Purge(){
  m_systems->PurgeEntities();
  for(auto& entity : m_entities){
    for(auto &component : entity.second.second){delete component;}
    entity.second.second.clear();
    entity.second.first.Clear();
  }
  m_entities.clear();
  m_idCounter = 0;
}
```

The system manager is notified to remove all of its entities first. While iterating over all of the entities in storage, it frees up the memory of every single component. The component container is then cleared. Lastly, the entity container itself is cleared and the identification counter is set back to 0.

The factory pattern

With complex data structures such as entities, chances are the programmer will not be setting up and initializing every single component by hand. Setting up entities with any arrangement of components quickly and with as little repeated code as possible is very much the goal here. Luckily, a programming pattern exists to solve this particular problem. It is simply referred to as the **factory** pattern.

The philosophy of use for this neat pattern is quite simple. There exists a class with some abstract method that takes in one or two arguments, pertaining to some vague identifying qualities. This class then generates, based on the information it was given, a class or a number of classes and returns a handle to them, effectively cutting out the part where data allocation or member initialization is done by hand. In other words, it is given a blueprint and produces a product based on it, hence the name "factory". This functionality was already achieved in a way by creating entities based on a bitmask, however, no actual data was initialized, only the defaults. Having a more pristine way of actually setting up these entities requires a more elaborate blueprint, so why not use text files? For example:

```
Name Player
Attributes 63
|Component|ID|Individual attributes|
Component 0 0 0 1
...
```

This format would allow everything there is to an entity to be stored in plain text as a blueprint and loaded at any time to produce any number of entities with exactly the same qualities. Let's take a look at how processing entity files could be achieved:

```
int EntityManager::AddEntity(const std::string& l_entityFile){
  int EntityId = -1;

  std::ifstream file;
  file.open(Utils::GetWorkingDirectory() +
    "media/Entities/" + l_entityFile + ".entity");
  if (!file.is_open()){
    std::cout << "! Failed to load entity: "
      << l_entityFile << std::endl;
    return -1;
  }
  std::string line;
  while(std::getline(file,line)){
    if (line[0] == '|'){ continue; }
    std::stringstream keystream(line);
    std::string type;
    keystream >> type;
    if(type == "Name"){

    } else if(type == "Attributes"){
      if (EntityId != -1){ continue; }
      Bitset set = 0;
      Bitmask mask;
      keystream >> set;
```

```
        mask.SetMask(set);
        EntityId = AddEntity(mask);
        if(EntityId == -1){ return -1; }
    } else if(type == "Component"){
        if (EntityId == -1){ continue; }
        unsigned int c_id = 0;
        keystream >> c_id;
        C_Base* component = GetComponent<C_Base>
            (EntityId,(Component)c_id);
        if (!component){ continue; }
        keystream >> *component;
        if(component->GetType() == Component::SpriteSheet){
            C_SpriteSheet* sheet = (C_SpriteSheet*)component;
            sheet->Create(m_textureManager);
        }
    }
  }
}
file.close();
return EntityId;
}
```

Loading entity files isn't much different from any other files we've processed in the past. For now, reading entity names hasn't yet been implemented. The attributes line is simply the numeric value that the bitmask has with the desired components enabled. Once that value is read in, we pass it in to the other version of AddEntity, in order to create it and have all of the components properly allocated.

Reading in the actual components is slightly more complicated. First, we must make sure that the entity has been created. This means that the "Attributes" line has to come before the individual component data in the entity file. If the entity ID is greater than -1, we proceed with reading in the component ID and obtaining the actual object based on it. The overloaded >> operator comes in handy here, since it greatly simplifies actually streaming in the component data.

Lastly, due to the nature of resource handling, the component type has to be checked in order to provide its instance with a pointer to the texture manager class, if it needs it. We haven't yet created such components, however one of them will be the sprite sheet component that will represent some entities.

Designing the systems

With the data side of this paradigm being accounted for, the last remaining component remains to be the **system**. As the name loosely implies, systems are responsible for handling all of the logic that takes place inside and between components. Things ranging from sprites being rendered to collision checks are all handled by their own, respective systems to ensure complete separation between non-overlapping parts of the game. At least, that's how it should play out in an ideal world. In reality, as hard as one tries to decouple and categorize logic or data, some things still remain loosely connected, which is just the nature of the beast. Information still has to be traded between systems, however. Certain functionality also needs to be invoked as a consequence of a totally unrelated system's actions. To put it simply, there needs to be a way for systems to talk to each other without them knowing anything about how the other one works.

Entity events

A fairly simplistic, and as it happens, necessary approach to handling inter-system relations is dispatching events. Every other system could be listening for those events and performing their own logic, completely separate from everything else, in response to a certain event taking place. Let's take a look at a possible list of entity events:

```
enum class EntityEvent{
   Spawned, Despawned, Colliding_X, Colliding_Y,
   Moving_Left, Moving_Right, Moving_Up, Moving_Down,
   Elevation_Change, Became_Idle, Began_Moving
};
```

This should give you a pretty good idea of how system communication will take place. Let's say that an entity is moving in the left direction. The "movement system" starts dispatching events, saying that it's in motion. The "animation system" listens for those events, and when they're received, it proceeds to increase frames in the entity's sprite sheet. Keep in mind that all of these chunks of logic are still completely separate from one another. The "movement system" is not increasing the frames of the entity's sprite sheet. It's simply saying to all of the other systems "Hello, I am moving entity x to the left," while they listen and react. It sounds like we can benefit from the "event queue."

Entity event queue

The **event queue** is a programming pattern, which is used to decouple when an event is fired from when it's actually processed. This illustration should capture the essence of it:

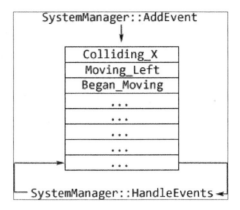

A queue is what's referred to as a First-In-First-Out data container. The data that is pushed onto it earliest is removed first. This serves our needs nicely. As the definition of the event queue states, its events are processed at a completely different time in relation to them being added. With that in mind, let's start designing the EventQueue class:

```cpp
using EventID = unsigned int;

class EventQueue{
public:
  void AddEvent(const EventID& l_event){m_queue.push(l_event);}

  bool ProcessEvents(EventID& l_id){
    if (m_queue.empty()){ return false; }
    l_id = m_queue.front();
    m_queue.pop();
    return true;
  }

  void Clear(){ while(!m_queue.empty()){ m_queue.pop(); }}
private:
  std::queue<EventID> m_queue;
};
```

The event identifier is represented with an unsigned integer. In order to store the actual events, we'll be using, appropriately enough, a `queue` container. Adding an event to it is as simple as any other STL container. This class offers a method that can be used with while loops in order to simplify event processing. It returns a Boolean value in order to break the loop when the event queue is empty and its sole argument is taken by reference, in order to modify it each time the method is called. This is similar to the way SFML handles events.

The base system

In order to begin implementing our systems, they must first have a common base class, which not only provides a common interface that must be implemented, but also eliminates code redundancy. Much like most other classes we build, it will have its own data types defined:

```
using EntityList = std::vector<EntityId>;
using Requirements = std::vector<Bitmask>;
```

The system identifier, just like the component identifier, is represented by an unsigned integer. All of the entity identifiers will be stored in a vector container, much like the requirement bitmasks. The reason we would ever want to have more than one requirement bitmask is to have the ability to define combinations of different types of components that could still belong to the same system. A good example of that would be different drawable types belonging to the same rendering system.

Let's take a look at the header of our system base class:

```
class SystemManager;
class S_Base{
public:
  S_Base(const System& l_id, SystemManager* l_systemMgr);
  virtual ~S_Base();

  bool AddEntity(const EntityId& l_entity);
  bool HasEntity(const EntityId& l_entity);
  bool RemoveEntity(const EntityId& l_entity);

  System GetId();

  bool FitsRequirements(const Bitmask& l_bits);
  void Purge();

  virtual void Update(float l_dT) = 0;
  virtual void HandleEvent(const EntityId& l_entity,
    const EntityEvent& l_event) = 0;
```

```
protected:
    System m_id;
    Requirements m_requiredComponents;
    EntityList m_entities;

    SystemManager* m_systemManager;
};
```

We want every single system to have its own update method, as well as its own version of event handling. Additionally, systems having access to their own manager is also desired. Everything else that is not system-specific, like checking requirement bitmasks, is handled by the base class.

Implementing the base system

Because all systems require a pointer to the system manager, there's an issue of cross-inclusion. A forward declaration of it right before the class header and the inclusion of the system manager header in the implementation file takes care of the issue:

```
#include "System_Manager.h"
```

Time to go down the list of methods to implement, starting with the constructor and destructor:

```
S_Base::S_Base(const System& l_id, SystemManager* l_systemMgr)
    : m_id(l_id), m_systemManager(l_systemMgr){}


S_Base::~S_Base(){ Purge(); }
```

Each system has to have its own identifier, much like all of the components. That gets passed in the argument list to the constructor, along with a pointer to the system manager. Aside from setting the appropriate data members to these values in an initializer list, the constructor of a base system does nothing else.

The destructor, following the typical fashion, invokes the `Purge` method to do the cleanup.

```
bool S_Base::AddEntity(const EntityId& l_entity){
    if (HasEntity(l_entity)){ return false; }
    m_entities.emplace_back(l_entity);
    return true;
}
```

Adding an entity to a system is fairly easy. If the identifier that was provided as an argument doesn't already exist within the said system, it simply gets pushed into the vector. How does a system determine if it has an entity with such an identifier? Let's find out:

```
bool S_Base::HasEntity(const EntityId& l_entity){
  return std::find(m_entities.begin(),
    m_entities.end(), l_entity) != m_entities.end();
}
```

Utilizing the `std::find` function allows us to sum up this method in a single line. Removing an entity also takes advantage of a similar function:

```
bool S_Base::RemoveEntity(const EntityId& l_entity){
  auto entity = std::find_if(m_entities.begin(), m_entities.end(),
    [&l_entity](EntityId& id){ return id = l_entity; });
  if (entity == m_entities.end()){ return false; }
  m_entities.erase(entity);
  return true;
}
```

In this case, we're using the `std::find_if` function, which takes a predicate as the third argument. A predicate is just another function that compares two elements together in order to find a match. In this case, we simply construct a lambda function that takes in an `EntityId` and returns a Boolean value, which will tell the find function whether a match was found. If it was, the entity is then removed.

Each system has to make sure that an entity has all the required components in order to be added to it. That's where this method comes in:

```
bool S_Base::FitsRequirements(const Bitmask& l_bits){
  return std::find_if(m_requiredComponents.begin(),
    m_requiredComponents.end(), [&l_bits](Bitmask& b){
      return b.Matches(l_bits, b.GetMask());
    }) != m_requiredComponents.end();
}
```

It takes in a bitmask as an argument and utilizes the same `std::find_if` function in conjunction with a lambda to locate a match. Very few systems will even need to define more than one bitmask for its required components, however it's nice to have this functionality when the need for it arises.

Lastly, here's the method for cleaning up:

```
void S_Base::Purge(){ m_entities.clear(); }
```

Because there's no actual dynamic memory being allocated here, it's safe to just empty the container of all the entity identifiers.

Handling messages

Entity events, while useful for a lot of situations, aren't perfect for everything. For instance, carrying data between systems is impossible using the event queue. The events are also being delivered to every single system, which can be wasteful. Instead, why not have an additional method of communication that not only carries data around, but also allows systems to pick and choose what they want to receive? Entity component system messaging serves exactly that purpose, and there just so happens to be yet another programming pattern, which allows easy implementation of the message-subscription approach.

The observer pattern

As the name entails, the **observer** pattern allows its users to pick and choose what they will be notified of. In other words, the observer will lay dormant after subscribing to information types it wishes to receive, and will only be notified if those types are encountered. Let's take a look at a very basic implementation of the `Observer` base class:

```
class Observer{
public:
    virtual ~Observer(){}
    virtual void Notify(const Message& l_message) = 0;
};
```

The `Observer` class is simply an interface, the inheritors of which must define a single method in order to use it. Although it looks simple, many features we desire in our game wouldn't be possible without it. Let's take a look at what these observers will be notified with:

```
using MessageType = unsigned int;
struct TwoFloats{ float m_x; float m_y; };

struct Message{
    Message(const MessageType& l_type) : m_type(l_type){}

    MessageType m_type;
    int m_sender;
    int m_receiver;

    union{
        TwoFloats m_2f;
        bool m_bool;
        int m_int;
    };
};
```

Aside from holding the information about the sender and receiver entities, as well as the message type, it employs a `union` in order to avoid inheritance. That essentially means that all of the data members within this union will be sharing the same space in memory, and only one of them can be valid at a time.

The last piece of the puzzle is containing all possible observers in a `Communicator` class. For this, we'll be using a vector:

```
using ObserverContainer = std::vector<Observer*>;
```

Because this class has relatively simple methods that simply deal with managing a vector container, let's take a look at the full class definition head to toe:

```
class Communicator{
public:
  ~Communicator(){ m_observers.clear(); }

  bool AddObserver(Observer* l_observer){
    if (HasObserver(l_observer)){ return false; }
    m_observers.emplace_back(l_observer);
    return true;
  }

  bool RemoveObserver(Observer* l_observer){
    auto observer = std::find_if(m_observers.begin(),
      m_observers.end(), [&l_observer](Observer* o){
        return o == l_observer; });
    if (observer == m_observers.end()){ return false; }
    m_observers.erase(observer);
    return true;
  }

  bool HasObserver(const Observer* l_observer){
    return (std::find_if(m_observers.begin(), m_observers.end(),
      [&l_observer](Observer* o){
        return o == l_observer;
      }) != m_observers.end());
  }

  void Broadcast(const Message& l_msg){
    for(auto& itr : m_observers){ itr->Notify(l_msg); }
  }

private:
  ObserverContainer m_observers;
};
```

The basic methods for adding, removing and looking for an observer are all typical. One thing to note, however, is the `Broadcast` method, which simply invokes the `Notify` method of an observer and passes in a message to send.

Last, and definitely the least amount of code is responsible for actually putting the observer approach to use:

```
class S_Base : public Observer{ ... }
```

Because the base system class has virtual methods, it doesn't need to implement its own version of `Notify`. That will be the job for all the systems that inherit from this class.

The message handler class

We have all of the pieces to build a cohesive messaging system. Let's take a look at some data types that will be used to store message subscription information:

```
using Subscribtions = std::unordered_map<
    EntityMessage,Communicator>;
```

Each possible message type will have its own communicator that will broadcast the message to all of its observers. Using an `unordered_map` is perfect for expressing such a relationship.

The message handler is a very simple class, so let's take a look at its entire implementation:

```
class MessageHandler{
public:
  bool Subscribe(const EntityMessage& l_type
    Observer* l_observer)
  {
    return m_communicators[l_type].AddObserver(l_observer);
  }

  bool Unsubscribe(const EntityMessage& l_type,
    Observer* l_observer)
  {
    return m_communicators[l_type].RemoveObserver(l_observer);
  }

  void Dispatch(const Message& l_msg){
    auto itr = m_communicators.find(
      (EntityMessage)l_msg.m_type);
```

```
      if (itr == m_communicators.end()){ return; }
      itr->second.Broadcast(l_msg);
   }
 private:
   Subscriptions m_communicators;
 };
```

Subscribing and unsubscribing to message types is simply done by manipulating the unordered map data container. When a message is dispatched, the message type in the subscription container is queried. If it is found, the communicator's `Broadcast` method is invoked with the message passed in as the argument.

At this point you might be wondering what kind of messages we'll be handling. Let's take a gander at the `EntityMessages.h` file:

```
enum class EntityMessage{
    Move, Is_Moving, State_Changed, Direction_Changed,
    Switch_State, Attack_Action, Dead
};
```

The purpose of a messaging system quickly becomes clear, even by simply reading the names of message types. Every one of them lends itself to either needing to contain extra data or only ever applying to a single system.

Managing systems

Finally, we've arrived at the last stop on the entity component system route: handling systems themselves. Let's quickly review our custom data types for this class:

```
using SystemContainer = std::unordered_map<System,S_Base*>;
using EntityEventContainer = std::unordered_map<
   EntityId,EventQueue>;
```

The first data type, `SystemContainer`, is really hard to misinterpret. An unordered map is used to link system identifiers to actual systems. The second type definition here is responsible for storage of entity events. It also uses an unordered map and links entity identifiers to `EventQueue` instances, that all hold events for a specific entity until they're processed.

It's time to design the system manager class:

```
class EntityManager;
class SystemManager{
public:
   SystemManager();
```

```
    ~SystemManager();

    void SetEntityManager(EntityManager* l_entityMgr);
    EntityManager* GetEntityManager();
    MessageHandler* GetMessageHandler();

    template<class T>
    T* GetSystem(const System& l_system){...}

    void AddEvent(const EntityId& l_entity, const EventID& l_event);

    void Update(float l_dT);
    void HandleEvents();
    void Draw(Window* l_wind, unsigned int l_elevation);

    void EntityModified(const EntityId& l_entity,
      const Bitmask& l_bits);
    void RemoveEntity(const EntityId& l_entity);

    void PurgeEntities();
    void PurgeSystems();
  private:
    SystemContainer m_systems;
    EntityManager* m_entityManager;
    EntityEventContainer m_events;
    MessageHandler m_messages;
  };
```

As expected, it needs to have methods for adding and handling events, updating and drawing the systems, notifying them of entity changes and removal requests, and obtaining them as well. The template method for getting a particular system is implemented this way:

```
template<class T>
T* GetSystem(const System& l_system){
  auto itr = m_systems.find(l_system);
  return(itr != m_systems.end() ?
    dynamic_cast<T*>(itr->second) : nullptr);
}
```

Just like the entity manager's method of obtaining components, this method relies on the use of templates and dynamic casting in order to obtain a system in the correct form.

Implementing the system manager

Cross-inclusion peaks its ugly head once more, so we must combat it with forward declarations and inclusions of headers in the implementation files:

```
#include "Entity_Manager.h"
```

With that out of the way, we can now start implementing the constructor and destructor:

```
SystemManager::SystemManager(): m_entityManager(nullptr){
    m_systems[System::State] = new S_State(this);
    m_systems[System::Control] = new S_Control(this);
    m_systems[System::Movement] = new S_Movement(this);
    m_systems[System::Collision] = new S_Collision(this);
    m_systems[System::SheetAnimation] = new S_SheetAnimation(this);
    m_systems[System::Renderer] = new S_Renderer(this);
}

SystemManager::~SystemManager(){
    PurgeSystems();
}
```

The constructor sets up a pointer to an entity manager class before initializing all of the systems it holds. The destructor performs its usual job of cleaning up the mess, which is entrusted to the `PurgeSystems` method.

Because the system manager needs to have a pointer to the entity manager and vice versa, the one that's instantiated first will not simply be able to take a pointer to the other class in its constructor, hence the need for the `SetEntityManager` method:

```
void SystemManager::SetEntityManager(EntityManager* l_entityMgr){
    if(!m_entityManager){ m_entityManager = l_entityMgr; }
}
```

With a class so broadly applied, it needs to provide getter methods for its data members:

```
EntityManager* SystemManager::GetEntityManager(){
    return m_entityManager;
}

MessageHandler* SystemManager::GetMessageHandler(){
    return &m_messages;
}
```

This ensures that all systems have access to the message handler, as well as the entity handler.

Speaking of system access, they also must be able to add events to any entity:

```
void SystemManager::AddEvent(const EntityId& l_entity,
  const EventID& l_event)
{
    m_events[l_entity].AddEvent(l_event);
}
```

Using an `unordered_map` structure here really makes this method simple and neat. The entity identifier being the key, it's easy to access its individual event queue and add to it.

Providing we want those systems to tick, an update loop is in order:

```
void SystemManager::Update(float l_dT){
  for(auto &itr : m_systems){
    itr.second->Update(l_dT);
  }
  HandleEvents();
}
```

Here, every single system's update method is invoked and the elapsed time is passed in. The event handling takes place after all of the systems have been updated. Time to dissect that method:

```
void SystemManager::HandleEvents(){
  for(auto &event : m_events){
    EventID id = 0;
    while(event.second.ProcessEvents(id)){
      for(auto &system : m_systems)
      {
        if(system.second->HasEntity(event.first)){
          system.second->HandleEvent(event.first,(EntityEvent)id);
        }
      }
    }
  }
}
```

We begin by iterating over the event queues of different entities. An event identifier variable is set up and used in a `while` loop by reference, in order to obtain information from the queue. Every system in the manager is iterated over and checked for having the entity of interest. If it does, the system's `HandleEvent` method is invoked and the relevant information is passed in. That, in a nutshell, concludes event management on a larger scale. Now every individual system only has to worry about which events it wants to handle and how it wants to respond to them.

In order to populate the dark void of the screen with entities, we're going to need a `Draw` method:

```
void SystemManager::Draw(Window* l_wind,
  unsigned int l_elevation)
{
  auto itr = m_systems.find(System::Renderer);
  if (itr == m_systems.end()){ return; }
  S_Renderer* system = (S_Renderer*)itr->second;
  system->Render(l_wind, l_elevation);
}
```

For most needs, having a single system devoted to rendering entities more than suffices. Ergo, the renderer system is located in the system container and type-cast up from the base class. Its `Render` method is then invoked with relevant arguments, one of which is the current elevation that's being rendered. Drawing it this way allows the feel of "depth" to be achieved within our game.

As entities are not static in their composure, systems must be aware of these changes and properly take in or dispose of them, given the circumstances. This specific method has already been brought up multiple times during the implementation of the entity manager class, so let's take a look at how it works:

```
void SystemManager::EntityModified(const EntityId& l_entity,
  const Bitmask& l_bits)
{
  for(auto &s_itr : m_systems){
    S_Base* system = s_itr.second;
    if(system->FitsRequirements(l_bits)){
      if(!system->HasEntity(l_entity)){
        system->AddEntity(l_entity);
      }
    } else {
      if(system->HasEntity(l_entity)){
        system->RemoveEntity(l_entity);
      }
    }
  }
}
```

Upon any changes regarding entities taking place, the `EntityModified` method must be invoked with the identifier of the entity and its new bitmask passed in as arguments. Every system is then iterated over. Their respective `FitsRequirements` methods are invoked with the new bitmask as the argument. If the entity fits the requirements of a system and it doesn't belong to it, it is added. If, however, the entity does not fit these requirements but a system still has this entity, it's removed. The use of this simple concept allows entities to be dynamic in structure. Any given entity can lose or gain a component and immediately "transform" into something else.

Removal of entities is quite simple:

```cpp
void SystemManager::RemoveEntity(const EntityId& l_entity){
  for(auto &system : m_systems){
    system.second->RemoveEntity(l_entity);
  }
}
```

All that needs to happen here is the `RemoveEntity` method of every system being invoked, which is quite similar to purging all entities:

```cpp
void SystemManager::PurgeEntities(){
  for(auto &system : m_systems){
    system.second->Purge();
  }
}
```

Getting rid of all systems in the system manager is also a cake walk:

```cpp
void SystemManager::PurgeSystems(){
  for (auto &system : m_systems){
    delete system.second;
  }
  m_systems.clear();
}
```

Because systems are dynamically allocated, the memory has to be freed for each of them. The system container is then simply cleared.

This last method marks the completion of our system manager, as well as the core structure of the entity component system paradigm. All of the basic tools for shaping our game are now present, so let's implement the first and most important system in the game: the renderer.

Implementing the rendering system

In order for entities to be drawn on screen, they must have a component that represents them visually. After some careful planning, one can deduce that an entity will probably not have just one possible choice for a graphical representation. For example, instead of a sprite sheet, an entity can be a simple shape with a single color fill. In order to make that happen, we need a common interface for drawable components. Let's see what we can come up with:

```cpp
class C_Drawable : public C_Base{
public:
  C_Drawable(const Component& l_type) : C_Base(l_type){}
  virtual ~C_Drawable(){}

  virtual void UpdatePosition(const sf::Vector2f& l_vec) = 0;
  virtual const sf::Vector2u& GetSize() = 0;
  virtual void Draw(sf::RenderWindow* l_wind) = 0;
private:

};
```

The first thing to note here is that the constructor of this class also takes in a component type, and simply passes it to the base class. Since C_Drawable only has purely virtual methods, it can never be instantiated and will only be used as a mold to shape other drawable components. It requires all derived classes to implement a method for updating the drawable's position, obtaining its size and drawing it on screen.

The sprite sheet component

With the base class set up, it's time to take a look at creating the sprite sheet component:

```cpp
class C_SpriteSheet : public C_Drawable{
public:
    ...
private:
    SpriteSheet* m_spriteSheet;
    std::string m_sheetName;
};
```

This component will, of course, be utilizing the `SpriteSheet` class we built in the past as one of its data members. We also want to hold on to the sprite sheet name in order to properly allocate resources after the time of de-serialization. Let's begin implementing the sprite sheet component:

```
C_SpriteSheet(): C_Drawable(Component::SpriteSheet),
    m_spriteSheet(nullptr){}

~C_SpriteSheet(){
    if(m_spriteSheet){ delete m_spriteSheet; }
}
```

So far, nothing is out of the ordinary. The constructor uses the initializer list to set up the component type and set the sprite sheet pointer to NULL, while the destructor takes care of de-allocating the memory that's taken up by said sprite sheet.

Next, let's handle reading in the component data, which only consists of the sprite sheet name:

```
void ReadIn(std::stringstream& l_stream){
    l_stream >> m_sheetName;
}
```

Due to the nature of this particular drawable component, it needs access to the texture manager. In order to set up the sprite sheet properly, the `Create` method is introduced:

```
void Create(TextureManager* l_textureMgr,
    const std::string& l_name = "")
{
    if (m_spriteSheet){ return; }
    m_spriteSheet = new SpriteSheet(l_textureMgr);
    m_spriteSheet->LoadSheet("media/Spritesheets/" +
        (l_name != "" ? l_name : m_sheetName) + ".sheet");
}
```

As seen previously, this particular method is used to set up the sprite sheet component during entity loading. It first checks if the memory for the `m_spriteSheet` data member hasn't already been allocated. If it hasn't, a new `SpriteSheet` object is created with the texture manager pointer passed in as its sole argument. The rest of the code deals with the second, optional argument. The name of the texture can be passed to the `Create` method itself, or it can use the `m_sheetName` data member that has been read in from the entity file.

Lastly, all of the virtual methods of the `C_Drawable` class must be implemented here:

```
SpriteSheet* GetSpriteSheet(){ return m_spriteSheet; }
void UpdatePosition(const sf::Vector2f& l_vec){
  m_spriteSheet->SetSpritePosition(l_vec);
}

const sf::Vector2u& GetSize(){
  return m_spriteSheet->GetSpriteSize();
}
void Draw(sf::RenderWindow* l_wind){
  if (!m_spriteSheet){ return; }
  m_spriteSheet->Draw(l_wind);
}
```

All of the work done on the `SpriteSheet` class in the past makes this pretty easy. One thing to note is that due to the nature of loading sprite sheet components, it may be wise to check if it has actually been allocated, before attempting to draw it.

The renderer

With the simple part out of the way, let's focus on creating our first system ever built, the renderer:

```
class S_Renderer : public S_Base{
public:
  S_Renderer(SystemManager* l_systemMgr);
  ~S_Renderer();

  void Update(float l_dT);
  void HandleEvent(const EntityId& l_entity,
    const EntityEvent& l_event);
  void Notify(const Message& l_message);
  void Render(Window* l_wind, unsigned int l_layer);
private:
  void SetSheetDirection(const EntityId& l_entity,
    const Direction& l_dir);
  void SortDrawables();
};
```

The header for all of the other systems will look very much like this one, with the exception of private methods, specific to the function that each individual system performs. Each system must implement its own `Update` and `HandleEvent` methods. Additionally, being an observer requires a unique implementation of the `Notify` method as well. Time to take a stab at implementing the renderer system:

```
S_Renderer::S_Renderer(SystemManager* l_systemMgr)
  :S_Base(System::Renderer, l_systemMgr)
{
  Bitmask req;
  req.TurnOnBit((unsigned int)Component::Position);
  req.TurnOnBit((unsigned int)Component::SpriteSheet);
  m_requiredComponents.push_back(req);
  req.Clear();

  m_systemManager->GetMessageHandler()->
    Subscribe(EntityMessage::Direction_Changed,this);
}
S_Renderer::~S_Renderer(){}
```

After invoking the base system's constructor and passing in the appropriate type, along with a pointer to the system manager, the renderer sets up a bitmask of requirements an entity has to meet in order to belong to this system. As you can see, it only needs to have the position and sprite sheet components. Once the requirement bitmask is added to the system, it also subscribes to the `Direction_Changed` message type. This utilizes the observer pattern discussed previously.

Let's take a look at the update method:

```
void S_Renderer::Update(float l_dT){
  EntityManager* entities = m_systemManager->GetEntityManager();
  for(auto &entity : m_entities)
  {
    C_Position* position = entities->
      GetComponent<C_Position>(entity, Component::Position);
    C_Drawable* drawable = nullptr;
    if (entities->HasComponent(entity, Component::SpriteSheet)){
      drawable = entities->
        GetComponent<C_Drawable>(entity, Component::SpriteSheet);
    } else { continue; }
    drawable->UpdatePosition(position->GetPosition());
  }
}
```

During iteration over all of the entities that belong to this system, the position and drawable components are obtained through the entity manager. The drawable's position is then updated through the use of its `UpdatePosition` method. This method can obviously be expanded if additional drawable types are added in the future.

Next, let's handle the appropriate events:

```
void S_Renderer::HandleEvent(const EntityId& l_entity,
  const EntityEvent& l_event)
{
  if (l_event == EntityEvent::Moving_Left ||
    l_event == EntityEvent::Moving_Right ||
    l_event == EntityEvent::Moving_Up ||
    l_event == EntityEvent::Moving_Down ||
    l_event == EntityEvent::Elevation_Change ||
    l_event == EntityEvent::Spawned)
  {
    SortDrawables();
  }
}
```

If the system encounters any events of entities spawning, changing their position or elevation, their drawable representations have to be re-sorted in order to assure the correct layering. The result of this is quite worth the trouble:

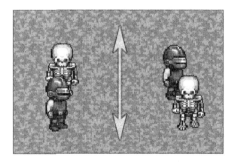

The code for message handling here is as follows:

```
void S_Renderer::Notify(const Message& l_message){
  if(HasEntity(l_message.m_receiver)){
    EntityMessage m = (EntityMessage)l_message.m_type;
    switch(m){
    case EntityMessage::Direction_Changed:
      SetSheetDirection(l_message.m_receiver,
        (Direction)l_message.m_int);
```

```
            break;
        }
    }
}
```

Since messages are globally broadcasted to every system regardless of what entities they have, and the renderer only deals with a single message type that pertains to specific entities only, a check takes place in order to make sure the entity exists within the renderer system. The sole message type we care about so far is the direction being altered, in which case a private method is invoked to adjust it.

Now, let's address the main purpose the renderer system exists:

```
void S_Renderer::Render(Window* l_wind, unsigned int l_layer)
{
    EntityManager* entities = m_systemManager->GetEntityManager();
    for(auto &entity : m_entities){
        C_Position* position = entities->
            GetComponent<C_Position>(entity, Component::Position);
        if(position->GetElevation() < l_layer){ continue; }
        if(position->GetElevation() > l_layer){ break; }
        C_Drawable* drawable = nullptr;
        if (!entities->HasComponent(entity,
            Component::SpriteSheet))
        {
            continue;
        }
        drawable = entities->
            GetComponent<C_Drawable>(entity, Component::SpriteSheet);
        sf::FloatRect drawableBounds;
        drawableBounds.left = position->GetPosition().x -
            (drawable->GetSize().x / 2);
        drawableBounds.top = position->GetPosition().y -
            drawable->GetSize().y;
        drawableBounds.width = drawable->GetSize().x;
        drawableBounds.height = drawable->GetSize().y;
        if (!l_wind->GetViewSpace().intersects(
            drawableBounds))
        {
            continue;
        }
        drawable->Draw(l_wind->GetRenderWindow());
    }
}
```

Each entity is iterated over, much like any other system. The main difference here is the layer argument the method takes in. Because we want to have a map that has many different layers entities can be, for the lack of better term, "sandwiched" in, rendering elevation by elevation is necessary in order to maintain the correct draw order and offer the feeling of depth, as illustrated here:

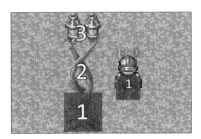

The second half of the `Render` method is devoted to entity culling. First, a rectangle structure is created in order to represent the boundaries of a drawable. In the case of a sprite sheet, we know that its origin is set at the point of half its width and its full height. Using this information, the rectangle structure is properly set up and inspected for intersections with the view space, which essentially means the sprite is on screen and should be drawn.

Re-using code as much as possible makes life easier in the long run, hence the existence of many private methods amongst multiple systems, regarding modifications of entity components. For example:

```
void S_Renderer::SetSheetDirection(const EntityId& l_entity,
  const Direction& l_dir)
{
  EntityManager* entities = m_systemManager->GetEntityManager();
  if (!entities->HasComponent(l_entity,
    Component::SpriteSheet))
  {
    return;
  }
  C_SpriteSheet* sheet = entities->
    GetComponent<C_SpriteSheet>(l_entity,Component::SpriteSheet);
  sheet->GetSpriteSheet()->SetDirection(l_dir);
}
```

The `SetSheetDirection` method simply fetches the sprite sheet component and changes its direction.

The last feature we want to work on implementing is the render order of drawables in order to simulate depth. Drawing entities in a correct sequence requires them being sorted. This is where the `SortDrawables` method comes in:

```
void S_Renderer::SortDrawables(){
  EntityManager* e_mgr = m_systemManager->GetEntityManager();
  std::sort(m_entities.begin(), m_entities.end(),
    [e_mgr](unsigned int l_1, unsigned int l_2)
  {
    auto pos1 = e_mgr->
      GetComponent<C_Position>(l_1, Component::Position);
    auto pos2 = e_mgr->
      GetComponent<C_Position>(l_2, Component::Position);
    if (pos1->GetElevation() == pos2->GetElevation()){
      return pos1->GetPosition().y < pos2->GetPosition().y;
    }
    return pos1->GetElevation() < pos2->GetElevation();
  });
}
```

Here, we simply invoke the `std::sort` function, with the last argument being the predicate lambda that we've already seen before. Elevation is given top priority when entity sprites are being sorted. Anything with a higher elevation will be drawn on top, while sprites on the same elevation are sorted based on their Y coordinate.

With that, the rendering system is now complete! Putting all of the pieces together is the final step in employing the entity component system pattern in our game.

Putting the ECS to work

Due to the part this paradigm plays in the overall structure of our application, we want the system manager and entity manager classes to be accessible to the majority of our code base. Having these objects be part of the shared context is the best way to do so:

```
struct SharedContext{
    SharedContext():
        ...
        m_systemManager(nullptr),
        m_entityManager(nullptr),
        ...{}
    ...
    SystemManager* m_systemManager;
```

```
    EntityManager* m_entityManager;
    ...
};
```

Adjusting the shared context means we have two extra classes to keep track of in Game.h:

```
class Game{
...
private:
    ...
    SystemManager m_systemManager;
    EntityManager m_entityManager;
    ...
};
```

These classes have to be properly initialized, which is done in Game.cpp:

```
Game::Game(): m_window("Chapter 8", sf::Vector2u(800,600)),
  m_entityManager(&m_systemManager, &m_textureManager),
  m_stateManager(&m_context)
{
    ...
  m_systemManager.SetEntityManager(&m_entityManager);
  m_context.m_systemManager = &m_systemManager;
  m_context.m_entityManager = &m_entityManager;
    ...
}
```

Notice that the entity manager is initialized in the initializer list. The system manager is then given a pointer to the entity manager, and both of these classes are added to the shared context.

Next up, some changes have to be made to the game state:

```
class State_Game : public BaseState{
public:
    ...
    void PlayerMove(EventDetails* l_details);
    ...
private:
    ...
    Void UpdateCamera();
    int m_player;
};
```

The game state currently keeps track of the player's entity identifier in addition to providing a new method for updating the camera, as well as moving the player, which will be set up as a callback like so:

```
void State_Game::OnCreate(){
  ...
  evMgr->AddCallback(StateType::Game, "Player_MoveLeft",
    &State_Game::PlayerMove, this);
  evMgr->AddCallback(StateType::Game, "Player_MoveRight",
    &State_Game::PlayerMove, this);
  evMgr->AddCallback(StateType::Game, "Player_MoveUp",
    &State_Game::PlayerMove, this);
  evMgr->AddCallback(StateType::Game, "Player_MoveDown",
    &State_Game::PlayerMove, this);
  ...
  m_player = m_gameMap->GetPlayerId();
}
```

After the game map is loaded, the player entity identifier is obtained through the Map class, which stores this information during map loading.

The next task is getting the camera to follow our hero. This can be accomplished by first calling our UpdateCamera method in the Update method of our game state:

```
void State_Game::Update(const sf::Time& l_time){
  SharedContext* context = m_stateMgr->GetContext();
  UpdateCamera();
  m_gameMap->Update(l_time.asSeconds());
  context->m_systemManager->Update(l_time.asSeconds());
}
```

The actual UpdateCamera method itself is implemented like so:

```
void State_Game::UpdateCamera(){
  if (m_player == -1){ return; }
  SharedContext* context = m_stateMgr->GetContext();
  C_Position* pos = m_stateMgr->GetContext()->m_entityManager->
    GetComponent<C_Position>(m_player, Component::Position);

  m_view.setCenter(pos->GetPosition());
  context->m_wind->GetRenderWindow()->setView(m_view);

  sf::FloatRect viewSpace = context->m_wind->GetViewSpace();
  if (viewSpace.left <= 0){
    m_view.setCenter(viewSpace.width / 2, m_view.getCenter().y);
    context->m_wind->GetRenderWindow()->setView(m_view);
```

```
    } else if (viewSpace.left + viewSpace.width >
      (m_gameMap->GetMapSize().x) * Sheet::Tile_Size)
    {
      m_view.setCenter(
        ((m_gameMap->GetMapSize().x) * Sheet::Tile_Size) -
        (viewSpace.width / 2), m_view.getCenter().y);
      context->m_wind->GetRenderWindow()->setView(m_view);
    }

    if (viewSpace.top <= 0){
      m_view.setCenter(m_view.getCenter().x, viewSpace.height / 2);
      context->m_wind->GetRenderWindow()->setView(m_view);
    } else if (viewSpace.top + viewSpace.height >
      (m_gameMap->GetMapSize().y) * Sheet::Tile_Size)
    {
      m_view.setCenter(m_view.getCenter().x,
        ((m_gameMap->GetMapSize().y) * Sheet::Tile_Size) -
        (viewSpace.height / 2));
      context->m_wind->GetRenderWindow()->setView(m_view);
    }
}
```

The player identifier first is verified of being a non-negative value, which would signify an error. The position component of the player entity is then obtained and used for updating the position of the current view. The rest of the code deals with adjusting the view to fit within the boundaries of the map, if it wanders outside of it. This is also where the system manager update method must be invoked.

Drawing our game world also needs revising:

```
void State_Game::Draw(){
  for(unsigned int i = 0; i < Sheet::Num_Layers; ++i){
    m_gameMap->Draw(i);
    m_stateMgr->GetContext()->m_systemManager->Draw(
      m_stateMgr->GetContext()->m_wind, i);
  }
}
```

First, a `for` loop iterates over each layer that might be used in the game. The `Num_Layers` value is part of the `Sheet` enumeration, which is defined in the `Map` class header. We'll be covering that shortly. The map `Draw` method now needs to know which layer to draw, as they're not all drawn at the same time anymore. After the appropriate layer is rendered, all of the entities that occupy the same elevation are also rendered on screen, giving the impression of depth in the game, like so:

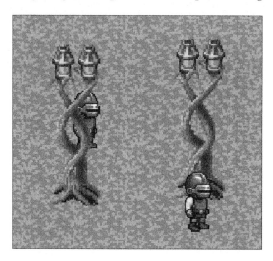

Lastly, we need to define the callback method for moving a player:

```
void State_Game::PlayerMove(EventDetails* l_details){
  Message msg((MessageType)EntityMessage::Move);
  if (l_details->m_name == "Player_MoveLeft"){
    msg.m_int = (int)Direction::Left;
  } else if (l_details->m_name == "Player_MoveRight"){
    msg.m_int = (int)Direction::Right;
  } else if (l_details->m_name == "Player_MoveUp"){
    msg.m_int = (int)Direction::Up;
  } else if (l_details->m_name == "Player_MoveDown"){
    msg.m_int = (int)Direction::Down;
  }
  msg.m_receiver = m_player;
  m_stateMgr->GetContext()->m_systemManager->
    GetMessageHandler()->Dispatch(msg);
}
```

A message of type `Move` is created and set up in order to hold the direction in its `m_int` data member. The receiver of the message is also set to be the player, and the message is dispatched through the system manager's message handler. This message will be handled by one of the systems we'll be building in a later chapter.

The last change from our previous project is the number of directions an entity can move in. Given the format of our new entity spritesheets, let's modify `Directions.h`:

```
enum class Direction{ Up = 0, Left, Down, Right };
```

Since the direction is used as a way to offset numbers of rows in sprite sheets for obtaining correct animations, the values set here are important. This small change concludes building and setting up the core of our component entity system! All that's left now is adjusting the `Map` class to satisfy and complement the new, shiny features of our game.

The new and improved map

For as good as the second project of this book looked, a lot of things about it were fairly primitive. Among its other shortcomings, the map design lacked complexity due to its inability to support tile layers. Having a more complex scene requires tiles being able to layer over each other, in a manner best represented by this illustration:

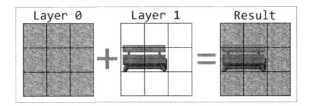

Adding layer support, as well as loading entity information after re-designing the way entities are handled requires some changes to be made to the map file format. Let's take a look at an example:

```
SIZE 32 32
DEFAULT_FRICTION 1.0 1.0
|ENTITY|Name|x|y|elevation|
ENTITY Player 256.0 256.0 1
...
|TILE|ID|x|y|layer|solid|
TILE 3 0 0 0 0
...
```

While some map properties remain in place, things like gravity or background images have been removed, as it no longer suits the genre of the game we're making. The main changes here are the entity and tile lines.

Loading an entity is as simple as providing the name of its entity file and a few pieces of data, relevant to maps, such as its position and elevation.

Tile loading is also slightly different now. In addition to its identifier and position, a tile now also requires having a layer, as well as a flag for solidity, which will be covered more in depth in the next chapter.

Amongst some of the bigger changes, a new value inside the *Sheet* enumeration is defined. It represents the maximum possible number of layers in any given map:

```
enum Sheet{
   Tile_Size = 32, Sheet_Width = 256,
   Sheet_Height = 256, Num_Layers = 4
};
```

Also, in order to allow individual solidity options, each tile now carries a solidity flag that can be turned on or off:

```
struct Tile{
   ...
   bool m_solid; // Is the tile a solid.
};
```

Working with an extra piece of information, the tile layer, requires certain modifications to be made to the `GetTile` and `ConvertCoords` methods:

```
class Map{
public:
   ...
   Tile* GetTile(unsigned int l_x, unsigned int l_y,
      unsigned int l_layer);
   ...
   void Draw(unsigned int l_layer);
private:
   unsigned int ConvertCoords(unsigned int l_x, unsigned int l_y,
      unsigned int l_layer)const;
   ...
   int m_playerId;
   ...
};
```

Note the `m_playerId` data member. It keeps track of what entity ID the player has been given after loading the map file.

Adjusting the Map class

It's time to start implementing all of these changes! First, let's take a look at the
method used for obtaining map tiles:

```
Tile* Map::GetTile(unsigned int l_x, unsigned int l_y,
  unsigned int l_layer)
{
  if(l_x < 0 || l_y < 0 || l_x >= m_maxMapSize.x ||
    l_y >= m_maxMapSize.y || l_layer < 0 ||
    l_layer >= Sheet::Num_Layers)
  {
    return nullptr;
  }
  auto itr = m_tileMap.find(ConvertCoords(l_x,l_y,l_layer));
  if (itr == m_tileMap.end()){ return nullptr; }
  return itr->second;
}
```

The biggest difference here is the check for accessing tiles that are out of boundaries
of the map. The method itself takes an additional argument that represents the tile
layer, which it then passes into the ConvertCoords method. Working with tile layers
would require having a third dimension added to a 2D array of tiles. Since we're
storing all of this information in a one-dimensional array, some additional math
has to be done in order to perform the conversion:

```
unsigned int Map::ConvertCoords(unsigned int l_x,
  unsigned int l_y, unsigned int l_layer)const
{
  return ((l_layer*m_maxMapSize.y+l_y) * m_maxMapSize.x + l_x);
}
```

If you previously visualized the map as a 2D grid, it's now becoming a 3D cube, with
the layer value representing its depth.

The desired functionality of the updated Draw method has been outlined quite
clearly in the game state Draw method. Let's implement that:

```
void Map::Draw(unsigned int l_layer){
  if (l_layer >= Sheet::Num_Layers){ return; }
  sf::RenderWindow* l_wind = m_context->m_wind->GetRenderWindow();
  sf::FloatRect viewSpace = m_context->m_wind->GetViewSpace();

  sf::Vector2i tileBegin(
    floor(viewSpace.left / Sheet::Tile_Size),
```

```
      floor(viewSpace.top / Sheet::Tile_Size));
  sf::Vector2i tileEnd(
    ceil((viewSpace.left + viewSpace.width) / Sheet::Tile_Size),
    ceil((viewSpace.top + viewSpace.height) / Sheet::Tile_Size));

  unsigned int count = 0;
  for(int x = tileBegin.x; x <= tileEnd.x; ++x){
    for(int y = tileBegin.y; y <= tileEnd.y; ++y){
      Tile* tile = GetTile(x,y,l_layer);
      if (!tile){ continue; }
      sf::Sprite& sprite = tile->m_properties->m_sprite;
      sprite.setPosition(x * Sheet::Tile_Size,
        y * Sheet::Tile_Size);
      l_wind->draw(sprite);
      ++count;
    }
  }
}
```

Before we get into any actual rendering, we must make sure that the provided layer argument does not exceed the defined maximum. Aside from that, the only real difference here is that we're passing the layer argument into the GetTile method now. That's quite a simple adjustment.

Lastly, the way tiles and entities are loaded has to be fixed. Let's take a look at snippets from the LoadMap method:

```
if(type == "TILE"){
  ...
  sf::Vector2i tileCoords;
  unsigned int tileLayer = 0;
  unsigned int tileSolidity = 0;
  keystream >> tileCoords.x >> tileCoords.y >>
    tileLayer >> tileSolidity;
  if (tileCoords.x > m_maxMapSize.x ||
    tileCoords.y > m_maxMapSize.y ||
    tileLayer >= Sheet::Num_Layers)
  {
    std::cout << "! Tile is out of range: " <<
      tileCoords.x << " " << tileCoords.y << std::endl;
    continue;
  }
  Tile* tile = new Tile();
```

```
// Bind properties of a tile from a set.
tile->m_properties = itr->second;
tile->m_solid = (bool)tileSolidity;
if(!m_tileMap.emplace(ConvertCoords(
  tileCoords.x,tileCoords.y,tileLayer),tile).second)
{
  ...
}
...
} else if ...
```

The majority of this code remains unchanged. Reading in the layer and solidity data has been added, as well as checking if the layer value is valid, together with the coordinate values. The entity side of things, however, is quite different:

```
} else if(type == "ENTITY"){
// Set up entity here.
std::string name;
keystream >> name;
if (name == "Player" && m_playerId != -1){ continue; }
int entityId = m_context->m_entityManager->AddEntity(name);
if (entityId < 0){ continue; }
if(name == "Player"){ m_playerId = entityId; }
C_Base* position = m_context->m_entityManager->
  GetComponent<C_Position>(entityId,Component::Position);
if(position){ keystream >> *position; }
} else ...
```

The name of an entity is read in first. If it's a player entity and it hasn't yet been set up based on the m_playerId data member, or if it's just any other entity, an attempt is made to add it. Upon successfully doing so, its name is checked once more in order to make sure the player entity identifier is caught and stored. The position component is then obtained and its data is read in directly from the map file.

Once the `Map` class is finished, compiling and rendering our project and loading in a valid map should leave us with a few entities standing around peacefully:

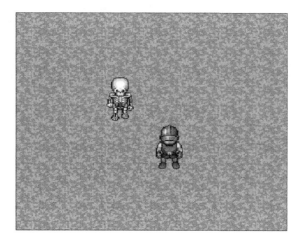

Summary

With the invention of all the tools we need, we will next be working on adding the most common game elements to our final project and bringing it to life, not to mention actually flexing the backend functionality we built. Although this chapter has come to an end, this is by no means the last of us discovering and applying new programming patterns, should a need ever arise again to use one.

A good code-base is one that can handle new features and expansion of old ones with ease. The fruition of this chapter marks the point, at which the games we make are no longer bound to be simplistic due to design restrictions or inconvenient expansion. At this point, the question is no longer "How?", it's "Why not?" Seeing as you have made it this far, why not keep going? See you in the next chapter!

A Breath of Fresh Air – Entity Component System Continued

In the previous chapter, we discussed the benefits of using aggregation versus simple inheritance. While not necessarily intuitive at first glance, entities composed of multiple components and operated on by systems inarguably enable higher flexibility and re-usability of code, not to mention a more convenient environment for future growth. Well, "The future is now!" as the popular expression states. A house is useless without a good foundation, just as much as a good foundation is useless without a house built on top of it. Since we already have a solid foundation, laying bricks until a proper structure emerges is what's next.

In this chapter, we will be:

- Implementing basic movement
- Developing a system for updating sprite sheets
- Revisiting and implementing entity states
- Studying the collision within the entity component system paradigm

Adding entity movement

Within the entity component system paradigm, movement of a particular body is quantified by all the forces imposed on it. The collection of these forces can be represented by a movable component:

```
class C_Movable : public C_Base{
public:
    ...
private:
    sf::Vector2f m_velocity;
```

```
    float m_velocityMax;
    sf::Vector2f m_speed;
    sf::Vector2f m_acceleration;
    Direction m_direction;
};
```

This component takes away physics elements from the second project of this book, namely the velocity, speed and acceleration attributes. In order to simplify the code, the velocity cap is represented by a single float this time, as it is unlikely we will ever need to limit the velocity differently based on its axis.

Let's take a look at the rest of the movable component class:

```
C_Movable() : C_Base(Component::Movable),
    m_velocityMax(0.f), m_direction((Direction)0)
{}
```

The constructor here initializes the data members to some default values, which are later replaced by ones from de-serialization:

```
void ReadIn(std::stringstream& l_stream){
    l_stream >> m_velocityMax >> m_speed.x >> m_speed.y;

    unsigned int dir = 0;
    l_stream >> dir;
    m_direction = (Direction)dir;
}
```

For purposes of easily manipulating velocity within a certain range, we provide the `AddVelocity` method:

```
void AddVelocity(const sf::Vector2f& l_vec){
  m_velocity += l_vec;
  if(std::abs(m_velocity.x) > m_velocityMax){
    m_velocity.x = m_velocityMax *
      (m_velocity.x / std::abs(m_velocity.x));
  }

  if(std::abs(m_velocity.y) > m_velocityMax){
    m_velocity.y = m_velocityMax *
      (m_velocity.y / std::abs(m_velocity.y));
  }
}
```

After adding the provided argument velocity, the end result is checked for being higher than the maximum allowed value on each axis. If it is, the velocity is capped at the maximum allowed value with the appropriate sign.

```
void ApplyFriction(const sf::Vector2f& l_vec){
  if(m_velocity.x != 0 && l_vec.x != 0){
    if(std::abs(m_velocity.x) - std::abs(l_vec.x) < 0){
      m_velocity.x = 0;
    } else {
      m_velocity.x += (m_velocity.x > 0 ? l_vec.x * -1 : l_vec.x);
    }
  }

  if(m_velocity.y != 0 && l_vec.y != 0){
    if(std::abs(m_velocity.y) - std::abs(l_vec.y) < 0){
      m_velocity.y = 0;
    } else {
      m_velocity.y += (m_velocity.y > 0 ? l_vec.y * -1 : l_vec.y);
    }
  }
}
```

Applying friction to the current velocity is also regulated. In order to avoid friction forcing the velocity to change its sign, it's checked to not be equal to zero, as well as if the difference between absolute values of current velocity and provided friction isn't going to be negative. If it is, the velocity is set to zero. Otherwise, the friction value is added to current velocity with an appropriate sign.

In order for an entity to move, it has to be accelerated. Let's supply a method for that:

```
void Accelerate(const sf::Vector2f& l_vec){
    m_acceleration += l_vec;
}
void Accelerate(float l_x, float l_y){
    m_acceleration += sf::Vector2f(l_x,l_y);
}
```

For the sake of convenience, we provide the same method, overloaded to take in two types of arguments: a float vector and two separate float values. All it does is simply add the argument values to current acceleration.

Lastly, entities can also be moved based on a provided direction, instead of calling the `Accelerate` method manually:

```
void Move(const Direction& l_dir){
  if(l_dir == Direction::Up){
    m_acceleration.y -= m_speed.y;
  } else if (l_dir == Direction::Down){
    m_acceleration.y += m_speed.y;
  } else if (l_dir == Direction::Left){
    m_acceleration.x -= m_speed.x;
  } else if (l_dir == Direction::Right){
    m_acceleration.x += m_speed.x;
  }
}
```

Based on the direction provided as an argument, the entity's speed is added to the acceleration vector.

The movement system

With the movement component designed, let's take a stab at implementing the actual system that will move our entities around:

```
enum class Axis{ x, y };
class Map;
class S_Movement : public S_Base{
public:
  ...
  void SetMap(Map* l_gameMap);
private:
  void StopEntity(const EntityId& l_entity,
    const Axis& l_axis);
  void SetDirection(const EntityId& l_entity,
    const Direction& l_dir);
  const sf::Vector2f& GetTileFriction(unsigned int l_elevation,
    unsigned int l_x, unsigned int l_y);
  void MovementStep(float l_dT, C_Movable* l_movable,
    C_Position* l_position);
  Map* m_gameMap;
};
```

First, an `Axis` enumeration is created, in order to simply the code in one of the private helper methods of this class. We then forward-declare a `Map` class, in order to be able to use it in the header. With that, comes a `Map` data member, as well as a public method for providing the movement system with an instance of `Map`. A few private helper methods are also needed in order to make the code more readable. Let's begin by setting up our constructor:

```
S_Movement::S_Movement(SystemManager* l_systemMgr)
  : S_Base(System::Movement,l_systemMgr)
{
  Bitmask req;
  req.TurnOnBit((unsigned int)Component::Position);
  req.TurnOnBit((unsigned int)Component::Movable);
  m_requiredComponents.push_back(req);
  req.Clear();

  m_systemManager->GetMessageHandler()->
    Subscribe(EntityMessage::Is_Moving,this);

  m_gameMap = nullptr;
}
```

The requirements for this system consist of two components: position and movable. In addition to that, this system also subscribes to the `Is_Moving` message type, in order to respond to it.

Next, let's update our entity information:

```
void S_Movement::Update(float l_dT){
  if (!m_gameMap){ return; }
  EntityManager* entities = m_systemManager->GetEntityManager();
  for(auto &entity : m_entities){
    C_Position* position = entities->
      GetComponent<C_Position>(entity, Component::Position);
    C_Movable* movable = entities->
      GetComponent<C_Movable>(entity, Component::Movable);
    MovementStep(l_dT, movable, position);
    position->MoveBy(movable->GetVelocity() * l_dT);
  }
}
```

As the requirements of this system suggest, it will be operating on the position component, as well as the movable component. For every entity that belongs to this system, we want to update its physics and adjust its position in accordance to its velocity and the time that has passed in between frames, producing movement based on forces.

Let's take a look at the movement step method:

```
void S_Movement::MovementStep(float l_dT, C_Movable* l_movable,
  C_Position* l_position)
{
  sf::Vector2f f_coefficient =
    GetTileFriction(l_position->GetElevation(),
    floor(l_position->GetPosition().x / Sheet::Tile_Size),
    floor(l_position->GetPosition().y / Sheet::Tile_Size));

  sf::Vector2f friction(l_movable->GetSpeed().x * f_coefficient.x,
    l_movable->GetSpeed().y * f_coefficient.y);

  l_movable->AddVelocity(l_movable->GetAcceleration() * l_dT);
  l_movable->SetAcceleration(sf::Vector2f(0.0f, 0.0f));
  l_movable->ApplyFriction(friction * l_dT);

  float magnitude = sqrt(
    (l_movable->GetVelocity().x * l_movable->GetVelocity().x) +
    (l_movable->GetVelocity().y * l_movable->GetVelocity().y));

  if (magnitude <= l_movable->GetMaxVelocity()){ return; }
  float max_V = l_movable->GetMaxVelocity();
  l_movable->SetVelocity(sf::Vector2f(
    (l_movable->GetVelocity().x / magnitude) * max_V,
    (l_movable->GetVelocity().y / magnitude) * max_V));
}
```

The friction value of the tile an entity is standing on is obtained first. It gets applied to the entity's movable component right after its velocity is updated based on the acceleration value.

Next, we must make sure that diagonal movement is handled correctly. Consider the following illustration:

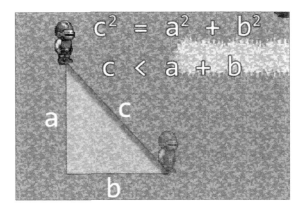

According to the Pythagorean theorem, the squared hypotenuse of a right triangle, which represents diagonal movement, is equal to the sum of its squared sides. In other words, its hypotenuse is shorter than the sum of both of its sides. Characters that move down-right, for example, would appear to move faster than they do in a single direction, unless we cap their velocity based on the magnitude of the velocity vector, also known as the hypotenuse of the triangle in our illustration. Once the magnitude is calculated, it is checked for exceeding the maximum possible velocity of an entity. If it does, it gets normalized and multiplied by the value of maximum velocity, in order to impose slower diagonal movement.

Obtaining the tile friction can be done like so:

```
const sf::Vector2f& S_Movement::GetTileFriction(
  unsigned int l_elevation, unsigned int l_x, unsigned int l_y)
{
  Tile* t = nullptr;
  while (!t && l_elevation >= 0){
    t = m_gameMap->GetTile(l_x, l_y, l_elevation);
    --l_elevation;
  }

  return(t ? t->m_properties->m_friction :
    m_gameMap->GetDefaultTile()->m_friction);
}
```

A tile pointer is set up before a `while` loop is initiated. It will keep trying to fetch a tile at a provided location while decreasing the elevation each time. This means that tile friction is effectively yielded from the top-most tile that a player is over. If a tile hasn't been found, the default friction value is returned instead.

As you might be able to guess by now, the movement system needs to respond to quite a few events, due to its importance:

```
void S_Movement::HandleEvent(const EntityId& l_entity,
  const EntityEvent& l_event)
{
  switch(l_event){
  case EntityEvent::Colliding_X:
    StopEntity(l_entity,Axis::x); break;
  case EntityEvent::Colliding_Y:
    StopEntity(l_entity, Axis::y); break;
  case EntityEvent::Moving_Left:
    SetDirection(l_entity, Direction::Left); break;
  case EntityEvent::Moving_Right:
    SetDirection(l_entity, Direction::Right); break;
  case EntityEvent::Moving_Up:
    {
      C_Movable* mov = m_systemManager->GetEntityManager()->
        GetComponent<C_Movable>(l_entity,Component::Movable);
      if(mov->GetVelocity().x == 0){
        SetDirection(l_entity, Direction::Up);
      }
    }
    break;
  case EntityEvent::Moving_Down:
    {
      C_Movable* mov = m_systemManager->GetEntityManager()->
        GetComponent<C_Movable>(l_entity,Component::Movable);
      if(mov->GetVelocity().x == 0){
        SetDirection(l_entity, Direction::Down);
      }
    }
    break;
  }
}
```

First, it handles two colliding events, to which it responds by calling the private `StopEntity` method in order to halt an entity on a specified axis. Next, we have four movement events. In cases of `Moving_Left` and `Moving_Right`, the private `SetDirection` method is invoked in order to update the direction of an entity. Moving up and down, however, is a little bit different. We want the entity's direction to only change if it has no velocity on the x axis. Otherwise, it ends up moving rather cheesily.

Next up, message handling:

```
void S_Movement::Notify(const Message& l_message){
    EntityManager* eMgr = m_systemManager->GetEntityManager();
    EntityMessage m = (EntityMessage)l_message.m_type;
    switch(m){
    case EntityMessage::Is_Moving:
        {
        if (!HasEntity(l_message.m_receiver)){ return; }
        C_Movable* movable = eMgr->GetComponent<C_Movable>
            (l_message.m_receiver, Component::Movable);
        if (movable->GetVelocity() != sf::Vector2f(0.0f, 0.0f))
        {
            return;
        }
        m_systemManager->AddEvent(l_message.m_receiver,
            (EventID)EntityEvent::Became_Idle);
        }
        break;
    }
}
```

Here, we're only concerned with a single message type: `Is_Moving`. It's a message, designed to trigger another one being sent when the entity becomes idle. First, the system is checked for having the entity in question. Its movable component is then acquired, the velocity of which is checked for being at absolute zero. Given that that's the case, an event is created to signify the entity becoming idle.

All we have left now are the private helper methods. It's all of the redundant logic, the existence of which within methods saves us from code duplication. The first one we'll examine is responsible for halting an entity:

```
void S_Movement::StopEntity(const EntityId& l_entity,
    const Axis& l_axis)
{
    C_Movable* movable = m_systemManager->GetEntityManager()->
        GetComponent<C_Movable>(l_entity,Component::Movable);
    if(l_axis == Axis::x){
        movable->SetVelocity(sf::Vector2f(
            0.f, movable->GetVelocity().y));
    } else if(l_axis == Axis::y){
        movable->SetVelocity(sf::Vector2f(
            movable->GetVelocity().x, 0.f));
    }
}
```

After obtaining its movable component, the entity then has its velocity set to zero on an axis, provided as the argument to this method.

```
void S_Movement::SetDirection(const EntityId& l_entity,
  const Direction& l_dir)
{
  C_Movable* movable = m_systemManager->GetEntityManager()->
    GetComponent<C_Movable>(l_entity,Component::Movable);
  movable->SetDirection(l_dir);

  Message msg((MessageType)EntityMessage::Direction_Changed);
  msg.m_receiver = l_entity;
  msg.m_int = (int)l_dir;
  m_systemManager->GetMessageHandler()->Dispatch(msg);
}
```

The `SetDirection` method updates the direction of a movable component. A message is then dispatched to notify all the other systems of this change.

Finally, we're down to a single setter method for the `Map` class:

```
void S_Movement::SetMap(Map* l_gameMap){ m_gameMap = l_gameMap; }
```

In order for entities to have dynamic friction, the movement system has to have access to the `Map` class, so it gets set up in the game state:

```
void State_Game::OnCreate(){
  ...
  m_stateMgr->GetContext()->m_systemManager->
    GetSystem<S_Movement>(SYSTEM_MOVEMENT)->SetMap(m_gameMap);
}
```

This last code snippet concludes the implementation of the movement system. Our entities are now able to move, based on the forces inflicted on them. Having support for movement, however, does not actually generate movement. This is where the entity state system comes in.

Implementing states

Movement, much like many other actions and events that are relevant to entities are contingent upon their current state being satisfactory. A dying player should not be able to move around. Relevant animations should be played, based on its current state. Enforcing those laws requires the entity to have a state component:

```
enum class EntityState{ Idle, Walking, Attacking, Hurt, Dying };
class C_State : public C_Base{
```

```
public:
  C_State(): C_Base(Component::State){}
  void ReadIn(std::stringstream& l_stream){
    unsigned int state = 0;
    l_stream >> state;
    m_state = (EntityState)state;
  }

  EntityState GetState(){ return m_state; }
  void SetState(const EntityState& l_state){
    m_state = l_state;
  }
private:
  EntityState m_state;
};
```

As you can tell already, this is a very simple chunk of code. It defines its own enumeration of possible entity states. The component class itself simply provides a setter and a getter, as well as the required method for de-serialization. The rest is, as always, left up to the system to hash out.

The state system

Since most of the system headers from here on out are going to look pretty much the same, they will be omitted. With that said, let's begin by implementing the constructor and destructor of our state system:

```
S_State::S_State(SystemManager* l_systemMgr)
  : S_Base(System::State,l_systemMgr)
{
  Bitmask req;
  req.TurnOnBit((unsigned int)Component::State);
  m_requiredComponents.push_back(req);

  m_systemManager->GetMessageHandler()->
    Subscribe(EntityMessage::Move,this);
  m_systemManager->GetMessageHandler()->
    Subscribe(EntityMessage::Switch_State,this);
}
```

All this system requires is the state component. It also subscribes to two message types: `Move` and `Switch_State`. While the latter is self-explanatory, the `Move` message is what gets sent by the methods in the game state in order to move the player. Because movement is entirely dependent on the entity state, this is the only system that handles this type of message and determines whether the state is appropriate for motion.

Next, let's take a look at the `Update` method:

```
void S_State::Update(float l_dT){
  EntityManager* entities = m_systemManager->GetEntityManager();
  for(auto &entity : m_entities){
    C_State* state = entities->
      GetComponent<C_State>(entity, Component::State);
    if(state->GetState() == EntityState::Walking){
      Message msg((MessageType)EntityMessage::Is_Moving);
      msg.m_receiver = entity;
      m_systemManager->GetMessageHandler()->Dispatch(msg);
    }
  }
}
```

All that happens here is a simple check of the entity's current state. If it's in motion, a message `Is_Moving` is dispatched. If you recall, this type of message is handled by the movement system, which fires an event when the entity becomes idle. That event is handled by our state system:

```
void S_State::HandleEvent(const EntityId& l_entity,
  const EntityEvent& l_event)
{
  switch(l_event){
  case EntityEvent::Became_Idle:
    ChangeState(l_entity,EntityState::Idle,false);
    break;
  }
}
```

All it does is invoke a private method `ChangeState`, which alters the current state of an entity to `Idle`. The third argument here is simply a flag for whether the state change should be forced or not.

The last public method we'll be dealing with here is `Notify`:

```
void S_State::Notify(const Message& l_message){
  if (!HasEntity(l_message.m_receiver)){ return; }
  EntityMessage m = (EntityMessage)l_message.m_type;
  switch(m){
  case EntityMessage::Move:
    {
      C_State* state = m_systemManager->GetEntityManager()->
        GetComponent<C_State>(l_message.m_receiver,
        Component::State);
      if (state->GetState() == EntityState::Dying){ return; }
      EntityEvent e;
      if (l_message.m_int == (int)Direction::Up){
        e = EntityEvent::Moving_Up;
      } else if (l_message.m_int == (int)Direction::Down){
        e = EntityEvent::Moving_Down;
      } else if(l_message.m_int == (int)Direction::Left){
        e = EntityEvent::Moving_Left;
      } else if (l_message.m_int == (int)Direction::Right){
        e = EntityEvent::Moving_Right;
      }

      m_systemManager->AddEvent(l_message.m_receiver, (EventID)e);
      ChangeState(l_message.m_receiver,
        EntityState::Walking,false);
    }
    break;
  case EntityMessage::Switch_State:
    ChangeState(l_message.m_receiver,
      (EntityState)l_message.m_int,false);
    break;
  }
}
```

The `Move` message is handled by obtaining the state of an entity it targets. If the entity isn't dying, a `Moving_X` event is constructed based on which direction the message holds. Once the event is dispatched, the entity's state is changed to `Walking`.

The `Switch_State` message simply alters the current state of an entity without forcing it, by invoking this private method:

```
void S_State::ChangeState(const EntityId& l_entity,
  const EntityState& l_state, const bool& l_force)
{
```

```
EntityManager* entities = m_systemManager->GetEntityManager();
C_State* state = entities->
  GetComponent<C_State>(l_entity, Component::State);
if (!l_force && state->GetState() == EntityState::Dying){
  return;
}
state->SetState(l_state);
Message msg((MessageType)EntityMessage::State_Changed);
msg.m_receiver = l_entity;
msg.m_int = (int)l_state;
m_systemManager->GetMessageHandler()->Dispatch(msg);
}
```

After the state is obtained, the `l_force` flag is checked. If it's set to `false`, the state is only altered if the entity isn't currently DYING. We don't want anything to snap entities out of death randomly. The state is changed regardless of that, if the `l_force` flag is set to `true`.

Now we have control over what can happen to an entity, based on its current state. With that in place, the entities are now ready to be controlled.

The entity controller

The idea behind having a separate system be responsible for moving an entity around is not only that we get to decide which entities are capable of being moved, but also further separation of logic, and hooks for future A.I. implementations. Let's take a look at the controller component:

```
class C_Controller : public C_Base{
public:
    C_Controller() : C_Base(COMPONENT_CONTROLLER){}
    void ReadIn(std::stringstream& l_stream){}
};
```

Yes, it's just an empty component, that is simply used as a way to tell the control system that the entity it belongs to can be controlled. There might be some additional information it needs to store in the future, but for now, it's simply a "flag."

The actual control system is extremely simple to implement. Let's begin with the constructor:

```
S_Control::S_Control(SystemManager* l_systemMgr)
  :S_Base(System::Control,l_systemMgr)
{
  Bitmask req;
```

```
req.TurnOnBit((unsigned int)Component::Position);
req.TurnOnBit((unsigned int)Component::Movable);
req.TurnOnBit((unsigned int)Component::Controller);
m_requiredComponents.push_back(req);
req.Clear();
}
```

It imposes requirements for position, movable and controller components, in order to be able to move the entity, which is the only purpose of this system. The actual movement is handled by processing entity events like so:

```
void S_Control::HandleEvent(const EntityId& l_entity,
  const EntityEvent& l_event)
{
  switch(l_event){
  case EntityEvent::Moving_Left:
    MoveEntity(l_entity,Direction::Left); break;
  case EntityEvent::Moving_Right:
    MoveEntity(l_entity, Direction::Right); break;
  case EntityEvent::Moving_Up:
    MoveEntity(l_entity, Direction::Up); break;
  case EntityEvent::Moving_Down:
    MoveEntity(l_entity, Direction::Down); break;
  }
}
```

All four events invoke the same private method, which simply calls the `Move` method of a movable component and passes in the appropriate direction:

```
void S_Control::MoveEntity(const EntityId& l_entity,
  const Direction& l_dir)
{
  C_Movable* mov = m_systemManager->GetEntityManager()->
    GetComponent<C_Movable>(l_entity, Component::Movable);
  mov->Move(l_dir);
}
```

After this humble addition to our code-base, we can finally move the player around with the keyboard:

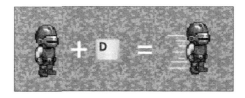

The only problem now is entities looking like they're sliding on ice, due to complete lack of animations. To resolve this issue, the animation system must be introduced.

Animating the entities

If you recall from previous chapters, the SpriteSheet class we built already has great support for animations. There is no reason to annex that at this point, especially since we're only dealing with sprite-sheet based graphics. This saves us a lot of time and allows sprite-sheet animations to be handled by a single system, with no additional component overhead.

Let's start implementing the sprite sheet animation system, as always, by getting the constructor out of the way:

```
S_SheetAnimation::S_SheetAnimation(SystemManager* l_systemMgr)
  : S_Base(System::SheetAnimation,l_systemMgr)
{
  Bitmask req;
  req.TurnOnBit((unsigned int)Component::SpriteSheet);
  req.TurnOnBit((unsigned int)Component::State);
  m_requiredComponents.push_back(req);

  m_systemManager->GetMessageHandler()->
    Subscribe(EntityMessage::State_Changed,this);
}
```

Since entity animations are, so far, entirely state-based, this system requires a state component, in addition to the sprite sheet component. It also subscribes to the State_Changed message type in order to respond to state changes by playing the appropriate animation. Updating all of the entities is the area where this system has most of its logic, so let's take a look at the Update method:

```
void S_SheetAnimation::Update(float l_dT){
  EntityManager* entities = m_systemManager->GetEntityManager();
  for(auto &entity : m_entities){
    C_SpriteSheet* sheet = entities->
      GetComponent<C_SpriteSheet>(entity, Component::SpriteSheet);
    C_State* state = entities->
      GetComponent<C_State>(entity, Component::State);

    sheet->GetSpriteSheet()->Update(l_dT);

    const std::string& animName = sheet->
      GetSpriteSheet()->GetCurrentAnim()->GetName();
```

```
        if(animName == "Attack"){
          if(!sheet->GetSpriteSheet()->GetCurrentAnim()->IsPlaying())
          {
            Message msg((MessageType)EntityMessage::Switch_State);
            msg.m_receiver = entity;
            msg.m_int = (int)EntityState::Idle;
            m_systemManager->GetMessageHandler()->Dispatch(msg);
          } else if(sheet->GetSpriteSheet()->
              GetCurrentAnim()->IsInAction())
          {
            Message msg((MessageType)EntityMessage::Attack_Action);
            msg.m_sender = entity;
            m_systemManager->GetMessageHandler()->Dispatch(msg);
          }
        } else if(animName == "Death" &&
          !sheet->GetSpriteSheet()->GetCurrentAnim()->IsPlaying())
        {
          Message msg((MessageType)EntityMessage::Dead);
          msg.m_receiver = entity;
          m_systemManager->GetMessageHandler()->Dispatch(msg);
        }
      }
    }
```

First, both the sprite sheet and state components are obtained. The sprite sheet is then updated and the current name of the animation is retrieved. If an attack animation is no longer playing, a message of `Switch_State` type is sent out in order to put the entity back to an `Idle` state. Otherwise, the animation is checked for currently being within the "action" frame range, which is specified in the sprite sheet file. If it is, an `Attack_Action` message is sent out to the current entity, which can later be used by different systems to implement combat. On the other hand, if the death animation has concluded, a `Dead` message is dispatched.

Next, let's work on handling messages:

```
void S_SheetAnimation::Notify(const Message& l_message){
  if(HasEntity(l_message.m_receiver)){
    EntityMessage m = (EntityMessage)l_message.m_type;
    switch(m){
    case EntityMessage::State_Changed:
      {
        EntityState s = (EntityState)l_message.m_int;
        switch(s){
        case EntityState::Idle:
```

```
                    ChangeAnimation(l_message.m_receiver,"Idle",true,true);
                    break;
                case EntityState::Walking:
                    ChangeAnimation(l_message.m_receiver,"Walk",true,true);
                    break;
                case EntityState::Attacking:
                    ChangeAnimation(l_message.m_receiver,
                        "Attack",true,false);
                    break;
                case EntityState::Hurt: break;
                case EntityState::Dying:
                    ChangeAnimation(l_message.m_receiver,
                        "Death",true,false);
                    break;
                }
            }
            break;
        }
    }
}
```

All possible messages this system would be interested in deal with specific entities, so that check is made first. For now, we'll only be dealing with a single message type: State_Changed. Every time a state is changed, we'll be altering the animation of the entity. The only possible exception here is the Hurt state, which will be dealt with later.

The last bit of code we need is the private ChangeAnimation method:

```
void S_SheetAnimation::ChangeAnimation(const EntityId& l_entity,
    const std::string& l_anim, bool l_play, bool l_loop)
{
    C_SpriteSheet* sheet = m_systemManager->GetEntityManager()->
        GetComponent<C_SpriteSheet>(l_entity,Component::SpriteSheet);
    sheet->GetSpriteSheet()->SetAnimation(l_anim,l_play,l_loop);
}
```

After obtaining the entity's sprite sheet component, it simply invokes its SetAnimation method to change the current animation that's playing. This code is redundant enough to warrant a separate method.

Upon successful compilation, we can see that our entities are now animated:

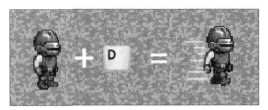

Handling collisions

Making entities bump into each other, as well as into all the lush environments we'll be building is a mechanic, without which most games out there would not be able to function. In order for that to be possible, these animated images zooming around the screen must have a component, which represents their solidity. Bounding boxes worked really well for us in the past, so let's stick to them and begin constructing the collidable body component:

```
enum class Origin{ Top_Left, Abs_Centre, Mid_Bottom };

class C_Collidable : public C_Base{
public:
    ...
private:
    sf::FloatRect m_AABB;
    sf::Vector2f m_offset;
    Origin m_origin;

    bool m_collidingOnX;
    bool m_collidingOnY;
};
```

Every collidable entity must have a bounding box that represents the solid portion of it. That's exactly where the m_AABB rectangle comes in. In addition to that, the bounding box itself can be offset by a number of pixels, based on what kind of entity it is, as well as have a different origin. Lastly, we want to keep track of whether an entity is currently colliding on any given axis, which warrants the use of m_collidingOnX and m_collidingOnY flags.

The constructor of this component might look a little something like this:

```
C_Collidable(): C_Base(Component::Collidable),
  m_origin(Origin::Mid_Bottom), m_collidingOnX(false),
  m_collidingOnY(false)
{}
```

After initializing the default values to some of its data members, this component, like many others, needs to have a way to be de-serialized:

```
void ReadIn(std::stringstream& l_stream){
    unsigned int origin = 0;
    l_stream >> m_AABB.width >> m_AABB.height >> m_offset.x
      >> m_offset.y >> origin;
    m_origin = (Origin)origin;
}
```

Here are a few unique setter and getter methods that we'll be using:

```
void CollideOnX(){ m_collidingOnX = true; }
void CollideOnY(){ m_collidingOnY = true; }
void ResetCollisionFlags(){
    m_collidingOnX = false;
    m_collidingOnY = false;
}
void SetSize(const sf::Vector2f& l_vec){
    m_AABB.width     = l_vec.x;
    m_AABB.height    = l_vec.y;
}
```

Finally, we arrive at the key method of this component, SetPosition:

```
void SetPosition(const sf::Vector2f& l_vec){
    switch(m_origin){
    case(Origin::Top_Left):
        m_AABB.left = l_vec.x + m_offset.x;
        m_AABB.top  = l_vec.y + m_offset.y;
        break;
    case(Origin::Abs_Centre):
        m_AABB.left = l_vec.x - (m_AABB.width / 2) + m_offset.x;
        m_AABB.top  = l_vec.y - (m_AABB.height / 2) + m_offset.y;
        break;
    case(Origin::Mid_Bottom):
        m_AABB.left = l_vec.x - (m_AABB.width / 2) + m_offset.x;
        m_AABB.top  = l_vec.y - m_AABB.height + m_offset.y;
        break;
    }
}
```

In order to support different types of origins, the position of the bounding box rectangle must be set differently. Consider the following illustration:

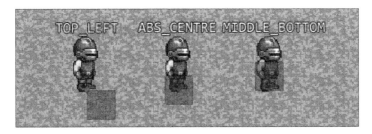

The origin of the actual bounding box rectangle is always going to be the top-left corner. To position it correctly, we use its width and height to compensate for differences between several possible origin types.

The collision system

The actual collision magic doesn't start happening until we have a system responsible for accounting for every collidable body in the game. Let's begin by taking a look at the data types that are going to be used in this system:

```
struct CollisionElement{
  CollisionElement(float l_area, TileInfo* l_info,
    const sf::FloatRect& l_bounds):m_area(l_area),
    m_tile(l_info), m_tileBounds(l_bounds){}
  float m_area;
  TileInfo* m_tile;
  sf::FloatRect m_tileBounds;
};

using Collisions = std::vector<CollisionElement>;
```

For proper collision detection and response, we're also going to need a data structure that is capable of holding collision information, which can later be sorted and processed. For that, we're going to be using a vector of `CollisionElement` data types. It's a structure, consisting of a float, representing area of collision, a pointer to a `TileInfo` instance, which carries all of the information about a tile, and a simple float rectangle, which holds the bounding box information of a map tile.

In order to detect collisions between entities and tiles, the collision system needs to have access to a `Map` instance. Knowing all of that, let's get started on implementing the class!

Implementing the collision system

As always, we're going to be setting up the component requirements right inside the constructor of this class:

```
S_Collision::S_Collision(SystemManager* l_systemMgr)
  :S_Base(System::Collision,l_systemMgr)
{
  Bitmask req;
  req.TurnOnBit((unsigned int)Component::Position);
  req.TurnOnBit((unsigned int)Component::Collidable);
  m_requiredComponents.push_back(req);
  req.Clear();

  m_gameMap = nullptr;
}
```

As you can see, this system imposes requirements of position and collidable components on entities. Its m_gameMap data member is also initialized to `nullptr`, until it gets set up via the use of this method:

```
void S_Collision::SetMap(Map* l_map){ m_gameMap = l_map; }
```

Next up is the oh-so-common update method that makes everything behave as it should:

```
void S_Collision::Update(float l_dT){
  if (!m_gameMap){ return; }
  EntityManager* entities = m_systemManager->GetEntityManager();
  for(auto &entity : m_entities){
    C_Position* position = entities->
      GetComponent<C_Position>(entity, Component::Position);
    C_Collidable* collidable = entities->
      GetComponent<C_Collidable>(entity, Component::Collidable);
    collidable->SetPosition(position->GetPosition());
    collidable->ResetCollisionFlags();
    CheckOutOfBounds(position, collidable);
    MapCollisions(entity, position, collidable);
  }
  EntityCollisions();
}
```

For clarity, the update method uses two other helper methods: `CheckOutOfBounds` and `MapCollisions`. While iterating over all collidable entities, this system obtains their position and collidable component. The latter is updated, using the entity's latest position. It also has its Boolean collision flags reset. After all entities have been updated, the private `EntityCollisions` method is invoked to process entity-on-entity intersection tests. Note the very beginning of this method. It immediately returns in case the map instance hasn't been properly set up.

First, the entity is checked for being outside the boundaries of our map:

```
void S_Collision::CheckOutOfBounds(C_Position* l_pos,
  C_Collidable* l_col)
{
  unsigned int TileSize = m_gameMap->GetTileSize();

  if (l_pos->GetPosition().x < 0){
    l_pos->SetPosition(0.0f, l_pos->GetPosition().y);
    l_col->SetPosition(l_pos->GetPosition());
  } else if (l_pos->GetPosition().x >
    m_gameMap->GetMapSize().x * TileSize)
  {
    l_pos->SetPosition(m_gameMap->GetMapSize().x * TileSize,
      l_pos->GetPosition().y);
    l_col->SetPosition(l_pos->GetPosition());
  }

  if (l_pos->GetPosition().y < 0){
    l_pos->SetPosition(l_pos->GetPosition().x, 0.0f);
    l_col->SetPosition(l_pos->GetPosition());
  } else if (l_pos->GetPosition().y >
    m_gameMap->GetMapSize().y * TileSize)
  {
    l_pos->SetPosition(l_pos->GetPosition().x,
      m_gameMap->GetMapSize().y * TileSize);
    l_col->SetPosition(l_pos->GetPosition());
  }
}
```

If the entity has somehow ended up outside the map, its position gets reset.

At this point, we begin running the tile-on-entity collision test:

```
void S_Collision::MapCollisions(const EntityId& l_entity,
  C_Position* l_pos, C_Collidable* l_col)
{
  unsigned int TileSize = m_gameMap->GetTileSize();
  Collisions c;

  sf::FloatRect EntityAABB = l_col->GetCollidable();
  int FromX = floor(EntityAABB.left / TileSize);
  int ToX = floor((EntityAABB.left + EntityAABB.width)/TileSize);
  int FromY = floor(EntityAABB.top / TileSize);
  int ToY = floor((EntityAABB.top + EntityAABB.height)/TileSize);
  ...
}
```

A collision information vector named c is set up. It will contain all the important information about what the entity is colliding with, the size of the collision area and properties of the tile it's colliding with. The entity's bounding box is then obtained from the collidable component. A range of coordinates to be checked is calculated, based on that bounding box, as shown here:

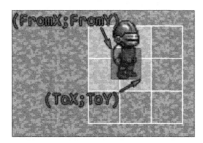

Those coordinates are immediately put to use, as we begin iterating over the calculated range of tiles, checking for collisions:

```
for (int x = FromX; x <= ToX; ++x){
  for (int y = FromY; y <= ToY; ++y){
    for (int l = 0; l < Sheet::Num_Layers; ++l){
      Tile* t = m_gameMap->GetTile(x, y, l);
      if (!t){ continue; }
      if (!t->m_solid){ continue; }
      sf::FloatRect TileAABB(x*TileSize, y*TileSize,
        TileSize, TileSize);
      sf::FloatRect Intersection;
      EntityAABB.intersects(TileAABB, Intersection);
      float S = Intersection.width * Intersection.height;
```

```
        c.emplace_back(S, t->m_properties, TileAABB);
        break;
      }
    }
  }
```

Once a solid tile is encountered, its bounding box, tile information and area of intersection details are gathered and inserted into the vector c. It's important to stop the layer loop if a solid tile is detected, otherwise collision detection may not function properly.

After all the solids the entity collides with in the calculated range have been found, they all must be sorted:

```
if (c.empty()){ return; }
std::sort(c.begin(), c.end(),
  [](CollisionElement& l_1, CollisionElement& l_2){
    return l_1.m_area > l_2.m_area;
});
```

After sorting, we can finally begin resolving collisions:

```
for (auto &col : c){
  EntityAABB = l_col->GetCollidable();
  if (!EntityAABB.intersects(col.m_tileBounds)){ continue; }
  float xDiff = (EntityAABB.left + (EntityAABB.width / 2)) -
    (col.m_tileBounds.left + (col.m_tileBounds.width / 2));
  float yDiff = (EntityAABB.top + (EntityAABB.height / 2)) -
    (col.m_tileBounds.top + (col.m_tileBounds.height / 2));
  float resolve = 0;
  if (std::abs(xDiff) > std::abs(yDiff)){
    if (xDiff > 0){
      resolve = (col.m_tileBounds.left + TileSize) -
        EntityAABB.left;
    } else {
      resolve = -((EntityAABB.left + EntityAABB.width) -
        col.m_tileBounds.left);
    }
    l_pos->MoveBy(resolve, 0);
    l_col->SetPosition(l_pos->GetPosition());
    m_systemManager->AddEvent(l_entity,
      (EventID)EntityEvent::Colliding_X);
    l_col->CollideOnX();
  } else {
    if (yDiff > 0){
      resolve = (col.m_tileBounds.top + TileSize) -
```

```
        EntityAABB.top;
      } else {
        resolve = -((EntityAABB.top + EntityAABB.height) -
          col.m_tileBounds.top);
      }
      l_pos->MoveBy(0, resolve);
      l_col->SetPosition(l_pos->GetPosition());
      m_systemManager->AddEvent(l_entity,
        (EventID)EntityEvent::Colliding_Y);
      l_col->CollideOnY();
    }
  }
}
```

Since resolution of one collision could potentially resolve another as well, the bounding box of an entity must be checked for intersections here as well, before we commit to resolving it. The actual resolution is pretty much the same as it was in *Chapter 7, Rediscovering Fire – Common Game Design Elements*.

Once the resolution details are calculated, the position component is moved based on it. The collidable component has to be updated here as well, because it would end up getting resolved multiple times and moved incorrectly otherwise. The last bit we need to worry about is adding a collision event to the entity's event queue and calling the CollideOnX or CollideOnY method in the collidable component to update its flags.

Now for entity-on-entity collisions:

```
void S_Collision::EntityCollisions(){
  EntityManager* entities = m_systemManager->GetEntityManager();
  for(auto itr = m_entities.begin();
    itr != m_entities.end(); ++itr)
  {
    for(auto itr2 = std::next(itr);
      itr2 != m_entities.end(); ++itr2){
      C_Collidable* collidable1 = entities->
        GetComponent<C_Collidable>(*itr, Component::Collidable);
      C_Collidable* collidable2 = entities->
        GetComponent<C_Collidable>(*itr2, Component::Collidable);
      if(collidable1->GetCollidable().intersects(
        collidable2->GetCollidable()))
      {
        // Entity-on-entity collision!
      }
    }
  }
}
```

This method checks all entities against all other entities for collisions between their bounding boxes, by using the `intersects` method, kindly provided by SFML's rectangle class. For now, we don't have to worry about responding to these types of collisions, however, we will be using this functionality in future chapters.

Lastly, just like its movement counterpart, the collision system requires a pointer to the `Map` class, so let's give it one in the game state's `OnCreate` method:

```
void State_Game::OnCreate(){
  ...
  m_stateMgr->GetContext()->m_systemManager->
    GetSystem<S_Collision>(SYSTEM_COLLISION)->SetMap(m_gameMap);
  ...
}
```

This final code snippet gives the collision system all of the power it needs, in order to keep the entities from walking through solid tiles, as so:

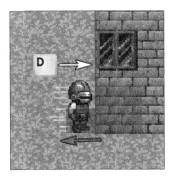

Summary

Upon completing this chapter, we've successfully moved away from inheritance-based entity design and reinforced our code-base with a much more modular approach, thus avoiding many pitfalls that composition leaves behind. A chain is only as strong as its weakest link, and now we can rest assured that the entity segment will hold.

In the next two chapters, we will be discussing how to make the game more interactive and user friendly by adding a GUI system, as well as adding a few different types of elements, managing their events and providing room for them to be graphically customizable. See you there!

10
Can I Click This? – GUI Fundamentals

What do humans and machines really have in common, in the non-Turing sense of the word? It seems like the everyday life of an average human nowadays is almost synonymous with operating the large number of contraptions our species has created, yet most of us don't even speak the same language as the devices we use, which creates a need for some kind of translation. Now it's not as if we can't learn how to speak to machines directly, but it's simply too tedious and time-consuming as our brains work in a completely different way to a common processor. A gray area exists in which relatively intuitive actions performed by humans can also be understood and interpreted by machines without the need for ever getting involved with the underlying complexities - the means of interfacing.

In this chapter, we will cover the following topics:

- Implementation of core data types for all GUI elements
- Utilizing SFML's render textures to achieve GUI layering
- Laying down the fundamentals of smooth and responsive GUI interactions by using stylistic attributes

There is quite a bit of ground to cover so let's get started!

Use of copyrighted resources

Before we begin, it's only fair to credit the true creators of the fonts and images used in the next two chapters:

Fantasy UI Elements by *Ravenmore* at `http://dycha.net/` under the CC-BY 3.0 license:

`http://opengameart.org/content/fantasy-ui-elements-by-ravenmore`

Vegur font by *Arro* under the CC0 license (public domain):

`http://www.fontspace.com/arro/vegur`

More information about all of the licenses that apply to these resources can be found here:

`http://creativecommons.org/publicdomain/zero/1.0/`

`http://creativecommons.org/licenses/by/3.0/`

What is a GUI?

A GUI, short for **Graphical User Interface**, is a visual intermediary between the user and a piece of software which serves as a control mechanism for digital devices or computer programs. Using this type of interface is faster and easier than relying on text-based controls, such as typing commands.

Before any code is written, we need to outline the desired features of our GUI system, which is going to consist of three major components:

- **Element**: Every GUI surface that is drawn onto the screen
- **Interface**: A special kind of element that serves as a container for other elements and can be moved around as well as scrolled
- **Manager**: The class that is in charge of keeping GUI interfaces in line and behaving

All of the elements in this system need to be able to adapt to a different state when they are hovered over by a mouse or clicked on. Style-sets also need to be applied to different states, resulting in interfaces becoming responsive. Lastly, you must be able to load the interfaces from files at runtime and tie them to code based on an event or a set of events taking place within them.

GUI style

Unifying the way styles are applied and used on GUI surfaces is crucial if you need customization and flexibility. To put it simply, modifying and applying every single stylistic attribute of every possible type of element manually would be a nightmare and any kind of code re-use would be impossible. This calls for a custom data type that can be used all across the board: the GUI_Style structure.

First things first, any and all GUI elements should be able to support the three following states:

```
enum class GUI_ElementState{ Neutral, Focused, Clicked };
```

Although these states are not only meant for graphical purposes, each one of them is also defined as a set of visual properties in order to simulate interaction and fluidity, represented by a set of style attributes:

```
struct GUI_Style{
    ...
    sf::Vector2f m_size; // Element size.
    // Background properties.
    sf::Color m_backgroundColor;
    sf::Color m_elementColor;
    std::string m_backgroundImage;
    sf::Color m_backgroundImageColor;
    // Text properties.
    sf::Color m_textColor;
    std::string m_textFont;
    sf::Vector2f m_textPadding;
    unsigned int m_textSize;
    bool m_textCenterOrigin;
    // Glyph properties.
    std::string m_glyph;
    sf::Vector2f m_glyphPadding;
};
```

An element or interface can alter every single one of these properties and adjust itself to look completely different based on the state it's in. If they are not defined, the default values set in the constructor take precedence, as shown here:

```
GUI_Style(): m_textSize(12), m_textCenterOrigin(false),
    m_backgroundImageColor(255,255,255,255)
{
    sf::Color none     = sf::Color(0, 0, 0, 0);
    m_backgroundColor = none;
    m_elementColor     = none;
    m_textColor        = none;
}
```

All of this is useless if we don't have drawable objects to modify, so let's fix that:

```
struct GUI_Visual{
    sf::RectangleShape m_backgroundSolid;
    sf::Sprite m_backgroundImage;
    sf::Sprite m_glyph;
    sf::Text m_text;
};
```

This basic structure will be a part of every single element and interface allowing them to be represented by any combination of these four drawable elements.

Expansion of utility functions

In order to keep things simple and easy to read, it's always a good idea to create utility-type functions out of any code that is going to be used frequently. When dealing with interface de-serialization, many elements have to read in parameters that have spaces in them. Our solution to this problem is to put the string in double quotes and define an inline function to read the data. The perfect spot for that is in the Utilities.h file:

```
inline void ReadQuotedString(std::stringstream& l_stream,
    std::string& l_string)
{
    l_stream >> l_string;
    if (l_string.at(0) == '"'){
        while (l_string.at(l_string.length() - 1) != '"' ||
            !l_stream.eof())
        {
            std::string str;
            l_stream >> str;
            l_string.append(" " + str);
        }
    }
    l_string.erase(std::remove(l_string.begin(),
        l_string.end(), '"'), l_string.end());
}
```

A word is loaded from the string stream object into the string provided as an argument. Its first character is checked to see if it is a double quote. If it is, a while loop keeps reading in words and appends them to the argument string until either its last character is a double quote or the end of the stream is reached.

Following that, all of the double quotes in the string are erased.

Font management

Before we start to build the structure of our graphical user interface, we need a way to manage and handle the loading and unloading of fonts automatically, just like we did with textures. The effort we put into the resource manager written back in *Chapter 6, Set It in Motion! – Animating and Moving around Your World*, is about to pay off. In order to manage fonts, all we need to do is create a `FontManager.h` file and write the following code:

```
class FontManager : public ResourceManager<FontManager, sf::Font>{
public:
  FontManager() : ResourceManager("fonts.cfg"){}

  sf::Font* Load(const std::string& l_path){
    sf::Font* font = new sf::Font();
    if (!font->loadFromFile(
      Utils::GetWorkingDirectory() + l_path))
    {
      delete font;
      font = nullptr;
      std::cerr << "! Failed to load font: "
        << l_path << std::endl;
    }
    return font;
  }
};
```

This defines the font resource configuration file in the constructor, as well as the specific way of loading font files using the `Load` method. The resource manager class that we implemented earlier makes this process very simple, so let's keep going!

The core of all elements

The `GUI_Element` class is the core of every single element and interface. It provides key functionality that higher level objects rely on, as well as enforcing the implementation of necessary methods, which leads to several distinctive element types.

A definition of the different element types is a good place to start:

```
enum class GUI_ElementType{ Window, Label, Button, Scrollbar,
  Textfield };
```

Each element has to hold different styles it can switch to, based on its state. The `unordered_map` data structure suits our purposes pretty well:

```
using ElementStyles = std::unordered_map<
  GUI_ElementState, GUI_Style>;
```

A forward declaration of the owner class is also necessary to prevent cross-inclusion:

```
class GUI_Interface;
```

Next, we can begin shaping the `GUI_Element` class:

```
class GUI_Element{
  friend class GUI_Interface;
public:
  GUI_Element(const std::string& l_name,
    const GUI_ElementType& l_type, GUI_Interface* l_owner);
  virtual ~GUI_Element();

  // Event methods.
  virtual void ReadIn(std::stringstream& l_stream) = 0;
  virtual void OnClick(const sf::Vector2f& l_mousePos) = 0;
  virtual void OnRelease() = 0;
  virtual void OnHover(const sf::Vector2f& l_mousePos) = 0;
  virtual void OnLeave() = 0;
  virtual void Update(float l_dT) = 0;
  virtual void Draw(sf::RenderTarget* l_target) = 0;

  virtual void UpdateStyle(const GUI_ElementState& l_state,
    const GUI_Style& l_style);
  virtual void ApplyStyle();
  ... // Getters/setters
  friend std::stringstream& operator >>(
    std::stringstream& l_stream, GUI_Element& b)
  {
    b.ReadIn(l_stream);
    return l_stream;
  }
protected:
  void ApplyTextStyle();
  void ApplyBgStyle();
  void ApplyGlyphStyle();

  void RequireTexture(const std::string& l_name);
  void RequireFont(const std::string& l_name);
  void ReleaseTexture(const std::string& l_name);
```

```
    void ReleaseFont(const std::string& l_name);
    void ReleaseResources();
    std::string m_name;
    sf::Vector2f m_position;
    ElementStyles m_style; // Style of drawables.
    GUI_Visual m_visual; // Drawable bits.
    GUI_ElementType m_type;
    GUI_ElementState m_state;
    GUI_Interface* m_owner;

    bool m_needsRedraw;
    bool m_active;
    bool m_isControl;
};
```

The most essential part of any GUI element is how it responds to events. This is where the magic of pure-virtual methods comes in. Style application methods, however, are not purely virtual. An element doesn't handle its style any differently to a default element.

Every element also needs to have a name, a position, a set of styles for every possible state, a visual component that can be drawn, a type and state identifiers, and a pointer to an owner class. It also needs to keep track of whether it needs to be re-drawn, its active status, and a flag that denotes whether it is a control or not. These properties are represented by a set of private data members of the GUI_Element class.

With a rough idea of this structure hammered out, let's shape the finer details of the element class.

Implementing the GUI element class

The class we're about to begin implementing is a cornerstone of every single interface and element. It will define how our GUI system behaves. With that in mind, let's start by taking a look at the constructor, as we have quite a bit to initialize:

```
GUI_Element::GUI_Element(const std::string& l_name,
    const GUI_ElementType& l_type, GUI_Interface* l_owner)
    : m_name(l_name), m_type(l_type), m_owner(l_owner),
    m_state(GUI_ElementState::Neutral), m_needsRedraw(false),
    m_active(true), m_isControl(false){}
```

The element name, type, and a pointer to the owner class arguments are taken in and passed to the appropriate data members. Other additional flags are also initialized to the default values. There's nothing out of the ordinary so far. Let's take a look at how this class is destroyed:

```
GUI_Element::~GUI_Element(){ ReleaseResources(); }
```

Since there is no dynamic memory allocation going on anywhere in this class, releasing resources is also fairly simple. The method for that specific purpose is simply invoked here. It looks a little like this:

```
void GUI_Element::ReleaseResources(){
  for (auto &itr : m_style){
    ReleaseTexture(itr.second.m_backgroundImage);
    ReleaseTexture(itr.second.m_glyph);
    ReleaseFont(itr.second.m_textFont);
  }
}
```

We only have to concern ourselves with those textures and fonts that are required by the element itself, so each style is iterated over and its resources are released by the respective methods, which all look similar to the one shown:

```
void GUI_Element::ReleaseTexture(const std::string& l_name){
  if (l_name == ""){ return; }
  m_owner->GetManager()->GetContext()->
    m_textureManager->ReleaseResource(l_name);
}
```

If a font is released, the only difference is the manager that is being used.

Speaking of styles, we need to have a regulated way of modifying them. The `UpdateStyle` method takes care of that job:

```
void GUI_Element::UpdateStyle(const GUI_ElementState& l_state,
  const GUI_Style& l_style)
{
  // Resource management.
  if (l_style.m_backgroundImage !=
    m_style[l_state].m_backgroundImage)
  {
    ReleaseTexture(m_style[l_state].m_backgroundImage);
    RequireTexture(l_style.m_backgroundImage);
  }
```

```
    if (l_style.m_glyph != m_style[l_state].m_glyph){
      ReleaseTexture(m_style[l_state].m_glyph);
      RequireTexture(l_style.m_glyph);
    }

    if (l_style.m_textFont != m_style[l_state].m_textFont){
      ReleaseFont(m_style[l_state].m_textFont);
      RequireFont(l_style.m_textFont);
    }
    // Style application.
    m_style[l_state] = l_style;
    if (l_state == m_state){ SetRedraw(true); ApplyStyle(); }
  }
```

Two arguments are expected by this method: the state being modified and a style
structure that will be used to replace the existing structure. While overwriting
the relevant style is as simple as using the assignment operator, some resource
management has to take place before that happens. We need to know if the style
being replaced requires different resources to the other one. If it does, the older
textures and fonts are released, while the new ones are reserved by using two
more helper methods which both look something like this:

```
  void GUI_Element::RequireTexture(const std::string& l_name){
    if (l_name == ""){ return; }
    m_owner->GetManager()->GetContext()->
      m_textureManager->RequireResource(l_name);
  }
```

The font equivalent for this method uses a different manager but is otherwise
identical.

Once the style is overwritten, we check if the state being modified is the same
state as the element. If so, this particular element is marked to be re-drawn via the
`SetRedraw` method, and its style is applied via the `ApplyStyle` method, which is
what we'll take a look at next:

```
  void GUI_Element::ApplyStyle(){
    ApplyTextStyle();
    ApplyBgStyle();
    ApplyGlyphStyle();
    if (m_owner != this && !IsControl()){
      m_owner->AdjustContentSize(this);
    }
  }
```

This chunk of code is responsible for connecting the style of an element to its visual representation. It first invokes a few helper methods which help us break down the code into smaller, more manageable chunks. The owner interface needs to be alerted afterwards because any modification of the element style may result in size changes. If the element is not an interface control and isn't its own owner, the `AdjustContentSize` method of the `GUI_Interface` class is called, with the `this` keyword passed in as an argument. We will get to implement it soon.

Let's take a look at the first helper method, which deals with text style:

```
void GUI_Element::ApplyTextStyle(){
  FontManager* fonts = m_owner->GetManager()->
    GetContext()->m_fontManager;
  const GUI_Style& CurrentStyle = m_style[m_state];
  if (CurrentStyle.m_textFont != ""){
    m_visual.m_text.setFont(
      *fonts->GetResource(CurrentStyle.m_textFont));
    m_visual.m_text.setColor(CurrentStyle.m_textColor);
    m_visual.m_text.setCharacterSize(CurrentStyle.m_textSize);
    if (CurrentStyle.m_textCenterOrigin){
      sf::FloatRect rect = m_visual.m_text.getLocalBounds();
      m_visual.m_text.setOrigin(rect.left + rect.width / 2.0f,
        rect.top + rect.height / 2.0f);
    } else {
      m_visual.m_text.setOrigin(0.f, 0.f);
    }
  }
  m_visual.m_text.setPosition(m_position +
    CurrentStyle.m_textPadding);
}
```

A different font, color, and character size can be applied to the text for each distinct style that an element can have. The text's origin also needs to be re-calculated every time this happens because these attributes can be manipulated at any point. The position of the text is then updated with the padding value of the current style being factored in.

Background style application follows the same basic idea:

```
void GUI_Element::ApplyBgStyle(){
  TextureManager* textures = m_owner->GetManager()->
    GetContext()->m_textureManager;
  const GUI_Style& CurrentStyle = m_style[m_state];
  if (CurrentStyle.m_backgroundImage != ""){
    m_visual.m_backgroundImage.setTexture(
```

```
    *textures->GetResource(CurrentStyle.m_backgroundImage));
  m_visual.m_backgroundImage.setColor(
    CurrentStyle.m_backgroundImageColor);
}
m_visual.m_backgroundImage.setPosition(m_position);
m_visual.m_backgroundSolid.setSize(
  sf::Vector2f(CurrentStyle.m_size));
m_visual.m_backgroundSolid.setFillColor(
  CurrentStyle.m_backgroundColor);
m_visual.m_backgroundSolid.setPosition(m_position);
}
```

This shows how we add support for the background image and solid elements. Both of these elements are adjusted by applying the visual attributes of a current style and having their positions re-set.

Finally, the glyph of an element is altered in the same fashion:

```
void GUI_Element::ApplyGlyphStyle(){
  const GUI_Style& CurrentStyle = m_style[m_state];
  TextureManager* textures = m_owner->GetManager()->
    GetContext()->m_textureManager;
  if (CurrentStyle.m_glyph != ""){
    m_visual.m_glyph.setTexture(
      *textures->GetResource(CurrentStyle.m_glyph));
  }
  m_visual.m_glyph.setPosition(m_position +
    CurrentStyle.m_glyphPadding);
}
```

Next, let's take a look at the changing element states:

```
void GUI_Element::SetState(const GUI_ElementState& l_state){
  if (m_state == l_state){ return; }
  m_state = l_state;
  SetRedraw(true);
}
```

The element must be marked for re-drawing if its state is changed as different states may have style elements that are also different. That, however, is only done if the state provided as an argument does not match the current state, which is done to conserve resources.

Setting the element position also deserves some attention:

```
void GUI_Element::SetPosition(const sf::Vector2f& l_pos){
    m_position = l_pos;
    if (m_owner == nullptr || m_owner == this){ return; }
    const auto& padding = m_owner->GetPadding();
    if (m_position.x < padding.x){ m_position.x = padding.x; }
    if (m_position.y < padding.y){ m_position.y = padding.y; }
}
```

Since all elements are owned by a container structure, their positions must also honor the padding of those containers. Once the element position is set, the padding of the container interface is obtained. If the element position on either axis is less than that padding, the position is set to be at least as far away from the edge as the interface allows it to be.

Here's an important bit of code that can make or break interactions with any GUI surface:

```
bool GUI_Element::IsInside(const sf::Vector2f& l_point) const{
    sf::Vector2f position = GetGlobalPosition();
    return(l_point.x >= position.x &&
        l_point.y >= position.y &&
        l_point.x <= position.x + m_style.at(m_state).m_size.x &&
        l_point.y <= position.y + m_style.at(m_state).m_size.y);
}
```

The `IsInside` method is used to determine whether a certain point in space is inside an element. Calculating intersections using its normal position yields incorrect results because of its relativity to its owner. Instead, it uses a `GetGlobalPosition` method to fetch the element's position in screen space, as opposed to local space, in the render texture of the owner interface. With a bit of basic bounding box collision magic, it then determines if a point provided as an argument is within the element, based on the size of its current style.

Obtaining global positions of elements can be done like so:

```
sf::Vector2f GUI_Element::GetGlobalPosition() const{
    sf::Vector2f position = GetPosition();
    if (m_owner == nullptr || m_owner == this){ return position; }
    position += m_owner->GetGlobalPosition();
    if (IsControl()){ return position; }
    position.x -= m_owner->m_scrollHorizontal;
    position.y -= m_owner->m_scrollVertical;
    return position;
}
```

Firstly, the element's local position is grabbed. The method then determines if this element has an owner and if does not own itself. If it does, the fetched position is simply the final result and is returned. Otherwise, the owner's global position is obtained through the use of this very method and added to the local position. Furthermore, if the element is not a control type, the horizontal and vertical scroll values are subtracted from its position in order to honor interface scrolling.

To cap things off, here are a few setters and getters that are not straightforward:

```
Const sf::Vector2f& GUI_Element::GetSize() const{
    return m_style.at(m_state).m_size;
}
void GUI_Element::SetActive(const bool& l_active){
    if (l_active != m_active){
     m_active = l_active;
        SetRedraw(true);
    }
}
std::string GUI_Element::GetText() const{
    return m_visual.m_text.getString();
}
void GUI_Element::SetText(const std::string& l_text){
    m_visual.m_text.setString(l_text);
    SetRedraw(true);
}
```

 Note the methods SetActive and SetText. Whenever an element is modified, we must set its re-draw flag to true, otherwise it won't be updated until another event requires it.

Defining GUI events

Providing fluid interactivity with the interface and a painless way of associating changes with actions inside your application may be the most important criterion to separate good GUI systems from bad ones. As we are already learning SFML, we can use the SFML method and omit events.

Firstly, we have to define all the possible events that could take place in an interface. Create a GUI_Event.h file and construct an enumeration, as shown here:

```
enum class GUI_EventType{ None, Click, Release, Hover, Leave };
```

We must also define a custom structure in the same file that is used to hold event information:

```
struct ClickCoordinates{
    float x, y;
};

struct GUI_Event{
    GUI_EventType m_type;
    const char* m_element;
    const char* m_interface;
    union{
        ClickCoordinates m_clickCoords;
    };
};
```

The first thing to talk about here is the structure. It should be possible to merely use `sf::Vector2f` here. That would work fine under most circumstances but, a few lines below that, you see the importance of `ClickCoordinates`. Based on the type of event we're going to be working with, it's going to need to store different data in the `GUI_Event` structure. By using a *union* inside this structure, we're going to avoid allocating additional memory, but that comes at a price. Unions cannot have members that have member functions, virtual functions, or are derivatives of other classes. It is because of this restriction that we are forced to define our own `struct` that holds two *floats* and represents a point.

> The boost library could potentially be useful in a situation like this as it provides `boost::variant`, which is a type-safe union container that doesn't have these limitations. It also has little or no overhead.

The actual event structure holds an event type that is used to determine which member of the union is active, as well as names of the element and interface the event originated from. If you have a good eye for detail, you may have asked yourself by now why we're using `const char*` data types instead of `std::string`. Simplifying data types of data members is another sign that this structure will be incorporated into a union. Unfortunately, `std::string` falls into the same trap as `sf::Vector2f` and cannot be used in a union without extra work.

The interface class

An interface, in its simplest meaning, is a container of elements. It's a window that can be moved around and scrolled and has all of the same features and event hooks as a regular element. Efficiency is also a great concern, as dealing with lots of elements in a single window is a definite possibility. Those problems can be dealt with by carefully designing a way of drawing elements at the appropriate time.

The way we want our interfaces to draw content is by using three separate textures for different purposes, as shown below:

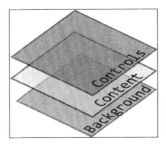

- The **background** layer is used for drawing backdrop elements
- The **content** layer is where all of the elements of the interface are drawn
- The **controls** layer hosts elements such as scrollbars that manipulate the content layer and don't need to be scrolled

With the design details out of the way, element storage deserves some attention. As it happens, the `std::unordered_map` structure serves this purpose well:

```
using Elements = std::unordered_map<std::string,GUI_Element*>;
```

Next, a forward declaration of the owner class is needed to prevent cross-inclusion:

```
class GUI_Manager;
```

All of this brings us to the `GUI_Interface` class:

```
class GUI_Interface : public GUI_Element{
  friend class GUI_Element;
  friend class GUI_Manager;
public:
  ...
private:
  void DefocusTextfields();
  Elements m_elements;
  sf::Vector2f m_elementPadding;
```

```
    GUI_Interface* m_parent;
    GUI_Manager* m_guiManager;

    sf::RenderTexture* m_backdropTexture;
    sf::Sprite m_backdrop;

    // Movement.
    sf::RectangleShape m_titleBar;
    sf::Vector2f m_moveMouseLast;
    bool m_showTitleBar;
    bool m_movable;
    bool m_beingMoved;
    bool m_focused;

    // Variable size.
    void AdjustContentSize(const GUI_Element* l_reference= nullptr);
    void SetContentSize(const sf::Vector2f& l_vec);
    sf::RenderTexture* m_contentTexture;
    sf::Sprite m_content;
    sf::Vector2f m_contentSize;
    int m_scrollHorizontal;
    int m_scrollVertical;
    bool m_contentRedraw;

    // Control layer.
    sf::RenderTexture* m_controlTexture;
    sf::Sprite m_control;
    bool m_controlRedraw;
};
```

 Note the declarations of `friend` classes. Both the GUI_Element and GUI_Manager need to have access to private and protected members of this class.

For now, let's only focus on the private members and leave the public ones for the implementation section of this chapter.

In addition to having an element container, an interface also defines the amount of padding it has that elements most honor, a pointer to its parent class if it has one, as well as the manager class and a set of textures that represent its different layers. The rest of the data members, as well as the omitted methods, can't be fully understood unless we talk about implementation details, so let's get right to it!

Implementing the interface class

A nice place to start, as always, is with the class constructor:

```
GUI_Interface::GUI_Interface(const std::string& l_name,
  GUI_Manager* l_guiManager)
  : GUI_Element(l_name, GUI_ElementType::Window, this),
  m_parent(nullptr), m_guiManager(l_guiManager), m_movable(false),
  m_beingMoved(false), m_showTitleBar(false), m_focused(false),
  m_scrollHorizontal(0),m_scrollVertical(0),m_contentRedraw(true),
  m_controlRedraw(true)
{
  m_backdropTexture = new sf::RenderTexture();
  m_contentTexture = new sf::RenderTexture();
  m_controlTexture = new sf::RenderTexture();
}
```

Quite a lot of data members are initialized through the initializer list here. Firstly, the parent class `GUI_Element` needs to know the name, type, and owner of the interface. One of the `GUI_Interface` arguments is its name, which gets passed to the `GUI_Element` constructor. The type is, of course, set to `Window`, and the `this` keyword is passed in as the owner of the interface. Additionally, the parent of the interface is initialized to its default value `nullptr` and a pointer to the `GUI_Manager` class is stored inside the `m_guiManager` data member.

After the data member initialization, we enter the constructor's body, in which three `sf::RenderTexture` objects are allocated dynamically. These are the textures that are used to render the background, content, and control layers of an interface.

Next, let's take a look at freeing up all of these resources in the destructor:

```
GUI_Interface::~GUI_Interface(){
  delete m_backdropTexture;
  delete m_contentTexture;
  delete m_controlTexture;
  for (auto &itr : m_elements){
    delete itr.second;
  }
}
```

The three texture instances, of course, have to be deleted, as well as every single element that still resides in the element container at the time of destruction. Afterwards, the element container is cleared.

Setting the position of an interface is slightly more complex, so let's take a look:

```
void GUI_Interface::SetPosition(const sf::Vector2f& l_pos){
    GUI_Element::SetPosition(l_pos);
    m_backdrop.setPosition(l_pos);
    m_content.setPosition(l_pos);
    m_control.setPosition(l_pos);
    m_titleBar.setPosition(m_position.x,
        m_position.y - m_titleBar.getSize().y);
    m_visual.m_text.setPosition(m_titleBar.getPosition()
        + m_style[m_state].m_textPadding);
}
```

Firstly, the `SetPosition` method of the parent class is invoked in order to adjust the actual position. There is no need to fix what isn't broken. Next, the three sprites that represent the background, content, and control layers have their positions adjusted as well. Lastly, you set up the title bar. The solid background shape's position is set to be right above the interface, while the text of the visual component is used as a title and adjusted to take the same position as the title bar background, except with text padding included.

Empty windows aren't very useful or entertaining, so let's provide a way in which elements can be added to them:

```
bool GUI_Interface::AddElement(const GUI_ElementType& l_type,
    const std::string& l_name)
{
    if (m_elements.find(l_name) != m_elements.end()){return false;}
    GUI_Element* element = nullptr;
    element = m_guiManager->CreateElement(l_type, this);
    if (!element){ return false; }
    element->SetName(l_name);
    element->SetOwner(this);
    m_elements.emplace(l_name, element);
    m_contentRedraw = true;
    m_controlRedraw = true;
    return true;
}
```

It is important to avoid name clashes so check the name provided as the second argument against the element container in order to prevent duplicates. If none are found, a `CreateElement` method of the `GUI_Manager` class is used to create an element of the relevant type on the heap and return its memory address. After verifying that it has indeed been created, the element's name and owner properties are set before it gets inserted into the element container. The interface then sets two flags to re-draw the content and control layers.

Any interface needs to have a way to provide access to its elements. That's where the GetElement method comes in:

```
GUI_Element* GUI_Interface::GetElement(const std::string& l_name)
const{
    auto itr = m_elements.find(l_name);
    return(itr != m_elements.end() ? itr->second : nullptr);
}
```

It simply locates the element in the std::unordered_map using its find method and returns it. If the element isn't found, nullptr is returned instead. Easy.

Next, we need to have a way to remove elements from interfaces:

```
bool GUI_Interface::RemoveElement(const std::string& l_name){
    auto itr = m_elements.find(l_name);
    if (itr == m_elements.end()){ return false; }
    delete itr->second;
    m_elements.erase(itr);
    m_contentRedraw = true;
    m_controlRedraw = true;
    AdjustContentSize();
    return true;
}
```

Following the same example as the GetElement method, the element is first located inside the container. The dynamic memory is then de-allocated by using the delete operator and the element itself is removed from the container. The interface is marked to re-draw its content and control layers and the AdjustContentSize method is invoked to re-size the content texture, if needed.

We need to override the original IsInside method because interfaces occupy additional space due to their title bars, as shown here:

```
bool GUI_Interface::IsInside(const sf::Vector2f& l_point) const{
    if (GUI_Element::IsInside(l_point)){ return true; }
    return m_titleBar.getGlobalBounds().contains(l_point);
}
```

The parent class method is invoked first to determine if l_point is inside the space an interface is occupying. If not, the result of the title bar bounding box's contains method is returned to determine if l_point is inside that.

Next is shown the de-serialization portion of the code:

```
void GUI_Interface::ReadIn(std::stringstream& l_stream){
    std::string movableState;
    std::string titleShow;
    std::string title;
    l_stream >> m_elementPadding.x >> m_elementPadding.y
       >> movableState >> titleShow;
    Utils::ReadQuotedString(l_stream, title);
    m_visual.m_text.setString(title);
    if (movableState == "Movable"){ m_movable = true; }
    if (titleShow == "Title"){ m_showTitleBar = true; }
}
```

All interfaces first read in the element padding *x* and *y* values, as well as the state and title parameters. It then uses the `ReadQuotedText` utility function which we defined earlier to read in the actual title of the interface. Based on the strings read in, it then sets the `m_movable` and `m_showTitleBar` flags to reflect those values.

Now comes the fun part. Let's define what happens when an interface is clicked:

```
void GUI_Interface::OnClick(const sf::Vector2f& l_mousePos){
  DefocusTextfields();
  if (m_titleBar.getGlobalBounds().contains(l_mousePos) &&
    m_movable && m_showTitleBar)
  {
    m_beingMoved = true;
  } else {
    GUI_Event event;
    event.m_type = GUI_EventType::Click;
    event.m_interface = m_name.c_str();
    event.m_element = "";
    event.m_clickCoords.x = l_mousePos.x;
    event.m_clickCoords.y = l_mousePos.y;
    m_guiManager->AddEvent(event);
    for (auto &itr : m_elements){
      if (!itr.second->IsInside(l_mousePos)){ continue; }
      itr.second->OnClick(l_mousePos);
      event.m_element = itr.second->m_name.c_str();
      m_guiManager->AddEvent(event);
    }
    SetState(GUI_ElementState::Clicked);
  }
}
```

Firstly, we invoke one of the private helper methods responsible for removing focus from all of the Textfield GUI elements. This will be covered in more depth later. Another problem is dragging, when a click is detected in an interface. If the mouse position is in the title bar area and the interface itself is movable, we set the m_beingMoved flag to true to indicate interface dragging.

In a case of it just being a regular click anywhere else within the interface boundaries, we first set up an event that is going to be dispatched, indicating that a click has happened. The type is set to Click, the interface name is copied as a *c string*, and the mouse coordinates are also set up. The AddEvent method of the GUI_Manager class is invoked with our newly created event as an argument. This first event indicates that a click happened within the interface itself and not in any particular element.

That is quickly followed by a loop that iterates over every single element in the interface. Their IsInside method is called to determine whether the click that took place was also within any of the elements. If so, the OnClick method of that particular element is invoked with the mouse position passed in as an argument. The same event that was set up before the loop is then slightly modified to contain the name of the element and is fired again, indicating that the click also affects it. The interface's state is then changed to CLICKED. The result of this is quite appealing to the eye:

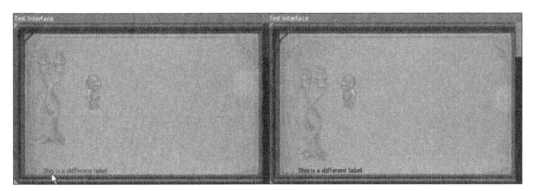

Next, let's take a look at the opposite side of clicking—the OnRelease method:

```
void GUI_Interface::OnRelease(){
  GUI_Event event;
  event.m_type = GUI_EventType::Release;
  event.m_interface = m_name.c_str();
  event.m_element = "";
  m_guiManager->AddEvent(event);
  for (auto &itr : m_elements){
    if (itr.second->GetState() != GUI_ElementState::Clicked)
    {
```

```
            continue;
        }
        itr.second->OnRelease();
        event.m_element = itr.second->m_name.c_str();
        m_guiManager->AddEvent(event);
    }
    SetState(GUI_ElementState::Neutral);
}
```

Just like before, an event is set up and fired, indicating that a release happened within this specific interface. Every element is then iterated over and their states are checked. If the element is in a `Clicked` state, its `OnRelease` method is called and another event is fired, indicating the release of the left mouse button within that element. The state of the interface is then set to `Neutral`.

An interface also needs to deal with text being entered:

```
void GUI_Interface::OnTextEntered(const char& l_char){
    for (auto &itr : m_elements){
        if (itr.second->GetType() != GUI_ElementType::Textfield){
            continue;
        }
        if (itr.second->GetState() != GUI_ElementState::Clicked){
            continue;
        }
        if (l_char == 8){
            // Backspace.
            const auto& text = itr.second->GetText();
            itr.second->SetText(text.substr(0, text.length() -1));
            return;
        }
        if (l_char < 32 || l_char > 126){ return; }
        std::string text = itr.second->GetText();
        text.push_back(l_char);
        itr.second->SetText(text);
        return;
    }
}
```

This method is going to be invoked whenever an SFML event `sf::Event::TextEntered` is received by our window. Each element is iterated over until we find one that is of the type `Textfield` and is currently in a `Clicked` state. The backspace key being pressed is handled by having the last character of our element's text attribute trimmed. Note that we're returning from the method in multiple places in order to avoid several `Textfield` elements receiving the same text that is being entered.

Lastly, we need to check the boundaries of the character value that has been received. Any characters below ID `32` or above `126` are reserved for other purposes and we're not interested in those. If a regular letter or number is typed in, we want to update our text attribute by adding that character to it.

 The full table of ASCII characters can be found here: `http://www.asciitable.com/`

Since we're on the subject of handling text field elements, let's take a look at a method that we used before when handling a `Click` event:

```
void GUI_Interface::DefocusTextfields(){
  GUI_Event event;
  event.m_type = GUI_EventType::Release;
  event.m_interface = m_name.c_str();
  event.m_element = "";
  for (auto &itr : m_elements){
    if (itr.second->GetType() != GUI_ElementType::Textfield){
      continue;
    }
    itr.second->SetState(GUI_ElementState::Neutral);
    event.m_element = itr.second->m_name.c_str();
    m_guiManager->AddEvent(event);
  }
}
```

When handling text fields, it's important to bear in mind that they lose focus every time a mouse is left-clicked. If that wasn't so, we would end up with text entered across multiple textboxes, and that is no good. Making a text field lose focus is as simple as constructing a `Release` event and sending it to every `Textfield` element that an interface possesses.

The next two methods are grouped together due to their similarities:

```
void GUI_Interface::OnHover(const sf::Vector2f& l_mousePos){
  GUI_Event event;
  event.m_type = GUI_EventType::Hover;
  event.m_interface = m_name.c_str();
  event.m_element = "";
  event.m_clickCoords.x = l_mousePos.x;
  event.m_clickCoords.y = l_mousePos.y;
  m_guiManager->AddEvent(event);
```

```
      SetState(GUI_ElementState::Focused);
  }
  void GUI_Interface::OnLeave(){
    GUI_Event event;
    event.m_type = GUI_EventType::Leave;
    event.m_interface = m_name.c_str();
    event.m_element = "";
    m_guiManager->AddEvent(event);

    SetState(GUI_ElementState::Neutral);
  }
```

An event is constructed including the mouse coordinates when the mouse hovers over an interface, as opposed to when the mouse leaves the interface area as in the `OnLeave` method. `OnHover` and `OnLeave` are only called once per event as they do not deal with elements. That job is left to the `Update` method:

```
  void GUI_Interface::Update(float l_dT){
    sf::Vector2f mousePos = sf::Vector2f(
      m_guiManager->GetContext()->m_eventManager->GetMousePos(
      m_guiManager->GetContext()->m_wind->GetRenderWindow()));

    if (m_beingMoved && m_moveMouseLast != mousePos){
      sf::Vector2f difference = mousePos - m_moveMouseLast;
      m_moveMouseLast = mousePos;
      sf::Vector2f newPosition = m_position + difference;
      SetPosition(newPosition);
    }
    ...
  }
```

After the mouse position is obtained, the `m_beingMoved` flag is checked to determine whether or not an interface is currently being dragged. If it is, and the saved position of the mouse is different to where the mouse is currently located, that difference is calculated and the interface's location is adjusted based on it. With that out of the way, let's take a look at the omitted chunk of code:

```
  for (auto &itr : m_elements){
    if (itr.second->NeedsRedraw()){
      if (itr.second->IsControl()){ m_controlRedraw = true; }
      else { m_contentRedraw = true; }
    }
    if (!itr.second->IsActive()){ continue; }
    itr.second->Update(l_dT);
    if (m_beingMoved){ continue; }
```

```
    GUI_Event event;
    event.m_interface = m_name.c_str();
    event.m_element = itr.second->m_name.c_str();
    event.m_clickCoords.x = mousePos.x;
    event.m_clickCoords.y = mousePos.y;
    if (IsInside(mousePos) && itr.second->IsInside(mousePos)
      && !m_titleBar.getGlobalBounds().contains(mousePos))
    {
      if (itr.second->GetState() != GUI_ElementState::Neutral){
        continue;
      }
      itr.second->OnHover(mousePos);
      event.m_type = GUI_EventType::Hover;
    } else if (itr.second->GetState() == GUI_ElementState::Focused){
      itr.second->OnLeave();
      event.m_type = GUI_EventType::Leave;
    }
    m_guiManager->AddEvent(event);
  }
```

We begin by checking if the current element needs to be re-drawn. The relevant flag for re-drawing the entire interface is set to `true` if one is encountered, while taking into account whether it's a control element or not.

When iterating over the list of all elements, their active status is checked. If an element is active, it gets updated. If the interface currently isn't being moved and the mouse is inside both the interface and the element, but not the title bar, the element's current state is checked. A `Hover` event needs to be dispatched and the `OnHover` method needs to be called if the element's current state is `Neutral`. However, if the mouse is not over the element, or the current interface's state is `Focused`, a `Leave` event is created and submitted, along with the `OnLeave` method being invoked.

Now, let's bring all of this hard work to the screen and render the interface:

```
  void GUI_Interface::Draw(sf::RenderTarget* l_target){
    l_target->draw(m_backdrop);
    l_target->draw(m_content);
    l_target->draw(m_control);

    if (!m_showTitleBar){ return; }
    l_target->draw(m_titleBar);
    l_target->draw(m_visual.m_text);
  }
```

This is quite simple, thanks to our design involving three different render textures. In order to draw an interface successfully, the sprites for the background, content, and control layers have to be drawn in that specific order. If the `m_showTitleBar` flag is set to `true`, the title background must also be drawn along with the text.

Whereas the `Update` method does most of the work, moving interfaces requires a bit more preparation. Let's begin by defining two helper methods for movement, starting with the one used to initiate the process:

```
void GUI_Interface::BeginMoving(){
  if (!m_showTitleBar || !m_movable){ return; }
  m_beingMoved = true;
  SharedContext* context = m_guiManager->GetContext();
  m_moveMouseLast = sf::Vector2f(context->m_eventManager->
    GetMousePos(context->m_wind->GetRenderWindow()));
}
```

If the conditions to move an interface are met, this method is invoked in order to save the mouse position at the point where dragging began.

We also have a simple line of code to stop interface movement:

```
void GUI_Interface::StopMoving(){ m_beingMoved = false; }
```

Since interfaces are quite different from normal GUI elements, they have to define their own way of obtaining their global position, as shown here:

```
sf::Vector2f GUI_Interface::GetGlobalPosition() const{
    sf::Vector2f pos = m_position;
    GUI_Interface* i = m_parent;
    while (i){
        pos += i->GetPosition();
        i = i->m_parent;
    }
    return pos;
}
```

When it obtains its actual position, it needs to follow through the chain of parent interfaces and sum all of their positions. A `while` loop serves as a nice way of doing this; the final position is returned when it concludes.

The style application of an interface also differs from the usual element types. Let's take a look:

```
void GUI_Interface::ApplyStyle(){
    GUI_Element::ApplyStyle(); // Call base method.
    m_visual.m_backgroundSolid.setPosition(0.f,0.f);
```

```
        m_visual.m_backgroundImage.setPosition(0.f,0.f);
        m_titleBar.setSize(sf::Vector2f(
            m_style[m_state].m_size.x, 16.f));
        m_titleBar.setPosition(m_position.x,
            m_position.y - m_titleBar.getSize().y);
        m_titleBar.setFillColor(m_style[m_state].m_elementColor);
        m_visual.m_text.setPosition(m_titleBar.getPosition()
          + m_style[m_state].m_textPadding);
        m_visual.m_glyph.setPosition(m_titleBar.getPosition()
          + m_style[m_state].m_glyphPadding);
    }
```

The `ApplyStyle` method is invoked first because the parent class does a great job of setting up most of the visual components correctly. The background elements then need to be changed to have positions with absolute zero values because interfaces render these drawables to a texture and not to a screen. Regardless of the position of the interface, the positions of these elements will not change.

Next, the title bar background is set up to match the size of the interface on the x axis and should have a height of 16 pixels on the y axis. This hardcoded value can be tweaked at any time. Its position is then set to be right above the interface. The fill color of the title background is defined by the element color property of its style.

The last four lines set up the position of the title bar text and glyph. The position of the title bar background is summed together with the relevant padding to obtain the final position of these two attributes.

Rendering time! Let's draw all of these visuals onto their respective textures, starting with the background layer:

```
void GUI_Interface::Redraw(){
  if (m_backdropTexture->getSize().x!=m_style[m_state].m_size.x ||
    m_backdropTexture->getSize().y != m_style[m_state].m_size.y)
  {
    m_backdropTexture->create(m_style[m_state].m_size.x,
      m_style[m_state].m_size.y);
  }
  m_backdropTexture->clear(sf::Color(0, 0, 0, 0));
  ApplyStyle();
  m_backdropTexture->draw(m_visual.m_backgroundSolid);

  if (m_style[m_state].m_backgroundImage != ""){
    m_backdropTexture->draw(m_visual.m_backgroundImage);
  }
```

```
    m_backdropTexture->display();
    m_backdrop.setTexture(m_backdropTexture->getTexture());
    m_backdrop.setTextureRect(sf::IntRect(0, 0,
      m_style[m_state].m_size.x, m_style[m_state].m_size.y));
    SetRedraw(false);
}
```

Firstly, a check is made in order to be sure that the background texture is the same size as the current style dictates. If it isn't, the texture is recreated with the correct size.

The next line is extremely important for good looking results. At first glance, it simply clears the texture to the color black. If you look closely, however, you will notice that it has four arguments instead of three. The last argument is the **alpha channel**, or the transparency value for the color. The texture cleared to black appears as a large black square, and that's not what we want. Instead, we want it to be completely empty before drawing elements to it, which is what the alpha value of *0* will do.

Next, the `ApplyStyle` method is invoked in order to adjust the visual parts of the interface to match the current style. The background solid and the background image are then drawn onto the background texture. The texture's `display` method *must* be called in order to show all of the changes made to it, just like the render window.

Lastly, the background sprite is bound to the background texture and its visible area is cropped to the interface size in order to prevent overflow. The redraw flag is set to `false` to indicate that this process is complete.

A very similar process also needs to occur for the content layer:

```
void GUI_Interface::RedrawContent(){
  if (m_contentTexture->getSize().x != m_contentSize.x ||
    m_contentTexture->getSize().y != m_contentSize.y)
  {
    m_contentTexture->create(m_contentSize.x, m_contentSize.y);
  }

  m_contentTexture->clear(sf::Color(0, 0, 0, 0));

  for (auto &itr : m_elements){
    GUI_Element* element = itr.second;
    if (!element->IsActive() || element->IsControl()){ continue; }
    element->ApplyStyle();
    element->Draw(m_contentTexture);
    element->SetRedraw(false);
```

```
    }

    m_contentTexture->display();
    m_content.setTexture(m_contentTexture->getTexture());

    m_content.setTextureRect(sf::IntRect(
        m_scrollHorizontal, m_scrollVertical,
        m_style[m_state].m_size.x, m_style[m_state].m_size.y));
    m_contentRedraw = false;
}
```

The content texture is checked for dimensions. The only difference here is that we're keeping a manual track of its size in the m_contentSize float vector, which will be covered later.

After the texture is cleared, we iterate over all of the elements inside the interface and check whether they are active or a control element. If all of these conditions are satisfied, the element's style is applied and it is rendered onto the content texture, which gets passed in as the argument of the Draw method. Its re-draw flag is then set to false.

After displaying the texture and binding it to a relevant sprite, it too gets cropped, except that, this time, we use the m_scrollHorizontal and m_scrollVertical data members as the first two arguments in order to account for scrolling. Consider the following illustration:

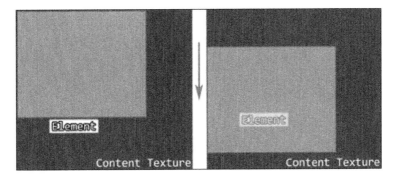

Scrolling an interface means moving the cropped rectangle across the content texture. The m_contentRedraw flag then gets set to false to signify that the re-draw process has concluded. It leaves us with a result that looks like this:

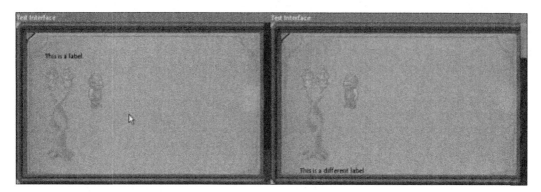

The final layer of the interface follows an almost identical path:

```
void GUI_Interface::RedrawControls(){
  if (m_controlTexture->getSize().x!=m_style[m_state].m_size.x ||
    m_controlTexture->getSize().y != m_style[m_state].m_size.y)
  {
    m_controlTexture->create(m_style[m_state].m_size.x,
      m_style[m_state].m_size.y);
  }
  m_controlTexture->clear(sf::Color(0, 0, 0, 0));

  for (auto &itr : m_elements){
    GUI_Element* element = itr.second;
    if (!element->IsActive() || !element->IsControl()){ continue; }
    element->ApplyStyle();
    element->Draw(m_controlTexture);
    element->SetRedraw(false);
  }

  m_controlTexture->display();
  m_control.setTexture(m_controlTexture->getTexture());
  m_control.setTextureRect(sf::IntRect(0, 0,
    m_style[m_state].m_size.x, m_style[m_state].m_size.y));
  m_controlRedraw = false;
}
```

The main difference here is that the texture is aiming to match the size of the current style, just like the background layer. Only the control elements are drawn this time.

The subject of interface scrolling keeps popping up, so let's take a look at how it is done:

```
void GUI_Interface::UpdateScrollHorizontal(
unsigned int l_percent)
{
  if (l_percent > 100){ return; }
  m_scrollHorizontal = ((m_contentSize.x - GetSize().x) / 100) *
    l_percent;
  sf::IntRect rect = m_content.getTextureRect();
  m_content.setTextureRect(sf::IntRect(
    m_scrollHorizontal, m_scrollVertical,rect.width,rect.height));
}

void GUI_Interface::UpdateScrollVertical(unsigned int l_percent){
  if (l_percent > 100){ return; }
  m_scrollVertical = ((m_contentSize.y - GetSize().y) / 100) *
    l_percent;
  sf::IntRect rect = m_content.getTextureRect();
  m_content.setTextureRect(sf::IntRect(
    m_scrollHorizontal, m_scrollVertical,rect.width,rect.height));
}
```

Both the horizontal and vertical adjustment methods take in a percentage value that tells the interface how much it should be scrolled. The actual amount of pixels an interface should be offset by is calculated by first dividing the difference of its content size on the relevant axis and the size of the interface itself by a hundred, and multiplying the result by the percentage argument. The texture rectangle is then obtained to maintain the proper width and height of the content area, which is then re-set with the scroll values as the first two arguments. This effectively simulates the scroll sensation of an interface.

Adding, removing, or manipulating different elements inside an interface may alter its size. Here's a method to solve those problems:

```
void GUI_Interface::AdjustContentSize(
  const GUI_Element* l_reference)
{
  if (l_reference){
    sf::Vector2f bottomRight =
      l_reference->GetPosition() + l_reference->GetSize();
    if (bottomRight.x > m_contentSize.x){
      m_contentSize.x = bottomRight.x;
      m_controlRedraw = true;
    }
```

```
        if (bottomRight.y > m_contentSize.y){
          m_contentSize.y = bottomRight.y;
          m_controlRedraw = true;
        }
        return;
      }

    sf::Vector2f farthest = GetSize();

    for (auto &itr : m_elements){
      GUI_Element* element = itr.second;
      if (!element->IsActive() || element->IsControl()){ continue; }
      sf::Vector2f bottomRight =
        element->GetPosition() + element->GetSize();
      if (bottomRight.x > farthest.x){
        farthest.x = bottomRight.x;
        m_controlRedraw = true;
      }
      if (bottomRight.y > farthest.y){
        farthest.y = bottomRight.y;
        m_controlRedraw = true;
      }
    }
    SetContentSize(farthest);
  }
```

Before examining it in depth, I can show you that, inside the class definition, this method looks like this:

```
void AdjustContentSize(const GUI_Element* l_reference = nullptr);
```

Its only argument has a default value of `nullptr`, which enables the method to detect size changes with or without a reference element.

If an element is provided as an argument, which usually happens when one is added to an interface, its bottom-right corner coordinates are calculated using its position and size. If these coordinates are somewhere outside of the content size boundaries, the content size is adjusted to be larger and the control redraw flag is set to `true` because the physical dimensions of the sliders will be changing. The method then returns in order to prevent the rest of the logic from being executed.

Without a reference element, a float vector is set up to keep track of the farthest point within the interface texture, the original value of which is the interface size. Every active non-control element is then iterated over and checked to see if it exceeds the furthest point in the texture, which simply gets overwritten on a relevant axis. If an element is found that pokes outside of these boundaries, its bottom-right corner position is stored and the control layer is marked for re-drawing. The content size itself is set to the farthest corner of the interface after all of the elements have been checked.

This final code snippet concludes the interface class.

Summary

Just as a book without binding is simply a stack of papers, the code we've written doesn't become what it needs to be unless it is properly incorporated and managed. The groundwork we've laid down in this chapter will aid us greatly in implementing a fully functional GUI system but it only represents all the pieces being laid out.

So far, we have covered the basic design of GUI elements and windows, as well as implementing quite a few useful features that different types of elements can use. While that is a lot of code, we're not quite done yet. In the next chapter, we will be bringing all of the pieces we worked on together, as well as creating actual GUI elements. See you there!

11
Don't Touch the Red Button!
– Implementing the GUI

We covered the fundamentals and created the building blocks necessary for graphical user interface assembly in the course of the last chapter. Although that might seem like lots of code, a lot more goes into making it tick. Proper management of interfaces, good support from the rest of the code base, and user-friendly semantics of the GUI system itself are all paramount. Let's finish our goal set in *Chapter 10, Can I Click This? – GUI Fundamentals*, and finally provide our users with a means of interfacing.

In this chapter, we will cover the following topics:

- Management of interfaces and their events
- Expansion of the event manager class for additional GUI support
- Creation of our first element type
- Integration and use of our GUI system

With all the pieces in place, let's bring our interfaces to life!

The GUI manager

The puppet master in the background, in charge of the entire show in this case, has to be the `GUI_Manager` class. It is responsible for storing all the interfaces in the application as well as maintaining their states. All mouse input processing originates from this class and is passed down the ownership tree. Let's begin by getting some type definitions out of the way:

```
using GUI_Interfaces = std::unordered_map<std::string,
  GUI_Interface*>;
using GUI_Container = std::unordered_map<StateType,
```

```
    GUI_Interfaces>;
using GUI_Events = std::unordered_map<StateType,
  std::vector<GUI_Event>>;
using GUI_Factory = std::unordered_map<GUI_ElementType,
  std::function<GUI_Element*(GUI_Interface*)>>;
using GUI_ElemTypes = std::unordered_map<std::string,
  GUI_ElementType>;
```

We will use the `std::unordered_map` data structure that indexes them by name to store the interface data. The interface data containers also need to be grouped by game states, which is what the next type definition is for. Similarly, GUI events need to be indexed by their relevant game state. The events themselves are stored in a `std::vector`.

Additionally, since we will be creating elements in a factory-like fashion, much like we did before, a factory type definition is created. The main difference here is that the `lambda` functions we'll be storing need to take in a pointer to the owner interface in order to be constructed correctly.

Lastly, we're going to be mapping element type strings to actual enumeration values for the same. Once again, the `std::unordered_map` type comes to the rescue.

Now, here is the class definition itself:

```
struct SharedContext; // Forward declaration.
class GUI_Manager{
  friend class GUI_Interface;
public:
  GUI_Manager(EventManager* l_evMgr, SharedContext* l_context);
  ~GUI_Manager();
  ...
  template<class T>
  void RegisterElement(const GUI_ElementType& l_id){
    m_factory[l_id] = [](GUI_Interface* l_owner) -> GUI_Element*
    { return new T("",l_owner); };
  }
private:
  GUI_Element* CreateElement(const GUI_ElementType& l_id,
    GUI_Interface* l_owner);
  GUI_ElementType StringToType(const std::string& l_string);
  bool LoadStyle(const std::string& l_file,
    GUI_Element* l_element);

  GUI_Container m_interfaces;
  GUI_Events m_events;
```

```
        SharedContext* m_context;
        StateType m_currentState;
        GUI_Factory m_factory;
        GUI_ElemTypes m_elemTypes;
    };
```

Right off the bat, we can tell that the factory method for elements is going to be used due to the presence of a `RegisterElement` method. It stores a `lambda` function with an owner interface pointer as its sole argument, which returns a `GUI_Element` type with a blank name, constructed from a given type denoted by the `l_id` argument. Its private method friend, `CreateElement`, will use the stored `lambda` functions and return pointers to newly created memory.

One last thing to note before diving into the implementation of this class is the existence of a `LoadStyle` method that takes in a `GUI_Element` type. The manager class is responsible for de-serializing style files and properly setting up elements based on them to avoid cluttering up the element and interface classes.

Implementing the GUI manager

With the class header out of the way, we can dive right into implementing our GUI manager. The constructor of the `GUI_Manager` class is defined like this:

```
GUI_Manager::GUI_Manager(EventManager* l_evMgr,
    SharedContext* l_shared): m_eventMgr(l_evMgr),
    m_context(l_shared), m_currentState(StateType(0))
{
    RegisterElement<GUI_Label>(GUI_ElementType::Label);
    RegisterElement<GUI_Scrollbar>(GUI_ElementType::Scrollbar);
    RegisterElement<GUI_Textfield>(GUI_ElementType::Textfield);
    m_elemTypes.emplace("Label", GUI_ElementType::Label);
    m_elemTypes.emplace("Button", GUI_ElementType::Button);
    m_elemTypes.emplace("Scrollbar", GUI_ElementType::Scrollbar);
    m_elemTypes.emplace("TextField", GUI_ElementType::Textfield);
    m_elemTypes.emplace("Interface", GUI_ElementType::Window);

    m_eventMgr->AddCallback(StateType(0),
        "Mouse_Left", &GUI_Manager::HandleClick, this);
    m_eventMgr->AddCallback(StateType(0),
        "Mouse_Left_Release", &GUI_Manager::HandleRelease, this);
    m_eventMgr->AddCallback(StateType(0),
        "Text_Entered", &GUI_Manager::HandleTextEntered, this);
}
```

It requires a pointer to the event manager and shared context structures as arguments and sets them up through the initializer list, along with a default value for the current state. Inside the body, we can see that this class first registers three element types that we're going to be working with. It also populates the element type map, which will be used for checks further down the line. Finally, it registers three callbacks: two for the left mouse button being pressed and released and one for text being entered. Note that these callbacks are registered to be called regardless of the state the application is in.

```
GUI_Manager::~GUI_Manager(){
  m_eventMgr->RemoveCallback(StateType(0), "Mouse_Left");
  m_eventMgr->RemoveCallback(StateType(0), "Mouse_Left_Release");
  m_eventMgr->RemoveCallback(StateType(0), "Text_Entered");

  for (auto &itr : m_interfaces){
    for (auto &itr2 : itr.second){
      delete itr2.second;
    }
  }
}
```

The destructor removes all of the callbacks registered in the constructor and iterates over every single interface for proper de-allocation of dynamically allocated memory. The interface and event containers are then cleared.

Let's take a look at how an interface is added to the GUI manager:

```
bool GUI_Manager::AddInterface(const StateType& l_state,
  const std::string& l_name)
{
  auto s = m_interfaces.emplace(l_state, GUI_Interfaces()).first;
  GUI_Interface* temp = new GUI_Interface(l_name, this);
  if (s->second.emplace(l_name, temp).second){ return true; }
  delete temp;
  return false;
}
```

Dynamic memory for an interface is allocated and an attempt to insert it is made when a valid application state and an unused interface name is provided. Any issues when inserting are caught by the return value of the `emplace` method, which gets stored in the `i` variable. If it fails, the memory is de-allocated and `false` is returned to signify failure. Otherwise, `true` is returned.

Obtaining an interface is as simple as it gets:

```
GUI_Interface* GUI_Manager::GetInterface(const StateType& l_state,
  const std::string& l_name)
{
  auto s = m_interfaces.find(l_state);
  if (s == m_interfaces.end()){ return nullptr; }
  auto i = s->second.find(l_name);
  return (i != s->second.end() ? i->second : nullptr);
}
```

If a state provided as an argument is found, and an interface with the name provided is also located, it gets returned. Failure to find either a valid state or the correct interface is represented by a return value of `nullptr`.

Removing an interface is achieved by manipulating the container structure:

```
bool GUI_Manager::RemoveInterface(const StateType& l_state,
  const std::string& l_name)
{
  auto s = m_interfaces.find(l_state);
  if (s == m_interfaces.end()){ return false; }
  auto i = s->second.find(l_name);
  if (i == s->second.end()){ return false; }
  delete i->second;
  return s->second.erase(l_name);
}
```

Note that the `delete` keyword appears if both the state and the interface are found. Sometimes, it's very easy to forget the de-allocation of no longer used memory on the heap, which results in memory leaks.

Since the GUI manager needs to keep track of the current application state, the following method is necessary:

```
void GUI_Manager::SetCurrentState(const StateType& l_state){
  if (m_currentState == l_state){ return; }
  HandleRelease(nullptr);
  m_currentState = l_state;
}
```

In addition to changing the current state data member, it also invokes the `HandleRelease` method to prevent sticky interface and element states. If an element is clicked and the state suddenly changes, that same element will remain in the `CLICKED` state until it is hovered over unless `HandleRelease` is called.

Now, let's handle the mouse input to provide interaction with our interfaces:

```cpp
void GUI_Manager::HandleClick(EventDetails* l_details){
  auto state = m_interfaces.find(m_currentState);
  if (state == m_interfaces.end()){ return; }
  sf::Vector2i mousePos = m_eventMgr->
    GetMousePos(m_context->m_wind->GetRenderWindow());
  for (auto itr = state->second.rbegin();
    itr != state->second.rend(); ++itr)
  {
    if (!itr->second->IsInside(sf::Vector2f(mousePos))){continue;}
    if (!itr->second->IsActive()){ return; }
    itr->second->OnClick(sf::Vector2f(mousePos));
    itr->second->Focus();
    if (itr->second->IsBeingMoved()){itr->second->BeginMoving();}
    return;
  }
}
```

This method, just like its `HandleRelease` brother, takes in a single argument of the type `EventDetails`. For now, simply ignore that as it does not affect `GUI_Manager` at all and will be dealt later in this chapter.

Firstly, it obtains the current mouse position relative to the window. Next, an iterator to the interface container is obtained and checked for validity. Every interface that belongs to the current state is then iterated over in reverse order, which gives newly added interfaces priority. If it is active and the mouse position falls within its boundaries, its `OnClick` method is invoked, with the mouse position passed in as the argument. The interface's `m_beingMoved` flag is then checked because the click might've been within the boundaries of its title bar. If so, the `BeginMoving` method is called to complete the drag operation. At this point, we simply return from the method in order to prevent a left click from affecting more than one interface at a time.

Handling the left mouse button release follows the same convention:

```cpp
void GUI_Manager::HandleRelease(EventDetails* l_details){
  auto state = m_interfaces.find(m_currentState);
  if (state == m_interfaces.end()){ return; }
  for (auto &itr : state->second){
    GUI_Interface* i = itr.second;
```

```
    if (!i->IsActive()){ continue; }
    if (i->GetState() == GUI_ElementState::Clicked)
    {
      i->OnRelease();
    }
    if (i->IsBeingMoved()){ i->StopMoving(); }
  }
}
```

The only difference here is that every interface which is in a `Clicked` state has its `OnRelease` method called, as well as the `StopMoving` method if it is in a state of being dragged.

Lastly, let's not forget about our text field elements as they need to be notified whenever some text is entered:

```
void GUI_Manager::HandleTextEntered(EventDetails* l_details){
  auto state = m_interfaces.find(m_currentState);
  if (state == m_interfaces.end()){ return; }
  for (auto &itr : state->second){
    if (!itr.second->IsActive()){ continue; }
    if (!itr.second->IsFocused()){ continue; }
    itr.second->OnTextEntered(l_details->m_textEntered);
    return;
  }
}
```

This is a quite simple snippet of code. Whenever text is entered, we attempt to find an active and focused element. Once we find one, its `OnTextEntered` method is invoked with the text information passed in as the argument.

Adding GUI events is as simple as pushing them back onto a `std::vector` data structure:

```
void GUI_Manager::AddEvent(GUI_Event l_event){
    m_events[m_currentState].push_back(l_event);
}
```

In order to properly handle these events, we must have a way to obtain them:

```
bool GUI_Manager::PollEvent(GUI_Event& l_event){
  if (m_events[m_currentState].empty()){ return false; }
  l_event = m_events[m_currentState].back();
  m_events[m_currentState].pop_back();
  return true;
}
```

This is similar to the way SFML handles events, in that it takes in a reference to a `GUI_Event` data type and overwrites it with the last event in the event vector, right before popping it. It also returns a Boolean value to provide an easy way for it to be used in a `while` loop.

Next, let's work on updating the interfaces:

```
void GUI_Manager::Update(float l_dT){
  sf::Vector2i mousePos = m_eventMgr->
    GetMousePos(m_context->m_wind->GetRenderWindow());

  auto state = m_interfaces.find(m_currentState);
  if (state == m_interfaces.end()){ return; }
  for (auto itr = state->second.rbegin();
    itr != state->second.rend(); ++itr)
  {
    GUI_Interface* i = itr->second;
    if (!i->IsActive()){ continue; }
    i->Update(l_dT);
    if (i->IsBeingMoved()){ continue; }
    if (i->IsInside(sf::Vector2f(mousePos)))
    {
      if (i->GetState() == GUI_ElementState::Neutral){
        i->OnHover(sf::Vector2f(mousePos));
      }
      return;
    } else if (i->GetState() == GUI_ElementState::Focused){
      i->OnLeave();
    }
  }
}
```

After the current mouse position is obtained, every interface that belongs to the current application state is iterated over. If the interface is currently active, it gets updated. The `Hover` and `Leave` events are only considered if the interface in question is not currently being dragged, as we did with the smaller GUI elements inside interfaces.

Now it's time to draw all of these interfaces onto the screen:

```
void GUI_Manager::Render(sf::RenderWindow* l_wind){
  auto state = m_interfaces.find(m_currentState);
  if (state == m_interfaces.end()){ return; }
  for (auto &itr : state->second){
    GUI_Interface* i = itr.second;
```

```
        if (!i->IsActive()){ continue; }
        if (i->NeedsRedraw()){ i->Redraw(); }
        if (i->NeedsContentRedraw()){ i->RedrawContent(); }
        if (i->NeedsControlRedraw()){ i->RedrawControls(); }
        i->Draw(l_wind);
    }
}
```

Once again, this method iterates over all interfaces that belong to the current application state. If they're active, each re-draw flag is checked and the appropriate re-draw methods are invoked. Finally, a pointer to the `sf::RenderWindow` is passed into the `Draw` method of an interface so it can draw itself.

It would be good to have a method for creating these types automatically because we're working with factory-produced element types:

```
GUI_Element* GUI_Manager::CreateElement(
    const GUI_ElementType& l_id, GUI_Interface* l_owner)
{
    if (l_id == GUI_ElementType::Window){
        return new GUI_Interface("", this);
    }
    auto f = m_factory.find(l_id);
    return (f != m_factory.end() ? f->second(l_owner) : nullptr);
}
```

If the provided element type is a `Window`, a new interface is created, to which a pointer of `GUI_Manager` is passed as its second argument. In the case of any other element type being passed in, the factory container is searched and the stored `lambda` function is invoked with the `l_owner` argument passed in to it.

Lastly, let's discuss the de-serialization of interfaces. A method is needed to load files formatted in this way:

```
Interface name Style.style 0 0 Immovable NoTitle "Title"
Element Label name 100 0 Style.style "Label text"
...
```

Next, let's work on loading our interfaces from a file. We're not going to cover how the file itself is read as it's pretty much identical to how we usually do it:

```
bool GUI_Manager::LoadInterface(const StateType& l_state,
    const std::string& l_interface, const std::string& l_name)
{
    ...
}
```

Let's start with creating an interface:

```
if (key == "Interface"){
  std::string style;
  keystream >> InterfaceName >> style;
  if (!AddInterface(l_state, l_name)){
    std::cout << "Failed adding interface: "
      << l_name << std::endl;
    return false;
  }
  GUI_Interface* i = GetInterface(l_state, l_name);
  keystream >> *i;
  if (!LoadStyle(style, i)){
    std::cout << "Failed loading style file: "
      << style << " for interface " << l_name << std::endl;
  }
  i->SetContentSize(i->GetSize());
} else if ...
```

As suggested by the file format, it first needs to read in its name and the name of the style file. If adding an interface with the loaded name fails, an error is printed out and the file reading is stopped. Otherwise, a pointer to this freshly added window is obtained and its overloaded **>>** operator is used to read in additional information from the stream, which we covered back in the interface section of this chapter.

Next, an attempt is made to load the style file that was read in earlier by calling the `LoadStyle` method, which we will be covering shortly. If it fails, an error message is printed out. Lastly, its content size is adjusted based on its current style.

Handling element de-serialization, in its most basic form, is quite similar:

```
} else if (key == "Element"){
  if (InterfaceName == ""){
    std::cout << "Error: 'Element' outside or before
      declaration of 'Interface'!" << std::endl;
    continue;
  }
  std::string type;
  std::string name;
  sf::Vector2f position;
  std::string style;
  keystream >> type >> name >> position.x >> position.y >> style;
  GUI_ElementType eType = StringToType(type);
  if (eType == GUI_ElementType::None){
    std::cout << "Unknown element('" << name
```

```
      << "') type: '" << type << "'" << std::endl;
    continue;
  }

  GUI_Interface* i = GetInterface(l_state, l_name);
  if (!i){ continue; }
  if (!i->AddElement(eType, name)){ continue; }
  GUI_Element* e = i->GetElement(name);
  keystream >> *e;
  e->SetPosition(position);
  if (!LoadStyle(style, e)){
    std::cout << "Failed loading style file: " << style
      << " for element " << name << std::endl;
    continue;
  }
}
```

The element type, the name, position, and the style values are read in from the file. An element type is obtained after running the text that was read into the `type` variable through our helper method `StringToType`. An interface that the element needs to be added to is obtained by using the name passed in as an argument to the `LoadInterface` method. The `AddElement` method of the obtained interface is called in order to create the appropriate element type on the heap. If it's successful, the element is obtained by name and its additional information is read in by utilizing its overloaded `>>` operator. The `LoadStyle` method is invoked once again in order to read the style of an element from a file. Let's take a look at what this looks like:

```
State Neutral
Size 64 32
TextColor 0 0 0 255
TextSize 12
Font Main
TextPadding 0 0
/State

State Hover
TextColor 255 255 255 255
/State

State Clicked
TextColor 255 0 0 255
/State
```

With this serving as an example, it's time to try and read it in. Once again, we're going to skip the code that reads the file as it is redundant. With that in mind, let's take a look:

```cpp
bool GUI_Manager::LoadStyle(const std::string& l_file,
  GUI_Element* l_element)
{
  ...
  std::string currentState;
  GUI_Style ParentStyle;
  GUI_Style TemporaryStyle;
  ...
}
```

Note the two `GUI_Style` structures that are set up here: they keep track of the main style that serves as a parent and the temporary style that's currently being read in. Let's keep moving further down this method, inside the actual `while` loop:

```cpp
if (type == "State"){
  if (currentState != ""){
    std::cout << "Error: 'State' keyword found
      inside another state!" << std::endl;
    continue;
  }
  keystream >> currentState;
} else if ...
```

If a `State` keyword is encountered and `currentState` is not set up, the name of the state is read in. Otherwise, we print out an error message:

```cpp
} else if (type == "/State"){
  if (currentState == ""){
    std::cout << "Error: '/State' keyword found
      prior to 'State'!" << std::endl;
    continue;
  }
  GUI_ElementState state = GUI_ElementState::Neutral;
  if (currentState == "Hover"){state = GUI_ElementState::Focused;}
  else if (currentState == "Clicked"){
    state = GUI_ElementState::Clicked;
  }

  if (state == GUI_ElementState::Neutral){
    ParentStyle = TemporaryStyle;
    l_element->UpdateStyle(
      GUI_ElementState::Neutral, TemporaryStyle);
```

```
    l_element->UpdateStyle(
      GUI_ElementState::Focused, TemporaryStyle);
    l_element->UpdateStyle(
      GUI_ElementState::Clicked, TemporaryStyle);
  } else {
    l_element->UpdateStyle(state, TemporaryStyle);
  }
  TemporaryStyle = ParentStyle;
  currentState = "";
} else { ...
```

When encountering a /State keyword, we can safely assume that the style currently being processed has ceased. The state is then determined based on the string that was read in denoting it.

If the state is Neutral, we need to set it to be the parent style, which means that every unset property of the other styles will also be inherited from this one. The UpdateStyle method is then invoked for each of the three supported states in order to overwrite the default values. If it is anything other than Neutral, the UpdateStyle method is only invoked once for that state. The TemporaryStyle variable is then overwritten with ParentStyle to simulate inheritance.

Finally, let's see how every different style feature is supported:

```
} else {
  // Handling style information.
  if (currentState == ""){
    std::cout << "Error: '" << type
      << "' keyword found outside of a state!" << std::endl;
    continue;
  }
  if (type == "Size"){
    keystream >>TemporaryStyle.m_size.x >>TemporaryStyle.m_size.y;
  } else if (type == "BgColor"){
    int r, g, b, a = 0;
    keystream >> r >> g >> b >> a;
    TemporaryStyle.m_backgroundColor = sf::Color(r,g,b,a);
  } else if (type == "BgImage"){
    keystream >> TemporaryStyle.m_backgroundImage;
  } else if (type == "BgImageColor"){
    int r, g, b, a = 0;
    keystream >> r >> g >> b >> a;
    TemporaryStyle.m_backgroundImageColor = sf::Color(r, g, b, a);
  } else if (type == "TextColor"){
    int r, g, b, a = 0;
```

```
        keystream >> r >> g >> b >> a;
        TemporaryStyle.m_textColor = sf::Color(r, g, b, a);
    } else if (type == "TextSize"){
        keystream >> TemporaryStyle.m_textSize;
    } else if (type == "TextOriginCenter"){
        TemporaryStyle.m_textCenterOrigin = true;
    } else if (type == "Font"){
        keystream >> TemporaryStyle.m_textFont;
    } else if (type == "TextPadding"){
        keystream >> TemporaryStyle.m_textPadding.x
            >> TemporaryStyle.m_textPadding.y;
    } else if (type == "ElementColor"){
        int r, g, b, a = 0;
        keystream >> r >> g >> b >> a;
        TemporaryStyle.m_elementColor = sf::Color(r, g, b, a);
    } else if (type == "Glyph"){
        keystream >> TemporaryStyle.m_glyph;
    } else if (type == "GlyphPadding"){
        Keystream >> TemporaryStyle.m_glyphPadding.x
            >> TemporaryStyle.m_glyphPadding.y;
    } else {
        std::cout << "Error: style tag '" << type
            << "' is unknown!" << std::endl;
    }
}
}
```

Every color value is first read in as four separate integers and then stored in a
sf::Color structure which gets assigned to the appropriate data member of the
style structure. Padding and text values are simply streamed in. One exception to
this is the TextOriginCenter tag. It does not contain any additional information
and its mere existence simply means that the origin of the text element should
always be centered.

The label element

A label element is the simplest GUI type yet. It supports all of the default stylistic
features but it doesn't do much else other than contain a certain string value that
can be loaded in or set at runtime.

Let's take a look at its constructor and destructor:

```
GUI_Label::GUI_Label(const std::string& l_name,
    GUI_Interface* l_owner)
    : GUI_Element(l_name, GUI_ElementType::Label, l_owner){}
```

This is nothing short of child's play in comparison to the code we've written before. Its name, type, and owner are set up in the initializer list and there's nothing else to it.

The de-serialization of this type of element is also fairly simple. Recall the following line from an interface file:

```
Element Label TestLabel 0 0 Default.style "Some text"
```

Since the `GUI_Manager` class takes care of all of this information except the last part, the `ReadIn` method of this element might look like this:

```
void GUI_Label::ReadIn(std::stringstream& l_stream){
    std::string content;
    Utils::ReadQuotedString(l_stream, content);
    m_visual.m_text.setString(content);
}
```

Now, we have to implement the event methods of this element. In this case, it's nothing more than simply adjusting the state of the label:

```
void GUI_Label::OnClick(const sf::Vector2f& l_mousePos){
  SetState(GUI_ElementState::Clicked);
}
void GUI_Label::OnRelease(){
  SetState(GUI_ElementState::Neutral);
}
void GUI_Label::OnHover(const sf::Vector2f& l_mousePos){
  SetState(GUI_ElementState::Focused);
}
void GUI_Label::OnLeave(){
  SetState(GUI_ElementState::Neutral);
}
```

The final bit of code is responsible for how this element is drawn:

```
void GUI_Label::Draw(sf::RenderTarget* l_target){
  l_target->draw(m_visual.m_backgroundSolid);
  if (m_style[m_state].m_glyph != ""){
    l_target->draw(m_visual.m_glyph);
  }
  l_target->draw(m_visual.m_text);
}
```

After the background rectangle is drawn, the glyph is checked to see whether it needs to be drawn as well. Lastly, the text is rendered right on top of the last two visual attributes.

The text field element

In order to implement a text field element successfully, we need to define how it responds to input correctly. Firstly, let's set up a new element type by creating the text field element class and implementing the constructor, as shown here:

```
GUI_Textfield::GUI_Textfield(const std::string& l_name,
  GUI_Interface* l_owner)
  : GUI_Element(l_name, GUI_ElementType::Textfield , l_owner){}
```

This element can also have a default text value when loaded, so let's express that by providing a custom version of the ReadIn method:

```
void GUI_Textfield::ReadIn(std::stringstream& l_stream){
  std::string content;
  Utils::ReadQuotedString(l_stream, content);
  m_visual.m_text.setString(content);
}
```

As you probably know, text fields do not change state if a mouse button is released. This allows them to be focused until a mouse click is registered elsewhere. We have already implemented that functionality in the GUI_Interface class as the DefocusTextfields method. All that's left to do now is ignore release events:

```
void GUI_Textfield::OnRelease(){}
```

Lastly, let's take a look at drawing this element:

```
void GUI_Textfield::Draw(sf::RenderTarget* l_target){
  l_target->draw(m_visual.m_backgroundSolid);
  if (m_style[m_state].m_glyph != ""){
    l_target->draw(m_visual.m_glyph);
  }
  l_target->draw(m_visual.m_text);
}
```

It is quite simple in nature. So far, we have only worried about drawing the background solid behind the text that this element holds. The glyph is also supported here but we're not going to be using it.

The scrollbar element

All of that support for interface scrolling and control elements implies the existence of the scrollbar element. Its purpose is to move around the visible area of the content texture in order to reveal elements that are positioned further out than its size allows, which could be along any axis. With that knowledge, let's take a stab at working out the basic class definition of the scrollbar element:

```
enum class SliderType{ Horizontal, Vertical };

class GUI_Scrollbar : public GUI_Element{
public:
    ...
    void SetPosition(const sf::Vector2f& l_pos);
    void ApplyStyle();
    void UpdateStyle(const GUI_ElementState& l_state,
        const GUI_Style& l_style);
private:
    SliderType m_sliderType;
    sf::RectangleShape m_slider;
    sf::Vector2f m_moveMouseLast;
    int m_percentage;
};
```

Firstly, we enumerate both possible types of sliders: horizontal and vertical. The actual GUI_Scrollbar class overwrites three of the original methods the parent class provides, in addition to implementing all of the purely virtual ones.

Among its private data members, the scrollbar keeps track of its own type, which contains another drawable object to represent the slider and maintains information about the last known mouse coordinates, as well as the percentage value of scroll it's currently at.

Let's start with the easy part – the constructor:

```
GUI_Scrollbar::GUI_Scrollbar(const std::string& l_name,
    GUI_Interface* l_owner)
    : GUI_Element(l_name, GUI_ElementType::Scrollbar, l_owner)
{
    m_isControl = true;
}
```

It's pretty straightforward so far. The element type is set to Scrollbar and the m_isControl flag is set to true to tell the owner interface which layer to draw it on.

Next up, the `SetPosition` method needs to be overwritten to make sure that the scrollbar is positioned correctly:

```
void GUI_Scrollbar::SetPosition(const sf::Vector2f& l_pos){
  GUI_Element::SetPosition(l_pos);
  if (m_sliderType == SliderType::Horizontal){ m_position.x = 0; }
  else { m_position.y = 0; }
}
```

Due to the nature of this particular element, one axis has to be always set to 0 in order to keep it positioned on the right edge.

For now, the type of a scrollbar will be read in from the interface file. To make that happen, we may want to handle de-serialization like this:

```
void GUI_Scrollbar::ReadIn(std::stringstream& l_stream){
  std::string type;
  l_stream >> type;
  if (type == "Horizontal"){m_sliderType =SliderType::Horizontal;}
  else { m_sliderType = SliderType::Vertical; }

  if (m_sliderType == SliderType::Horizontal){
    m_slider.setPosition(0, GetPosition().y);
  }
  else { m_slider.setPosition(GetPosition().x, 0); }
}
```

Let's handle the events next, starting with `OnClick`:

```
void GUI_Scrollbar::OnClick(const sf::Vector2f& l_mousePos){
  if (!m_slider.getGlobalBounds().contains(
    l_mousePos - m_owner->GetPosition()))
  {
    return;
  }
  SetState(GUI_ElementState::Clicked);
  m_moveMouseLast = l_mousePos;
}
```

Since we only want scrolling to happen when the slider part is being dragged, the state of this element is only set to `Clicked` if the mouse coordinates are inside the slider. They then get stored in the `m_moveMouseLast` data member to prevent the slider from jumping.

The remaining three events are not needed for anything other than adjusting the state:

```
void GUI_Scrollbar::OnRelease(){
  SetState(GUI_ElementState::Neutral);
}
void GUI_Scrollbar::OnHover(const sf::Vector2f& l_mousePos){
  SetState(GUI_ElementState::Focused);
}
void GUI_Scrollbar::OnLeave(){
  SetState(GUI_ElementState::Neutral);
}
```

The style updating also has to be altered to maintain the desired functionality of the scrollbar:

```
void GUI_Scrollbar::UpdateStyle(const GUI_ElementState& l_state,
  const GUI_Style& l_style)
{
  GUI_Element::UpdateStyle(l_state, l_style);
  if (m_sliderType == SliderType::Horizontal){
    m_style[l_state].m_size.x = m_owner->GetSize().x;
  }
  else { m_style[l_state].m_size.y = m_owner->GetSize().y; }
}
```

The size of the scrollbar is set to match the size of the owner interface on the relevant axis after the parent `UpdateStyle` is called.

Next, we have to define a custom way of applying style attributes to scrollbar elements, due to their unique nature:

```
void GUI_Scrollbar::ApplyStyle(){
  GUI_Element::ApplyStyle();
  m_slider.setFillColor(m_style[m_state].m_elementColor);
  bool horizontal = m_sliderType == SliderType::Horizontal;
  auto& bgSolid = m_visual.m_backgroundSolid;
  SetPosition((horizontal ?
    sf::Vector2f(0, m_owner->GetSize().y - bgSolid.getSize().y) :
    sf::Vector2f(m_owner->GetSize().x - bgSolid.getSize().x, 0)));
  bgSolid.setSize((horizontal ?
   sf::Vector2f(m_owner->GetSize().x,m_style[m_state].m_size.y) :
   sf::Vector2f(m_style[m_state].m_size.x,m_owner->GetSize().y)));
  m_slider.setPosition(
    (horizontal ? m_slider.getPosition().x : GetPosition().x),
```

```
      (horizontal ? GetPosition().y : m_slider.getPosition().y));
   float SizeFactor = (horizontal ?
     m_owner->GetContentSize().x / m_owner->GetSize().x :
     m_owner->GetContentSize().y / m_owner->GetSize().y);
   if (SizeFactor < 1.f){ SizeFactor = 1.f; }
   float SliderSize = (horizontal ?
     m_owner->GetSize().x : m_owner->GetSize().y) / SizeFactor;
   m_slider.setSize((horizontal ?
     sf::Vector2f(SliderSize,bgSolid.getSize().y) :
     sf::Vector2f(bgSolid.getSize().x, SliderSize)));
   bgSolid.setPosition(GetPosition());
}
```

After the parent `ApplyStyle` is invoked and the slider color is set, the position of the element is overwritten to keep it at 0 on the axis of action and right near the edge on the perpendicular axis. The size of the background solid is determined by the size of the interface on the scroll axis. Its style attributes determine the other size value.

The position of the slider is modified on the non-operational axis to always match the position of the element itself. Calculating its size along the scrolling axis is as simple as dividing the size of the owner window by the result of dividing its content size by the same window size.

With the style part of this element complete, let's work on moving it and affecting its owner interface:

```
void GUI_Scrollbar::Update(float l_dT){
   // Mouse-drag code.
   if (GetState() != GUI_ElementState::Clicked){ return; }
   SharedContext* context = m_owner->GetManager()->GetContext();
   sf::Vector2f mousePos =
     sf::Vector2f(context->m_eventManager->GetMousePos(
     context->m_wind->GetRenderWindow()));
   if (m_moveMouseLast == mousePos){ return; }
   sf::Vector2f difference = mousePos - m_moveMouseLast;
   m_moveMouseLast = mousePos;

   bool horizontal = m_sliderType == SliderType::Horizontal;
   m_slider.move((horizontal ? difference.x : 0),
     (horizontal ? 0 : difference.y));
   if (horizontal && m_slider.getPosition().x < 0){
     m_slider.setPosition(0, m_slider.getPosition().y);
   } else if (m_slider.getPosition().y < 0){
     m_slider.setPosition(m_slider.getPosition().x, 0);
   }
```

```
if (horizontal&&(m_slider.getPosition().x+m_slider.getSize().x >
  m_owner->GetSize().x))
{
  m_slider.setPosition(
    m_owner->GetSize().x - m_slider.getSize().x,
    m_slider.getPosition().y);
} else if (m_slider.getPosition().y + m_slider.getSize().y >
  m_owner->GetSize().y)
{
  m_slider.setPosition(m_slider.getPosition().x,
    m_owner->GetSize().y - m_slider.getSize().y);
}
float WorkArea = (horizontal ?
  m_owner->GetSize().x - m_slider.getSize().x :
  m_owner->GetSize().y - m_slider.getSize().y);
int percentage = ((horizontal ?
  m_slider.getPosition().x : m_slider.getPosition().y) /
  WorkArea) * 100;
if (horizontal){ m_owner->UpdateScrollHorizontal(percentage); }
else { m_owner->UpdateScrollVertical(percentage); }
SetRedraw(true);
}
```

All of the code above only needs to be executed if the state of this element is Clicked. It's then obvious that the slider of the scrollbar is being dragged up and down. If the current mouse position is not the same as the last position from a previous iteration, the difference between them is calculated and the current position of the mouse is stored for later reference.

Firstly, the slider is moved by the difference of the mouse positions between the last two iterations. It is then checked to see if it is outside the boundaries of the interface, in which case, its position gets reset to the closest edge.

Lastly, the scroll percentage value is calculated by dividing the slider's position on the relevant axis by the difference of the window size and the slider size. The relevant update method for scrolling is then invoked and this element is marked to be re-drawn to reflect its changes.

The last thing we need to do is define how the scrollbar element is drawn:

```
void GUI_Scrollbar::Draw(sf::RenderTarget* l_target){
    l_target->draw(m_visual.m_backgroundSolid);
    l_target->draw(m_slider);
}
```

For now, it only uses two rectangle shapes, however, this can easily be expanded to support textures as well.

Integrating the GUI system

In order to use the GUI system, it needs to first exist. Just like in previous chapters, we need to instantiate and update the GUI classes we built. Let's start by adding the GUI manager and the font manager to the `SharedContext.h` file:

```
struct SharedContext{
  SharedContext():
    ...
    m_fontManager(nullptr),
    ...
    m_guiManager(nullptr){}
     ...
      FontManager* m_fontManager;
   GUI_Manager* m_guiManager;
};
```

We need to keep a pointer to the GUI manager and the font manager in the `Game` class, as with all of the other classes that are shared through the `SharedContext` structure, starting with the header:

```
class Game{
public:
    ...
private:
    ...
    FontManager m_fontManager;
    ...
    GUI_Manager m_guiManager;
};
```

These pointers are, of course meaningless, unless they actually point to valid objects in memory. Let's take care of the allocation and de-allocation of resources in the `Game.cpp` file:

```
Game::Game() : m_window("Chapter 11", sf::Vector2u(800, 600)),
  m_entityManager(&m_systemManager, &m_textureManager),
  m_stateManager(&m_context),
  m_guiManager(m_window.GetEventManager(),&m_context)
{
  ...
  m_context.m_guiManager = &m_guiManager;
  ...
  m_fontManager.RequireResource("Main");
}
```

```
Game::~Game(){
  m_fontManager.ReleaseResource("Main");
}
```

Next, we can look at updating all of the interfaces in the application and handling GUI events:

```
void Game::Update(){
    ...
    m_context.m_guiManager->Update(m_elapsed.asSeconds());
    GUI_Event guiEvent;
    while (m_context,m_guiManager->PollEvent(guiEvent)){
        m_window.GetEventManager()->HandleEvent(guiEvent);
    }
}
```

Note that the GUI_Event instance is forwarded to the EventManager class. We're going to be expanding it soon.

Finally, let's handle drawing our interfaces:

```
void Game::Render(){
    ...
    m_stateManager.Draw();

    sf::View CurrentView = m_window.GetRenderWindow()->getView();
    m_window.GetRenderWindow()->setView(
        m_window.GetRenderWindow()->getDefaultView());
    m_context.m_guiManager->Render(m_window->GetRenderWindow());
    m_window.GetRenderWindow()->setView(CurrentView);

    m_window.EndDraw();
}
```

In order for the GUI to be always drawn above the rest of the scene, the window view has to be set to the default before the interfaces are drawn. It then needs to be set back in order to maintain a consistent camera position, which might look something like this:

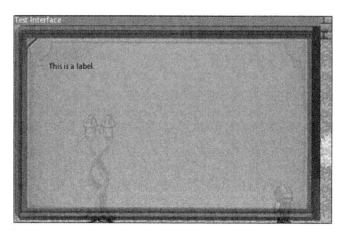

Expanding the event manager

GUI events need to be handled for every possible state of the application in order to keep them from piling up, much like SFML events. In order to avoid writing all of that extra code, we're going to use something that was built solely for the purpose of handling them: the event manager.

Let's start by expanding the `EventType` enumeration to support GUI events:

```
enum class EventType{
   ...
   Keyboard = sf::Event::Count + 1, Mouse, Joystick,
   GUI_Click, GUI_Release, GUI_Hover, GUI_Leave
};
```

It's important to keep these custom event types at the very bottom of the structure because of the way the code we've written in the past works.

Our previous raw implementation of the `EventManager` class relied on the fact that any given event can be represented simply by a numeric value. Most SFML events, such as key bindings, fit into that category but a lot of other event types, especially custom events, require additional information in order to be processed correctly.

Instead of using numbers, we need to switch to a lightweight data structure like this:

```
struct EventInfo{
    EventInfo(){ l_code = 0; }
    EventInfo(int l_event){ l_code = l_event; }
    EventInfo(GUI_Event l_guiEvent){ l_gui = l_guiEvent; }
    union{
        int l_code;
        GUI_Event l_gui;
    };
};
```

The union ensures that no memory is wasted and that we can still use numeric representations of event types, as well as custom data-types, such as the GUI_Event structure. GUI_Event belongs to a union, which is why it couldn't use std::string typed data members.

 If the boost library is used, all of this code can be reduced to boost::variant<int, GUI_Event>.

One additional change is that we want to be able to pass the GUI event information to the callback methods that are registered. This information will also be held by our EventDetails structure:

```
struct EventDetails{
    EventDetails(const std::string& l_bindName)
        : m_name(l_bindName){ Clear(); }
    ...
    std::string m_guiInterface; // GUI interface name.
    std::string m_guiElement; // GUI element name.
    GUI_EventType m_guiEvent; // GUI event type.

    void Clear(){
        ...
        m_guiInterface = "";
        m_guiElement = "";
        m_guiEvent = GUI_EventType::None;
    }
};
```

Now, let's adjust the `Binding` structure:

```
struct Binding{
  Binding(const std::string& l_name) : m_name(l_name),
    m_details(l_name), c(0){}
  ~Binding(){
    // GUI portion.
    for (auto itr = m_events.begin();
      itr != m_events.end(); ++itr)
    {
      if (itr->first == EventType::GUI_Click ||
        itr->first == EventType::GUI_Release ||
        itr->first == EventType::GUI_Hover ||
        itr->first == EventType::GUI_Leave)
      {
        delete [] itr->second.m_gui.m_interface;
        delete [] itr->second.m_gui.m_element;
      }
    }
  }
  ...
};
```

We had to use `const char*` data types to hold element and interface names because of union restrictions. While that only applies to GUI-related events, this memory still needs to be de-allocated. When a binding is being destroyed, all of the event information is iterated over and checked to see if it is any of the four GUI event types, in which case the memory is safely de-allocated.

Next, we need a separate method that handles just the GUI events. Overloading the `HandleEvent` method with a different argument type seems like a good choice here:

```
void HandleEvent(sf::Event& l_event);
void HandleEvent(GUI_Event& l_event);
```

We need to make sure that no GUI events are processed in the original `HandleEvent` method:

```
void EventManager::HandleEvent(sf::Event& l_event){
  ...
  for(auto &e_itr : bind->m_events){
    EventType sfmlEvent = (EventType)l_event.type;
    if (e_itr.first == EventType::GUI_Click ||
      e_itr.first == EventType::GUI_Release ||
      e_itr.first == EventType::GUI_Hover ||
```

```
          e_itr.first == EventType::GUI_Leave)
      {
        continue;
      }
      ...
    }
    ...
}
```

If the event is of one of the four GUI types, the iteration is skipped. Handling the GUI events themselves is quite simple and can be done in this manner:

```
void EventManager::HandleEvent(GUI_Event& l_event){
  for (auto &b_itr : m_bindings){
    Binding* bind = b_itr.second;
    for (auto &e_itr : bind->m_events)
    {
      if (e_itr.first != EventType::GUI_Click &&
        e_itr.first != EventType::GUI_Release &&
        e_itr.first != EventType::GUI_Hover &&
        e_itr.first != EventType::GUI_Leave)
      { continue; }
      if ((e_itr.first == EventType::GUI_Click &&
        l_event.m_type != GUI_EventType::Click) ||
        (e_itr.first == EventType::GUI_Release &&
        l_event.m_type != GUI_EventType::Release) ||
        (e_itr.first == EventType::GUI_Hover &&
        l_event.m_type != GUI_EventType::Hover) ||
        (e_itr.first == EventType::GUI_Leave &&
        l_event.m_type != GUI_EventType::Leave))
      { continue; }
      if (strcmp(e_itr.second.m_gui.m_interface,
        l_event.m_interface) ||
        strcmp(e_itr.second.m_gui.m_element, l_event.m_element))
      { continue; }
      bind->m_details.m_guiInterface = l_event.m_interface;
      bind->m_details.m_guiElement = l_event.m_element;
      ++(bind->c);
    }
  }
}
```

While iterating over the events inside bindings, their types are checked. Anything that is not a GUI event is skipped over. If the type of a processed event matches the type inside the binding, additional information is checked in the `EventInfo` structure, namely the interface and element names. If those match too, they are recorded as event details and the event count is incremented.

The last chunk of code that needs attention is the `LoadBindings` method. We need to adjust it to support interface and element name-loading from the `keys.cfg` file, which should look something like this:

```
Key_X 5:23
MainMenu_Play 27:MainMenu:Play
```

The first line represents a normal type of event, while the second line is a GUI event, which requires two identifiers to be loaded instead of just one. Let's adjust it:

```
void EventManager::LoadBindings(){
  ...
  while(!keystream.eof()){
    std::string keyval;
    keystream >> keyval;
    int start = 0;
    int end = keyval.find(delimiter);
    if (end == std::string::npos){
      delete bind;
      bind = nullptr;
      break;
    }
    EventType type = EventType(
      stoi(keyval.substr(start, end-start)));

    EventInfo eventInfo;
    if (type==EventType::GUI_Click ||
      type==EventType::GUI_Release ||
      type == EventType::GUI_Hover ||
      type == EventType::GUI_Leave)
    {
      start = end + delimiter.length();
      end = keyval.find(delimiter, start);
      std::string window = keyval.substr(start, end - start);
      std::string element;
      if (end != std::string::npos){
        start = end + delimiter.length();
        end = keyval.length();
        element = keyval.substr(start, end);
```

```
    }
    char* w = new char[window.length() + 1]; // +1 for \0
    char* e = new char[element.length() + 1];

    // Size in bytes is the same as character length.1 char = 1B.
    strcpy_s(w, window.length() + 1, window.c_str());
    strcpy_s(e, element.length() + 1, element.c_str());

    eventInfo.m_gui.m_interface = w;
    eventInfo.m_gui.m_element = e;
  } else {
    int code = stoi(keyval.substr(end + delimiter.length(),
      keyval.find(delimiter,end + delimiter.length())));
    eventInfo.m_code = code;
  }
  bind->BindEvent(type, eventInfo);
  }
  ...
}
```

After the event type is loaded in as usual, it is checked to see if it matches any of the four GUI events. The window and element strings are then read in and copied to the newly allocated memory of `char*` via the `std::strcpy` method.

> Keep in mind that when memory for `char*` types is allocated to match a given string, it also needs an additional space for the null-terminating character at the end.

Re-implementing the main menu

In order to demonstrate how much easier it is building interactivity in this way, let's re-construct the main menu, starting by creating its `.interface` file:

```
Interface MainMenu MainMenu.style 0 0 Immovable NoTitle "Main menu"
Element Label Title 100 0 MainMenuTitle.style "Main menu:"
Element Label Play 0 32 MainMenuLabel.style "PLAY"
Element Label Credits 0 68 MainMenuLabel.style "CREDITS"
Element Label Quit 0 104 MainMenuLabel.style "EXIT"
```

The interface is set to have zero padding on both axes, be immovable, and have no title bar. All three buttons in this interface, as well as its title, can be represented by labels with different styles. Speaking of which, let's take a look at the style of our main menu interface:

```
State Neutral
Size 300 150
TextSize 12
Font Main
/State
```

As you can see, it only defines the most basic attributes and does not aim to be visually responsive by itself. The button label style, however, is a little different:

```
State Neutral
Size 300 32
BgColor 255 0 0 255
TextColor 255 255 255 255
TextSize 14
Font Main
TextPadding 150 16
TextOriginCenter
/State

State Hover
BgColor 255 100 0 255
/State

State Clicked
BgColor 255 150 0 255
/State
```

When its state changes, the label's background color is adjusted as well, unlike the label that represents the title of the main menu:

```
State Neutral
Size 118 32
TextColor 255 255 255 255
TextSize 24
Font Main
/State
```

With all of the visual elements out of the way, let's adjust the main menu state to load and maintain this interface:

```
class State_MainMenu : public BaseState{
public:
    ...
    void Play(EventDetails* l_details); // Callback.
    void Quit(EventDetails* l_details); // Callback.
};
```

In addition to all of the required methods that a state has to implement, we only need two callbacks to handle GUI clicks. This is all set up in the `OnCreate` method of the main menu state:

```
void State_MainMenu::OnCreate(){
  GUI_Manager* gui = m_stateMgr->GetContext()->m_guiManager;
  gui->LoadInterface(StateType::MainMenu,
    "MainMenu.interface", "MainMenu");
  gui->GetInterface(StateType::MainMenu,
    "MainMenu")->SetPosition(sf::Vector2f(250.f, 168.f));
  EventManager* eMgr = m_stateMgr->GetContext()->m_eventManager;
  eMgr->AddCallback(StateType::MainMenu,
    "MainMenu_Play", &State_MainMenu::Play, this);
  eMgr->AddCallback(StateType::MainMenu,
    "MainMenu_Quit", &State_MainMenu::Quit, this);
}
```

Firstly, the main menu interface is loaded from a file and placed on screen. The event manager is then used to set up callbacks for the **Play** and **Quit** button actions. This is already much cleaner than the previous approach.

Once the state is destroyed, the interface and two callbacks must be removed, as shown here:

```
void State_MainMenu::OnDestroy(){
  m_stateMgr->GetContext()->m_guiManager->
    RemoveInterface(StateType::MainMenu, "MainMenu");
  EventManager* eMgr = m_stateMgr->GetContext()->m_eventManager;
  eMgr->RemoveCallback(StateType::MainMenu, "MainMenu_Play");
  eMgr->RemoveCallback(StateType::MainMenu, "MainMenu_Quit");
}
```

The text of the **Play** button must be changed if a GAME state exists:

```
void State_MainMenu::Activate(){
  auto& play = *m_stateMgr->GetContext()->m_guiManager->
    GetInterface(StateType::MainMenu, "MainMenu")->
    GetElement("Play");
  if (m_stateMgr->HasState(StateType::Game)){
    // Resume
    play.SetText("Resume");
  } else {
    // Play
    play.SetText("Play");
  }
}
```

That leaves us with our two callbacks, which look like this:

```
void State_MainMenu::Play(EventDetails* l_details){
    m_stateMgr->SwitchTo(StateType::Game);
}
void State_MainMenu::Quit(EventDetails* l_details){
    m_stateMgr->GetContext()->m_wind->Close();
}
```

This illustrates perfectly how easy it is to use our new GUI with an improved event manager for fast and responsive results. The main menu was created with roughly 20 lines of code, or fewer, and looks like this:

Summary

At the beginning of *Chapter 10, Can I Click This? – GUI Fundamentals*, our main goal was to achieve a simple yet powerful means of interfacing with our own application. Throughout this chapter, additional topics such as interface and event management, creation and integration of new element types, and expansion of existing code were covered in depth. The effectiveness of all the work that was put into the GUI cannot be measured in any other way but success. We are now left with a system that is capable of producing efficient, responsive, and fast results with the minimum amount of effort and code. Furthermore, you should now have the skills necessary to build even more element types that will enable this system to do amazing things.

In the next chapter, we're going to be covering the management and usage of sound and music elements in SFML. See you there!

12
Can You Hear Me Now? – Sound and Music

There's nothing quite like the enjoyment of being immersed in a virtual environment. From the movies we watch to the games we play, appeal to and usage of as many human senses as possible can either make or break the captivation that a form of media can hold. Creating a living and breathing atmosphere can rarely, if ever, be only down to visual effects. Throughout this chapter, we will briefly close our eyes and engage in the auditory side of this project by covering subjects such as:

- Basics of sound and music in SFML
- Placement of sounds and the listener in 3D space
- Proper management and recycling of sound instances
- Expansion of the entity component system to allow for sounds

We have a long way to go until our first sonic boom, so let's dive right in!

Use of copyrighted resources

Before we jump into managing sounds, let's give credit where it is due. Throughout this chapter, we're going to use the following resources:

- *Fantozzi's Footsteps (Grass/Sand & Stone)* by *Fantozzi* under the CC0 license (public domain): `http://opengameart.org/content/fantozzis-footsteps-grasssand-stone`
- *Electrix* (NES Version) by *Snabisch* under the CC-BY 3.0 license: `http://opengameart.org/content/electrix-nes-version`
- *Town Theme RPG* by *cynicmusic* under the CC-BY 3.0 license: `http://opengameart.org/content/town-theme-rpg`

Preparing the project for sound

In order to successfully compile a project that uses SFML audio, we need to make sure these additional dependency `.lib` files are included:

- `sfml-audio-s.lib`
- `openal32.lib`
- `flac.lib`
- `ogg.lib`
- `vorbis.lib`
- `vorbisenc.lib`
- `vorbisfile.lib`

Additionally, the executable file must always be accompanied by the `openal32.dll` file, which comes with SFML and can be found inside the `bin` folder of the library.

Basics of SFML sound

Anything audio related falls into one of two categories within SFML: `sf::Sound` that represents short sound effects, or `sf::Music` that is used to play longer audio tracks. It's prudent that we understand how these two classes are used before continuing further. Let's talk about each one individually.

Playing sounds

The `sf::Sound` class is extremely lightweight and should only ever be used to play short sound effects that don't take up a lot of memory. The way it stores and utilizes actual audio files is by using a `sf::SoundBuffer` instance. It is analogous to `sf::Sprite` and the way it uses an instance of `sf::Texture` for drawing. The `sf::SoundBuffer` is used to hold audio data in memory, which the `sf::Sound` class then reads and plays from. It can be used as follows:

```
sf::SoundBuffer buffer;
buffer.loadFromFile("SomeSound.ogg");

sf::Sound sound(buffer);
sound.setBuffer(buffer); // Alternative.
```

As you can see, a sound buffer can be attached to an instance of `sf::Sound` by either passing it to the sound's constructor or by using the `setBuffer` method of a sound instance.

As long as the sound is expected to be playing, the `sf::SoundBuffer` instance *shouldn't* be destroyed!

After the sound buffer loads the sound file and is attached to an instance of `sf::Sound`, it can be played by invoking the `play()` method:

```
sound.play(); // Play the sound!
```

It can also be paused and stopped by using the appropriately named `pause()` and `stop()` methods:

```
sound.pause(); // Pause the sound.
sound.stop(); // Stop the sound.
```

Obtaining the current status of a sound to determine if it's playing, paused, or stopped can be done like this:

```
sf::SoundSource::Status status = sound.getStatus();
```

The status it returns is a simple enumeration of three values: `stopped`, `paused`, and `playing`.

Lastly, we can adjust the sound's volume, pitch, whether it loops or not, and how far the sound has progressed by using these methods respectively:

```
sound.setVolume(100.f); // Takes in a float.
sound.setPitch(1.f); // Takes in a float.
sound.setLoop(true); // Takes in a Boolean.
sound.setPlayingOffset(sf::seconds(5.f)); // Takes in sf::Time.
```

Audio pitch is simply a numeric value that represents frequency of the sound. Values above 1 will result in the sound playing at a higher pitch, while anything below 1 has the opposite effect. If the pitch is changed, it also changes the sound's playing speed.

Playing music

Any `sf::Music` instance supports all of the methods discussed previously, except `setBuffer`. As you already know, `sf::Sound` uses instances of `sf::SoundBuffer` that it reads from. This means that the entire sound file has to be loaded in memory for it to be played. With larger files, this quickly becomes inefficient, and that's the reason `sf::Music` exists. Instead of using buffer objects, it streams the data from the file itself as the music plays, only loading as much data as it needs for the time being.

Let's take a look at an example:

```
sf::Music music;
music.openFromFile("SomeMusic.ogg");
music.play();
...
music.stop();
```

Notice the name of the method `openFromFile`. In contrast, where sound buffers load files, `sf::Music` merely opens it and reads from it.

A very important thing to mention here is that `sf::Music` is a non-copyable class! This means that any sort of assignment by value will automatically result in an error:

```
sf::Music music;
sf::Music music2 = music; // ERROR!
```

Passing a music instance to a function or a method by value would also produce the same results.

Sound spatialization

Both `sf::Sound` and `sf::Music` also support spatial positioning. It takes advantage of left and right audio channels and makes it feel like the sound is actually playing around you. There is a catch, though. Every sound or music instance that is desired to be spatial has to only have a single channel. It is more commonly known as a monophonic or mono sound, as opposed to stereo that already decides how the speakers are used.

The way sounds are perceived in three-dimensional space is manipulated through a single, static class: `sf::Listener`. It's static because there can only ever be one listener per application. The main two aspects of this class we're interested in are the position and direction of the listener. Keep in mind that although we may be working on a 2D game, SFML sounds exist in 3D space. Let's take a look at an example:

```
sf::Listener::setPosition(5.f, 0.f, 5.f);
sf::Listener::setDirection(1.f, 0.f, 0.f);
```

First, let's address the three-dimensional coordinates. In SFML, the default up vector is on the positive Y axis. Look at the following figure:

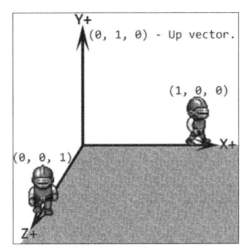

Each axis the character is on represents a direction vector in three dimensions

This arrangement of axes is known as a *right-handed Cartesian coordinate system* and is the standard for OpenGL, which is the basis of SFML. What this means is that what we've been calling the Y axis in two dimensions is really the Z axis in a three dimensional space. That's important to keep in mind if we want to have correct results when moving sound through space.

The listener direction is represented by something called a unit vector, also referred to as a normalized vector, which means it can only have a maximum magnitude of 1. When setting the listener's direction, the vector provided is normalized again, so these two lines of code would produce equivalent results of a south-east direction:

```
sf::Listener::setDirection(1.f, 0.f, 1.f);
sf::Listener::setDirection(0.5f, 0.f, 0.5f);
```

For our purposes, however, we're not going to need to use diagonal directions, as our main character, who will obviously be the sole listener, can only face four possible directions.

Placing sounds in space

Much like how sprites are positioned in two-dimensional space, sounds can be positioned as well by using the method with the same name:

```
sf::Sound sound;
sound.setPosition(5.f, 0.f, 5.f);
```

Let's say that the listener is facing in the positive *X* direction *(1.f, 0.f, 0.f)*. The sound that we just placed at coordinates *(5.f, 0.f, 5.f)* would be five units ahead and five units to the right of our listener and would be heard through the right speaker. How loud would it have to be, though? That's where the minimum sound distance and attenuation come in:

```
sound.setMinDistance(6.f);
sound.setAttenuation(2.f);
```

Sound minimum distance is the threshold at which the sound begins to lose volume and gets quieter. In the preceding example, if the listener is closer or exactly six units of distance away from the sound source, full volume of the sound will be heard. Otherwise, the sound begins to fade. How fast it fades is determined by the attenuation factor. Consider this figure:

The circle with a radius of Min_Distance represents an area, where the sound can be heard at maximum volume. After the minimum distance is exceeded, the attenuation factor is applied to the volume.

Attenuation is simply a multiplicative factor. The higher it is, the faster sound fades over distance. Setting attenuation to 0 would result in a sound heard everywhere, while a value like 100 would mean that it is heard only when the listener is very close to it.

Remember that although we're not going to be taking advantage of it, music in SFML behaves under the same rules of spatialization as sound, as long as it only has one channel.

Audio manager

Similar to what we did for textures and fonts, we're going to need a way to manage `sf::SoundBuffer` instances easily. Luckily, our `ResourceManager` class is there to make it extremely convenient, so let's create the `AudioManager.h` file and define the way sound buffers are set up:

```cpp
class AudioManager : public ResourceManager<
  AudioManager, sf::SoundBuffer>
{
public:
  AudioManager() : ResourceManager("audio.cfg"){}

  sf::SoundBuffer* Load(const std::string& l_path){
    sf::SoundBuffer* sound = new sf::SoundBuffer();
    if (!sound->loadFromFile(
      Utils::GetWorkingDirectory() + l_path))
    {
      delete sound;
      sound = nullptr;
      std::cerr << "! Failed to load sound: "
        << l_path << std::endl;
    }
    return sound;
  }
};
```

As you can tell already, the sound interface is pretty much exactly the same as that of textures or fonts. Similar to the previous resource managers, we also provide a file that paths are loaded from. In this case, it is the `audio.cfg` file:

```
Footstep media/Audio/footstep.ogg
TownTheme media/Audio/TownTheme.ogg
```

Once again, it is just like dealing with textures or fonts. So far, so good!

Defining sound properties

Sound, much like any other medium, has a few different properties of interest that are up for tweaking. The effects we're going to be playing in our game don't just have varying sources, but also different volumes, pitch values, the distance a sound can cover, and a factor that represents how fast that sound fades. How we're going to store this information is defined in `SoundProps.h`:

```
struct SoundProps{
    SoundProps(const std::string& l_name): m_audioName(l_name),
        m_volume(100), m_pitch(1.f), m_minDistance(10.f),
        m_attenuation(10.f){}
    std::string m_audioName;
    float m_volume;
    float m_pitch;
    float m_minDistance;
    float m_attenuation;
};
```

In addition to the qualities described earlier, it is also necessary to store the identifier of the audio file that a sound is going to be using. A typical sound file for our application would look something like `footstep.sound`:

```
Audio Footstep
Volume 25
Pitch 1.0
Distance 150
Attenuation 2
```

With this out of the way, we can actually jump right into managing the `sf::Sound` instances!

Managing sounds

Due to the limitations on the number of sounds we can have in an application, it's best to have a centralized way of handling and recycling them. This is where the `SoundManager` class comes in. Let's begin aliasing a data type for sound IDs:

```
using SoundID = int;
```

A simple integer type is more than qualified for the job of keeping sounds identified.

Additionally, we'll want to store some information with the sound instance:

```
struct SoundInfo{
    SoundInfo(const std::string& l_name):
        m_name(l_name), m_manualPaused(false){}
    std::string m_name;
    bool m_manualPaused;
};
```

In order to properly deallocate resources when it counts, we're going to want to store the string identifier of the audio file that the sound is using. Keeping track of whether the sound has been paused automatically or not is important for consistency. That's what the m_manualPaused Boolean flag is there for.

Lastly, before we delve deeper into the sound manager, looking at a few type definitions used here is essential:

```
using SoundProperties = std::unordered_map<std::string,
    SoundProps>;
using SoundContainer = std::unordered_map<SoundID,
    std::pair<SoundInfo, sf::Sound*>>;
using Sounds = std::unordered_map<StateType, SoundContainer>;
using RecycledSounds = std::vector<std::pair<
    std::pair<SoundID, std::string>, sf::Sound*>>;
using MusicContainer = std::unordered_map<StateType,
    std::pair<SoundInfo, sf::Music*>>;
```

The SoundProperties type is just a map that associates the name of a sound to a structure that contains its properties. SoundContainer is another map that ties a SoundID to a pair that contains the SoundInfo structure, as well as the actual instance of the sf::Sound object. The Sounds data type is responsible for grouping these sound containers by State.

Further down the line, as sounds get recycled, they need to be moved to a different container of type RecycledSounds. It stores the sound ID and name alongside the sf::Sound instance.

The last type definition we're going to be dealing with here is a container for sf::Music instances. Just like sounds, they're grouped by states. One major difference here is the fact that we're only allowing one instance of sf::Music per state, which is stored together with a SoundInfo structure.

Now that we have everything we need, let's take a look at the sound manager header file:

```
class SoundManager{
public:
  SoundManager(AudioManager* l_audioMgr);
  ~SoundManager();

  void ChangeState(const StateType& l_state);
  void RemoveState(const StateType& l_state);

  void Update(float l_dT);

  SoundID Play(const std::string& l_sound,
    const sf::Vector3f& l_position,
    bool l_loop = false,
    bool l_relative = false);
  bool Play(const SoundID& l_id);
  bool Stop(const SoundID& l_id);
  bool Pause(const SoundID& l_id);

  bool PlayMusic(const std::string& l_musicId,
    float l_volume = 100.f, bool l_loop = false);
  bool PlayMusic(const StateType& l_state);
  bool StopMusic(const StateType& l_state);
  bool PauseMusic(const StateType& l_state);

  bool SetPosition(const SoundID& l_id, const sf::Vector3f& l_pos);
  bool IsPlaying(const SoundID& l_id);
  SoundProps* GetSoundProperties(const std::string& l_soundName);

  static const int Max_Sounds = 150;
  static const int Sound_Cache = 75;
private:
  bool LoadProperties(const std::string& l_file);
  void PauseAll(const StateType& l_state);
  void UnpauseAll(const StateType& l_state);

  sf::Sound* CreateSound(SoundID& l_id,
    const std::string& l_audioName);
  void SetUpSound(sf::Sound* l_snd, const SoundProps* l_props,
    bool l_loop = false, bool l_relative = false);
  bool RecycleSound(const SoundID& l_id, sf::Sound* l_snd,
    const std::string& l_name);
```

```
    void Cleanup();

    Sounds m_audio;
    MusicContainer m_music;
    RecycledSounds m_recycled;
    SoundProperties m_properties;
    StateType m_currentState;

    SoundID m_lastID;
    unsigned int m_numSounds;
    float m_elapsed;

    AudioManager* m_audioManager;
};
```

As mentioned previously, it's a good idea to keep the number of sf::Sound and sf::Music instances in your application down to a designated limit that never exceeds 256. In this case, we're playing it pretty safe by using static data members for setting a limit of 150 sounds loaded in memory at the same time. In addition to that, we're also setting a limit to how many sound instances can be recycled before they're used again, which is 75. These values can obviously be tweaked to your liking.

Let's talk about the private data members of this class before we get into implementation details. As expected, the sound and music containers are stored in this class under the names m_audio and m_music. Additionally, we're storing all of the sound properties in this class, alongside the recycled sound container. Because sound functionality is state based, the m_currentState data member is necessary for keeping tabs on what state the application is running in.

In order to assign sound IDs properly, keeping track of the last ID is a good idea, hence m_lastID. Also, since enforcing restrictions on how many instances of sf::Sound and sf::Music can be "alive" at the same time is of paramount importance; m_numSounds is used to keep track of every instance of these two classes. We're also going to need to check time passage in our application, which is what m_elapsed will be used for.

Finally, a pointer to the audio manager is kept around for resource management and retrieval.

Implementing the sound manager

Let's begin, as always, by looking at the constructor and destructor of this class:

```
SoundManager::SoundManager(AudioManager* l_audioMgr)
    : m_lastID(0), m_audioManager(l_audioMgr),
    m_elapsed(0.f), m_numSounds(0){}

SoundManager::~SoundManager(){ Cleanup(); }
```

A pointer to an `AudioManager` instance is obtained through the argument list of the constructor and initialized in the initializer list, alongside other data members and their default values. The destructor simply invokes another method called `Cleanup()`, which is responsible for the de-allocation of memory. It will be covered shortly.

We have already discussed the role that application states play in sound management. Now, let's take a look at actually defining the behavior of sound when states are changed:

```
void SoundManager::ChangeState(const StateType& l_state){
   PauseAll(m_currentState);
   UnpauseAll(l_state);
   m_currentState = l_state;

   if (m_music.find(m_currentState) != m_music.end()){ return; }
   SoundInfo info("");
   sf::Music* music = nullptr;
   m_music.emplace(m_currentState, std::make_pair(info, music));
}
```

Upon the application state being altered, a `PauseAll` method is invoked with the argument of `m_currentState`. It's responsible for effectively silencing every sound that is currently playing. We don't want to be hearing fights and explosions of the in-game action while we're in the main menu. The `UnpauseAll` method is called next, with the identifier of the state being changed to being passed in as the argument. Obviously, if we're in the main menu and we're switching back to the game state, we want all of the action to resume and this includes all of the sound effects. The data member that holds the current state information is then altered.

The last few lines of code in this method are responsible for making sure that the music container has information about the new state. If nothing is found, some blank information is inserted into the `m_music` container in order to signify that the current state currently has no music playing.

Next, let's talk about what happens when a state is removed from the application:

```
void SoundManager::RemoveState(const StateType& l_state){
  auto& StateSounds = m_audio.find(l_state)->second;
  for (auto &itr : StateSounds){
    RecycleSound(itr.first, itr.second.second,
      itr.second.first.m_name);
  }
  m_audio.erase(l_state);
  auto music = m_music.find(l_state);
  if (music == m_music.end()){ return; }
  if (music->second.second){
    delete music->second.second;
    --m_numSounds;
  }
  m_music.erase(l_state);
}
```

The sound container is first obtained for the state that is being removed. Every sound in that state is then iterated over and recycled via the `RecycleSound` method, which takes in the sound ID, pointer to the `sf::Sound` instance, and the sound name. Once that is done, all of the state information is erased from the `m_audio` container. Additionally, if an instance of `sf::Music` is found in that state, the memory for it is deallocated and the number of sounds currently existing in memory is decreased.

Good memory management is extremely important in an application and is one of the main reasons we're using manager classes instead of simply having resources scattered all over the place. The method responsible for cleaning up the mess in this case might look a little something like this:

```
void SoundManager::Cleanup(){
  for (auto &state : m_audio){
    for (auto &sound : state.second){
      m_audioManager->ReleaseResource(sound.second.first.m_name);
      delete sound.second.second;
    }
  }
  m_audio.clear();
  for (auto &recycled : m_recycled){
    m_audioManager->ReleaseResource(recycled.first.second);
    delete recycled.second;
  }
  m_recycled.clear();
  for (auto &music : m_music){
    if (music.second.second){
```

```
        delete music.second.second;
      }
    }
    m_music.clear();

    m_properties.clear();
    m_numSounds = 0;
    m_lastID = 0;
  }
```

First, we iterate over the container of currently playing sounds and release the audio resources that are being used. The dynamic memory for the sound is then deleted safely instead of being recycled. The exact same process is repeated one more time for all of the sounds that exist in the `m_recycled` container. Finally, all of the music instances are also deleted. Once all containers are properly cleared, the number of sounds is set back to 0, along with the last sound ID.

Now that we've covered all of the "housekeeping" details, let's take a look at how we can make a system like this tick through its `Update` method:

```
    void SoundManager::Update(float l_dT){
      m_elapsed += l_dT;
      if (m_elapsed < 0.33f){ return; }
      // Run once every third of a second.
      m_elapsed = 0;
      auto& container = m_audio[m_currentState];
      for (auto itr = container.begin(); itr != container.end();){
        if (!itr->second.second->getStatus()){
          RecycleSound(itr->first, itr->second.second,
            itr->second.first.m_name);
          itr = container.erase(itr); // Remove sound.
          continue;
        }
        ++itr;
      }
      auto music = m_music.find(m_currentState);
      if (music == m_music.end()){ return; }
      if (!music->second.second){ return; }
      if (music->second.second->getStatus()){ return; }
      delete music->second.second;
      music->second.second = nullptr;
      --m_numSounds;
    }
```

An important thing to keep in mind here is that we really don't need to run this chunk of code every single tick of the application. Instead, we keep track of time passing and check the `m_elapsed` data member each cycle to see if it's time to run our code yet. The `0.33f` value is arbitrary in this case and can be set to anything within a reasonable range.

If enough time has passed, we loop over every sound in the current state and check its status. If the sound has stopped, we can safely recycle it by invoking the `RecycleSound` method and then remove it from our primary sound container.

When an element in an STL container is removed, all iterators of said container become invalid. If left unattended, this can lead to elements being skipped or out of bounds accesses. It can be addressed by setting the iterator to the return value of the `erase` method, as it returns a valid iterator to an element *after* the one that has been erased. It increments the iterator only if an element hasn't been erased during the current cycle of the loop.

In this system, music follows the exact same treatment and is removed if it's no longer playing.

Next, let's look at providing a way for the users of this class to play sounds:

```
SoundID SoundManager::Play(const std::string& l_sound,
  const sf::Vector3f& l_position, bool l_loop, bool l_relative)
{
  SoundProps* props = GetSoundProperties(l_sound);
  if (!props){ return -1; } // Failed to load sound properties.
  SoundID id;
  sf::Sound* sound = CreateSound(id, props->m_audioName);
  if (!sound){ return -1; }
  // Sound created successfully.
  SetUpSound(sound, props, l_loop, l_relative);
  sound->setPosition(l_position);
  SoundInfo info(props->m_audioName);
  m_audio[m_currentState].emplace(id,std::make_pair(info, sound));
  sound->play();
  return id;
}
```

We begin by obtaining a pointer to the sound properties structure by using the `GetSoundProperties` method, which we will be covering later. If it returned a `nullptr` value, -1 is returned by the `Play` method to signify a loading error. Otherwise, we proceed by creating a sound ID instance that is going to be passed in *by reference* to the `CreateSound` method, along with the identifier of the audio sound buffer. If the sound was created successfully, it returns a pointer to the `sf::Sound` instance that is ready to be used.

The `SetUpSound` method is then invoked with pointers to the `sf::Sound` instance and properties being passed in as arguments, as well as two Boolean flags for whether the sound should loop and be relative to the listener. The latter two are passed in as arguments to the `Play` method we're currently implementing. The sound is then positioned in space and stored in the `m_audio` container, along with the `SoundInfo` structure that is set up just one line before and holds the audio identifier.

The final step is then calling the `play()` method of our sound instance and returning the ID of said sound for later manipulations.

As the header file suggests, there are two versions of the `Play` method. Let's cover the other one now:

```
bool SoundManager::Play(const SoundID& l_id){
    auto& container = m_audio[m_currentState];
    auto sound = container.find(l_id);
    if (sound == container.end()){ return false; }
    sound->second.second->play();
    sound->second.first.m_manualPaused = false;
    return true;
}
```

This version of the `Play` method only takes in a single argument of the sound ID and returns a Boolean flag. It's meant to start an already existing sound, which begins by it being located in the sound container. If the sound has been found, its `play` method is invoked and the `m_manualPaused` flag is set to `false`, showing that it is no longer paused.

Stopping a sound works in a very similar fashion:

```
bool SoundManager::Stop(const SoundID& l_id){
    auto& container = m_audio[m_currentState];
    auto sound = container.find(l_id);
    if (sound == container.end()){ return false; }
    sound->second.second->stop();
    sound->second.first.m_manualPaused = true;
    return true;
}
```

The only difference here is that the `stop` method is invoked instead, and the `m_manualPaused` flag is set to `true` to signify that it has been paused in a non-automatic fashion.

One more method that follows the exact same pattern is the `Pause` method:

```
bool SoundManager::Pause(const SoundID& l_id){
  auto& container = m_audio[m_currentState];
  auto sound = container.find(l_id);
  if (sound == container.end()){ return false; }
  sound->second.second->pause();
  sound->second.first.m_manualPaused = true;
  return true;
}
```

Now it's time to move on from sound and to music, specifically how it can be played:

```
bool SoundManager::PlayMusic(const std::string& l_musicId,
  float l_volume, bool l_loop)
{
  auto s = m_music.find(m_currentState);
  if (s == m_music.end()){ return false; }
  std::string path = m_audioManager->GetPath(l_musicId);
  if (path == ""){ return false; }
  if (!s->second.second){
    s->second.second = new sf::Music();
    ++m_numSounds;
  }
  sf::Music* music = s->second.second;
  if (!music->openFromFile(Utils::GetWorkingDirectory() + path)){
    delete music;
    --m_numSounds;
    s->second.second = nullptr;
    std::cerr << "[SoundManager] Failed to load music from file: "
      << l_musicId << std::endl;
    return false;
  }
  music->setLoop(l_loop);
  music->setVolume(l_volume);
  music->setRelativeToListener(true); // Always relative.
  music->play();
  s->second.first.m_name = l_musicId;
  return true;
}
```

First, the music element for the current state is located. The path to the actual audio file is then obtained by using our newly added Get Path method and checked for being blank. If it isn't, we check whether an actual instance of sf::Music exists for the current state and create one if it doesn't. The openFromFile method of the sf::Music instance is then called in an if statement in order to check if it was successful or not. If it wasn't, the sf::Music instance is deleted and the number of sounds is decreased. Otherwise, the music instance is set to the volume and loop preferences provided as arguments and played. Note that we're setting every music instance to also be relative to the listener. While it is possible to make music positional, we have no need for it at this point.

Because we want the same functionality for music as we do for any given sound, we have a fairly similar line-up of methods for manipulating music as well:

```
bool SoundManager::PlayMusic(const StateType& l_state){
    auto music = m_music.find(m_currentState);
    if (music == m_music.end()){ return false; }
    if (!music->second.second){ return false; }
    music->second.second->play();
    music->second.first.m_manualPaused = false;
    return true;
}
bool SoundManager::StopMusic(const StateType& l_state){
    auto music = m_music.find(m_currentState);
    if (music == m_music.end()){ return false; }
    if (!music->second.second){ return false; }
    music->second.second->stop();
    delete music->second.second;
    music->second.second = nullptr;
    --m_numSounds;
    return true;
}
bool SoundManager::PauseMusic(const StateType& l_state){
    auto music = m_music.find(m_currentState);
    if (music == m_music.end()){ return false; }
    if (!music->second.second){ return false; }
    music->second.second->pause();
    music->second.first.m_manualPaused = true;
    return true;
}
```

Let's get back to sound now. Since we're going to be utilizing its spatial qualities, it's a good idea to have a method that can be used for setting its position in space:

```
bool SoundManager::SetPosition(const SoundID& l_id,
  const sf::Vector3f& l_pos)
{
  auto& container = m_audio[m_currentState];
  auto sound = container.find(l_id);
  if (sound == container.end()){ return false; }
  sound->second.second->setPosition(l_pos);
  return true;
}
```

This method simply locates the sound instance in its container and sets its position to the one provided as an argument.

What if we want to check if a sound is still playing? No problem! That's what the IsPlaying method is for:

```
bool SoundManager::IsPlaying(const SoundID& l_id){
  auto& container = m_audio[m_currentState];
  auto sound = container.find(l_id);
  return (sound != container.end() ?
    sound->second.second->getStatus() : false);
}
```

Due to the fact that sound status is a simple enumeration table, it can be forced into a Boolean value. Since we don't care about the "paused" state, returning the status as a Boolean works just fine.

Next, we have a way for obtaining the sound properties:

```
SoundProps* SoundManager::GetSoundProperties(
  const std::string& l_soundName)
{
  auto& properties = m_properties.find(l_soundName);
  if (properties == m_properties.end()){
    if (!LoadProperties(l_soundName)){ return nullptr; }
    properties = m_properties.find(l_soundName);
  }
  return &properties->second;
}
```

Because sound properties aren't loaded during start-up, simply not finding the right information might simply mean that it was never loaded. If that's the case, the LoadProperties method is invoked. It returns a Boolean value that informs us of a failure, in which case a nullptr value is returned. Otherwise, the properties structure is searched for again and then returned at the end of this method.

As we're on the subject of loading properties, let's actually take a look at how they're loaded from the .sound file:

```cpp
bool SoundManager::LoadProperties(const std::string& l_name){
  std::ifstream file;
  file.open(Utils::GetWorkingDirectory() +
    "media/Sounds/" + l_name + ".sound");
  if (!file.is_open()){
    std::cerr << "Failed to load sound: " << l_name << std::endl;
    return false;
  }
  SoundProps props("");
  std::string line;
  while (std::getline(file, line)){
    if (line[0] == '|'){ continue; }
    std::stringstream keystream(line);
    std::string type;
    keystream >> type;
    if (type == "Audio"){
      keystream >> props.m_audioName;
    } else if (type == "Volume"){
      keystream >> props.m_volume;
    } else if (type == "Pitch"){
      keystream >> props.m_pitch;
    } else if (type == "Distance"){
      keystream >> props.m_minDistance;
    } else if (type == "Attenuation"){
      keystream >> props.m_attenuation;
    } else {
      // ?
    }
  }
  file.close();
  if (props.m_audioName == ""){ return false; }
  m_properties.emplace(l_name, props);
  return true;
}
```

Having loaded many files in the past, this should be nothing new. So, let's just breeze right through it. A temporary `SoundProps` instance called `props` is created on the stack with a default audio name that is blank. The file is then processed and checked line by line for relevant keywords. The information is then loaded directly into the temporary properties instance using the `>>` operator.

For extra credit, the `if else` chain could be replaced with some sort of associative container of lambda functions, but let's keep the logic as it is for the sake of simplicity.

Once the file has all been read in, it is closed and the audio name of the properties instance is checked for not being a blank, as it should've been loaded during the process. If the name is, in fact, something other than a blank, the `SoundProps` instance is inserted into the property container and true is returned for success.

As we were covering changing states, a few methods for pausing and starting all sounds were introduced. Let's take a look at one of them now:

```
void SoundManager::PauseAll(const StateType& l_state){
  auto& container = m_audio[l_state];
  for (auto itr = container.begin(); itr != container.end();){
    if (!itr->second.second->getStatus()){
      RecycleSound(itr->first, itr->second.second,
        itr->second.first.m_name);
      itr = container.erase(itr);
      continue;
    }
    itr->second.second->pause();
    ++itr;
  }
  auto music = m_music.find(l_state);
  if (music == m_music.end()){ return; }
  if (!music->second.second){ return; }
  music->second.second->pause();
}
```

The `PauseAll` method first obtains the container of all sounds for the provided state. It iterates over each one and checks if the sound is actually stopped or not. If it is, the sound is simply recycled and the element is erased. Otherwise, the sound's `pause` method is called. Music for the provided state is also paused, provided that it exists.

The `UnpauseAll` method is simpler, as it has no reason to recycle sounds:

```
void SoundManager::UnpauseAll(const StateType& l_state){
  auto& container = m_audio[l_state];
  for (auto &itr : container){
    if (itr.second.first.m_manualPaused){ continue; }
    itr.second.second->play();
  }

  auto music = m_music.find(l_state);
  if (music == m_music.end()){ return; }
  if (!music->second.second ||music->second.first.m_manualPaused){
    return;
  }
  music->second.second->play();
}
```

The catch here is that the sounds and music are only played again if they weren't manually paused by their respective `Pause` methods.

Now, let's implement arguably the most important piece of this class that is responsible for actual creation and recycling of the `sf::Sound` instances:

```
sf::Sound* SoundManager::CreateSound(SoundID& l_id,
  const std::string& l_audioName)
{
  sf::Sound* sound = nullptr;
  if (!m_recycled.empty() && (m_numSounds >= Max_Sounds ||
    m_recycled.size() >= Sound_Cache))
  {
    auto itr = m_recycled.begin();
    while (itr != m_recycled.end()){
      if (itr->first.second == l_audioName){ break; }
      ++itr;
    }
    if (itr == m_recycled.end()){
      // If a sound with the same name hasn't been found!
      auto element = m_recycled.begin();
      l_id = element->first.first;
      m_audioManager->ReleaseResource(element->first.second);
      m_audioManager->RequireResource(l_audioName);
      sound = element->second;
      sound->setBuffer(*m_audioManager->GetResource(l_audioName));
      m_recycled.erase(element);
    } else {
```

```
        l_id = itr->first.first;
        sound = itr->second;
        m_recycled.erase(itr);
    }
    return sound;
}
if (m_numSounds < Max_Sounds){
    if (m_audioManager->RequireResource(l_audioName)){
        sound = new sf::Sound();
        l_id = m_lastID;
        ++m_lastID;
        ++m_numSounds;
        sound->setBuffer(*m_audioManager->GetResource(l_audioName));
        return sound;
    }
}
std::cerr << "[SoundManager] Failed to create sound."
    << std::endl;
return nullptr;
}
```

A local variable named `sound` is first set up with the value of `nullptr`, and it will be manipulated throughout the rest of this method. The size of the recycled sound container is then checked, along with whether the number of maximum sounds overall or maximum cached sounds has been exceeded.

If the number of sounds is too high on either count and the recycled container isn't empty, we know we're going to be recycling an already existing sound. This process begins by first attempting to find a sound that already uses the same `sf::SoundBuffer` instance. In the case of such sound not existing, we simply pop the first element from the recycled container, store its ID in the variable `l_id` and release the resource that was used by the sound being recycled. The `l_id` argument takes a reference to a `SoundID` that it modifies, which serves as a way to let the outside code know the ID that has been assigned to the sound instance. The new resource that our sound is going to use is then reserved and our sound variable is set to point to the recycled sound instance, which is then set to use a new sound buffer. Our refurbished sound is removed from the recycled container. On the other hand, if a sound that uses the same `sf::SoundBuffer` instance was found, it doesn't need any additional setting up and can simply be returned after its ID is stored and it's erased from the `m_recycled` container.

If there were no recycled sounds available or we had extra space to spare, a new sound is created instead of using a recycled one. The ID of the sound is set to match that of m_lastID, which is then incremented (same as m_numSounds). After the sound's buffer is set up, it can safely be returned for further processing, such as in the SetUpSound method:

```
void SoundManager::SetUpSound(sf::Sound* l_snd,
  const SoundProps* l_props, bool& l_loop, bool& l_relative)
{
    l_snd->setVolume(l_props->m_volume);
    l_snd->setPitch(l_props->m_pitch);
    l_snd->setMinDistance(l_props->m_minDistance);
    l_snd->setAttenuation(l_props->m_attenuation);
    l_snd->setLoop(l_loop);
    l_snd->setRelativeToListener(l_relative);
}
```

The main idea of this method is simply reducing code wherever possible. It sets up the volume, pitch, minimum distance, attenuation, looping, and relativity of the sound all based on the arguments provided.

Let's wrap this class up with a relatively simple yet commonly used piece of code:

```
void SoundManager::RecycleSound(const SoundID& l_id,
  sf::Sound* l_snd, const std::string& l_name)
{
  m_recycled.emplace_back(std::make_pair(l_id, l_name), l_snd);
}
```

This method is only responsible for pushing the information provided as arguments into the recycled container for later use.

Adding support for sound

In order to make our entities emit sounds, some preparations have to be made. For now, we're only going to concern ourselves with simply adding the sound of footsteps whenever a character walks. Doing so requires a slight modification of the EntityMessage enumeration in EntityMessages.h:

```
enum class EntityMessage{
  Move, Is_Moving, Frame_Change, State_Changed, Direction_Changed,
  Switch_State, Attack_Action, Dead
};
```

The highlighted bits are what we're going to be focusing on. `Frame_Change` is a new type of message that's been added in this chapter, and `Direction_Changed` will be used to manipulate the sound listener's direction. In order to detect when a frame changes during the animation process, however, we're going to need to make a few more adjustments to our code base.

Animation system hooks

In order to have the ability to send out the `Frame_Change` message we've just created, our animation system is going to need a few minor additions, starting with `Anim_Base.h`:

```
class Anim_Base{
public:
    ...
    bool CheckMoved();
    ...
protected:
    ...
    bool m_hasMoved;
    ...
};
```

Here, we're adding a new data member and a method to check if the current frame of an animation has recently been changed. Let's actually integrate this code in `Anim_Base.cpp`:

```
Anim_Base::Anim_Base()...,m_hasMoved(false){ ... }

bool Anim_Base::CheckMoved(){
    bool result = m_hasMoved;
    m_hasMoved = false;
    return result;
}
```

In the constructor, it's important to remember to set the newly added data member to a default value, which in this case is `false`. The actual `CheckMoved` method is a very basic chunk of code that returns the value of `m_hasMoved` but sets it to `false` at the same time in order to avoid false positives.

Now that we have an active flag that is going to be used to check for frame changes, all that's missing is simply setting it to `true` in the `SetFrame` method:

```
bool Anim_Base::SetFrame(const unsigned int& l_frame){
    if((l_frame >= m_frameStart && l_frame <= m_frameEnd)||
      (l_frame >= m_frameEnd && l_frame <= m_frameStart))
    {
        m_frameCurrent = l_frame;
        m_hasMoved = true;
        return true;
    }
    return false;
}
```

Notice the return value is now a Boolean instead of void. This additional change makes it very easy to do error checking, which is very important for making our last alteration in `Anim_Directional.cpp`:

```
void Anim_Directional::FrameStep(){
  bool b = SetFrame(m_frameCurrent +
    (m_frameStart <= m_frameEnd ? 1 : -1));
  if (b){ return; }
  if (m_loop){ SetFrame(m_frameStart); }
  else { SetFrame(m_frameEnd); Pause(); }
}
```

The difference here is subtle but relevant. We essentially went from incrementing the current frame by hand by using `m_frameCurrent` to only using the `SetFrame` method.

Entity component system expansion

With adjustments made previously, we can now put down our last piece of the puzzle in making this work by sending out the `Frame_Change` message in `S_SheetAnimation.cpp`:

```
void S_SheetAnimation::Update(float l_dT){
  EntityManager* entities = m_systemManager->GetEntityManager();
  for(auto &entity : m_entities){
    ...
    if (sheet->GetSpriteSheet()->GetCurrentAnim()->CheckMoved()){
      int frame = sheet->GetSpriteSheet()->
        GetCurrentAnim()->GetFrame();
      Message msg((MessageType)EntityMessage::Frame_Change);
      msg.m_receiver = entity;
```

```
            msg.m_int = frame;
            m_systemManager->GetMessageHandler()->Dispatch(msg);
        }
    }
}
```

The `Update` method, as you might recall, already handles other types of messages that are related to entities attacking and dying, so this is already gift-wrapped for us. The `CheckMoved` method we added earlier comes in handy and aids us in checking for changes. If there has been a change, the current frame is obtained and stored in the message, which is shortly followed by a `Dispatch` call.

The sound emitter component

Within the entity component system paradigm, every possible entity parameter or feature is represented as a component. Emitting sounds is definitely one of those features. In order for that to happen, we do have some setting up to do, starting with creating and implementing it in the `C_SoundEmitter.h` header. Before that, however, let's define the types of sounds an entity can have:

```
enum class EntitySound{ None = -1, Footstep, Attack, Hurt,Death };
```

As you can see, we're only going to be working with four types of sound, one of which is going to be implemented in this chapter. A `None` value is also set up in order to make error checking easier.

Every sound that an entity can emit will most likely have different frames it plays during, which calls for a new data structure that encapsulates such information:

```
struct SoundParameters{
    static const int Max_SoundFrames = 5;
    SoundParameters(){
        for (int i = 0; i < Max_SoundFrames; ++i){ m_frames[i] = -1; }
    }
    std::string m_sound;
    std::array<int, Max_SoundFrames> m_frames;
};
```

Since sounds are going to be tied to specific frames of animation, we need to define the maximum possible number of frames that can have sounds attached to them. The static constant named `Max_SoundFrames` is used for that purpose here.

The constructor of the `SoundParameters` structure initializes the entire array of frames to a value of -1. This is going to allow us to check this information in a slightly more efficient way, as the check can be over whenever the first -1 value is encountered. In addition to an array of frame numbers, this structure also stores the name of the sound that is to be emitted.

Now, we can finally begin implementing the sound emitter component:

```
class C_SoundEmitter : public C_Base{
public:
    static const int Max_EntitySounds = 4;
    ...
private:
    SoundID m_soundID;
    std::array<SoundParameters, Max_EntitySounds> m_params;
};
```

First, another static constant is created in order to denote the number of entity sounds that are going to exist. The component itself only has two data members. The first one is a sound ID that will be used for emitting sounds that should not be played repeatedly and have to wait until the previous sound is finished. The second data member is an array of sound parameters for each possible type of entity sound.

Let's begin implementing the component, starting with its constructor:

```
C_SoundEmitter(): C_Base(Component::SoundEmitter), m_soundID(-1){}
```

Apart from the typical invocation of the `C_Base` constructor with the component type passed in, the sound ID data member is initialized to -1 as well to signify that this component currently is not playing any sounds.

In order for the future sound system to know what sounds to play, we're going to provide a way sound information can be extracted from this component:

```
const std::string& GetSound(const EntitySound& l_snd){
  static std::string empty = "";
  return((int)l_snd < Max_EntitySounds ?
    m_params[(int)l_snd].m_sound : empty);
}
```

By simply providing one of the enumerated values of `EntitySound` as an argument, outside classes can retrieve information about which sound to play given the circumstances.

Additionally, in order to know if a sound should be played or not, the sound system will need a way to tell if the current frame of animation should be emitting sound or not. This is where the `IsSoundFrame` method comes in:

```
bool IsSoundFrame(const EntitySound& l_snd, int l_frame){
  if ((int)l_snd >= Max_EntitySounds){ return false; }
  for (int i = 0; i < SoundParameters::Max_SoundFrames; ++i){
    if (m_params[(int)l_snd].m_frames[i] == -1){ return false; }
    if (m_params[(int)l_snd].m_frames[i] == l_frame){return true;}
  }
  return false;
}
```

If the provided sound argument is larger than the highest supported entity sound ID, `false` is returned. Otherwise, all of the frames for the given sound are iterated over. If a -1 value is encountered, `false` is returned right away. However, if the frame provided as an argument matches a sound frame in the array, this method returns `true`.

Next, we're going to need a few helper methods to set and get certain information:

```
SoundID GetSoundID(){ return m_soundID; }
void SetSoundID(const SoundID& l_id){ m_soundID = l_id; }
SoundParameters* GetParameters(){ return &m_params[0]; }
```

Before we get to reading in this component's information from the entity file, let's take a gander at what it might look like. This snippet can be found inside `Player.entity`:

```
Name Player
...
Component 6 footstep:1,4
```

After the component ID, we're going to be reading in the name of the sound effect to be played, followed by a set of frames delimited by commas. The name of the sound itself is separated from the frame information by a colon. Let's write this:

```
void ReadIn(std::stringstream& l_stream){
  std::string main_delimiter = ":";
  std::string frame_delimiter = ",";
  for (int i = 0; i < Max_EntitySounds; ++i){
    std::string chunk;
    l_stream >> chunk;
    if (chunk == ""){ break; }
```

```cpp
std::string sound = chunk.substr(0,
    chunk.find(main_delimiter));
std::string frames = chunk.substr(
    chunk.find(main_delimiter) + main_delimiter.length());
m_params[i].m_sound = sound;
size_t pos = 0;
unsigned int frameNum = 0;
while (frameNum < SoundParameters::Max_SoundFrames){
    pos = frames.find(frame_delimiter);
    int frame = -1;
    if (pos != std::string::npos){
        frame = stoi(frames.substr(0, pos));
        frames.erase(0, pos + frame_delimiter.length());
    } else {
        frame = stoi(frames);
        m_params[i].m_frames[frameNum] = frame;
        break;
    }
    m_params[i].m_frames[frameNum] = frame;
    ++frameNum;
}
}
}
```

After the delimiter information is set up, we iterate once for each possible entity sound and read in the contents of the next segment of the line into a string named chunk. If that string is actually empty, we break out of the loop as there's clearly no more information to be loaded. Otherwise, the chunk is split into two parts right at the colon delimiter: sound and frames. The entity sound is then stored inside the parameters structure.

Lastly, it's necessary to process the frame information, which is delimited by commas. Two local variables are set up to help us with this: pos that stores the position of the comma delimiter if one is found and frameNum that is used to make sure the Max_SoundFrames limit is honored. Inside the while loop, the frame delimiter is first located using the find method of the std::string class. If a delimiter was found, the frame is extracted from the string and converted to an integer, which is stored inside the variable frame. That entire segment, including the delimiter, is then erased from the string frames and the extracted information is stored inside the parameters structure. In a case where a delimiter wasn't found, however, the loop is stopped right after the frame information has been extracted.

The sound listener component

In order to properly implement spatial sounds, there has to be a listener within our game world. That listener is, of course, the player of the game. Fortunately, there isn't a lot of information we need to process or store when creating a component for an audio listener:

```
class C_SoundListener : public C_Base{
public:
    C_SoundListener() : C_Base(Component::SoundListener){}
    void ReadIn(std::stringstream& l_stream){}
private:

};
```

Yes, that's it! In its most essential form, this class simply represents a sign that its owner entity should be treated as a listener in the auditory world.

Implementing the sound system

With both sound emitter and sound listener components out of the way, we have a green light to begin implementing the sound system that is going to bring all of this code to life. Let's get it started!

```
class S_Sound : public S_Base{
public:
  S_Sound(SystemManager* l_systemMgr);
  ~S_Sound();

  void Update(float l_dT);
  void HandleEvent(const EntityId& l_entity,
    const EntityEvent& l_event);
  void Notify(const Message& l_message);

  void SetUp(AudioManager* l_audioManager,
    SoundManager* l_soundManager);
private:
  sf::Vector3f MakeSoundPosition(const sf::Vector2f& l_entityPos,
    unsigned int l_elevation);
  void EmitSound(const EntityId& l_entity,
    const EntitySound& l_sound, bool l_useId, bool l_relative,
    int l_checkFrame = -1);
  AudioManager* m_audioManager;
  SoundManager* m_soundManager;
};
```

Apart from the typical methods that a system is required to implement and a few custom ones, we also have two data members that point to instances of the `AudioManager` and `SoundManager` classes. Let's begin actually implementing the sound system:

```
S_Sound::S_Sound(SystemManager* l_systemMgr)
  : S_Base(System::Sound, l_systemMgr), m_audioManager(nullptr),
  m_soundManager(nullptr)
{
  Bitmask req;
  req.TurnOnBit((unsigned int)Component::Position);
  req.TurnOnBit((unsigned int)Component::SoundEmitter);
  m_requiredComponents.push_back(req);
  req.ClearBit((unsigned int)Component::SoundEmitter);
  req.TurnOnBit((unsigned int)Component::SoundListener);
  m_requiredComponents.push_back(req);

  m_systemManager->GetMessageHandler()->
    Subscribe(EntityMessage::Direction_Changed, this);
  m_systemManager->GetMessageHandler()->
    Subscribe(EntityMessage::Frame_Change, this);
}
```

The constructor, predictably enough, sets up two possible versions of the requirement bitmask, both of which require the position component to be present. It then subscribes to the two message types we discussed previously.

Since we're going to need access to both the audio manager and sound manager, a method like this can definitely come in handy:

```
void S_Sound::SetUp(AudioManager* l_audioManager,
    SoundManager* l_soundManager)
{
    m_audioManager = l_audioManager;
    m_soundManager = l_soundManager;
}
```

Next, let's take a jab at implementing the `Update` method:

```
void S_Sound::Update(float l_dT){
  EntityManager* entities = m_systemManager->GetEntityManager();
  for (auto &entity : m_entities){
    C_Position* c_pos = entities->
      GetComponent<C_Position>(entity, Component::Position);
    sf::Vector2f position = c_pos->GetPosition();
    unsigned int elevation = c_pos->GetElevation();
```

```
    bool IsListener = entities->
      HasComponent(entity, Component::SoundListener);
    if (IsListener){
      sf::Listener::setPosition(
        MakeSoundPosition(position, elevation));
    }

    if (!entities->HasComponent(
      entity, Component::SoundEmitter))
    {
      continue;
    }
    C_SoundEmitter* c_snd = entities->GetComponent<C_SoundEmitter>
      (entity,Component::SoundEmitter);
    if (c_snd->GetSoundID() == -1){ continue; }
    if (!IsListener){
      if (!m_soundManager->SetPosition(c_snd->GetSoundID(),
        MakeSoundPosition(position, elevation)))
      {
        c_snd->SetSoundID(-1);
      }
    } else {
      if (!m_soundManager->IsPlaying(c_snd->GetSoundID())){
        c_snd->SetSoundID(-1);
      }
    }
  }
}
```

Each entity in this system first has its position and elevation obtained and stored inside a few local variables. It also determines if the current entity is the sound listener or not and stores that information inside a Boolean variable.

If the current entity has a sound emitter component and its sound ID is not equal to -1, it's safe to deduce that the sound is currently still being played. If the current entity is not a sound listener, we attempt to update the sound's position and catch the result of that in an `if` statement. If the position update fails, the sound ID is set back to -1, since it means the sound is no longer active. If the entity is, in fact, a listener, we don't need to update the sound's position at all. Instead, we determine if the sound is still playing or not by calling the `IsPlaying` method.

Afterwards, it's necessary to update the position of the sf::Listener class if the current entity has the listener component. Note the use of the MakeSoundPosition method here, as well as in the previous chunk of code. It returns a sf::Vector3f based on the position and elevation of an entity. We're going to cover this method shortly.

Let's work on handling both of the message types we've discussed previously next:

```
void S_Sound::Notify(const Message& l_message){
  if (!HasEntity(l_message.m_receiver)){ return; }
  EntityManager* entities = m_systemManager->GetEntityManager();
  bool IsListener = entities->
    HasComponent(l_message.m_receiver, Component::SoundListener);
  EntityMessage m = (EntityMessage)l_message.m_type;
  switch (m){
  case EntityMessage::Direction_Changed:
  {
    if (!IsListener){ return; }
    Direction dir = (Direction)l_message.m_int;
    switch (dir){
    case Direction::Up: sf::Listener::setDirection(0, 0, -1);
      break;
    case Direction::Down: sf::Listener::setDirection(0, 0, 1);
      break;
    case Direction::Left: sf::Listener::setDirection(-1, 0, 0);
      break;
    case Direction::Right: sf::Listener::setDirection(1, 0, 0);
      break;
    }
  }
    break;
  case EntityMessage::Frame_Change:
    if (!entities->HasComponent(l_message.m_receiver,
      Component::SoundEmitter))
    {
      return;
    }
    EntityState state = entities->GetComponent<C_State>
      (l_message.m_receiver, Component::State)->GetState();
    EntitySound sound = EntitySound::None;
    if (state==EntityState::Walking){sound=EntitySound::Footstep;}
      else if(state == EntityState::Attacking){
        sound = EntitySound::Attack;
      } else if (state==EntityState::Hurt){sound=EntitySound::Hurt;}
```

```
      else if (state==EntityState::Dying){sound=EntitySound::Death;}
      if (sound == EntitySound::None){ return; }
      EmitSound(l_message.m_receiver, sound, false,
        IsListener, l_message.m_int);
      break;
    }
  }
}
```

In case the entity's direction has changed and it is the sound listener, we obviously need to change the direction of the `sf::Listener` to match the one that is carried inside the message. On the other hand, if we receive a message about a frame changing, the `EmitSound` method is called with the entity ID, sound type, two Boolean flags indicating whether the sound should loop and whether it should be relative to the listener or not, and the current frame the animation is in all passed in as arguments. The sound relativity to the listener in the scene is simply decided by whether the current entity itself is a listener or not.

Positioning sounds in space is also a huge part of this whole system working correctly. Let's take a look at the `MakeSoundPosition` method:

```
sf::Vector3f S_Sound::MakeSoundPosition(
  const sf::Vector2f& l_entityPos, unsigned int l_elevation)
{
  return sf::Vector3f(l_entityPos.x,
    l_elevation * Sheet::Tile_Size, l_entityPos.y);
}
```

Due to the default up vector in SFML being the positive Y axis, the two dimensional coordinates of an entity position are passed in as X and Z arguments. Meanwhile, the Y argument is simply the entity's elevation multiplied by the `Tile_Size` value, found inside the `Map.h` header, which results in entity elevation simulating the height.

Last but definitely not least, we have a chunk of code that is responsible for entities emitting all their sounds that we need to take a look at:

```
void S_Sound::EmitSound(const EntityId& l_entity,
  const EntitySound& l_sound, bool l_useId, bool l_relative,
  int l_checkFrame)
{
  if (!HasEntity(l_entity)){ return; }
  if (!m_systemManager->GetEntityManager()->
    HasComponent(l_entity, Component::SoundEmitter))
  {
    return;
  }
```

```
// Is a sound emitter.
EntityManager* entities = m_systemManager->GetEntityManager();
C_SoundEmitter* c_snd = entities->GetComponent<C_SoundEmitter>
  (l_entity, Component::SoundEmitter);
if (c_snd->GetSoundID() != -1 && l_useId){ return; }
// If sound is free or use of ID isn't required.
if (l_checkFrame != -1 &&
  !c_snd->IsSoundFrame(l_sound, l_checkFrame))
{
  return;
}
// Frame is irrelevant or correct.
C_Position* c_pos = entities->
  GetComponent<C_Position>(l_entity, Component::Position);
sf::Vector3f pos = (l_relative ?
  sf::Vector3f(0.f, 0.f, 0.f) :
  MakeSoundPosition(c_pos->GetPosition(),
  c_pos->GetElevation()));
if (l_useId){
  c_snd->SetSoundID(m_soundManager->
    Play(c_snd->GetSound(l_sound), pos));
} else {
  m_soundManager->Play(c_snd->GetSound(l_sound),
    pos, false, l_relative);
}
}
```

The first task is obviously checking if the sound system has an entity with the provided ID, and if the entity is a sound emitter. If it is, the sound emitter component is obtained and the sound ID it stores is checked for being equal to -1. The code still proceeds, however, if an entity is already emitting another sound but the `l_useId` argument is set to `false`, which tells us that a sound should be emitted regardless. Next, the frame passed in as an argument is checked for either being equal to -1, which means the sound should be played regardless, or for it being one of the sound frames defined inside the sound emitter component.

Once we commit to playing the sound, the entity's position component is obtained and used to calculate the position of the sound. If it should be relative to the listener, the position is simply set to be at the absolute zero coordinate of all axes.

If we want to only keep a single instance of a particular sound, the `Play` method of the sound manager is invoked within the `SetSoundID` argument list of the sound emitter component to catch the returned ID. It only has two arguments passed in, as the other two Boolean flags hold the default values of `false`. Otherwise, if this particular sound should be played irrespective of whether the entity is already emitting another sound or not, the `Play` method of our sound manager is called by itself and the Boolean flag for sound being relative to the listener is passed in as the last argument.

Integrating our code

In order to prevent sounds or music from playing at inappropriate times, our state manager must notify the sound manager of any state changes:

```
void StateManager::SwitchTo(const StateType& l_type){
  ...
  m_shared->m_soundManager->ChangeState(l_type);
  ...
}
```

Since the sound manager also cares about states being removed, let's tell it when that happens:

```
void StateManager::RemoveState(const StateType& l_type){
  for (auto itr = m_states.begin();
    itr != m_states.end(); ++itr)
  {
    if (itr->first == l_type){
      ...
      m_shared->m_soundManager->RemoveState(l_type);
      return;
    }
  }
}
```

The only thing we have left to do now is actually integrating everything we worked on into the rest of our code base, starting with `SharedContext.h`:

```
...
#include "AudioManager.h"
#include "SoundManager.h"
...
struct SharedContext{
    SharedContext():
```

```
        ...
        m_audioManager(nullptr),
        m_soundManager(nullptr),
        ...
        {}

    ...
    AudioManager* m_audioManager;
    SoundManager* m_soundManager;
    ...
};
```

Next, instantiating and managing these two new classes inside the shared context is of utmost importance. Let's start by modifying the `Game.h` header:

```
class Game{
public:
    ...
private:
    ...
    AudioManager m_audioManager;
    SoundManager m_soundManager;
    ...
};
```

As always, we keep these manager classes inside `Game` in order to manage their lifetime properly. For some of them, however, merely existing isn't enough. They require to be set up like this:

```
Game::Game(): ..., m_soundManager(&m_audioManager)
{
  ...
  m_context.m_audioManager = &m_audioManager;
  m_context.m_soundManager = &m_soundManager;
  ...
  m_systemManager.GetSystem<S_Sound>(System::Sound)->
    SetUp(&m_audioManager, &m_soundManager);
  ...
}
```

After both classes are created, their addresses are passed to the shared context. One more important detail that's easy to overlook is actually setting up the sound system at this point. It needs to have access to both the audio and the sound manager.

Let's not forget to also update the sound manager properly during the flow of the entire application:

```
void Game::Update(){
    ...
    m_soundManager.Update(m_elapsed.asSeconds());
    ...
}
```

With the creation of new components and systems comes the responsibility of making sure they can actually be created automatically, by adding the component types to the entity manager:

```
EntityManager::EntityManager(SystemManager* l_sysMgr,
    TextureManager* l_textureMgr): ...
{
    ...
    AddComponentType<C_SoundEmitter>(Component::SoundEmitter);
    AddComponentType<C_SoundListener>(Component::SoundListener);
}
```

Our sound system also needs to be created inside the system manager:

```
SystemManager::SystemManager():...{
    ...
    m_systems[System::Sound] = new S_Sound(this);
}
```

Having all of that done, we can finally add some music to our game! Let's start by making sure we have an intro soundtrack by modifying State_Intro.cpp:

```
void State_Intro::OnCreate(){
    ...
    m_stateMgr->GetContext()->m_soundManager->
        PlayMusic("Electrix", 100.f, true);
}
```

Also, it would be nice to have some background music during actual game-play, so let's modify State_Game.cpp as follows:

```
void State_Game::OnCreate(){
    ...
    m_stateMgr->GetContext()->m_soundManager->
        PlayMusic("TownTheme", 50.f, true);
}
```

And voila! Just like that, we now have music and dynamic sound effects baked into our RPG!

Summary

With possibilities ranging anywhere from simple ambiance to complex musical scores tugging at the heart strings of the player, our game world starts to develop a sense of character and presence. All of the hard work we put in towards making sure our project isn't mute adds up to yet another major leap in the direction of quality. However, as we begin to approach the end of this book with only two chapters remaining, the most challenging part is still yet to come.

In the next chapter, we will be exploring the vast world of networking and how it can help us turn our lonely, quiet RPG into a battle zone of multiple other players. See you there!

13
We Have Contact! – Networking Basics

In today's world where everyone and everything is interconnected, playing games with your friends is not a new thing anymore. It has become a standard amongst many groups. Expressions such as "frag" or "camping" became buzzwords amongst gamers. Whether it's a 2-4 player LAN party or a massive multiplayer online game, networking obviously plays a huge role in the gaming circles. Introducing the element of other human players amplifies the content added, on top of making the game's universe seem much more alive and flourishing. In many instances, this sort of phenomenon actually brings people together and provides a very enjoyable experience, as long as it's not lagging. It's about time we harness the essence of multiplayer, and perhaps even propagate the six degrees of separation.

In this chapter, we're going to be covering:

- Fundamentals of networking applications
- Utilizing threads and ensuring data safety
- Implementing our own basic communication protocol
- Building a simple chat client and server

Let's break the isolation of your system and open it up to the outside world!

Basics of networking

First things first, let's cover a term that is pretty much synonymous with networking at this point: sockets. What is a socket? In its simplest terms, a socket is just an interface that is used for network communications. When two applications are communicating, at least two sockets are involved and data is exchanged between them. When data is sent from application A to application B, it first leaves from the socket of application A, travels throughout the internet, and hopefully reaches the socket of application B:

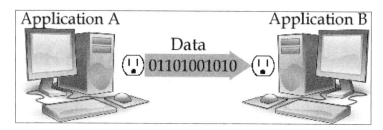

Each socket has to be bound to something referred to as a port, which can be imagined as a gateway to a system. Each gateway is used for different purposes and can only be used by one socket at a time. In the simplest terms, a port is just a 16-bit numerical value, which means a port number can be as high as 65535. While a service is using a specific port, another socket cannot bind to it until it's freed. The most commonly used ports are in a range of 20-1024. For example, port 80 is always used for HTTP traffic, which is what most website hosting servers operate on.

SFML networking

In order to access network constructs in SFML, we must first include the network header:

```
#include <SFML/Network.hpp>
```

Building a project that has networking capabilities also requires more library files in order to link properly, specifically `sfml-network.lib`, `ws2_32.lib`, and `winmm.lib`. Having these libraries included will ensure that the project compiles properly.

There are several types of sockets available out there, each with specific features, advantages, and disadvantages. SFML provides us with two basic types: TCP and UDP. **TCP** stands for **Transmission Control Protocol**, while **UDP** stands for **User Datagram Protocol**. Both of these protocols are capable of sending and receiving data, but they are fundamentally different from each other under the hood. It's fair to mention that while two sockets of the same type cannot bind to the same port, it can still be bound to by two different protocols.

TCP sockets

TCP is a connection-based protocol, which means that before data can be exchanged, a connection has to be established by having an application that attempts to initiate it (a client) connect to another application that is actively waiting for connections (a server). Let's take a look at a basic client application connection attempt:

```
sf::TcpSocket socket;
sf::Socket::Status status =
  socket.connect("192.168.1.2", 5600, sf::seconds(5.f));
if (status != sf::Socket::Done){
    // Connection failed.
}
```

First, we create a TCP socket instance. Its `connect` method is called next, with three arguments:

- The first argument is of the type `sf::IpAddress` and is exactly what it sounds like: the IP address we are trying to connect to, which has to be open and have a server accepting connections.

- The second argument is the port number.

- Lastly, we have the third argument, which is completely optional. It's the timeout value after which the socket should give up and throw an error. If this argument isn't provided, the default operating system time-out value is used.

The return value of the connect method is captured and stored in a `sf::Socket::Status` type, which is just an enumeration table that has a few useful values, such as `Done`, `NotReady`, `Partial`, `Disconnected`, and `Error`. Every method of both socket types that has to do with sending or receiving data, connecting or disconnecting, returns a status that we can use for error checking.

In order to accept a connection on the server side when using TCP, a special class is used: `sf::TcpListener`. It has to be bound to a specific port and cannot send or receive any data:

```
sf::TcpListener listener;
if (listener.listen(5600) != sf::Socket::Done)
{
    // Unable to bind to port.
}

sf::TcpSocket incoming;
```

```
if (listener.accept(incoming) != sf::Socket::Done)
{
    // Failed accepting an incoming connection.
}
```

After the socket is set up, the listener's `accept` method is called. Along with `connect` and a few other methods we'll be covering down the line, it actually stops the application from continuing until a connection comes through. This is what's referred to as `blocking`. A good example of a blocking function from an STL library is `std::cin`. Why is this important? Well, to put it simply, networking operations are rather unpredictable. There is no way of knowing exactly how long a connection attempt may take, as the host on the other end could be unreachable. During that time, your application will stand still and do absolutely nothing.

After a connection finally comes through, the incoming socket can be used to communicate with the client:

```
char data[100];
// ...
if (socket.send(data, 100) != sf::Socket::Done){
    // Sending data failed.
}
```

The send method has two variations: a low-level one that allows the user to send a raw array of bytes and a higher level one that uses a specialized class we're going to be covering shortly. The low-level version takes in a `void` pointer and the number of bytes it should send.

Keep in mind that sending data could also fail for a number of reasons. Make sure to always check the returned status for errors!

In order to receive data on the other end, a socket needs to listen:

```
char data[100];
std::size_t received;

if (socket.receive(data, 100, received) != sf::Socket::Done)
{
    // Failed receiving data.
}
```

When raw data is sent, a large-enough buffer must be provided along with the maximum size it can contain, which is the second argument of the receive method. The third argument is the number of bytes received, which is written over when data comes in. The receive method is also blocking by default. This means that it will halt the entire program until some data comes through.

Handling multiple connections

You might have noticed by now that all of the examples above focus on just one client connecting and sending data. In today's hyper-connected world that is almost never the case, so let's take a look at a way we can handle multiple TCP sockets at the same time:

```
sf::TcpSocket socket;
// ...
sf::SocketSelector selector;
selector.add(socket);
```

The `sf::SocketSelector` class provides a way for us to block on multiple sockets, instead of just one. It monitors every single socket that is added to it for incoming data, unlike the previous examples that only dealt with a single socket.

A very important thing to keep in mind is that the socket selector does not actually store the sockets added to it, but merely points to them. This means that although a socket has been added to a selector, it still must be stored in a data container of your choosing.

To handle incoming data from multiple sockets, the `wait` method of a socket selector class is used:

```
sf::SocketSelector selector;
std::vector<sf::TcpSocket> container;
// ...
sf::TcpSocket socket;
selector.add(socket);
container.push_back(socket);
if (selector.wait(sf::seconds(10))){
  for (auto &itr : container){
    if (selector.isReady(itr)){
      // Socket received data.
      char data[100];
      std::size_t received;
      sf::Socket::Status status= itr.receive(data, 100, received);
      if (status != sf::Socket::Done){
```

```
            // Failed receiving data...
        }
      }
    }
  } else {
    // Timed out...
  }
```

The argument provided in the `wait` method is, once again, optional. If one of the socket inside the selector receives something, *true* is returned and we can iterate over our data container to find the socket that received data, by using the `isReady` method.

TCP protocol specifics

One major difference between TCP and UDP is transmission reliability. The TCP protocol uses something called a three-way-handshake when establishing a connection. It looks a little something like this:

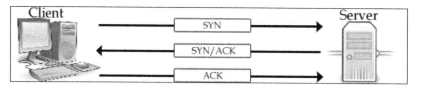

A **SYN (synchronize)** packet is first sent by the party attempting to establish a connection. The server responds with a **SYN/ACK (synchronize-acknowledgement)** packet, to which the client responds with an **ACK (acknowledgement)** packet. These three exchanges of data happen at the beginning of every connection. Afterwards, when actual data is being sent, it travels in a form of a SYN packet, to which the receiving party always replies with an ACK packet. If the party sending some data does not receive an ACK response, the same data is sent again after a specific time interval. All of this data being sent back and forth is also tagged with a sequence number, which enables the TCP protocol to also ensure that data arrives in order. This provides reliability, but at a price. Because of additional checks, waiting if some data got lost somewhere and additional data overhead, TCP ends up being slower and bulkier. If a packet gets lost somewhere, the receiving party has to wait until the same data is retransmitted in order to continue. For most applications and even certain types of games this difference is speed is negligible. However, some really fast-paced games that require highest possible efficiency and don't care about packet loss end up using UDP.

User datagram protocol

Both TCP and UDP sockets in SFML actually inherit from the same base class, which means a lot of the functionality that we saw with TCP carries over. One major difference, however, is that UDP is connectionless. This means that there is no such thing as a three-way-handshake for UDP and for that matter, no acknowledgement packets either. UDP is centered on data being sent. There are no order checks, no sequence numbers, no bloated packets, and no guarantee that what was sent out is going to reach its destination. This total elimination of error checking reduces the packet overhead from 20 bytes when using TCP all the way down to 8 bytes.

With all of that said, there are some limitations that UDP has, such as the maximum size of the data being sent out. Data in UDP is being sent out in datagrams instead of streams, which is how TCP handles it. The maximum imposed datagram size, which is a little less than 65536 bytes, cannot be exceeded.

Because UDP is connectionless, there is no equivalent of `sf::TcpListener` that can be used to accept incoming traffic. The socket must be bound to a specific port before it can be used though:

```
sf::UdpSocket socket;

// Bind to port 5600
if (socket.bind(5600) != sf::Socket::Done)
{
    // Binding failed.
}
```

Binding to a random port is also possible, thanks to `sf::Socket::AnyPort`, which can be passed into the bind method instead of a numerical constant. It can be retrieved later like this:

```
sf::UdpSocket socket;
// ...
unsigned int port = socket.getLocalPort();
```

Sending and receiving carries the same gist, except for having to provide additional arguments for an IP address and port that the data is being sent to or received from, on the count of UDP being connectionless:

```
sf::UdpSocket socket;
// ...
char data[100];
if (socket.send(data, 100, "192.168.1.2", 5600)
  != sf::Socket::Done)
{
```

```
        // Sending failed.
}
// ...
sf::IpAddress ipAddr;
unsigned short port;
std::size_t received;
if (socket.receive(data, 100, received, ipAddr, port)
   != sf::Socket::Done)
{
    // Receiving failed.
}
```

Lastly, UDP sockets do work with a `sf::SocketSelector` class, but given the nature of UDP, there are fewer instances where that actually come in handy, because all data can simply be sent and received by using one or two sockets at most.

Alternative to sending raw data

Simply sending raw bytes across a network can get quite tricky, not to mention problematic. The first and perhaps the biggest issue is the **endianness** of a machine. Some processors interpret data in a different order than others. In a big-endian family, the most significant byte is stored first, while a little-endian family machine would do the opposite. Raw data being sent from a big-endian machine to a little-endian machine would be interpreted differently and result in funky results.

On top of data being stored differently amongst all types of machines, the sizes of basic variables in C++ may vary between different machines and compilers. If that is not enough, the TCP protocol introduces additional headaches due to it not preserving message boundaries. Chunks of data being sent out can be split and combined, which can cause problems if they are not properly re-constructed by the receivers.

While all of this sounds fairly horrific, there are solutions to all of these problems. Data type size variations can be addressed by using SFML's fixed-size types, such as `sf::Int8`, `sf::Uint16`, and so on. They are simple type definitions, mapped to data types that are sure to have the expected size depending on the platform. Exchanging these types over the network instead re-assures data safety.

SFML packets

The endianness and message boundary problems require slightly more effort to resolve. Enter `sf::Packet`! It is a specialized, lightweight class that can be used to pack/extract data. SFML packets use the exact same interface as standard streams by using the `<<` and `>>` operators for data insertion and extraction, as seen here:

```
sf::Int16 n = 16;
float f = 32.f;
std::string str = "Aloha";

sf::Packet packet;
packet << n << f << str;
// ...
packet >> n >> f >> str;
```

While packing data is always guaranteed to work, extracting it can in fact fail. If it does, the packet error flag is set. Checking whether the flag is set or not is similar to testing a Boolean value, which is again similar to standard streams:

```
if(!(packet >> n)){
    // Failed extraction.
}
```

Both TCP and UDP packets do provide overloaded send and receive methods that work with instances of `sf::Packet`:

```
sf::Packet packet;
// TCP
tcpSocket.send(packet);
tcpSocket.receive(packet);
// UDP
udpSocket.send(packet, "192.168.1.2", 5600);
sf::IpAddress senderIP;
unsigned short senderPort;
udpSocket.receive(packet, senderIP, senderPort);
```

Custom data types can also be fed into or extracted from the `sf::Packet` structure, if overloads of `<<` and `>>` operators are provided, as follows:

```
struct SomeStructure{
    sf::Int32 m_int;
    std::string m_str;
};

sf::Packet& operator <<(sf::Packet& l_packet,
  const SomeStructure& l_struct)
```

```
{
    return l_packet << l_struct.m_int << l_struct.m_str;
}

sf::Packet& operator >>(sf::Packet& l_packet,
  SomeStructure& l_struct)
{
    return l_packet >> l_struct.m_int >> l_struct.m_str;
}
```

This enables easy insertion and extraction of a custom data type:

```
SomeStructure s;
sf::Packet packet;

packet << s;
packet >> s;
```

Using SFML packets with TCP sockets poses a small restriction. Due to the message boundaries having to be preserved, some extra data is sent in the packet. This means that data sent in a form of a SFML packet has to be received by using a SFML packet. UDP does not pose this restriction, as the protocol itself preserves message boundaries.

Non-blocking sockets

Both TCP and UDP sockets, as well as the TCP listener, are blocking by default. Their blocking mode can be changed to return immediately:

```
sf::TcpSocket tcp;
tcp.setBlocking(false);

sf::TcpListener tcpListener;
tcpListener.setBlocking(false);

sf::UdpSocket udp;
udp.setBlocking(false);
```

Receiving on a non-blocking socket that has no data incoming would return `sf::Socket::NotReady`, as well as trying to accept a TCP connection if there are none pending. Putting your sockets in a non-blocking mode is the easiest way to not halt your program's execution by instead checking the availability of data or connections each time it is updated.

Non-blocking TCP sockets are not guaranteed to send all of the data you pass to it, even when using instances of `sf::Packet`. If a `sf::Socket::Partial` status is returned, the data must be sent again at the exact byte offset of where the last call to `send` stopped. If raw data is sent, make sure to use this `send` overload:

```
send(const void* data, std::size_t size, std::size_t& sent)
```

It overwrites the third provided argument with the exact number of bytes sent out.

Sending `sf::Packet` instances does not require you to keep track of the byte offset, as it is stored in the packet itself. This means that you cannot destroy the packet instance until it has been successfully sent. Creating a new packet and filling it with the exact same data will not work, as the data offset that was stored internally inside the packet is lost.

Letting the traffic flow

There are a lot more subtleties to communicating over the internet than using the right code. As we discussed previously, the port number an application uses to send or receive data can be imagined as a gateway to your system, of which there are thousands. That gateway can either be open or closed. By default, it's more likely than not that whichever port you choose to use for your program is going to be closed on your system, which doesn't matter for local connections, but anything coming from the outside world through that particular port is not going to get through. Managing your ports can be done by visiting your router's settings page. The steps required to do so are different for each router out there. Luckily, http://portforward.com is there to help you! By visiting it and looking up the make and model of your router on this website, you can find detailed instructions on how any port can be opened or closed.

Sockets bound to `sf::Socket::AnyPort` will most likely end up binding to a port in a range of 49152 and 65535. Port forwarding works for ranges, as well as individual ports. Opening this particular range of ports will ensure that your SFML networking application works as intended when communicating over the World Wide Web.

Firewalls also tend to block this type of traffic by default. For example, the Windows firewall prompts users about allowing traffic to come through for an application that's being launched for the first time. Depending on your application, however, that prompt may never manifest due to the Windows firewall not being the most reliable piece of software ever written. If all of your key ports are open and a particular program still doesn't seem to be sending or receiving anything, make sure to add your client or server program to the "allowed list" of the Windows firewall, by going to **Control Panel**, clicking on **Windows Firewall**, selecting **Allow a program or feature through Windows Firewall** on the left side, clicking **Change settings**, and finally hitting the **Allow another program** button. This will bring up another window that can be used to add your client/server application by browsing for it and clicking on **Add** afterwards.

Multi-threading

Having blocking functions in your code can be a real nuisance. Listening for incoming network connections or data, asking users to input something into the console, or even loading game data, like textures, maps, or sounds, can block a program from executing until it's done. Have you ever wondered how certain games have a loading bar that actually moves while the data is being loaded? How can that be done with code that is executed sequentially? The answer to that is multi-threading. Your application runs all its code sequentially from top to bottom in something referred to as the main thread. It is not a program, as it can't exist by itself. Instead, a thread only runs within your application. The beauty of this is that multiple threads can exist and run all at once, which enables parallel code execution. Consider the following diagram:

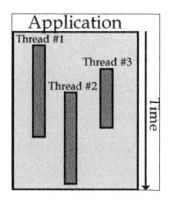

Let's say that the entire application space is the main thread, and all we do here is update and render the game. The example above is running three threads in addition to that. The first thread could be used to listen for incoming network connections. **Thread #2** is responsible for loading/unloading data when a new level is opened or closed. Lastly, thread three could be waiting for console input. Even if all three threads are blocked, the application still keeps rendering! Neat!

SFML provides us with a few fundamental types that can be used to create and control threads. Let's start by first giving a thread something to do:

```
void Test(){
    for (int i = 0; i < 10; ++i){
        std::cout << i << std::endl;
    }
}
```

This is just a basic function that we want to be executed in parallel to the main thread. How can that be done? By using the `sf::Thread`!

C++ also provides its own thread class, `std::thread`, as well its own locks and mutexes. It also provides a `std::future` class template, which is useful when accessing results of asynchronous operations.

First, it must be set up properly by providing a function or a member function pointer to its constructor:

```
sf::Thread thread1(Test);
```

The thread constructor actually provides four overloads and even takes in the return value of `std::bind` and lambda expressions, which allows us to provide any number of arguments to these functions. Once the thread is set up, it must be launched in order to execute the code:

```
thread1.launch();
```

Once the function that is executed returns, its thread is automatically stopped. The `sf::Thread` class provides a terminate method, but it really shouldn't be used unless you know what you're doing. It can produce unwanted behavior, including local variables not being destroyed on some operating systems. Instead, your code should be designed in a way that allows a thread to stop on its own when it's no longer needed. Terminating it by hand is not safe! You have been warned.

One last method that threads provide is the `wait` method:

```
thread1.wait();
```

The thread it is called on will halt until `thread1` is finished. This could be potentially dangerous. In the case of an infinite loop or a blocking function being called in `thread1` that never unblocks, the program will hang completely.

 Never destroy an instance of `sf::Thread` before it's done! This will cause the main thread to halt, as the destructor of a thread invokes its `wait` method. Your application will be stuck.

Shared data protection

Incidentally, the reason why threads are used is also the cause for most problems a user could potentially experience. Having chunks of code that run in parallel is great, but what happens if two threads attempt to read or modify the same data? In a scenario like that, crashes and data corruption are a distinct possibility. Imagine a scenario where the main thread holds a list of entities that are to be updated and rendered. So far, so good! Next, let's introduce a new thread that is going to be running network-specific code and has access to all of our entities. If this thread decided to remove an entity for whatever reason, there's a very good chance that it might happen during either the update or render cycle of the main thread. At this point, we all know too well what happens when an iterator you're using suddenly becomes invalid. Luckily, there are ways to ensure all operations in your code are thread-safe, by synchronizing them.

SFML provides us with an interesting little class called `sf::Mutex`. It stands for mutual exclusion and operates on a very basic principle of allowing only a single thread to execute certain bits of code, while making other threads wait until it's done. Let's take a look at a basic code example to help you better understand this idea:

```
sf::Mutex mutex;

void Test(){
    mutex.lock();
    for (int i = 0; i < 10; ++i){
        std::cout << i << std::endl;
    }
    mutex.unlock();
}
```

```
int main(){
    sf::Thread thread1(Test);
    thread1.launch();

    mutex.lock();
    // Do something data-sensitive here.
    mutex.unlock();
    return 0;
}
```

The `mutex` class provides us with two methods: `lock` and `unlock`. When a mutex is locked for the first time, the thread that locked it is given priority and is allowed to continue executing the code. If another thread calls the `lock` method of the *same* mutex while it's still locked, it's not allowed to move any further until the mutex is unlocked. Once it is, the waiting is over and the second thread is allowed to continue.

Let's analyze what happens in the code example above: `thread1` is bound to the `Test` function and launched immediately. The test function locks the mutex and because it hasn't been locked yet, the loop for printing numbers begins iterating. In the meantime, our main thread reaches the `mutex.lock();` line. A few numbers may have been printed out already by this point. Because the mutex is already locked, the main thread *halts* immediately. Once the last number of the `Test` function is printed out, the `mutex.unlock();` line is reached. This enables the main thread to lock the mutex for itself and continue. If any other thread was to invoke the lock method of the shared mutex, it would have to wait until the main thread is through. Finally, the mutex is unlocked and any possible thread that was waiting in the background can now resume.

There is a corner-case scenario where this could potentially be dangerous. The mutex has to be unlocked in order for the main thread to continue. What if the function that is bound to a thread suddenly throws an exception? What if it returns a value, or has a branch of if/else statements that return separate values? The `unlock` method could be called in each branch, but that just clutters the code, not to mention it doesn't solve the exception problem. Luckily, there is a very elegant solution to that: the `sf::Lock` class. All it does is take in a reference to a mutex in its constructor, at which point it's locked, and unlocks it in its destructor. Creating an object like that on the stack would solve all of these problems, as the mutex would just get unlocked as soon as the lock object is out of scope. Let's take a look at how it can be used:

```
sf::Mutex mutex;

void Test(){
    sf::Lock lock(mutex);
    for (int i = 0; i < 10; ++i){
        std::cout << i << std::endl;
```

```
        if (i == 5){ return; } // mutex.unlock() called.
    }
} // mutex.unlock() called.
```

This is a much safer piece of code. Even if there was a possibility of an exception being thrown, the shared mutex would be unlocked, allowing the rest of the program to continue.

Creating a simple communication protocol

Having covered all of the basics, we're finally ready to get designing! The first choice we need to make is which protocol suits our needs better. Losing packets in a real-time application like this is not a tragedy. It's more important that data is sent and received as quickly as possible in order to update the player and all of the entities in the game. Since TCP is a slower protocol and we would not benefit from the extra measures it takes to deliver data in order, the choice is clear. User datagram protocol is the way to go.

Let's flesh out some details of the system we're going to be building by first defining some packet types that are going to be exchanged between the server and client, as well as deciding on the type of the packet identifier. This information will be held inside the `PacketTypes.h` header:

```
using PacketID = sf::Int8;
enum class PacketType{
  Disconnect = -1, Connect, Heartbeat, Snapshot,
  Player_Update, Message, Hurt, OutOfBounds
};
void StampPacket(const PacketType& l_type, sf::Packet& l_packet);
```

Note the very last element inside the `PacketType` enumeration. It isn't an actual packet type that will be sent or received. Instead, it simply exists for convenience when checking whether a packet type is valid or not, which we'll cover soon enough. In addition to the enumeration, we're also providing a function for attaching a type to a packet. It's implemented in the `PacketTypes.cpp` file:

```
void StampPacket(const PacketType& l_type, sf::Packet& l_packet){
    l_packet << PacketID(l_type);
}
```

This function simply converts the provided type argument into a specific integer data type supplied by SFML prior to feeding it into the packet instance. Using a function to do it pays off in the long run, should we ever decide to change the communication protocol by adding additional data into the packet.

Next, let's create a header file that contains the most common bits of information shared between both the client and server. We'll simply call it `NetworkDefinitions.h`:

```
enum class Network{
  HighestTimestamp = 2147483647, ClientTimeout = 10000,
  ServerPort = 5600, NullID = -1
};
using ClientID = int;
using PortNumber = unsigned short;
```

These are simply all of the types and constants that both communicating sides are going to be using.

Keeping a UDP connection alive

Due to UDP sockets being connectionless, we're going to need to have a way to check if either one of the clients on the server side, or the server on the client side, has stopped responding, and therefore is deemed to have timed out. A common term for this type of mechanism is **heartbeat**. How it's implemented may differ from application to application, as well as your own sensibilities. In this case, we're going to cover a fairly basic strategy of not only maintaining a live connection, but also measuring the network delay between both sides.

For this purpose, it's always best to have the server initiate the heartbeat. It has two major benefits: less data being exchanged and a reduced risk of cheating. Let's take a look at the most conservative implementation of a server-client heartbeat:

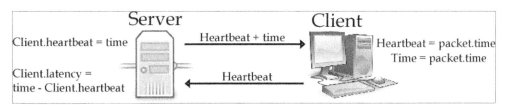

The server is going to keep track of when the last heartbeat to a client was sent. That combined with a predefined heartbeat interval enables us to send them at a constant rate. When it is time to send one, a heartbeat packet is constructed and the local server time is attached to it. It is then sent out to the client.

The client side of this operation is much simpler. It is always waiting for a heartbeat and when one is received, the local time of the client is updated and kept around for checking timeouts later. A response to the server is then sent back, acknowledging that a heartbeat was indeed received.

When our server receives a heartbeat response from the client, the delay between these two machines is measured by subtracting the time of when the last heartbeat packet was sent out from the current time. This delay, also known as latency, is the time it takes for data to make a round trip between two hosts.

Having a heartbeat mechanism in place ensures that we are not keeping around any clients that could've potentially disconnected and thereby wasting bandwidth by sending data to unreachable hosts.

Designing the client class

With all of the things happening on the client side, be it rendering sprites or playing sounds or processing user input, it only makes sense to have all of the networking code localized inside a single class. This will allow us to communicate with the server quickly and easily. Let's begin designing that class, by first taking a look at some necessary definitions inside the `Client.h` header:

```
#define CONNECT_TIMEOUT 5000 // Milliseconds.

class Client;
using PacketHandler = std::function<
  void(const PacketID&, sf::Packet&, Client*)>;
```

The first definition is the amount of milliseconds that it takes for a client to realize that it's no longer connected to a server. This value can obviously be tweaked at any time. Following that is a definition of a function type that will be used to handle packets on the client side. We're going to be providing the client class with a pointer to a function that is responsible for handling most of the incoming information.

With that out of the way, we can begin shaping the client class:

```
class Client{
public:
  Client();
  ~Client();
  bool Connect();
  bool Disconnect();
  void Listen();
  bool Send(sf::Packet& l_packet);
  const sf::Time& GetTime() const;
```

```
    const sf::Time& GetLastHeartbeat() const;
    void SetTime(const sf::Time& l_time);
    void SetServerInformation(const sf::IpAddress& l_ip,
      const PortNumber& l_port);

    template<class T>
    void Setup(void(T::*l_handler)
      (const PacketID&, sf::Packet&, Client*), T* l_instance)
    {
      m_packetHandler = std::bind(l_handler, l_instance,
        std::placeholders::_1, std::placeholders::_2,
        std::placeholders::_3);
    }

    void Setup(void(*l_handler)(const PacketID&,
      sf::Packet&, Client*));
    void UnregisterPacketHandler();
    void Update(const sf::Time& l_time);
    bool IsConnected() const;
    void SetPlayerName(const std::string& l_name);
    sf::Mutex& GetMutex();
  private:
    std::string m_playerName;

    sf::UdpSocket m_socket;
    sf::IpAddress m_serverIp;
    PortNumber m_serverPort;
    PacketHandler m_packetHandler;
    bool m_connected;
    sf::Time m_serverTime;
    sf::Time m_lastHeartbeat;

    sf::Thread m_listenThread;
    sf::Mutex m_mutex;
  };
```

There are a few things to note here. First, we're going to want to support both regular functions and member functions to serve as packet handlers, hence two `Setup` methods. The first one obviously has to be implemented in the header file due to having a template argument.

Second, this class keeps and manages its own instances of `sf::Mutex` and `sf::Thread`. This way, we can provide a common interface of thread synchronization to the outside code.

Implementing the client

With the class definition covered, it's time to actually make it do something, starting with the constructor and destructor:

```
Client::Client():m_listenThread(&Client::Listen, this){}
Client::~Client(){ m_socket.unbind(); }
```

In the client constructor's initializer list, we bind the listening thread to the `Listen` method of this class. Threads do not have a default empty constructor, which is why this is necessary. The destructor is simply used to unbind the socket we're using.

Now, let's take a stab at implementing the connection protocol:

```
bool Client::Connect(){
  if (m_connected){ return false; }
  m_socket.bind(sf::Socket::AnyPort);
  sf::Packet p;
  StampPacket(PacketType::Connect, p);
  p << m_playerName;
  if (m_socket.send(p, m_serverIp, m_serverPort) !=
    sf::Socket::Done)
  {
    m_socket.unbind();
    return false;
  }
  m_socket.setBlocking(false);
  p.clear();
  sf::IpAddress recvIP;
  PortNumber recvPORT;
  sf::Clock timer;
  timer.restart();
  while (timer.getElapsedTime().asMilliseconds()<CONNECT_TIMEOUT){
    sf::Socket::Status s = m_socket.receive(p, recvIP, recvPORT);
    if (s != sf::Socket::Done){ continue; }
    if (recvIP != m_serverIp){ continue; }
    PacketID id;
    if (!(p >> id)){ break; }
    if ((PacketType)id != PacketType::Connect){ continue; }
    m_packetHandler(id, p, this);
    m_connected = true;
    m_socket.setBlocking(true);
    m_lastHeartbeat = m_serverTime;
    m_listenThread.launch();
    return true;
```

```
    }
    std::cout << "Connection attempt failed! Server info: "
        << m_serverIp << ":" << m_serverPort << std::endl;
    m_socket.unbind();
    m_socket.setBlocking(true);
    return false;
}
```

The first and most obvious step is checking whether we're already connected to the server by checking out the `m_connected` data member.

Next, the socket we're using must be bound to a port. A specific port number could be used here, but that would limit the number of connections a single computer can have at the same time. You cannot bind a socket to the same port on the same protocol twice. By using `sf::Socket::AnyPort`, we're letting SFML pick a random port that isn't being used.

In order to establish a connection, the client must first send something to the server. Since SFML already provides an excellent helper class for easy data transfer, `sf::Packet`, we're going to be taking full advantage of it.

After assigning the type `Connect` to our packet, we also write in the player name and send the packet to the server.

The rest of the code is responsible for correctly handling timeouts. First, we set our socket to be in a non-blocking mode, because we're going to be handling this in a single thread. After clearing the packet we just sent out in order to use it again, a few local variables are set up in order to capture the IP address and port number of a response. Additionally, a clock is set up in order to help us determine whether we've been waiting too long for a response.

Next, the code loops as long as the timer stays underneath the predefined time-out value, `CONNECT_TIMEOUT`. In each iteration, we invoke the receive method of our socket and capture its status. If the returned status doesn't signify success or the IP address it was received from does not match that of our server, we simply skip the current iteration. Nobody wants to receive data from an unknown source!

After verifying that the packet contains an ID and that it matches `Connect`, we pass the received information to the packet handler, set the `m_connected` flag to `true`, put the socket back into blocking mode, set the last heartbeat value to the current time, launch the listening thread, and return `true` to show success. However, if the time to successfully connect runs out, the loop is ended, an error message is printed, and the socket is unbound and set to blocking mode again.

Once the client is connected to the server, the listening thread is launched. Let's take a look at what makes it tick:

```cpp
void Client::Listen(){
  sf::Packet packet;
  sf::IpAddress recvIP;
  PortNumber recvPORT;
  while (m_connected){
    packet.clear();
    sf::Socket::Status status =
      m_socket.receive(packet, recvIP, recvPORT);
    if (status != sf::Socket::Done){
      if (m_connected){
        std::cout << "Failed receiving a packet from "
          << recvIP << ":" << recvPORT << ". Status: "
          << status << std::endl;
        continue;
      } else {
        std::cout << "Socket unbound." << std::endl;
        break;
      }
    }
    if (recvIP != m_serverIp){
      // Ignore packets not sent from the server.
      continue;
    }
    PacketID p_id;
    if (!(packet >> p_id)){
      // Non-conventional packet.
      continue;
    }
    PacketType id = (PacketType)p_id;
    if (id<PacketType::Disconnect||id >=PacketType::OutOfBounds){
      // Invalid packet type.
      continue;
    }

    if (id == PacketType::Heartbeat){
      sf::Packet p;
      StampPacket(PacketType::Heartbeat, p);
      if (m_socket.send(p, m_serverIp, m_serverPort) !=
        sf::Socket::Done)
      {
        std::cout << "Failed sending a heartbeat!" << std::endl;
```

```
        }
        sf::Int32 timestamp;
        packet >> timestamp;
        SetTime(sf::milliseconds(timestamp));
        m_lastHeartbeat = m_serverTime;
      } else if(m_packetHandler){
        m_packetHandler((PacketID)id, packet, this); // Handle.
      }
    }
  }
}
```

After setting up some local variables to hold the packet, IP, and port information, the listening thread loop is entered. It runs as long as the client is connected to the server. Each time the loop iterates, the packet instance is cleared in order to receive new data. The status of the socket receive method is stored in a local variable, `status`, and checked for success. Because the socket is in blocking mode, the listening thread will halt at the `m_socket.receive(...)` line until some data comes in.

If the returned status denotes some kind of failure, an appropriate error message is printed, presuming that the client is still connected to the server. If it's not, the socket was unbound and the loop is immediately stopped so the thread can safely terminate.

Given that some data was properly received, the originating IP address is checked. If it does not match the IP of our server, the data is discarded by skipping the current loop iteration. Similarly enough, if we're unable to extract the packet ID, or if it does not fit within our predetermined boundaries, the same outcome takes place. We don't want any malformed or unwelcome packets.

Next, we check the ID of the packet that was just received. In this particular class, we only want to worry about a single type of packets: PACKET_HEARTBEAT. These are little messages that the server sends to all clients for two reasons: time synchronization and maintaining a valid connection. Due to unforeseen circumstances, time on the server side and the client side can start going out of sync, which eventually can cause serious problems. Overwriting the client time with a timestamp coming from the server every so often eliminates this problem. In addition to that, this is how both the client and server keep track of whether the connection is still alive or not. In the case of our client, `m_lastHeartbeat` holds the latest timestamp received from the server, which can be checked for timeouts later.

If the packet ID is something else, it simply gets passed into the packet handler function to be processed by a different class.

Now that we have all these ways of opening and maintaining a connection to the server, let's take a look at how it can be terminated:

```
bool Client::Disconnect(){
  if (!m_connected){ return false; }
  sf::Packet p;
  StampPacket(PacketType::Disconnect, p);
  sf::Socket::Status s =
    m_socket.send(p, m_serverIp, m_serverPort);
  m_connected = false;
  m_socket.unbind(); // Unbind to close the listening thread.
  if (s != sf::Socket::Done){ return false; }
  return true;
}
```

First, the state of the client is checked. We don't need to disconnect if there is no connection to begin with. A packet instance is then constructed with a type of `Disconnect` and sent to the server. After the `m_connected` flag is set to `false`, we unbind our socket and return `true` or `false`, based on whether sending the packet was successful or not.

> When a socket is in blocking mode, its `receive` method waits until some data arrives before continuing. Having something like that happen in a separate thread would leave it running, and therefore stop our program from quitting. One way to prevent that is by unbinding a socket that is being used. It makes the `receive` method return an error, which we have handled in the `Listen` method of our client class.

Sending data to the server is quite simple, as this next method shows:

```
bool Client::Send(sf::Packet& l_packet){
  if (!m_connected){ return false; }
  if (m_socket.send(l_packet, m_serverIp, m_serverPort) !=
    sf::Socket::Done)
  {
    return false;
  }
  return true;
}
```

We take in a reference to an existing packet that needs to be sent out. The method immediately returns `false` if we're not connected to the server or if the `send` method of our socket returns anything else than `sf::Socket::Done`.

We also need a way to provide a custom packet handler function that is to be used by this class. The member function version of this method was already implemented in the header file, and all that's left is handling a function pointer version:

```
void Client::Setup(void(*l_handler)
  (const PacketID&, sf::Packet&, Client*))
{
    m_packetHandler = std::bind(l_handler,
      std::placeholders::_1, std::placeholders::_2,
      std::placeholders::_3);
}
```

For balance, every positive needs a negative. Let's provide a way to remove any ties to functions that may no longer exist once the code starts wrapping up:

```
void Client::UnregisterPacketHandler(){
    m_packetHandler = nullptr;
}
```

Last but not least, the update method:

```
void Client::Update(const sf::Time& l_time){
  if (!m_connected){ return; }
  m_serverTime += l_time;
  if (m_serverTime.asMilliseconds() < 0){
    m_serverTime -= sf::milliseconds(
      sf::Int32(Network::HighestTimestamp));
    m_lastHeartbeat = m_serverTime;
    return;
  }
  if (m_serverTime.asMilliseconds() -
    m_lastHeartbeat.asMilliseconds() >=
      sf::Int32(Network::ClientTimeout))
  {
    // Timeout.
    std::cout << "Server connection timed out!" << std::endl;
    Disconnect();
  }
}
```

The main purpose of this method is keeping track of passing time by adding the time between updates to the server time.

Now, you might notice something strange in the next few lines. Why are we checking for the server time being below zero? Well, the amount of milliseconds that have passed since the beginning is represented by a signed 32-bit integer. Its maximum positive value is 2,147,483,647, after which it goes right to the negatives, -2,147,483,648 to be precise. Granted, this doesn't happen very often. In fact, the server would have to be running continuously for almost 25 whole days for the timestamp to reach the values we're talking about. Still, a corner-case scenario is not worthy of ignoring simply because it's unlikely to happen. Subtracting the highest possible value of a 32-bit integer from the server timestamp "wraps" the time around back into the positive realm and allows it to continue like nothing happened.

The update method is also where we check for our connection timing out. If the difference between current time and the last heartbeat received from the server is greater or equal to the timeout value in milliseconds, the `Disconnect` method is invoked.

The server class

Now, it's time to take a look at the way things are handled on the other side of the wire. Let's begin by defining some constants:

```
#define HEARTBEAT_INTERVAL 1000 // Milliseconds.
#define HEARTBEAT_RETRIES 5
```

Our server application is going to send out heartbeats every second and retry five times before it times out a client. Speaking of clients, there's additional information that we need to keep track of, which calls for a good data structure that holds it all:

```
struct ClientInfo{
    sf::IpAddress m_clientIP;
    PortNumber m_clientPORT;
    sf::Time m_lastHeartbeat;
    sf::Time m_heartbeatSent;
    bool m_heartbeatWaiting;
    unsigned short m_heartbeatRetry;
    unsigned int m_latency;

    ClientInfo(const sf::IpAddress& l_ip, const PortNumber& l_port,
        const sf::Time& l_heartbeat): m_clientIP(l_ip),
        m_clientPORT(l_port), m_lastHeartbeat(l_heartbeat),
        m_heartbeatWaiting(false), m_heartbeatRetry(0), m_latency(0)
    {}
```

```
ClientInfo& operator=(const ClientInfo& l_rhs){
    m_clientIP          = l_rhs.m_clientIP;
    m_clientPORT        = l_rhs.m_clientPORT;
    m_lastHeartbeat     = l_rhs.m_lastHeartbeat;
    m_heartbeatSent     = l_rhs.m_heartbeatSent;
    m_heartbeatWaiting  = l_rhs.m_heartbeatWaiting;
    m_heartbeatRetry    = l_rhs.m_heartbeatRetry;
    m_latency           = l_rhs.m_latency;
    return *this;
  }
};
```

Besides simply keeping track of the IP and port of a client, we also need to know when the last heartbeat was sent to them, whether the server is waiting for a heartbeat response, the number of heartbeat retries made, and the current latency the client has.

Keeping track of latency provides tons of potential benefits, ranging from assessing quality of service and accurate matchmaking to maximizing the accuracy of a network simulation.

Next, the data types we're going to be using throughout the `Server` class deserve a look:

```
using Clients = std::unordered_map<ClientID, ClientInfo>;
class Server;
using PacketHandler = std::function<void(sf::IpAddress&,
  const PortNumber&, const PacketID&, sf::Packet&, Server*)>;
using TimeoutHandler = std::function<void(const ClientID&)>;
```

As you can see, this class also uses a custom function that is going to be handling incoming packets. In addition to that, we're going to need to be able to process client timeouts outside of this class as well, which can also be done through means of using a function pointer.

We have everything we need, so let's write the `Server` class header:

```
class Server{
public:
    template <class T>
    Server(void(T::*l_handler)(sf::IpAddress&, const PortNumber&,
        const PacketID&, sf::Packet&, Server*),
        T* l_instance): m_listenThread(&Server::Listen, this)
    {
```

```
      m_packetHandler = std::bind(l_handler, l_instance,
         std::placeholders::_1, std::placeholders::_2,
         std::placeholders::_3, std::placeholders::_4,
         std::placeholders::_5);
   }

   Server(void(*l_handler)(sf::IpAddress&, const PortNumber&,
      const PacketID&, sf::Packet&, Server*));
   ~Server();

   template<class T>
   void BindTimeoutHandler(void(T::*l_handler)
      (const ClientID&), T* l_instance)
   {
      m_timeoutHandler = std::bind(l_handler, l_instance,
         std::placeholders::_1);
   }
   void BindTimeoutHandler(void(*l_handler)(const ClientID&));

   bool Send(const ClientID& l_id, sf::Packet& l_packet);
   bool Send(sf::IpAddress& l_ip, const PortNumber& l_port,
      sf::Packet& l_packet);
   void Broadcast(sf::Packet& l_packet,
      const ClientID& l_ignore = ClientID(Network::NullID));

   void Listen();
   void Update(const sf::Time& l_time);

   ClientID AddClient(const sf::IpAddress& l_ip,
      const PortNumber& l_port);
   ClientID GetClientID(const sf::IpAddress& l_ip,
      const PortNumber& l_port);
   bool HasClient(const ClientID& l_id);
   bool HasClient(const sf::IpAddress& l_ip,
      const PortNumber& l_port);
   bool GetClientInfo(const ClientID& l_id, ClientInfo& l_info);
   bool RemoveClient(const ClientID& l_id);
   bool RemoveClient(const sf::IpAddress& l_ip,
      const PortNumber& l_port);

   void DisconnectAll();
   bool Start();
   bool Stop();
```

```
    bool IsRunning();

    unsigned int GetClientCount();
    std::string GetClientList();

    sf::Mutex& GetMutex();
private:
    void Setup();
    ClientID m_lastID;

    sf::UdpSocket m_incoming;
    sf::UdpSocket m_outgoing;

    PacketHandler m_packetHandler;
    TimeoutHandler m_timeoutHandler;

    Clients m_clients;
    sf::Time m_serverTime;

    bool m_running;

    sf::Thread m_listenThread;
    sf::Mutex m_mutex;

    size_t m_totalSent;
    size_t m_totalReceived;
};
```

Just like the `Client` class, we want to support both member functions and regular functions being bound as packet and timeout handlers. Additionally, we also need an instance of a mutex and two sockets: one for listening and one for sending data. Having two sockets on the server side provides separation between different operations, which sometimes may result in runtime errors and data corruption. For an added bonus, we're also keeping track of all data sent and received.

Implementing server

Let's start by taking a look at the second constructor and the destructor of this class:

```
Server::Server(void(*l_handler)(sf::IpAddress&, const PortNumber&,
    const PacketID&, sf::Packet&, Server*))
    : m_listenThread(&Server::Listen, this)
{
    // Bind a packet handler function.
```

```
    m_packetHandler = std::bind(l_handler,
      std::placeholders::_1, std::placeholders::_2,
      std::placeholders::_3, std::placeholders::_4,
      std::placeholders::_5);
}


Server::~Server(){ Stop(); }
```

Nothing too interesting is happening here. The constructor simply binds the
provided packet handler function, while the destructor just invokes the `Stop`
method, which we are going to cover shortly. Speaking of binding, we also
need a function to handle client timeouts:

```
void Server::BindTimeoutHandler(void(*l_handler)
  (const ClientID&))
{
    m_timeoutHandler = std::bind(l_handler, std::placeholders::_1);
}
```

Simply having the client get disconnected is not always enough, depending on your
application. One of the main ways we're going to be taking advantage of this feature
is de-spawning entities in the game world.

Now, let's take a peek at how we start our server:

```
bool Server::Start(){
    if (m_running){ return false; }
    if(m_incoming.bind(SERVER_PORT) != sf::Socket::Done){
        return false;
    }
    m_outgoing.bind(sf::Socket::AnyPort);
    Setup();
    std::cout << "Incoming port: " <<
      m_incoming.getLocalPort() << ". Outgoing port: "
      << m_outgoing.getLocalPort() << std::endl;
    m_listenThread.launch();
    m_running = true;
    return true;
}
```

If the server is already running, or if we failed to bind the incoming socket to the predesignated port number, `false` is returned. Otherwise, the outgoing socket is bound to a random port, a `Setup` method is invoked to set up some data members, the listening thread is launched, and the m_running flag is set to true. You can stop the server like this:

```
bool Server::Stop(){
    if (!m_running){ return false; }
    DisconnectAll();
    m_running = false;
    m_incoming.unbind(); // Stops the listening thread.
    return true;
}
```

If the server is actually running, a `DisconnectAll` method is invoked to drop all the clients. The running flag is then set to `false` and the incoming socket is unbound, which in turn stops the listening thread from running, as the socket is in blocking mode.

Here's a little helper method that initializes some data members to their default states:

```
void Server::Setup(){
    m_lastID = 0;
    m_running = false;
    m_totalSent = 0;
    m_totalReceived = 0;
}
```

This is invoked every time a server is started, as demonstrated previously.

Sending data to clients is fairly straightforward, as you can see here:

```
bool Server::Send(const ClientID& l_id, sf::Packet& l_packet){
    sf::Lock lock(m_mutex);
    auto itr = m_clients.find(l_id);
    if (itr == m_clients.end()){ return false; }
    if (m_outgoing.send(l_packet, itr->second.m_clientIP,
        itr->second.m_clientPORT) != sf::Socket::Done)
    {
        std::cout << "Error sending a packet..." << std::endl;
        return false;
    }
    m_totalSent += l_packet.getDataSize();
    return true;
}
```

With a little bit of STL find magic, we retrieve the client's information from the container it's stored in and send the packet out.

 Note the mutex lock in the very first line. This is done to ensure that the client isn't removed from the container right in the middle of a send operation.

As a side bonus, it's also nice to keep track of how much data was sent and received. Here, we make use of the `getDataSize` method that `sf::Packet` provides to do just that.

For convenience, we could also write an overloaded version of the `Send` method that doesn't require a client:

```cpp
bool Server::Send(sf::IpAddress& l_ip,
  const PortNumber& l_port, sf::Packet& l_packet)
{
  if (m_outgoing.send(l_packet, l_ip, l_port) != sf::Socket::Done)
  {
    return false;
  }
  m_totalSent += l_packet.getDataSize();
  return true;
}
```

In plenty of occasions, sending data out to only one client isn't enough. Broadcasting it to all of the clients currently connected can be useful for sending out anything from chat messages to entity states. Let's write it:

```cpp
void Server::Broadcast(sf::Packet& l_packet,
  const ClientID& l_ignore)
{
  sf::Lock lock(m_mutex);
  for (auto &itr : m_clients)
  {
    if (itr.first != l_ignore){
      if (m_outgoing.send(l_packet, itr.second.m_clientIP,
        itr.second.m_clientPORT) != sf::Socket::Done)
      {
        std::cout << "Error broadcasting a packet to client: "
          << itr.first << std::endl;
        continue;
      }
```

```
      m_totalSent += l_packet.getDataSize();
    }
  }
}
```

Once again, it's quite basic. The client container is iterated over and each client's ID is checked for matching the l_ignore argument, which can be used to specify a client ID that shouldn't receive the packet being broadcasted. If data is successfully sent out, its size is added to the sent data counter.

Much like the client, our server is going to need a separate thread for processing incoming data. Let's take a look at the Listen method:

```
void Server::Listen(){
  sf::IpAddress ip;
  PortNumber port;
  sf::Packet packet;
  while (m_running){
    packet.clear();
    sf::Socket::Status status =
      m_incoming.receive(packet, ip, port);
    if (status != sf::Socket::Done){
      if (m_running){
        std::cout << "Error receiving a packet from: "
          << ip << ":" << port << ". Code: " <<
          status << std::endl;
        continue;
      } else {
        std::cout << "Socket unbound." << std::endl;
        break;
      }
    }

    m_totalReceived += packet.getDataSize();

    PacketID p_id;
    if (!(packet >> p_id)){
      continue;
    } // Non-conventional packet.
    PacketType id = (PacketType)p_id;
    if (id<PacketType::Disconnect || id>=PacketType::OutOfBounds){
      continue;
    } // Invalid packet type.
```

```
if (id == PacketType::Heartbeat){
  sf::Lock lock(m_mutex);
  for (auto &itr : m_clients){
    if (itr.second.m_clientIP != ip ||
      itr.second.m_clientPORT != port)
    {
      continue;
    }
    if (!itr.second.m_heartbeatWaiting){
      std::cout << "Invalid heartbeat packet received!"
        << std::endl;
      break;
    }
    itr.second.m_ping = m_serverTime.asMilliseconds() -
      itr.second.m_heartbeatSent.asMilliseconds();
    itr.second.m_lastHeartbeat = m_serverTime;
    itr.second.m_heartbeatWaiting = false;
    itr.second.m_heartbeatRetry = 0;
    break;
  }
} else if (m_packetHandler){
  m_packetHandler(ip, port, (PacketID)id, packet, this);
}
}
}
```

As you can see, it's quite similar to the way a client listener is implemented. After some local variables are set up for capturing incoming data, we enter a `while` loop, during which the packet is cleared and the blocking receive method of our incoming socket is invoked, capturing the status as well. Just as before, we break from the loop if the server is no longer running and the return status from the `receive` method was anything but `sf::Socket::Done`.

After all of the packet ID checks, we get to the heartbeat part of the code. A flag is set up to indicate whether a client that sent the heartbeat was located or not.

Note that we lock our mutex here, because we're about to start iterating over the list of clients in order to find the one that sent in the heartbeat response.

If the client with matching information has been found, we also check if the server is currently waiting for a heartbeat response from them. We only want clients to be able to send in heartbeat responses in order to both accurately measure latency and prevent potential cheating attempts.

Given that this is a valid heartbeat response, latency is calculated by subtracting the time a heartbeat was sent to this particular client from the current server time. The current timestamp is also stored in `m_lastHeartbeat`, which we'll be using to determine when to dispatch the next one. Afterwards, the heartbeat waiting flag is set to `false` and the retry counter is set back to 0.

Next, let's implement adding clients:

```
ClientID Server::AddClient(const sf::IpAddress& l_ip,
  const PortNumber& l_port)
{
  sf::Lock lock(m_mutex);
  for (auto &itr : m_clients){
    if (itr.second.m_clientIP == l_ip &&
      itr.second.m_clientPORT == l_port)
    {
      return ClientID(Network::NullID);
    }
  }
  ClientID id = m_lastID;
  ClientInfo info(l_ip, l_port, m_serverTime);
  m_clients.insert(std::make_pair(id, info));
  ++m_lastID;
  return id;
}
```

Once again, since we're modifying client data, we want to lock our mutex to ensure no other piece of code running in another thread will attempt to read or modify the data as well. Following that, we do a quick search through the client container and return -1 if a specified IP and port combination already exists. Otherwise, a new client ID is assigned and the client information is inserted into the container, followed by an increment operation of `m_lastID`.

Sometimes, we may need to obtain the client ID of a client by providing their IP address and port number. Let's write a way to do just that:

```
ClientID Server::GetClientID(const sf::IpAddress& l_ip,
  const PortNumber& l_port)
{
  sf::Lock lock(m_mutex);
  for (auto &itr : m_clients){
    if (itr.second.m_clientIP == l_ip &&
      itr.second.m_clientPORT == l_port)
    {
      return itr.first;
```

```
        }
    }
    return ClientID(Network::NullID);
}
```

As always, it simply iterates over each client and checks if their information matches the provided arguments. This is another instance where we need to lock the mutex in order to safely access this data.

Next up, we need some setters and getters:

```
bool Server::HasClient(const ClientID& l_id){
    return (m_clients.find(l_id) != m_clients.end());
}

bool Server::HasClient(const sf::IpAddress& l_ip,
    const PortNumber& l_port)
{
    return(GetClientID(l_ip, l_port) >= 0);
}

bool Server::IsRunning(){ return m_running; }
sf::Mutex& Server::GetMutex(){ return m_mutex; }
```

A way of obtaining client information from a client ID is also necessary:

```
bool Server::GetClientInfo(const ClientID& l_id,
    ClientInfo& l_info)
{
    sf::Lock lock(m_mutex);
    for (auto &itr : m_clients){
        if (itr.first == l_id){
            l_info = itr.second;
            return true;
        }
    }
    return false;
}
```

In this case, the provided reference to a ClientInfo structure is simply overwritten with the located information. It can be done in a single line of code, thanks to the overloaded assignment operator that ClientInfo provides. Once again, the mutex is locked because we're accessing data that can be removed or overwritten in the middle of the search otherwise.

When a client is no longer needed, it must be removed. For convenience, we provide two variations of the same method:

```
bool Server::RemoveClient(const ClientID& l_id){
  sf::Lock lock(m_mutex);
  auto itr = m_clients.find(l_id);
  if (itr == m_clients.end()){ return false; }
  sf::Packet p;
  StampPacket(PacketType::Disconnect, p);
  Send(l_id, p);
  m_clients.erase(itr);
  return true;
}
```

The first one simply locates client information by using the `find` method of a container it's stored in. If one was found, a disconnect packet is created and sent to the client before it gets erased. The second variation varies in its search method, but carries out the same basic idea:

```
bool Server::RemoveClient(const sf::IpAddress& l_ip,
  const PortNumber& l_port)
{
  sf::Lock lock(m_mutex);
  for (auto itr = m_clients.begin();
    itr != m_clients.end(); ++itr)
  {
    if (itr->second.m_clientIP == l_ip &&
      itr->second.m_clientPORT == l_port)
    {
      sf::Packet p;
      StampPacket(PacketType::Disconnect , p);
      Send(itr->first, p);
      m_clients.erase(itr);
      return true;
    }
  }
  return false;
}
```

Once again, the mutex is locked in both of them as data is being read and modified. Speaking of removing clients, how about having a method that kicks all of them out at the same time?

```
void Server::DisconnectAll(){
  if (!m_running){ return; }
  sf::Packet p;
  StampPacket(PacketType::Disconnect, p);
```

```
    Broadcast(p);
    sf::Lock lock(m_mutex);
    m_clients.clear();
}
```

It's quite a simple little bit of code. If the server is running, a disconnect packet is created, just like before, except it's broadcasted to all clients instead of just one. The mutex is then locked, right before the client container is cleared completely.

Last but definitely not least, here's the update method:

```
void Server::Update(const sf::Time& l_time){
  m_serverTime += l_time;
  if (m_serverTime.asMilliseconds() < 0){
    m_serverTime -= sf::milliseconds(HIGHEST_TIMESTAMP);
    sf::Lock lock(m_mutex);
    for (auto &itr : m_clients)
    {
      Itr.second.m_lastHeartbeat =
        sf::milliseconds(std::abs(
        itr.second.m_lastHeartbeat.asMilliseconds() -
        HIGHEST_TIMESTAMP));
    }
  }


  sf::Lock lock(m_mutex);
  for (auto itr = m_clients.begin(); itr != m_clients.end();){
    sf::Int32 elapsed =
      m_serverTime.asMilliseconds() -
      itr->second.m_lastHeartbeat.asMilliseconds();
    if (elapsed >= HEARTBEAT_INTERVAL){
      if (elapsed >= CLIENT_TIMEOUT
        || itr->second.m_heartbeatRetry > HEARTBEAT_RETRIES)
      {
        // Remove client.
        std::cout << "Client " <<
          itr->first << " has timed out." << std::endl;
        if (m_timeoutHandler){ m_timeoutHandler(itr->first); }
        itr = m_clients.erase(itr);
        continue;
      }
      if (!itr->second.m_heartbeatWaiting || (elapsed >=
        HEARTBEAT_INTERVAL * (itr->second.m_heartbeatRetry + 1)))
      {
        // Heartbeat
```

```
            if (itr->second.m_heartbeatRetry >= 3){
              std::cout << "Re-try(" << itr->second.m_heartbeatRetry
                << ") heartbeat for client "
                << itr->first << std::endl;
            }
            sf::Packet Heartbeat;
            StampPacket(PACKET_HEARTBEAT, Heartbeat);
            Heartbeat << m_serverTime.asMilliseconds();
            Send(itr->first, Heartbeat);
            if (itr->second.m_heartbeatRetry == 0){
              itr->second.m_heartbeatSent = m_serverTime;
            }
            itr->second.m_heartbeatWaiting = true;
            ++itr->second.m_heartbeatRetry;

            m_totalSent += Heartbeat.getDataSize();
          }
        }
        ++itr;
      }
    }
```

Similar to the client, the server also has to worry about the timestamp running out of bounds. Unlike the client, however, we need to reset the heartbeats of every client the server has, hence the mutex lock. Speaking of which, we also need to lock the mutex right before all of the update code, as it can potentially modify any of the clients, just like any other piece of code that runs in a different thread.

After the mutex lock, we begin iterating over clients and measuring the time elapsed between now and the last heartbeat. If this time exceeds or is equal to the interval we want heartbeats to be sent out at, we first check if it either also exceeds the timeout interval or if the number of heartbeat retries has exceeded the designated value. If so, the timeout handler is invoked and the client is erased from the container.

The heartbeat code itself is quite simple. If the server isn't waiting for a reply from the client, or if it's time to retry sending another heartbeat, a packet is constructed, the server time is attached to it, and it is sent out. If this is a first try sending it, the server time also gets stored inside the m_heartbeatSent data member of a client entry.

A simple chat application

We have the basic framework in place to handle connections, so let's build something with it! How about a neat little console-based chat program? Let's start with the server by creating a separate project and a new file called `Server_Main.cpp`. The first thing we're going to need is a packet handler:

```cpp
void Handler(sf::IpAddress& l_ip, const PortNumber& l_port,
  const PacketID& l_id, sf::Packet& l_packet, Server* l_server)
{
  ClientID id = l_server->GetClientID(l_ip, l_port);
  if (id >= 0){
    if ((PacketType)l_id == PacketType::Disconnect){
      l_server->RemoveClient(l_ip, l_port);
      sf::Packet p;
      StampPacket(PacketType::Message, p);
      std::string message;
      message = "Client left! " + l_ip.toString() +
        ":" + std::to_string(l_port);
      p << message;
      l_server->Broadcast(p, id);
    } else if ((PacketType)l_id == PacketType::Message){
      std::string receivedMessage;
      l_packet >> receivedMessage;
      std::string message = l_ip.toString() + ":" +
        std::to_string(l_port) + " :" + receivedMessage;
      sf::Packet p;
      StampPacket(PacketType::Message, p);
      p << message;
      l_server->Broadcast(p, id);
    }
  } else {
    if ((PacketType)l_id == PacketType::Connect){
      ClientID id = l_server->AddClient(l_ip, l_port);
      sf::Packet packet;
      StampPacket(PacketType::Connect, packet);
      l_server->Send(id, packet);
    }
  }
}
```

As we're going to be providing a pointer to this function to our `Server` class, the fingerprint has to match exactly. The function itself starts by first establishing whether the client ID for the provided IP address and port number exists. If it is indeed above or equal to zero, we're only interested in two types of packets: `Disconnect` and `Message`.

In a case of client disconnect, we create a message packet that is broadcasted to all clients except the one disconnecting. On the other hand, if there is an incoming message from one of the clients, it is first extracted and attached to a string that contains the client's IP address and port. We're not going to be using nicknames this time. The full message string is then attached to a message packet and broadcasted to every client, except the one that sent the message to begin with.

If a client wasn't found, however, all we care about is receiving connect packets. When one is received, the IP address and port are added and a connect packet is sent back to the client.

What kind of a server would it be if it didn't have the ability to process commands? Let's write a function that will be running in a separate thread and process user input:

```
void CommandProcess(Server* l_server){
    while (l_server->IsRunning()){
        std::string str;
        std::getline(std::cin, str);
        if (str == "!quit"){
            l_server->Stop();
            break;
        } else if (str == "dc"){
            l_server->DisconnectAll();
            std::cout << "DC..." << std::endl;
        } else if (str == "list"){
            std::cout << l_server->GetClientCount()
                << " clients online:" << std::endl;
            std::cout << l_server->GetClientList() << std::endl;
        }
    }
}
```

Note that `std::getline` is a blocking function. If the program stops running, the thread that this function is running on will still be blocking until some user input comes through. One way to get it to terminate is to implement a command that stops the server, which is what `"!quit"` does. Once the server `Stop` method is invoked, it also breaks the loop just to be safe.

The other two commands are pretty standard. One simply disconnects all users, while the other prints out a list of all connected clients. We haven't covered `GetClientCount` or `GetClientList`, since they're fairly basic and are not required for the server to run. You can find the implementation of these two methods in the source code of this book.

Now it's time to assemble and run our code:

```
int main(){
    Server server(Handler);

    if (server.Start()){
        sf::Thread c(&CommandProcess, &server);
        c.launch();

        sf::Clock clock;
        clock.restart();
        while (server.IsRunning()){
            server.Update(clock.restart());
        }
        std::cout << "Stopping server..." << std::endl;
    }

    system("PAUSE");
    return 0;
}
```

This is quite a basic setup for the entry point of an application like this. First, we create an instance of the `Server` class and provide a function pointer that is going to be handling packets in its constructor. We then attempt to start the server and catch the return value of that in an `if` statement. If a successful start took place, a command thread is set up and launched. An instance of `sf::Clock` is created and restarted before entering our main loop, which simply executes as long as the server is running and updates it with the elapsed time value between iterations. That's all we need to have in a chat server!

The chat client

Our server is quite useless if we don't have the means of connecting to it and sending messages back and forth. In a separate project, let's create a file named `Client_Main.cpp` and begin writing the client portion of the code, starting with a packet handler:

```
void HandlePacket(const PacketID& l_id,
    sf::Packet& l_packet, Client* l_client)
{
    if ((PacketType)l_id == PacketType::Message){
        std::string message;
        l_packet >> message;
        std::cout << message << std::endl;
```

```
    } else if ((PacketType)l_id == PacketType::Disconnect){
        l_client->Disconnect();
    }
}
```

As you can see, it's really quite a simple design when we have a proper support class to fall back on. The client responds to two types of packets: messages and disconnects. In case a message pops in, it's extracted and simply printed in the console window. If a disconnect packet arrives from the server, the client's `Disconnect` method is invoked.

Next, the function that will be running in a command thread:

```
void CommandProcess(Client* l_client){
    while (l_client->IsConnected()){
        std::string str;
        std::getline(std::cin, str);
        if (str != ""){
            if (str == "!quit"){
                l_client->Disconnect();
                break;
            }
            sf::Packet p;
            StampPacket(PacketType::Message, p);
            p << str;
            l_client->Send(p);
        }
    }
}
```

We're using the same basic principle of capturing console input with the `std::getline` function, except we're only going to be processing the quit command in this case. Anything else that gets entered is treated as a message and sent out to the server. Keep in mind that because the `std::getline` function is a blocking one, a user will have to press enter once if the client gets disconnected by the server, just to provide some input and get things moving again in order for the thread to be closed.

Lastly, let's put all of this code to work and implement the main loop of our chat client:

```
void main(int argc, char** argv){
    sf::IpAddress ip;
    PortNumber port;
    if (argc == 1){
        std::cout << "Enter Server IP: ";
        std::cin >> ip;
```

```
            std::cout << "Enter Server Port: ";
            std::cin >> port;
    } else if (argc == 3){
        ip = argv[1];
        port = atoi(argv[2]);
    } else {
        return;
    }

    Client client;
    client.SetServerInformation(ip, port);
    client.Setup(&HandlePacket);
    sf::Thread c(&CommandProcess, &client);
    if (client.Connect()){
        c.launch();
        sf::Clock clock;
        clock.restart();
        while (client.IsConnected()){
            client.Update(clock.restart());
        }
    } else {
        std::cout << "Failed to connect." << std::endl;
    }
    std::cout << "Quitting..." << std::endl;
    sf::sleep(sf::seconds(1.f));
}
```

We begin by setting up a few variables to hold the IP address and port of the server. For extra credit, let's add support for command line arguments. If none are provided, the user is simply prompted to enter the server information inside the console window. Otherwise, the command-line arguments are read in and used for the same purpose.

Moving further, we see that an instance of `Client` is created and set up with the server information that was provided, in addition to the packet handler function getting registered and a command thread being prepared. The client then attempts to connect to the server, and if the connection is successful, the command thread is launched, an instance of `sf::Clock` is created, and the main loop of the program is entered, where the client gets updated.

With this, we have a fairly simple yet functional chat application:

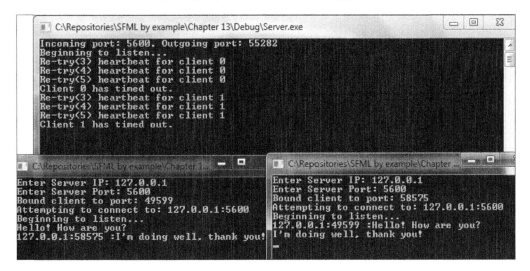

Summary

Congratulations on making it this far! Having covered the most important fundamentals, which includes the basics of socket programming, utilization of threads, and building the underlying layer of client-server communications, we're finally ready to tackle actual game networking! In the final chapter of this book, we're going to integrate this network code into our existing code base, turning a lonely single player RPG into an exciting arena of player versus player combat! See you there!

14
Come Play with Us! – Multiplayer Subtleties

Lots of great things in this world have incredibly humble beginnings. The contents of this book, from cover to cover, tell a story of a journey that began with nothing more than an interest and the will to create. Now that we're at the climax of our tale, why not end with a bang? Let's bring things back full circle and combine the framework we've developed with capabilities of networking to bring the third project of this book into new light! Let's connect our players not just through means of simple information exchange, but also through gameplay.

In this chapter, we're going to cover:

- Building a game server that supports previously implemented mechanics
- Exchanging entity data over a network
- Transforming existing game code into a client application
- Implementing player versus player combat
- Hiding network latency by smoothing out entity movement

There's a lot of code to cover, so let's get started!

Use of copyrighted resources

As always, it's fair to credit the artists who made the amazing graphics and sound effects that we're going to be using for our final project:

- *Simple small pixel hearts* by *C.Nilsson* under the CC-BY-SA 3.0 license: http://opengameart.org/content/simple-small-pixel-hearts
- *Grunt* by *n3b* under the CC-BY 3.0 license: http://opengameart.org/content/grunt

- *Swishes sound pack* by *artisticdude* under the CC0 license (public domain):
  `http://opengameart.org/content/swishes-sound-pack`

- *3 Item sounds* by *Michel Baradari* under the CC-BY 3.0 license:
  `http://opengameart.org/content/3-item-sounds`

Shared code

Since there are many instances where code we write is going to exist on both the client and the server side, let's discuss that first, starting with the way data exchange between both sides is made.

The most important part of our information exchange is updating entities on any and all connected clients. We do this by sending specialized structures back and forth, which contains relevant entity information. From now on, these structures are going to be referred to as snapshots. Let's see how they can be implemented, by taking a look at the `EntitySnapshot.h` file:

```
struct EntitySnapshot{
    std::string m_type;
    sf::Vector2f m_position;
    sf::Int32 m_elevation;
    sf::Vector2f m_velocity;
    sf::Vector2f m_acceleration;
    sf::Uint8 m_direction;
    sf::Uint8 m_state;
    sf::Uint8 m_health;
    std::string m_name;
};
```

The information we're going to be updating constantly for any given entity consists of its position and elevation, velocity, acceleration, the direction it's facing as well as the state it's in, and the entity's health and name. The type of an entity is also sent in a snapshot and used when creating the entity on the client side.

In this example, the order of the data members in the `EntitySnapshot` structure may not be the most efficient. Ordering data in your structures from biggest to smallest can help reduce their size, and therefore the bandwidth overhead. Structure alignment and packing are not going to be covered here, but it's a worthy subject to look into.

Something that helps a great deal in making our code more readable is overloading the *bitwise shift* operators of `sf::Packet` to support custom data types, such as `EntitySnapshot`:

```
sf::Packet& operator <<(sf::Packet& l_packet,
    const EntitySnapshot& l_snapshot);
sf::Packet& operator >>(sf::Packet& l_packet,
    EntitySnapshot& l_snapshot);
```

Actual implementation of these overloads exists inside the `EntitySnapshot.cpp` file:

```
sf::Packet& operator <<(sf::Packet& l_packet,
    const EntitySnapshot& l_snapshot)
{
    return l_packet << l_snapshot.m_type << l_snapshot.m_name
        << l_snapshot.m_position.x << l_snapshot.m_position.y
        << l_snapshot.m_elevation << l_snapshot.m_velocity.x
        << l_snapshot.m_velocity.y << l_snapshot.m_acceleration.x
        << l_snapshot.m_acceleration.y << l_snapshot.m_direction
        << l_snapshot.m_state << l_snapshot.m_health;
}

sf::Packet& operator >>(sf::Packet& l_packet,
    EntitySnapshot& l_snapshot)
{
    return l_packet >> l_snapshot.m_type >> l_snapshot.m_name
        >> l_snapshot.m_position.x >> l_snapshot.m_position.y
        >> l_snapshot.m_elevation >> l_snapshot.m_velocity.x
        >> l_snapshot.m_velocity.y >> l_snapshot.m_acceleration.x
        >> l_snapshot.m_acceleration.y >> l_snapshot.m_direction
        >> l_snapshot.m_state >> l_snapshot.m_health;
}
```

Other data exchanges are going to be more specific to the situation, so we're going to cover them later on. One thing we can do to prepare for that now, however, is updating the `Network` enumeration in the `NetworkDefinitions.h` file with a new value that is going to be used as a delimiter between different types of data in a specific packet:

```
enum class Network{
    HighestTimestamp = 2147483647, ClientTimeout = 10000,
    ServerPort = 5600, NullID = -1, PlayerUpdateDelim = -1
};
```

As we're going to work with the specific packet type that uses this delimiter on both the client and the server, its place is within the shared code space.

Additional components

First and foremost, entities that need to be synchronized between the server and client need to be marked and assigned a unique identifier. This is where the `C_Client` component comes in:

```
class C_Client : public C_Base{
public:
  C_Client(): C_Base(Component::Client),
    m_clientID((ClientID)Network::NullID){}
  void ReadIn(std::stringstream& l_stream){}

  ClientID GetClientID()const{ return m_clientID; }
  void SetClientID(const ClientID& l_id){ m_clientID = l_id; }
private:
  ClientID m_clientID;
};
```

It would also be nice to support entity names, in order to be able to store player nicknames. This can be accomplished by implementing a name component:

```
class C_Name : public C_Base{
public:
  C_Name() : C_Base(Component::Name){}
  void ReadIn(std::stringstream& l_stream){ l_stream >> m_name; }
  const std::string& GetName()const{ return m_name; }
  void SetName(const std::string& l_name){ m_name = l_name; }
private:
  std::string m_name;
};
```

It's a common thing in games to have a small cooldown period where an entity cannot be attacked, possibly also defining how long its hurting/death animation should last. Components that allow and define such functionality would ideally have to inherit from a base class, which simplifies the process of timing such events:

```
class C_TimedComponentBase : public C_Base{
public:
  C_TimedComponentBase(const Component& l_type)
    : C_Base(l_type), m_duration(sf::milliseconds(0)){}
  virtual ~C_TimedComponentBase(){}

  const sf::Time& GetTimer()const{ return m_duration; }
  void SetTimer(const sf::Time& l_time){ m_duration = l_time; }
  void AddToTimer(const sf::Time& l_time){ m_duration += l_time; }
```

```
    void Reset(){ m_duration = sf::milliseconds(0); }
  protected:
    sf::Time m_duration;
};
```

One component that will make use of the base timed class will be `C_Health`:

```
using Health = unsigned int;

class C_Health : public C_TimedComponentBase{
public:
  C_Health(): C_TimedComponentBase(Component::Health),
    m_hurtDuration(0), m_deathDuration(0){}
  void ReadIn(std::stringstream& l_stream){
    l_stream >> m_maxHealth >> m_hurtDuration >> m_deathDuration;
    m_health = m_maxHealth;
  }
  Health GetHealth()const{ return m_health; }
  Health GetMaxHealth()const{ return m_maxHealth; }
  void SetHealth(const Health& l_health){ m_health = l_health; }
  void ResetHealth(){ m_health = m_maxHealth; }

  sf::Uint32 GetHurtDuration(){ return m_hurtDuration; }
  sf::Uint32 GetDeathDuration(){ return m_deathDuration; }
private:
  Health m_health;
  Health m_maxHealth;
  sf::Uint32 m_hurtDuration;
  sf::Uint32 m_deathDuration;
};
```

As you can see, it holds values for the current entity health, its maximum health value, and a few data members that hold the expected duration of being hurt and dying.

Naturally, we're going to need more entity message and event types in order to express the process of combat. The newly added types are highlighted in the following code snippet:

```
enum class EntityMessage{
  Move, Is_Moving, Frame_Change, State_Changed,
  Direction_Changed, Switch_State, Attack,
  Being_Attacked, Hurt, Die, Respawn, Removed_Entity
};
enum class EntityEvent{
  Spawned, Despawned, Colliding_X, Colliding_Y,
```

```
    Moving_Left, Moving_Right, Moving_Up, Moving_Down,
    Elevation_Change, Became_Idle, Began_Moving, Began_Attacking
};
```

The `EntityManager` class is also going to be shared between both sides. Some adjustments have to be made to its `AddEntity` and `RemoveEntity` methods in order to let the rest of the entity component system know when an entity has been added or removed:

```
int EntityManager::AddEntity(const Bitmask& l_mask, int l_id){
    ...
    m_systems->EntityModified(entity,l_mask);
    m_systems->AddEvent(entity, (EventID)EntityEvent::Spawned);
    return entity;
}

bool EntityManager::RemoveEntity(const EntityId& l_id){
    ...
    Message msg((MessageType)EntityMessage::Removed_Entity);
    msg.m_receiver = l_id;
    msg.m_int = l_id;
    m_systems->GetMessageHandler()->Dispatch(msg);
    ... // Removing all components.
}
```

A lot more of the code we've written in previous chapters is actually going to need to be shared as well. Some of these classes, like the entity manager for example, have been slightly modified to serve as parents for derivatives of client and server implementations. We're not going to discuss that at length here, as the code files of this chapter should be more than helpful for familiarizing yourself with the code structure.

Building our game server

In *Chapter 13, We Have Contact! – Networking Basics,* we took a look at a very basic chat service that was supported by a server application and multiple clients connecting to it. Building a game server is quite similar to that. We have a piece of software that acts as a central point of interest to all its clients by doing all of the calculations and sending the results back to them in order to ensure proper and identical simulation is taking place across the board. Naturally, since we're not simply exchanging text messages, there is going to be a lot more data being sent back and forth, as well as more calculation on the server side.

First, we need to decide on a time interval value of sending entity snapshots. It has to be often enough to maintain smooth updates, but send as little information as possible to remain efficient. After some testing and tweaking, a sweet spot can be found pretty easily. For this particular project, let's say that an entity snapshot will be sent once every 100 milliseconds, which will be defined in `NetSettings.h`:

```
#define SNAPSHOT_INTERVAL 100
```

Sending 10 snapshots a second is enough to keep the clients happy and the server maintaining a relatively low bandwidth.

Additions to the entity component system

The majority of combat logic is going to take place on the server side. In order to support entities attacking one another, we need a new component to work with the `C_Attacker`:

```cpp
class C_Attacker : public C_TimedComponentBase{
public:
  C_Attacker(): C_TimedComponentBase(Component::Attacker),
    m_attacked(false), m_knockback(0.f), m_attackDuration(0){}
  void ReadIn(std::stringstream& l_stream){
    l_stream >> m_offset.x >> m_offset.y
      >> m_attackArea.width >> m_attackArea.height
      >> m_knockback >> m_attackDuration;
  }

  void SetAreaPosition(const sf::Vector2f& l_pos){
    m_attackArea.left = l_pos.x;
    m_attackArea.top = l_pos.y;
  }

  const sf::FloatRect& GetAreaOfAttack(){ return m_attackArea; }
  const sf::Vector2f& GetOffset(){ return m_offset; }
  bool HasAttacked(){ return m_attacked; }
  void SetAttacked(bool l_attacked){ m_attacked = l_attacked; }
  float GetKnockback(){ return m_knockback; }
  sf::Uint32 GetAttackDuration(){ return m_attackDuration; }
private:
  sf::FloatRect m_attackArea;
  sf::Vector2f m_offset;
  bool m_attacked;
  float m_knockback;
  sf::Uint32 m_attackDuration;
};
```

The attacker component holds information about the size and location of the entity's attack area and possible offset, a flag to check if the entity has hit something while attacking, the force of knockback that is to be applied to another entity being attacked by this one, and the duration of the attack.

Implementing combat

Entity-on-entity combat is going to be a fairly simple addition, since we already have a nice collision system in place. It only requires a few additional lines of code inside the EntityCollisions method:

```
void S_Collision::EntityCollisions(){
  EntityManager* entities = m_systemManager->GetEntityManager();
  for (auto itr = m_entities.begin();
    itr != m_entities.end(); ++itr)
  {
    for (auto itr2 = std::next(itr);
      itr2 != m_entities.end(); ++itr2)
    {
      ...
      C_Attacker* attacker1 = entities->
        GetComponent<C_Attacker>(*itr, Component::Attacker);
      C_Attacker* attacker2 = entities->
        GetComponent<C_Attacker>(*itr2, Component::Attacker);
      if (!attacker1 && !attacker2){ continue; }
      Message msg((MessageType)EntityMessage::Being_Attacked);
      if (attacker1){
        if (attacker1->GetAreaOfAttack().intersects(
          collidable2->GetCollidable()))
        {
          // Attacker-on-entity collision!
          msg.m_receiver = *itr2;
          msg.m_sender = *itr;
          m_systemManager->GetMessageHandler()->Dispatch(msg);
        }
      }
      if (attacker2){
        if (attacker2->GetAreaOfAttack().intersects(
          collidable1->GetCollidable()))
        {
          // Attacker-on-entity collision!
          msg.m_receiver = *itr;
          msg.m_sender = *itr2;
          m_systemManager->GetMessageHandler()->Dispatch(msg);
```

```
            }
          }
        }
      }
    }
```

First, both entities being checked get their attacker components fetched. If neither one of them has one, the iteration is skipped. Otherwise, a new message of type `Being_Attacked` is constructed. If the attacking entity's area of attach actually intersects the bounding box of another entity, this message is filled in with receiver and sender information and sent out.

In order to process and react properly to these collisions, as well as update all the entities that have potential to be in combat, we're going to need a new system: `S_Combat`! It doesn't have any additional methods other than the ones required to be implemented by the base system class, so there's really no need for us to examine its header. Let's take a look at its constructor and destructor instead:

```cpp
S_Combat::S_Combat(SystemManager* l_systemMgr)
  : S_Base(System::Combat, l_systemMgr)
{
  Bitmask req;
  req.TurnOnBit((unsigned int)Component::Position);
  req.TurnOnBit((unsigned int)Component::Movable);
  req.TurnOnBit((unsigned int)Component::State);
  req.TurnOnBit((unsigned int)Component::Health);
  m_requiredComponents.push_back(req);
  req.ClearBit((unsigned int)Component::Health);
  req.TurnOnBit((unsigned int)Component::Attacker);
  m_requiredComponents.push_back(req);

  m_systemManager->GetMessageHandler()->
    Subscribe(EntityMessage::Being_Attacked, this);
}
```

This system will hold any entity that has position, is a movable entity with a state, and has a health component or attack component or both. It also subscribes to the `Being_Attacked` message in order to process attack area collisions.

Naturally, the same attack area cannot be positioned identically for all four directions that an entity is facing. Consider the following example:

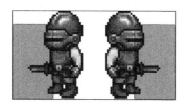

Repositioning the attack area for each entity based on its current direction is done inside the Update method of this system:

```
void S_Combat::Update(float l_dT){
  EntityManager* entities = m_systemManager->GetEntityManager();
  for (auto &entity : m_entities){
    C_Attacker* attack = entities->
      GetComponent<C_Attacker>(entity, Component::Attacker);
    if (!attack){ continue; }
    sf::Vector2f offset = attack->GetOffset();
    sf::FloatRect AoA = attack->GetAreaOfAttack();
    Direction dir = entities->GetComponent<C_Movable>
      (entity, Component::Movable)->GetDirection();
    sf::Vector2f position = entities->GetComponent<C_Position>
      (entity, Component::Position)->GetPosition();
    if (dir == Direction::Left){ offset.x -= AoA.width / 2; }
    else if (dir == Direction::Right){offset.x += AoA.width / 2; }
    else if (dir == Direction::Up){offset.y -= AoA.height / 2; }
    else if (dir == Direction::Down){offset.y += AoA.height / 2; }
    position -= sf::Vector2f(AoA.width / 2, AoA.height / 2);
    attack->SetAreaPosition(position + offset);
  }
}
```

If the current entity being checked has no C_Attacker component, the iteration is simply skipped. Otherwise, both the entity's area of attack and its offset are obtained, in addition to its current direction and position. In order to first center the attack area, half of its width and height is subtracted from the entity's position. The offset is then adjusted based on the direction the entity is facing, and the area of attack is moved to the latest position with it applied.

Let's take a look at a possible response to the message our collision system sends out:

```
void S_Combat::Notify(const Message& l_message){
  if (!HasEntity(l_message.m_receiver) ||
    !HasEntity(l_message.m_sender))
  {
    return;
  }
  EntityManager* entities = m_systemManager->GetEntityManager();
  EntityMessage m = (EntityMessage)l_message.m_type;
  switch (m){
  case EntityMessage::Being_Attacked:
    C_Health* victim = entities->GetComponent<C_Health>
      (l_message.m_receiver, Component::Health);
    C_Attacker* attacker = entities->GetComponent<C_Attacker>
      (l_message.m_sender, Component::Attacker);
    if (!victim || !attacker){ return; }
    S_State* StateSystem = m_systemManager->
      GetSystem<S_State>(System::State);
    if (StateSystem->GetState(l_message.m_sender) !=
      EntityState::Attacking)
    {
      return;
    }
    if (attacker->HasAttacked()){ return; }
    // Begin attacking.
    victim->SetHealth((victim->GetHealth() > 1 ?
      victim->GetHealth() - 1 : 0));
    attacker->SetAttacked(true);
    if (!victim->GetHealth()){
      StateSystem->ChangeState(l_message.m_receiver,
        EntityState::Dying, true);
    } else {
      Message msg((MessageType)EntityMessage::Hurt);
      msg.m_receiver = l_message.m_receiver;
      m_systemManager->GetMessageHandler()->Dispatch(msg);
    }

    // Knockback.
    Direction attackerDirection =entities->GetComponent<C_Movable>
      (l_message.m_sender, Component::Movable)->GetDirection();
    float Knockback = attacker->GetKnockback();
    sf::Vector2f KnockbackVelocity;
    if (attackerDirection == Direction::Left ||
```

```
      attackerDirection == Direction::Up)
  {
    Knockback = -Knockback;
  }
  if (attackerDirection == Direction::Left ||
    attackerDirection == Direction::Right)
  {
    KnockbackVelocity.x = Knockback;
  }
  else{ KnockbackVelocity.y = Knockback; }
  entities->GetComponent<C_Movable>
    (l_message.m_receiver, Component::Movable)->
    SetVelocity(KnockbackVelocity);
  break;
    }
  }
```

First, we check if the combat system has both the sender and receiver of this message. If that's the case, the `Being_Attacked` message is processed by first obtaining the health component of the entity being attacked, as well as the attacker component of the aggressor. The state of the attacking entity is then checked. If it is not currently attacking or if the entity has already attacked something else, the method is terminated by returning. Otherwise, the attack is initiated by first reducing the victim's health by *1*. The attacker is then flagged for having already attacked an entity. If the victim's health is at value 0, its state is changed to `Dying`. Otherwise, a `Hurt` message is dispatched.

The remaining few lines of code deal with the victim entity being knocked back slightly, as it's being attacked. Both the attacker's direction and knockback force are obtained and a `sf::Vector2f` variable, signifying the applied force is created. If the attacker is facing either left or up, the knockback value is inverted. Also, if the attacking entity is facing either left or right, the knockback is applied on the *X* axis. Otherwise, the *Y* axis is used. Then, the force is simply applied as velocity through the victim's `C_Movable` component.

Server action timing

One major difference between running the same code on a server and a client is how certain actions and events are timed. Since we have no animations happening, there is no way to simply check when the last frame was reached and terminate an attack or death, for example. This is where manually setting certain time values comes in. For this, we're going to need the `S_Timers` system. Since it also doesn't have any additional methods other than the required ones, the class definition is not necessary.

Let's start by taking a look at the constructor and destructor of this system:

```
S_Timers::S_Timers(SystemManager* l_systemMgr)
  : S_Base(System::Timers, l_systemMgr)
{
  Bitmask req;
  req.TurnOnBit((unsigned int)Component::State);
  req.TurnOnBit((unsigned int)Component::Attacker);
  m_requiredComponents.push_back(req);
  req.ClearBit((unsigned int)Component::Attacker);
  req.TurnOnBit((unsigned int)Component::Health);
  m_requiredComponents.push_back(req);
}
```

Once again, we simply subscribe to the state component as well as the attacker component, health component, or both. Nothing interesting happens here, so let's move on to the `Update` method that makes timing on the server side possible:

```
void S_Timers::Update(float l_dT){
  EntityManager* entities = m_systemManager->GetEntityManager();
  for (auto &entity : m_entities){
    EntityState state = entities->GetComponent<C_State>
      (entity, Component::State)->GetState();
    if (state == EntityState::Attacking){
      C_Attacker* attack = entities->GetComponent<C_Attacker>
        (entity, Component::Attacker);
      attack->AddToTimer(sf::seconds(l_dT));
      if (attack->GetTimer().asMilliseconds() <
        attack->GetAttackDuration())
      {
        continue;
      }
      attack->Reset();
      attack->SetAttacked(false);
    } else if (state == EntityState::Hurt ||
      state == EntityState::Dying)
    {
      C_Health* health = entities->
        GetComponent<C_Health>(entity, Component::Health);
      health->AddToTimer(sf::seconds(l_dT));
      if ((state == EntityState::Hurt &&
        health->GetTimer().asMilliseconds() <
        health->GetHurtDuration()) ||
        (state == EntityState::Dying &&
```

```
        health->GetTimer().asMilliseconds() <
        health->GetDeathDuration()))
      {
        continue;
      }

      health->Reset();
      if (state == EntityState::Dying){
        Message msg((MessageType)EntityMessage::Respawn);
        msg.m_receiver = entity;
        m_systemManager->GetMessageHandler()->Dispatch(msg);
        health->ResetHealth();
      }
    } else { continue; }
    m_systemManager->GetSystem<S_State>(System::State)->
      ChangeState(entity, EntityState::Idle, true);
  }
}
```

In this system, both the attacker and health components are checked to see whether they have reached specific time values that are provided in the entity file. If the entity is in an attacking state, the attacker component is obtained and the elapsed time is added to it. If the attack duration is passed, the timer is reset and the "attacked" flag is set back to false, making another attack possible.

If the entity is in either the hurting or dying state, the respectful time values are checked against predetermined durations and the timer is reset once again. If the entity is actually in a dying state, a Respawn message is sent out as well, in order to reset its animation, health and move the entity to a specific location where it "respawns".

Server network system

Handling entity networking on the server side can be made a lot easier by simply building a dedicated system that would already have access to entity data by design. This is where the server network system comes in.

Let's start with how entities are going to be controlled by players. In previous chapters, we simply used messaging to move entities around on the client side. Obviously, due to network delays and bandwidth restrictions, it would be problematic to simply send out a bunch of messages whenever a client moves. It's much more efficient to simply keep track of a player's input state, as this simple structure demonstrates:

```
struct PlayerInput{
    int m_movedX;
    int m_movedY;
```

```
    bool m_attacking;
    PlayerInput() : m_movedX(0), m_movedY(0), m_attacking(false){}
};
```

```
using PlayerInputContainer = std::unordered_map<EntityId,
  PlayerInput>;
```

The first two data members will contain the amount of times a player has been moved along either axis. On the client side, we're going to be sending input states to the server at a specific interval, which means we have the benefit of combining messages into neat packets, as well as process out redundant movement, such as moving left and right by the same amount. Additionally, clients are also going to be sending their attacking states. All of this information will be held in a container, which tethers it to a specific entity ID.

Now, let's take a look at the header file of the network system we're going to implement:

```
class S_Network : public S_Base{
public:
  S_Network(SystemManager* l_systemMgr);
  ~S_Network();

  void Update(float l_dT);
  void HandleEvent(const EntityId& l_entity,
    const EntityEvent& l_event);
  void Notify(const Message& l_message);

  bool RegisterClientID(const EntityId& l_entity,
    const ClientID& l_client);
  void RegisterServer(Server* l_server);
  ClientID GetClientID(const EntityId& l_entity);
  EntityId GetEntityID(const ClientID& l_client);

  void CreateSnapshot(sf::Packet& l_packet);
  void UpdatePlayer(sf::Packet& l_packet, const ClientID& l_cid);
private:
  PlayerInputContainer m_playerInput;
  Server* m_server;
};
```

As usual, we have the required methods implemented, as well as a few additional ones. Since we're going to link behavior between clients and entities, we have a few methods that help us register and obtain this relationship information. On top of that, a few helper methods exist for creating snapshots of entity states and updating a specific client's information from an incoming packet.

Implementing the network system

Let's start with the constructor and destructor of the network system:

```
S_Network::S_Network(SystemManager* l_systemMgr)
  : S_Base(System::Network, l_systemMgr)
{
  Bitmask req;
  req.TurnOnBit((unsigned int)Component::Client);
  m_requiredComponents.push_back(req);

  MessageHandler* messageHandler =
    m_systemManager->GetMessageHandler();
  messageHandler->Subscribe(EntityMessage::Removed_Entity, this);
  messageHandler->Subscribe(EntityMessage::Hurt, this);
  messageHandler->Subscribe(EntityMessage::Respawn, this);
}
```

This particular system is only going to require a single component: `C_Client`. It also subscribes to entity removal, hurt, and respawn messages.

Next, the `Update` method:

```
void S_Network::Update(float l_dT){
  EntityManager* entities = m_systemManager->GetEntityManager();
  for (auto &entity : m_entities){
    auto& player = m_playerInput[entity];
    if (player.m_movedX || player.m_movedY){
      if (player.m_movedX){
        Message msg((MessageType)EntityMessage::Move);
        msg.m_receiver = entity;
        if (player.m_movedX > 0){msg.m_int=(int)Direction::Right;}
        else { msg.m_int = (int)Direction::Left; }
        m_systemManager->GetMessageHandler()->Dispatch(msg);
      }

      if (player.m_movedY){
        Message msg((MessageType)EntityMessage::Move);
        msg.m_receiver = entity;
```

```
        if (player.m_movedY > 0){msg.m_int=(int)Direction::Down;}
        else { msg.m_int = (int)Direction::Up; }
        m_systemManager->GetMessageHandler()->Dispatch(msg);
      }
    }
    if (player.m_attacking){
      Message msg((MessageType)EntityMessage::Attack);
      msg.m_receiver = entity;
      m_systemManager->GetMessageHandler()->Dispatch(msg);
    }
  }
}
```

This is where we process the current control state of a client and apply it to the entity. Relevant messages are constructed and sent out, based on the state of a client's input.

Next, let's deal with those three message types that this system is subscribed to:

```
void S_Network::Notify(const Message& l_message){
  if (!HasEntity(l_message.m_receiver)){ return; }
  EntityMessage m = EntityMessage(l_message.m_type);
  if (m == EntityMessage::Removed_Entity){
    m_playerInput.erase(l_message.m_receiver);
    return;
  }
  if (m == EntityMessage::Hurt){
    sf::Packet packet;
    StampPacket(PacketType::Hurt, packet);
    packet << l_message.m_receiver;
    m_server->Broadcast(packet);
    return;
  }
  if (m == EntityMessage::Respawn){
    C_Position* position = m_systemManager->GetEntityManager()->
      GetComponent<C_Position>(l_message.m_receiver,
      Component::Position);
    if (!position){ return; }
    position->SetPosition(64.f, 64.f);
    position->SetElevation(1);
  }
}
```

First, if the entity is being removed, the player input information of the corresponding client in control of that entity gets erased. If a message about an entity getting hurt is received, a hurt packet is constructed and sent to all clients to notify them of an entity taking damage. Lastly, an entity respawn message is handled by resetting its position and elevation to some pre-defined values. These coordinates can easily be randomized or read in from the map file, but for demonstration purposes this works just fine.

When a client connects to our server and an entity for it is created, we need to have a method that allows us to express that relationship by binding the two values together, as shown here:

```
bool S_Network::RegisterClientID(const EntityId& l_entity,
  const ClientID& l_client)
  {
  if (!HasEntity(l_entity)){ return false; }
  m_systemManager->GetEntityManager()->GetComponent<C_Client>
    (l_entity, Component::Client)->SetClientID(l_client);
  return true;
}
```

Since we're going to be storing the client ID inside the client component, it's obtained through the entity manager and used in exactly that manner.

The network class is also going to need access to an instance of the Server class, hence the following method:

```
void S_Network::RegisterServer(Server* l_server){
    m_server = l_server;
}
```

Next, a few methods of convenience for obtaining client and entity IDs:

```
ClientID S_Network::GetClientID(const EntityId& l_entity){
  if (!HasEntity(l_entity)){ return (ClientID)Network::NullID; }
  return m_systemManager->GetEntityManager()->
    GetComponent<C_Client>(l_entity, Component::Client)->
    GetClientID();
}
EntityId S_Network::GetEntityID(const ClientID& l_client){
  EntityManager* e = m_systemManager->GetEntityManager();
  auto entity = std::find_if(m_entities.begin(), m_entities.end(),
    [&e, &l_client](EntityId& id){
      return e->GetComponent<C_Client>
```

```
        (id, Component::Client)->GetClientID() == l_client;
  });
  return(entity != m_entities.end() ?
    *entity : (EntityId)Network::NullID);
}
```

Snapshot creation itself also deserves its own method:

```
void S_Network::CreateSnapshot(sf::Packet& l_packet){
  sf::Lock lock(m_server->GetMutex());
  ServerEntityManager* e =
    (ServerEntityManager*)m_systemManager->GetEntityManager();
  StampPacket(PacketType::Snapshot, l_packet);
  l_packet << sf::Int32(e->GetEntityCount());
  if (e->GetEntityCount()){
    e->DumpEntityInfo(l_packet);
  }
}
```

Because we're accessing entity information that could be changed, the server mutex has to be locked before we access it. After assigning a snapshot type to the packet provided as an argument, we write the number of entities into it as well. If the number is above zero, a DumpEntityInfo method is invoked. This method is defined within our ServerEntityManager class and will be covered shortly.

Lastly, let's handle the incoming player update packets:

```
void S_Network::UpdatePlayer(sf::Packet& l_packet,
  const ClientID& l_cid)
{
  sf::Lock lock(m_server->GetMutex());
  EntityId eid = GetEntityID(l_cid);
  if (eid == -1){ return; }
  if (!HasEntity(eid)){ return; }
  sf::Int8 entity_message;
  m_playerInput[eid].m_attacking = false;
  while (l_packet >> entity_message){
    switch (entity_message){
    case sf::Int8(EntityMessage::Move):
    {
      sf::Int32 x = 0, y = 0;
      l_packet >> x >> y;
      m_playerInput[eid].m_movedX = x;
      m_playerInput[eid].m_movedY = y;
      break;
```

```
      }
      case sf::Int8(EntityMessage::Attack):
      {
        sf::Int8 attackState;
        l_packet >> attackState;
        if (attackState){ m_playerInput[eid].m_attacking = true; }
        break;
      }
      }
      sf::Int8 delim = 0;
      if (!(l_packet >> delim) || delim !=
        (sf::Int8)Network::PlayerUpdateDelim)
      {
        std::cout << "Faulty update!" << std::endl;
        break;
      }
    }
  }
```

Before anything can be done, we must make sure that the server mutex is locked and the client sending this packet has a valid entity attached to it. This is done by obtaining the entity ID and checking its validity in the next two lines. A local variable named `entity_message` is then created in order to hold the message type that the client is going to be sending to us. The attack state of the entity is then set to `false` by default and iterating over the packet's information begins.

Encountering a `Move` message is dealt with by extracting the X and Y values from the packet and overwriting our player movement information for the given entity with them. The `Attack` message has one less value to worry about. The player's `m_attacking` flag is set to `true` if the incoming player state contains anything else but zero.

Server entity and system management

The components and systems supported on the server side are obviously going to differ from those on the client side. On top of that, custom methods for both ends help out a great deal by allowing the base class to remain unmodified, while the derivatives can deal with side-specific logic. Let's take a look at our simple extension to the `EntityManager` class that runs on the server side:

```
ServerEntityManager::ServerEntityManager(SystemManager* l_sysMgr)
  : EntityManager(l_sysMgr)
{
  AddComponentType<C_Position>(Component::Position);
```

```
    AddComponentType<C_State>(Component::State);
    AddComponentType<C_Movable>(Component::Movable);
    AddComponentType<C_Controller>(Component::Controller);
    AddComponentType<C_Collidable>(Component::Collidable);
    AddComponentType<C_Client>(Component::Client);
    AddComponentType<C_Health>(Component::Health);
    AddComponentType<C_Name>(Component::Name);
    AddComponentType<C_Attacker>(Component::Attacker);
}
```

We're obviously not going to need any graphics or sound related component types here. It's the client's job to deal with those.

This class will also be useful when creating entity snapshots. All of the entity information is dumped into a provided instance of sf::Packet by using this method:

```
void ServerEntityManager::DumpEntityInfo(sf::Packet& l_packet){
  for (auto &entity : m_entities){
    l_packet << sf::Int32(entity.first);
    EntitySnapshot snapshot;
    snapshot.m_type = entity.second.m_type;
    const auto& mask = entity.second.m_bitmask;
    if (mask.GetBit((unsigned int)Component::Position)){
      C_Position* p = GetComponent<C_Position>(entity.first,
        Component::Position);
      snapshot.m_position = p->GetPosition();
      snapshot.m_elevation = p->GetElevation();
    }
    if (mask.GetBit((unsigned int)Component::Movable)){
      C_Movable* m = GetComponent<C_Movable>(entity.first,
        Component::Movable);
      snapshot.m_velocity = m->GetVelocity();
      snapshot.m_acceleration = m->GetAcceleration();
      snapshot.m_direction = sf::Uint8(m->GetDirection());
    }
    if (mask.GetBit((unsigned int)Component::State)){
      C_State* s = GetComponent<C_State>(entity.first,
        Component::State);
      snapshot.m_state = sf::Uint8(s->GetState());
    }
    if (mask.GetBit((unsigned int)Component::Health)){
      C_Health* h = GetComponent<C_Health>(entity.first,
        Component::Health);
      snapshot.m_health = h->GetHealth();
```

```
      }
      if (mask.GetBit((unsigned int)Component::Name)){
        C_Name* n = GetComponent<C_Name>(entity.first,
          Component::Name);
        snapshot.m_name = n->GetName();
      }
      l_packet << snapshot;
    }
  }
```

The entity ID is written into the packet instance first. An EntitySnapshot variable is created afterwards, and it is filled with relevant component information, provided these components exist at all. Once that's done, the snapshot instance is written to the packet, which is made incredibly easy thanks to its overloaded << and >> operators.

For system management on the server side, we only need to handle the systems that are added:

```
ServerSystemManager::ServerSystemManager(){
  AddSystem<S_Network>(System::Network);
  AddSystem<S_State>(System::State);
  AddSystem<S_Control>(System::Control);
  AddSystem<S_Movement>(System::Movement);
  AddSystem<S_Timers>(System::Timers);
  AddSystem<S_Collision>(System::Collision);
  AddSystem<S_Combat>(System::Combat);
}
```

Similar to what we did for components, we simply exclude anything graphical or sound related.

Main server class

Similar to the client side's Game class, a supervisor object is going to be needed on the server side as well. We're going to be keeping instances of the game map, entity, and server managers, and the Server class itself in a new class, simply called World. Let's start by taking a look at the header file:

```
class World{
public:
    World();
    ~World();

    void Update(const sf::Time& l_time);
    void HandlePacket(sf::IpAddress& l_ip,
```

```
        const PortNumber& l_port, const PacketID& l_id,
         sf::Packet& l_packet, Server* l_server);
      void ClientLeave(const ClientID& l_client);
      void CommandLine();

      bool IsRunning();
  private:
      sf::Time m_tpsTime;
      sf::Time m_serverTime;
      sf::Time m_snapshotTimer;
      sf::Thread m_commandThread;
      Server m_server;
      ServerSystemManager m_systems;
      ServerEntityManager m_entities;
      bool m_running;

      Map m_map;
      unsigned int m_tick;
      unsigned int m_tps;
  };
```

Similar to `Game`, it has an `Update` method where all of the time-related magic is going to happen. It also has methods for handling custom packet types, handling a client leaving, and processing command-line input.

Data member wise, we're looking at a few `sf::Time` instances for keeping track of the current server time, as well as delivery time for snapshots. A `sf::Thread` instance for the command line is also quite handy to have around.

Last but not least, the `m_tpsTime`, `m_tick` and `m_tps` data members exist for the simple convenience of measuring the update rate on the server. The number of updates per second, also known as ticks, is quite useful for tracking down and resolving performance issues.

Implementing the world class

Let's kick this class into gear, starting with the constructor and destructor:

```
World::World(): m_server(&World::HandlePacket, this),
  m_commandThread(&World::CommandLine, this), m_entities(nullptr),
  m_map(&m_entities), m_tick(0), m_tps(0), m_running(false)
{
  if (!m_server.Start()){ return; }
  m_running = true;
  m_systems.SetEntityManager(&m_entities);
```

```
    m_entities.SetSystemManager(&m_systems);
    m_map.LoadMap("media/Maps/map1.map");
    m_systems.GetSystem<S_Collision>(System::Collision)->
      SetMap(&m_map);
    m_systems.GetSystem<S_Movement>(System::Movement)->
      SetMap(&m_map);
    m_systems.GetSystem<S_Network>(System::Network)->
      RegisterServer(&m_server);
    m_server.BindTimeoutHandler(&World::ClientLeave, this);
    m_commandThread.launch();
}

    World::~World(){ m_entities.SetSystemManager(nullptr); }
```

Our `Server` instance is set up by providing a valid packet handler in the initializer list, where the command thread is also set up. In the actual body of the constructor, we first attempt to start the server and catch a possible failure in an `if` statement. Upon a successful start, the `m_running` flag is set to `true` and both the entity manager and system manager are provided with pointers to each other. The game map is then loaded and relevant systems are provided with its instance. After our network system is made available with an instance of `Server`, the `ClientLeave` method is fed in as the timeout handler and the command line thread is launched.

Upon destruction of the `World` class, all we really have to worry about is taking away the entity manager's access to the system manager.

Next, let's keep the action rolling by updating everything:

```
void World::Update(const sf::Time& l_time){
  if (!m_server.IsRunning()){ m_running = false; return; }
  m_serverTime += l_time;
  m_snapshotTimer += l_time;
  m_tpsTime += l_time;
  m_server.Update(l_time);
  m_server.GetMutex().lock();
  m_systems.Update(l_time.asSeconds());
  m_server.GetMutex().unlock();
  if (m_snapshotTimer.asMilliseconds() >= SNAPSHOT_INTERVAL){
    sf::Packet snapshot;
    m_systems.GetSystem<S_Network>(System::Network)->
      CreateSnapshot(snapshot);
    m_server.Broadcast(snapshot);
    m_snapshotTimer = sf::milliseconds(0);
  }
```

```
    if (m_tpsTime >= sf::milliseconds(1000)){
      m_tps = m_tick;
      m_tick = 0;
      m_tpsTime = sf::milliseconds(0);
    } else {
      ++m_tick;
    }
  }
}
```

The server instance is first checked for having stopped. If that's the case, the world class itself is stopped and the Update method is returned from. Otherwise, all of our time values are updated alongside the server class. The system manager's Update method is then invoked in order to update all of the entity information. The server mutex has to be locked while that happens, as entity information could potentially be changed.

Once everything is up to date, the snapshot timer is checked to see if it has exceeded the snapshot interval. With that being the case, a snapshot packet is created and filled in by using the CreateSnapshot method of S_Network. The packet is then broadcasted to every single client and the snapshot timer is reset to zero.

Ticks Per Second (**TPS**) are measured by increasing the m_tick data member every update, provided the TPS timer hasn't exceeded one second. If that's the case, m_tps is assigned the value of m_tick, which in turn gets set back to zero, alongside the TPS timer.

Handling incoming packets is the next piece of the puzzle:

```
void World::HandlePacket(sf::IpAddress& l_ip,
  const PortNumber& l_port, const PacketID& l_id,
  sf::Packet& l_packet, Server* l_server)
{
  ClientID id = l_server->GetClientID(l_ip, l_port);
  PacketType type = (PacketType)l_id;
  if (id >= 0){
    if (type == PacketType::Disconnect){
      ClientLeave(id);
      l_server->RemoveClient(l_ip, l_port);
    } else if (type == PacketType::Message){
      // ...
    } else if (type == PacketType::PlayerUpdate){
      m_systems.GetSystem<S_Network>(System::Network)->
        UpdatePlayer(l_packet, id);
    }
```

```
    } else {
      if (type != PacketType::Connect){ return; }
      std::string nickname;
      if (!(l_packet >> nickname)){ return; }
      ClientID cid = l_server->AddClient(l_ip, l_port);
      if (cid == -1){
        sf::Packet packet;
        StampPacket(PacketType::Disconnect, packet);
        l_server->Send(l_ip, l_port, packet);
        return;
      }
      sf::Lock lock(m_server.GetMutex());
      sf::Int32 eid = m_entities.AddEntity("Player");
      if (eid == -1){ return; }
      m_systems.GetSystem<S_Network>(System::Network)->
        RegisterClientID(eid, cid);
      C_Position* pos = m_entities.GetComponent<C_Position>
        (eid, Component::Position);
      pos->SetPosition(64.f, 64.f);
      m_entities.GetComponent<C_Name>(eid, Component::Name)->
        SetName(nickname);
      sf::Packet packet;
      StampPacket(PacketType::Connect, packet);
      packet << eid;
      packet << pos->GetPosition().x << pos->GetPosition().y;
      if (!l_server->Send(cid, packet)){
        std::cout << "Unable to respond to connect packet!"
          << std::endl;
        return;
      }
    }
  }
}
```

The client ID is first obtained from the originating IP address and port number. If a client with that information exists, we're interested in three packet types that can be received from it. First, the client disconnect packet is handled by invoking the `ClientLeave` method with the client ID passed in as the only argument. Next, the actual client is removed from the server class.

The next packet type, `Message`, is left unimplemented for now. We're not going to send chat messages between clients just yet, but this is where it would be implemented in the future. Following that is the player update packet type, in which case the packet is simply passed into the network system to be processed. We have already covered this.

If the origin information of the incoming data does not yield us a valid client ID, we're only interested in communications that attempt to connect. First, we attempt to extract a string from the packet, which would be the player nickname. If that fails, this method is returned from. Next, the client information is added and its success is checked by analyzing the returned client ID. In case of a failure, a `Disconnect` packet is sent back to the originating source and the method is returned from. Otherwise, the server mutex is locked and we attempt to add a new player entity. Failure to do that, once again, would result in returning from this method. The client ID is then registered in the network system and the position of our newly added player entity is set to some pre-defined values. The name component of the player entity is also adjusted to reflect the entered nickname. At this point, a connect packet is constructed as a response. It contains the entity ID of the player, as well as its spawn position. The packet is then sent out to our new client.

Leaving the server is a much simpler procedure in comparison to this. Let's take a look:

```
void World::ClientLeave(const ClientID& l_client){
    sf::Lock lock(m_server.GetMutex());
    S_Network* network = m_systems.
     GetSystem<S_Network>(System::Network);
    m_entities.RemoveEntity(network->GetEntityID(l_client));
}
```

The server mutex gets locked before this operation is performed. The network system is then obtained and the `RemoveEntity` method of our entity manager is invoked with the return value of network system's `GetEntityID` method. This effectively removes the entity.

Implementing some basic commands on the server side proves to be more than useful. Let's take a look at a very basic setup of a command-line thread:

```
void World::CommandLine(){
    while (m_server.IsRunning()){
        std::string str;
        std::getline(std::cin, str);
        if (str == "terminate"){
            m_server.Stop();
            m_running = false;
            break;
        } else if (str == "disconnectall"){
            std::cout << "Disconnecting all clients..." << std::endl;
            m_server.DisconnectAll();
            sf::Lock lock(m_server.GetMutex());
            m_entities.Purge();
```

```
        } else if (str.find("tps") != std::string::npos){
          std::cout << "TPS: " << m_tps << std::endl;
        } else if (str == "clients"){
          std::cout << m_server.GetClientCount()
              << " clients online:" << std::endl;
          std::cout << m_server.GetClientList()
              << std::endl;
        } else if (str == "entities"){
          std::cout << "Current entity count: "
              << m_entities.GetEntityCount() << std::endl;
        }
    }
}
```

First, a loop is entered and kept alive as long as the server is running. Next, the command line is prompted to obtain a line of input. The first command we process is `"terminate"`. This stops the server and breaks out of the command line loop, which is helpful. The following command disconnects every single client and purges all entities that currently exist. Notice that the server mutex gets locked before the purge. The next command simply displays the current tick per second rate. Typing in `"clients"` would result in a list of clients currently connected that contains their IP addresses, port numbers, and latency values. Lastly, the `"entities"` command simply prints out the number of entities that are currently in the world.

The last and definitely the least interesting method is useful for obtaining the current status of the world:

```
bool World::IsRunning(){ return m_running; }
```

Server entry point

Now let's put all of this effort to work. The following are the contents of our `Server_Main.cpp` file:

```
#include "World.h"

int main(){
    World world;
    sf::Clock clock;
    clock.restart();

    while (world.IsRunning()){
        world.Update(clock.restart());
    }
     return 0;
}
```

It couldn't get simpler than this. A new instance of the `World` class is created, alongside a clock that is promptly restarted. Our main `while` loop is entered with the condition that the world instance has to keep running. It gets updated every iteration with the return value of `clock.restart()`. After the loop is terminated, zero is returned to end the program successfully.

All of this brings us a very nice looking and capable console window that's ready to handle some incoming connections:

```
Incoming port: 5600. Outgoing port: 50979
Beginning to listen...
--- Loading a map: media/Maps/map1.map
--- Map Loaded! ---
clients
2 clients online:

ID        Client IP:PORT              Ping

0         127.0.0.1:50980             0ms.
1         127.0.0.1:50981             0ms.

Total data sent: 9kB. Total data received: 3kB
```

This by itself is, of course, completely useless without the client that draws all of the pretty images as a result of the server communicating with it. That is the next major task on our list.

Developing the game client

With proper backend support from the server, we can now focus entirely on client-side details and spoil ourselves a little with pretty visuals that always yield that sense of accomplishment a lot quicker than anything that runs in the background. Let's start by creating the client's own version of `NetSettings.h`:

```
#define NET_RENDER_DELAY 100 // ms.
#define PLAYER_UPDATE_INTERVAL 50 // ms
```

We have a couple of macros to work with here. First is the expected delay between what's being rendered on screen and real time. This means that technically we're going to be rendering all action about 100 milliseconds in the past. The second macro is the interval at which we're going to be sending updates to the server. 50 milliseconds gives us plenty of time to gather a few input states and let the server know what's going on.

Entity component system expansions

As in the case of the server, additional components and systems are necessary if we want to realize any of our goals. Unlike the server, however, these additions to the client entity component system are going to serve an entirely different purpose. It's going to be important for us to see the names and health values of all players in the game. We're going to shoot for something like this:

In order to easily maintain these glyphs floating above an entity, we're going to need a new type of component that describes exactly where they're supposed to be rendered:

```cpp
class C_UI_Element : public C_Base{
public:
  C_UI_Element() : C_Base(Component::UI_Element),
    m_showHealth(false), m_showName(false){}
  void ReadIn(std::stringstream& l_stream){
    l_stream >> m_offset.x >> m_offset.y;
  }

  const sf::Vector2f& GetOffset(){ return m_offset; }
  void SetOffset(const sf::Vector2f& l_offset){ m_offset = l_offset; }

  void SetShowHealth(bool l_show){ m_showHealth = l_show; }
  void SetShowName(bool l_show){ m_showName = l_show; }
  bool ShowHealth(){ return m_showHealth; }
  bool ShowName(){ return m_showName; }
private:
  sf::Vector2f m_offset;
  bool m_showHealth;
  bool m_showName;
};
```

The `C_UI_Element` component will read in two offset values, one for X and one for Y, from the entity file. This way, characters of different sizes can define their own rules of where this information will appear. We also included a couple of Boolean flags in case the health or name information ever needs to be disabled for some reason.

The component alone isn't going to do anything fancy, so let's create a new system that actually makes something happen:

```
class S_CharacterUI : public S_Base{
public:
    S_CharacterUI(SystemManager* l_systemMgr);
    ~S_CharacterUI();

    void Update(float l_dT);
    void HandleEvent(const EntityId& l_entity,
      const EntityEvent& l_event);
    void Notify(const Message& l_message);

    void Render(Window* l_wind);
private:
    sf::Sprite m_heartBar;
    sf::Text m_nickname;
    sf::RectangleShape m_nickbg;
    sf::Vector2u m_heartBarSize;
};
```

Note that this system has a `Render` method. We're not only going to update the position of the graphical elements, but also draw them on the screen. This includes a sprite that will be bound to whatever texture is chosen to represent health, an instance of `sf::Text` that will hold the entity's name, a rectangle background that will be rendered behind the name, and a data member that holds the size of the health bar texture.

With that out of the way, let's start implementing this system!

```
S_CharacterUI::S_CharacterUI(SystemManager* l_systemMgr)
  : S_Base(System::Character_UI, l_systemMgr)
{
  Bitmask req;
  req.TurnOnBit((unsigned int)Component::Position);
  req.TurnOnBit((unsigned int)Component::UI_Element);
  req.TurnOnBit((unsigned int)Component::Health);
  m_requiredComponents.push_back(req);
  req.ClearBit((unsigned int)Component::Health);
```

```
        req.TurnOnBit((unsigned int)Component::Name);
        m_requiredComponents.push_back(req);

        ClientSystemManager* mgr =(ClientSystemManager*)m_systemManager;
        mgr->GetTextureManager()->RequireResource("HeartBar");
        mgr->GetFontManager()->RequireResource("Main");
        sf::Texture* txtr = mgr->GetTextureManager()->
          GetResource("HeartBar");
        txtr->setRepeated(true);
        m_heartBarSize = txtr->getSize();
        m_heartBar.setTexture(*txtr);
        m_heartBar.setScale(0.5f, 0.5f);
        m_heartBar.setOrigin(m_heartBarSize.x / 2, m_heartBarSize.y);
        m_nickname.setFont(*mgr->GetFontManager()->GetResource("Main"));
        m_nickname.setCharacterSize(9);
        m_nickname.setColor(sf::Color::White);
        m_nickbg.setFillColor(sf::Color(100, 100, 100, 100));
    }
```

The first order of business here is, of course, setting up the component requirements. An entity has to have a position component and a UI element component, in addition to some combination of the health and name components. The rest of the constructor is used to set up the texture and font resources for our graphics. Our health bar texture is set to be repeated so we can represent any health value. The actual texture is only the size of a single heart.

The resources for these elements obviously have to be released when they're no longer needed. That's where the destructor comes in:

```
    S_CharacterUI::~S_CharacterUI(){
        ClientSystemManager* mgr =
          (ClientSystemManager*)m_systemManager;
        mgr->GetTextureManager()->ReleaseResource("HeartBar");
        mgr->GetFontManager()->ReleaseResource("Main");
    }
```

Lastly, the most important part of this system is contained within the Render method:

```
    void S_CharacterUI::Render(Window* l_wind){
      EntityManager* entities = m_systemManager->GetEntityManager();
      for (auto &entity : m_entities){
        C_Health* health = entities->
          GetComponent<C_Health>(entity, Component::Health);
        C_Name* name = entities->
          GetComponent<C_Name>(entity, Component::Name);
        C_Position* pos = entities->
```

```
      GetComponent<C_Position>(entity, Component::Position);
    C_UI_Element* ui = entities->
      GetComponent<C_UI_Element>(entity, Component::UI_Element);
    if (health){
      m_heartBar.setTextureRect(sf::IntRect(0, 0,
        m_heartBarSize.x * health->GetHealth(),
        m_heartBarSize.y));
      m_heartBar.setOrigin((
        m_heartBarSize.x * health->GetHealth())/2,
        m_heartBarSize.y);
      m_heartBar.setPosition(pos->GetPosition() +ui->GetOffset());
      l_wind->GetRenderWindow()->draw(m_heartBar);
    }
    if (name){
      m_nickname.setString(name->GetName());
      m_nickname.setOrigin(m_nickname.getLocalBounds().width / 2,
        m_nickname.getLocalBounds().height / 2);
      if (health){
        m_nickname.setPosition(m_heartBar.getPosition().x,
          m_heartBar.getPosition().y - (m_heartBarSize.y));
      } else {
        m_nickname.setPosition(pos->GetPosition() +
          ui->GetOffset());
      }
      m_nickbg.setSize(sf::Vector2f(
        m_nickname.getGlobalBounds().width + 2,
        m_nickname.getCharacterSize() + 1));
      m_nickbg.setOrigin(m_nickbg.getSize().x / 2,
        m_nickbg.getSize().y / 2);
      m_nickbg.setPosition(m_nickname.getPosition().x + 1,
        m_nickname.getPosition().y + 1);
      l_wind->GetRenderWindow()->draw(m_nickbg);
      l_wind->GetRenderWindow()->draw(m_nickname);
    }
  }
}
```

For each entity, we obtain all four components that we're going to be working with. Since there can be instances where either the name or health components exist without the other one present, both of them must be checked before we commit to rendering them.

The health bar portion is drawn by first resetting the texture rectangle of the sprite. Its width is changed to the result of multiplying the width of a single heart in the texture by the health value an entity has. The Y value is left unchanged. The origin of the sprite is then changed to be in the middle of it on the X axis and on the very bottom of the Y axis. Its position is then set to that of the entity's, but with the UI element's offset factored in. Because the texture is set up to repeat itself, this allows us to represent ridiculous amounts of health:

When an entity's name is rendered, the `sf::Text` instance is first set up by changing the string and its origin is manipulated to be exactly in the middle. Since we want our information to be nicely stacked and not drawn on top of each other, checking if the health was rendered is necessary.

If the health component is present, the name's position is obtained from the `m_heartBar` data member. The Y value of that position is modified by subtracting the height of the health bar in order to render the player name on top. Otherwise, the name's position is set to match the entity with the offset included. The name background is then set up to be slightly larger than the text that it will be drawn behind and its origin is set to the exact center. The position of the name background is slightly offset by a single pixel from the position of the actual name. The values used here can be perfected by simply trying out different things and getting the feel for the best result.

Lastly, the background and the entity's name are drawn in that order on screen.

Network class and interpolation

Showing our entities simply appearing on the screen isn't satisfactory at all. Even if we get them to move, you will quickly notice that due to the delay between the server and client, players would look more like they're skipping across the screen, rather than walking. A little more work has to be done on the client side in order to smooth it out. For that, we're going to rely on something called interpolation. Consider the following illustration:

What is interpolation? It's an estimation between two known data points. There are
many different types of interpolation out there, all with a different philosophy of
use. For our purposes, interpolating data simply comes down to finding a weighted
average between two values at a given time. In the preceding diagram, we have two
snapshots representing different places in time. Interpolating helps us find the state
of an entity somewhere in the middle of those two snapshots, and, in turn, smooths
out their movement by adjusting attributes such as position, velocity, and acceleration
based on the estimation, rather than actual snapshot data.

Finding a value at a specific point in time between two snapshots can be expressed
this way:

$$\text{value}(t_x) = \left(\frac{\Delta \text{value}}{\Delta t} * (t_x - t_1) \right) + \text{value}(t_1)$$

A value we want to find at a given time, tx, is simply the difference of the value
between both snapshots divided by the difference in time, multiplied by the time
that has passed since the first snapshot and then added to the value of the first
snapshot. In code, it can be expressed like this:

```
template<class T>
inline T Interpolate(const sf::Int32& T1, const sf::Int32& T2,
  const T& T1_val, const T& T2_val, const sf::Int32& T_X)
{
  return (((T2_val - T1_val) / (T2 - T1)) * (T_X - T1)) + T1_val;
}
```

Having a few extra methods for actually handling the snapshot and time types,
as well as comparing two snapshots together, would be useful:

```
void InterpolateSnapshot(const EntitySnapshot& l_s1,
  const sf::Int32& T1, const EntitySnapshot& l_s2,
  const sf::Int32& T2, EntitySnapshot& l_target,
  const sf::Int32& T_X);
```

```
bool CompareSnapshots(const EntitySnapshot& l_s1,
  const EntitySnapshot& l_s2, bool l_position = true,
  bool l_physics = true, bool l_state = true);
```

We're going to need some way of containing these snapshots, so it's time to define our data types:

```
using SnapshotMap = std::unordered_map<EntityId, EntitySnapshot>;
struct SnapshotDetails{
  SnapshotMap m_snapshots;
};
using SnapshotContainer = std::map<sf::Int32, SnapshotDetails>;
using OutgoingMessages = std::unordered_map<EntityMessage,
  std::vector<Message>>;
```

All of the snapshots are first stored with the entity ID being the key. The actual map itself is being held by a `SnapshotDetails` struct, which may prove to be useful later if we decide to add any additional snapshot information. All of the entity data is then stored in a map structure, where the timestamp of the snapshot is the key value. Notice that we're using a regular map here, as opposed to an unordered map. What's the benefit, you may ask. The regular map type may be a little bit slower, but it automatically sorts its entries by key. This means that newer snapshots will always go towards the end of the map. The reason why that's important will become apparent when we're performing entity interpolation.

The last data type we're going to need for the network class is some sort of container that holds outgoing messages we're going to send to the server. In this case, an unordered map works just fine.

So, what is our network system class going to look like? Let's take a look:

```
class S_Network : public S_Base{
public:
  S_Network(SystemManager* l_systemMgr);
  ~S_Network();

  void Update(float l_dT);
  void HandleEvent(const EntityId& l_entity,
    const EntityEvent& l_event);
  void Notify(const Message& l_message);

  void SetClient(Client* m_client);
  void SetPlayerID(const EntityId& l_entity);
```

```
    void AddSnapshot(const EntityId& l_entity,
      const sf::Int32& l_timestamp,
      EntitySnapshot& l_snapshot);
    void SendPlayerOutgoing();
    void ClearSnapshots();
  private:
    void ApplyEntitySnapshot(const EntityId& l_entity,
      const EntitySnapshot& l_snapshot,
      bool l_applyPhysics);

    void PerformInterpolation();
    SnapshotContainer m_entitySnapshots;
    EntityId m_player;
    OutgoingMessages m_outgoing;
    Client* m_client;
    sf::Time m_playerUpdateTimer;
};
```

Apart from the normal methods a system has to implement, we have a few setters for registering a `Client` instance, as well as keeping track of the entity ID that our client is going to be controlling as a player. A few helper methods for adding a received entity snapshot, as well as sending out player messages to the server also exist to make life just a little bit easier. For our private method selection, we have a total of two: one for applying a specific snapshot to an entity and another for performing interpolation. This is met by a standard number of data members that are responsible for containing received snapshots, keeping track of the player ID, containing outgoing messages to the server before they're sent out, and having access to the `Client` instance. To top that off, we're going to use another `sf::Time` data type in order to keep track of time passage for sending player updates to the server.

Implementing the client network class

Before we get to actually implementing the network system, let's complete the last two functions related to interpolation and comparison of entity snapshots:

```
    void InterpolateSnapshot(const EntitySnapshot& l_s1,
      const sf::Int32& T1, const EntitySnapshot& l_s2,
      const sf::Int32& T2, EntitySnapshot& l_target,
      const sf::Int32& T_X)
    {
      l_target.m_direction = l_s2.m_direction;
      l_target.m_health = l_s2.m_health;
      l_target.m_name = l_s2.m_name;
      l_target.m_state = l_s1.m_state;
```

```
l_target.m_elevation = l_s1.m_elevation;

l_target.m_position.x = Interpolate<float>(
  T1, T2, l_s1.m_position.x, l_s2.m_position.x, T_X);
l_target.m_position.y = Interpolate<float>(
  T1, T2, l_s1.m_position.y, l_s2.m_position.y, T_X);

l_target.m_velocity.x = Interpolate<float>(
  T1, T2, l_s1.m_velocity.x, l_s2.m_velocity.x, T_X);
l_target.m_velocity.y = Interpolate<float>(
  T1, T2, l_s1.m_velocity.y, l_s2.m_velocity.y, T_X);

l_target.m_acceleration.x = Interpolate<float>(
  T1, T2, l_s1.m_acceleration.x, l_s2.m_acceleration.x, T_X);
l_target.m_acceleration.y = Interpolate<float>(
  T1, T2, l_s1.m_acceleration.y, l_s2.m_acceleration.y, T_X);
}
```

We begin by overwriting some values that don't need to be interpolated. Note that the direction, health, and name values are overwritten with the latest available information from the second entity snapshot, rather than the first. This provides an overall smoother feel to entity movement and interactions. For the rest of the snapshot data, we use our handy `Interpolate` function, which provides a smooth transition between the two updates.

It's also quite useful to have a function that can compare two snapshots together, so we can know if any data has changed. `CompareSnapshots` comes to the rescue here:

```
bool CompareSnapshots(const EntitySnapshot& l_s1,
  const EntitySnapshot& l_s2, bool l_position,
  bool l_physics, bool l_state)
{
  if (l_position && (l_s1.m_position != l_s2.m_position ||
    l_s1.m_elevation != l_s2.m_elevation))
  { return false; }
  if (l_physics && (l_s1.m_velocity != l_s2.m_velocity ||
    l_s1.m_acceleration != l_s2.m_acceleration ||
    l_s1.m_direction != l_s2.m_direction))
  { return false; }
  if (l_state && (l_s1.m_state != l_s2.m_state))
  { return false; }
  return true;
}
```

It's not really necessary to check every single aspect of a snapshot here. All we really care about is the positional, kinematic, and state information of the entity. Three additional Boolean arguments can also be provided, telling this function which data is relevant.

With this out of the way, we can finally begin implementing the network system class, starting, of course, with the constructor and destructor:

```
S_Network::S_Network(SystemManager* l_systemMgr)
  : S_Base(System::Network, l_systemMgr), m_client(nullptr)
{
  Bitmask req;
  req.TurnOnBit((unsigned int)Component::Client);
  m_requiredComponents.push_back(req);

  m_systemManager->GetMessageHandler()->
    Subscribe(EntityMessage::Move, this);
  m_systemManager->GetMessageHandler()->
    Subscribe(EntityMessage::Attack, this);
  m_playerUpdateTimer = sf::milliseconds(0);
}
```

Much like on the server class, we only care about the entities that have client components in this system. Messages for entity movement and attacks are also subscribed to in order to properly store them and update the server later on.

Next up, we have the `Update` method:

```
void S_Network::Update(float l_dT){
  if (!m_client){ return; }
  sf::Lock lock(m_client->GetMutex());
  m_playerUpdateTimer += sf::seconds(l_dT);
  if (m_playerUpdateTimer.asMilliseconds() >=
    PLAYER_UPDATE_INTERVAL)
  {
    SendPlayerOutgoing();
    m_playerUpdateTimer = sf::milliseconds(0);
  }
  PerformInterpolation();
}
```

First, a check is made to make sure we have a valid pointer to the client class. If so, we lock the client mutex and add time to the player update timer. The `SendPlayerOutgoing` method is then invoked and the timer is reset if enough time has passed to update the server. Lastly, we call the private helper method of this class, which is responsible for interpolating between snapshots. Keeping this functionality separate from the actual update loop leaves us with nicer looking code and allows early return while interpolating.

Handling the messages this system is subscribed to is quite simple, as you will see here:

```
void S_Network::Notify(const Message& l_message){
  if (!HasEntity(l_message.m_receiver) ||
    l_message.m_receiver != m_player)
  {
    return;
  }
  if (l_message.m_type == (MessageType)EntityMessage::Attack &&
    m_outgoing.find(EntityMessage::Attack) != m_outgoing.end())
  {
    return;
  }
  m_outgoing[(EntityMessage)l_message.m_type].
    emplace_back(l_message);
}
```

At this point, all we care about is adding the message into our outgoing container, since we're not dealing with more complex types just yet. An additional check is performed in case an attack message is received. There really is no point of having multiple attack messages in this container at the same time, so the `Notify` method simply returns if an attack message is attempted to be inserted while one already exists in the container.

Next, we have some helper methods:

```
void S_Network::SetClient(Client* l_client){m_client = l_client;}
void S_Network::SetPlayerID(const EntityId& l_entity){
  m_player = l_entity;
}
void S_Network::AddSnapshot(const EntityId& l_entity,
  const sf::Int32& l_timestamp, EntitySnapshot& l_snapshot)
{
  sf::Lock lock(m_client->GetMutex());
  auto i = m_entitySnapshots.emplace(l_timestamp,
    SnapshotDetails());
  i.first->second.m_snapshots.emplace(l_entity, l_snapshot);
}
```

There's nothing too special going on here. One thing to note is that when a new snapshot is being added, the client mutex probably should be locked. Speaking of snapshots, let's look at how one could be applied to an entity:

```
void S_Network::ApplyEntitySnapshot(const EntityId& l_entity,
  const EntitySnapshot& l_snapshot, bool l_applyPhysics)
{
  ClientEntityManager* entities =
    (ClientEntityManager*)m_systemManager->GetEntityManager();
  C_Position* position = nullptr;
  C_Movable* movable = nullptr;
  S_Movement* movement_s = nullptr;
  S_State* state_s = nullptr;
  C_Health* health = nullptr;
  C_Name* name = nullptr;
  sf::Lock lock(m_client->GetMutex());
  if (position = entities->GetComponent<C_Position>(l_entity,
    Component::Position))
  {
    position->SetPosition(l_snapshot.m_position);
    position->SetElevation(l_snapshot.m_elevation);
  }
  if (l_applyPhysics){
    if (movable = entities->GetComponent<C_Movable>(l_entity,
      Component::Movable))
    {
      movable->SetVelocity(l_snapshot.m_velocity);
      movable->SetAcceleration(l_snapshot.m_acceleration);
    }
  }
  if (movement_s = m_systemManager->
    GetSystem<S_Movement>(System::Movement))
  {
    movement_s->SetDirection(l_entity,
      (Direction)l_snapshot.m_direction);
  }
  if (state_s = m_systemManager->
    GetSystem<S_State>(System::State))
  {
    state_s->ChangeState(l_entity,
      (EntityState)l_snapshot.m_state,true);
  }
  if (health = entities->GetComponent<C_Health>(l_entity,
    Component::Health))
```

```
    {
      health->SetHealth(l_snapshot.m_health);
    }
    if (name = entities->GetComponent<C_Name>(l_entity,
      Component::Name))
    {
      name->SetName(l_snapshot.m_name);
    }
  }
}
```

After we obtain a pointer to the entity manager and set up empty pointers to various components that the entity snapshot might contain information about, the client mutex is locked and we begin manipulating the component information carefully, by first attempting to retrieve a valid component address inside the `if` statements. This method also takes in a flag to let it know whether physics information, such as acceleration or velocity, should be applied, which can come in handy.

The following method is executed while updating the network system class, and it is responsible for sending player updates to the server:

```
void S_Network::SendPlayerOutgoing(){
  sf::Int32 p_x = 0, p_y = 0;
  sf::Int8 p_a = 0;

  for (auto &itr : m_outgoing){
    if (itr.first == EntityMessage::Move){
      sf::Int32 x = 0, y = 0;
      for (auto &message : itr.second){
        if (message.m_int == (int)Direction::Up){ --y; }
        else if (message.m_int == (int)Direction::Down){ ++y; }
        else if (message.m_int == (int)Direction::Left){ --x; }
        else if (message.m_int == (int)Direction::Right){ ++x; }
      }
      if (!x && !y){ continue; }
      p_x = x; p_y = y;
    } else if (itr.first == EntityMessage::Attack){ p_a = 1; }
  }

  sf::Packet packet;
  StampPacket(PacketType::PlayerUpdate, packet);
  packet << sf::Int8(EntityMessage::Move)
    << p_x << p_y << sf::Int8(Network::PlayerUpdateDelim);
  packet << sf::Int8(EntityMessage::Attack)
    << p_a << sf::Int8(Network::PlayerUpdateDelim);
```

```
    m_client->Send(packet);
    m_outgoing.clear();
  }
```

We begin by setting up some local variables that are going to be holding the number of times our player has moved in the X and Y directions. A smaller variable is also set up for the attack state. The next step is to iterate over all outgoing messages and process each type individually. In a case of a `Move` type, every single one of them is counted. If an `Attack` message is found, the attack state is simply set to 1.

The last step is, of course, sending this information out. A new packet is then constructed and marked as a player update. The movement and attack state information is then fed into the packet. Notice that we're adding in the `PlayerUpdateDelim` value at the end of each update type. Enforcing specific communication rules as such decreases the chances of our server processing invalid or damaged data. Once the update packet is sent in, the outgoing message container is cleared for the next time.

Lastly, we arrive at the key method for ensuring smooth entity movement:

```
void S_Network::PerformInterpolation(){
  if (m_entitySnapshots.empty()){ return; }
  ClientEntityManager* entities =
    (ClientEntityManager*)m_systemManager->GetEntityManager();
  sf::Time t = m_client->GetTime();
  auto itr = ++m_entitySnapshots.begin();
  while (itr != m_entitySnapshots.end()){
    if (m_entitySnapshots.begin()->first <=
      t.asMilliseconds() - NET_RENDER_DELAY &&
      itr->first >= t.asMilliseconds() - NET_RENDER_DELAY)
    {
      auto Snapshot1 = m_entitySnapshots.begin();
      auto Snapshot2 = itr;
      bool SortDrawables = false;
      for (auto snap = Snapshot1->second.m_snapshots.begin();
        snap != Snapshot1->second.m_snapshots.end();)
      {
        if (!entities->HasEntity(snap->first)){
          if (entities->AddEntity(snap->second.m_type,
            snap->first) == (int)Network::NullID)
          {
            std::cout << "Failed adding entity type: "
              << snap->second.m_type << std::endl;
            continue;
          }
          ApplyEntitySnapshot(snap->first, snap->second, true);
          ++snap;
```

```
                        continue;
                    }
                    auto snap2 =Snapshot2->second.m_snapshots.find(
                        snap->first);
                    if (snap2 == Snapshot2->second.m_snapshots.end()){
                        sf::Lock lock(m_client->GetMutex());
                        entities->RemoveEntity(snap->first);
                        snap = Snapshot1->second.m_snapshots.erase(snap);
                        continue;
                    }

                    EntitySnapshot i_snapshot;
                    InterpolateSnapshot(snap->second, Snapshot1->first,
                        snap2->second, Snapshot2->first,
                        i_snapshot, t.asMilliseconds() - NET_RENDER_DELAY);
                    ApplyEntitySnapshot(snap->first, i_snapshot, true);
                    if (!CompareSnapshots(snap->second, snap2->second,
                        true, false, false))
                    {
                        SortDrawables = true;
                    }
                    ++snap;
                }
                if (SortDrawables){
                    m_systemManager->GetSystem<S_Renderer>
                        (System::Renderer)->SortDrawables();
                }
                return;
            }
            m_entitySnapshots.erase(m_entitySnapshots.begin());
            itr = ++m_entitySnapshots.begin();
        }
    }
```

First and foremost, we must deal with the possibility of our client not having any snapshots at all. If that happens, this method is returned from immediately. If we have snapshots available, the next step is iterating over the snapshot container and finding two snapshots that we're currently between (time wise). Normally, this wouldn't be a likely outcome, but keep in mind that we're rendering things slightly in the past:

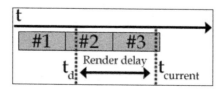

The benefit of rendering slightly in the past is that we will actually have more data that has arrived from the server, which in turn will allow us to smooth it out and provide nicer entity movement. This wouldn't be possible if we simply rendered everything in real time. This delay is represented by the NET_RENDER_DELAY macro.

Once we find the pair of snapshots that we're looking for, a local variable called SortDrawables is set up to keep track of whether or not we need to worry about re-sorting drawable components to represent depth correctly. All of the entities from the first (earlier) snapshot are then iterated over. Our first concern is making sure that an entity that exists in the snapshot also exists on our client. If it doesn't, a new entity is created from the type that the snapshot provides. All of its information is then applied to the newly created entity and we skip the current iteration of the snapshot loop as there's no need to interpolate anything.

The next step is making sure that the entity that exists in the earlier snapshot also exists in the later one, so an attempt to find it in the second snapshot container is made. Provided the entity has not been found, the client mutex is locked and the entity is removed from our client, prior to actually being erased from the snapshot container as well. The current iteration is then skipped, as we have no reason to interpolate once again.

If all of these checks yield no reason for us to skip an iteration, a new instance of EntitySnapshot is created. This is going to be our target for holding interpolated data. InterpolateSnapshot is then called with both snapshots and their time values, as well as the target snapshot and the current time *with the interpolation delay* factored in is passed in as arguments. After the target snapshot is filled in with the interpolated data, it is applied to the current entity. We also want to compare both snapshots we're interpolating between and set the SortDrawables variable to true if they have different positions. After all of the entity interpolation code, this variable is checked and the system renderer is instructed to re-sort the drawable components if it was indeed set to true at some point.

One last thing to take away from this is that if the time checking conditional in the very first loop ends up not being satisfied, the first element in the snapshot container is erased and the iterator is reset to point to the second value in it, ensuring a proper disposal of irrelevant snapshots.

Client entity and system management

Quite predictably, we're going to have different types of components and systems available on the client side than the server side, starting with component types:

```
ClientEntityManager::ClientEntityManager(SystemManager* l_sysMgr,
    TextureManager* l_textureMgr): EntityManager(l_sysMgr),
    m_textureManager(l_textureMgr)
{
    AddComponentType<C_Position>(Component::Position);
    AddComponentType<C_State>(Component::State);
    AddComponentType<C_Movable>(Component::Movable);
    AddComponentType<C_Controller>(Component::Controller);
    AddComponentType<C_Collidable>(Component::Collidable);
    AddComponentType<C_SpriteSheet>(Component::SpriteSheet);
    AddComponentType<C_SoundEmitter>(Component::SoundEmitter);
    AddComponentType<C_SoundListener>(Component::SoundListener);
    AddComponentType<C_Client>(Component::Client);
    AddComponentType<C_Health>(Component::Health);
    AddComponentType<C_Name>(Component::Name);
    AddComponentType<C_UI_Element>(Component::UI_Element);
}
```

After making sure all client-relevant component types are registered, let's implement our own version of loading an entity here, as it involves manipulating the renderable components it may have:

```
int ClientEntityManager::AddEntity(
    const std::string& l_entityFile, int l_id)
{
    ...
    while (std::getline(file, line)){
        ...
        } else if (type == "Component"){
            ...
            keystream >> *component;
            if (component->GetType() == Component::SpriteSheet){
                C_SpriteSheet* sheet = (C_SpriteSheet*)component;
                sheet->Create(m_textureManager);
            }
        }
    }
    ...
}
```

We have already seen this code in previous chapters, but it's still fair to emphasize that the highlighted snippet does not exist on the server side at all, yet is necessary here.

Next, the client's version of a system manager:

```
class ClientSystemManager : public SystemManager{
public:
    ClientSystemManager(TextureManager* l_textureMgr,
      FontManager* l_fontMgr);
    ~ClientSystemManager();

    TextureManager* GetTextureManager();
    FontManager* GetFontManager();
    void Draw(Window* l_wind, unsigned int l_elevation);
private:
    TextureManager* m_textureMgr;
    FontManager* m_fontMgr;
};
```

Naturally, the only additions we have here are, once again, related to graphics. We wouldn't need to draw anything on the server side, but it's necessary here.

The constructor of our client system manager handles adding systems that are relevant to the client performing as intended:

```
ClientSystemManager::ClientSystemManager(
    TextureManager* l_textureMgr, FontManager* l_fontMgr)
    : m_textureMgr(l_textureMgr), m_fontMgr(l_fontMgr)
{
    AddSystem<S_State>(System::State);
    AddSystem<S_Control>(System::Control);
    AddSystem<S_Movement>(System::Movement);
    AddSystem<S_Collision>(System::Collision);
    AddSystem<S_SheetAnimation>(System::SheetAnimation);
    AddSystem<S_Network>(System::Network);
    AddSystem<S_Sound>(System::Sound);
    AddSystem<S_Renderer>(System::Renderer);
    AddSystem<S_CharacterUI>(System::Character_UI);
}
```

Note the placement of the network system here. The order of adding these systems directly dictates the order in which they are updated. We don't want our network system sending or receiving any data before we get a chance to process our own.

Naturally, getters for texture and font managers would be useful on this side:

```
TextureManager* ClientSystemManager::GetTextureManager(){
    return m_textureMgr;
}
FontManager* ClientSystemManager::GetFontManager(){
    return m_fontMgr;
}
```

Lastly, we have a few systems that need to render something on screen:

```
void ClientSystemManager::Draw(Window* l_wind,
  unsigned int l_elevation)
{
  auto itr = m_systems.find(System::Renderer);
  if(itr != m_systems.end()){
    S_Renderer* system = (S_Renderer*)itr->second;
    system->Render(l_wind, l_elevation);
  }
  itr = m_systems.find(System::Character_UI);
  if (itr != m_systems.end()){
    S_CharacterUI* ui = (S_CharacterUI*)itr->second;
    ui->Render(l_wind);
  }
}
```

After the renderer system draws all of the entities on screen, we want to overlay their names and health graphics on top of that.

Putting the pieces into place

Because all of the networking and action is going to take place solely within the confines of the game state, that's the main class we're going to adjust, starting with the header file:

```
class State_Game : public BaseState{
    ...
private:
    Map* m_gameMap;
    int m_player;
    Client* m_client;
};
```

After making sure that the game state has a pointer to a `Client` instance, we must provide a way for the game to handle incoming packets:

```
void State_Game::HandlePacket(const PacketID& l_id,
  sf::Packet& l_packet, Client* l_client)
{
  ClientEntityManager* emgr = m_stateMgr->
    GetContext()->m_entityManager;
  PacketType type = (PacketType)l_id;
  if (type == PacketType::Connect){
    sf::Int32 eid;
    sf::Vector2f pos;
    if (!(l_packet >> eid) || !(l_packet >> pos.x) ||
      !(l_packet >> pos.y))
    {
      std::cout << "Faulty CONNECT response!" << std::endl;
      return;
    }
    std::cout << "Adding entity: " << eid << std::endl;
    m_client->GetMutex().lock();
    emgr->AddEntity("Player", eid);
    emgr->GetComponent<C_Position>
      (eid, Component::Position)->SetPosition(pos);
    m_client->GetMutex().unlock();
    m_player = eid;
    m_stateMgr->GetContext()->m_systemManager->
     GetSystem<S_Network>(System::Network)->SetPlayerID(m_player);
    emgr->AddComponent(eid, Component::SoundListener);
    return;
  }

  if (!m_client->IsConnected()){ return; }
  switch (type){
  case PacketType::Snapshot:
  {
    sf::Int32 entityCount = 0;
    if (!(l_packet >> entityCount)){
      std::cout << "Snapshot extraction failed."
        << std::endl;
      return;
    }
    sf::Lock lock(m_client->GetMutex());
    sf::Int32 t = m_client->GetTime().asMilliseconds();
    for (unsigned int i = 0; i < entityCount; ++i){
```

```
                  sf::Int32 eid;
                  EntitySnapshot snapshot;
                  if (!(l_packet >> eid) || !(l_packet >> snapshot)){
                    std::cout << "Snapshot extraction failed."
                      << std::endl;
                    return;
                  }
                  m_stateMgr->GetContext()->m_systemManager->
                    GetSystem<S_Network>(System::Network)->
                      AddSnapshot(eid, t, snapshot);
              }
              break;
          }
          case PacketType::Disconnect:
          {
              m_stateMgr->Remove(StateType::Game);
              m_stateMgr->SwitchTo(StateType::MainMenu);
              std::cout << "Disconnected by server!" << std::endl;
              break;
          }
          case PacketType::Hurt:
          {
              EntityId id;
              if (!(l_packet >> id)){ return; }
              Message msg((MessageType)EntityMessage::Hurt);
              msg.m_receiver = id;
              m_stateMgr->GetContext()->m_systemManager->
                GetMessageHandler()->Dispatch(msg);
              break;
          }
        }
      }
  }
```

First, we handle the connect packet that the server sends back to us after the client tries to reach it. If the entity ID and position were successfully extracted from the packet, the client mutex is locked while the player entity is added and its position is updated. The entity ID of our player is then stored in the `m_player` data member and passed in to our network system, which needs it. Note the very last line of code in this segment before we return. After the entity is successfully constructed, we're adding in a sound listener component to it. Naturally, there can only be one single sound listener on the client side, which is our player. This means that the `player.entity` file *does not* have its own sound listener component anymore. Instead, it must be added here in order to have correct audio positioning.

Next, if our client is already connected to the server, we're ready to process snapshot, hurt, and disconnect packets. If a snapshot is received, we first attempt to read the number of entities it contains and return if the reading fails. The client mutex is then locked and the current time is obtained in order to maintain continuity of entity snapshots. A new `for` loop is then constructed to run for each individual entity in the packet and extract its ID and snapshot data, which in turn is added to the network system for later processing.

If a disconnect packet is received from the server, we simply remove the game state and switch back to the main menu. Also, upon receiving a hurt packet, the entity ID in it is extracted and a `Hurt` message that is to be received by that entity is created and sent out.

Now, it's time to adjust the existing methods of our game state in order to have it try to establish a connection to the server upon creation:

```
void State_Game::OnCreate(){
  m_client->Setup(&State_Game::HandlePacket, this);
  if (m_client->Connect()){
    m_stateMgr->GetContext()->m_systemManager->
      GetSystem<S_Network>(System::Network)->SetClient(m_client);
    ...
    evMgr->AddCallback(StateType::Game, "Player_Attack",
      &State_Game::PlayerAttack, this);
    ...
  } else {
    std::cout << "Failed to connect to the game server!"
      << std::endl;
    m_stateMgr->Remove(StateType::Game);
    m_stateMgr->SwitchTo(StateType::MainMenu);
  }
}
```

First, the client's packet handler is assigned. We then attempt to connect to the server with whatever IP and port information exist inside the client class at this point. If the connection attempt was successful, we can start initializing our data members and add callbacks, one of which is a callback to a new method that handles the player attack button being pressed. If the connection wasn't successful, the game state is removed and we switch back to the main menu state instead.

If the game state is removed, some cleanup is in order:

```
void State_Game::OnDestroy(){
  m_client->Disconnect();
  m_client->UnregisterPacketHandler();
  S_Network* net = m_stateMgr->GetContext()->
    m_systemManager->GetSystem<S_Network>(System::Network);
  net->ClearSnapshots();
  net->SetClient(nullptr);
  net->SetPlayerID((int)Network::NullID);
  ...
  evMgr->RemoveCallback(StateType::Game, "Player_Attack");
  ...
}
```

In addition to the rest of the code that cleans up the game state, we must now also disconnect from the server and unregister the packet handler that is being used by the client class. The network system is also cleared of all snapshots it may currently hold, as well as any player information and pointers to the client class. The player attack callback is also removed here.

Naturally, we're going to want to alter the Update method of the game state a little as well:

```
void State_Game::Update(const sf::Time& l_time){
  if (!m_client->IsConnected()){
    m_stateMgr->Remove(StateType::Game);
    m_stateMgr->SwitchTo(StateType::MainMenu);
    return;
  }
  SharedContext* context = m_stateMgr->GetContext();
  UpdateCamera();
  m_gameMap->Update(l_time.asSeconds());
  {
    sf::Lock lock(m_client->GetMutex());
    context->m_systemManager->Update(l_time.asSeconds());
  }
}
```

The connection status of our client is first checked. Not being connected means we get to exit the game state and switch back to the main menu once again. Otherwise, we continue on with the updating. Note the curly brackets surrounding the system manager update call. They create a scope for any variables defined inside, which is useful for locking the client mutex with a sf::Lock instance, as it will fall out of scope once we're outside the brackets, in turn unlocking it.

Drawing things on screen also needs a slight adjustment:

```
void State_Game::Draw(){
  if (!m_gameMap){ return; }
  sf::Lock lock(m_client->GetMutex());
  for (int i = 0; i < Sheet::Num_Layers; ++i){
    m_gameMap->Draw(i);
    m_stateMgr->GetContext()->m_systemManager->
      Draw(m_stateMgr->GetContext()->m_wind, i);
  }
}
```

The only addition here is the client mutex lock right before we draw entities on different elevations in a `for` loop. We don't want another thread to manipulate any data that we may be currently accessing.

Lastly, the player attack button being pressed needs to be handled like this:

```
void State_Game::PlayerAttack(EventDetails* l_details){
  Message msg((MessageType)EntityMessage::Attack);
  msg.m_receiver = m_player;
  m_stateMgr->GetContext()->m_systemManager->
    GetMessageHandler()->Dispatch(msg);
}
```

It's quite simple. When an attack key is pressed, the entity component system has a new attack message sent to it. Our network system is subscribed to this message type and adds it to the player update container, which is going to be sent out to the server at a specific interval.

Main menu adjustments

Our client-server setup is now functional, but we are missing one more small addition in order to really make it work. We have no way of putting in our server information! Let's fix that by modifying the main menu interface file:

```
Interface MainMenu MainMenu.style 0 0 Immovable NoTitle "Main menu"
Element Label Title 100 0 MainMenuTitle.style "Main menu:"
Element Label IpLabel 0 32 DefaultLabel.style "IP:"
Element TextField IP 18 32 MainMenuTextfield.style "127.0.0.1"
Element Label PortLabel 150 32 DefaultLabel.style "Port:"
Element TextField PORT 175 32 MainMenuTextfield.style "5600"
Element Label NameLabel 50 56 DefaultLabel.style "Nickname:"
Element TextField Nickname 105 56 MainMenuTextfield.style "Player"
Element Label Play 0 80 MainMenuLabel.style "CONNECT"
```

```
Element Label Disconnect 0 116 MainMenuLabel.style "DISCONNECT"
Element Label Credits 0 152 MainMenuLabel.style "CREDITS"
Element Label Quit 0 188 MainMenuLabel.style "EXIT"
```

Quite a few new elements are added to the main menu here. We have three new text fields and some text labels that go next to them to let the user know what they're for. This is how server information, as well as the player nickname, is going to be entered. Let's make this happen by adding a few callbacks for the new buttons:

```cpp
void State_MainMenu::OnCreate(){
  SetTransparent(true); // Transparent for rendering.
  SetTranscendent(true); // Transcendent for updating.
  ...
  eMgr->AddCallback(StateType::MainMenu, "MainMenu_Play",
    &State_MainMenu::Play, this);
  eMgr->AddCallback(StateType::MainMenu, "MainMenu_Disconnect",
    &State_MainMenu::Disconnect, this);
  eMgr->AddCallback(StateType::MainMenu, "MainMenu_Quit",
    &State_MainMenu::Quit, this);
}

void State_MainMenu::OnDestroy(){
  ...
  gui->RemoveInterface(StateType::MainMenu, "MainMenu");
  eMgr->RemoveCallback(StateType::MainMenu, "MainMenu_Play");
  eMgr->RemoveCallback(StateType::MainMenu,"MainMenu_Disconnect");
  eMgr->RemoveCallback(StateType::MainMenu, "MainMenu_Quit");
}
```

To make the main menu feel interactive, we're going to want to update this interface each time the menu state is activated:

```cpp
void State_MainMenu::Activate(){
  GUI_Interface* menu = m_stateMgr->GetContext()->
    m_guiManager->GetInterface(StateType::MainMenu, "MainMenu");
  if(m_stateMgr->HasState(StateType::Game)){
    // Resume
    menu->GetElement("Play")->SetText("Resume");
    menu->GetElement("Disconnect")->SetActive(true);
    menu->GetElement("IP")->SetActive(false);
    menu->GetElement("PORT")->SetActive(false);
    menu->GetElement("IpLabel")->SetActive(false);
    menu->GetElement("PortLabel")->SetActive(false);
    menu->GetElement("NameLabel")->SetActive(false);
    menu->GetElement("Nickname")->SetActive(false);
```

```
      } else {
      // Play
      menu->GetElement("Play")->SetText("CONNECT");
      menu->GetElement("Disconnect")->SetActive(false);
      menu->GetElement("IP")->SetActive(true);
      menu->GetElement("PORT")->SetActive(true);
      menu->GetElement("IpLabel")->SetActive(true);
      menu->GetElement("PortLabel")->SetActive(true);
      menu->GetElement("NameLabel")->SetActive(true);
      menu->GetElement("Nickname")->SetActive(true);
   }
}
```

Depending on whether a game state exists or not, we set up the elements in our interface to reflect the current state of our connection.

Lastly, let's look at the callback methods of both connect and disconnect buttons:

```
void State_MainMenu::Play(EventDetails* l_details){
   if (!m_stateMgr->HasState(StateType::Game)){
      GUI_Interface* menu = m_stateMgr->GetContext()->
         m_guiManager->GetInterface(StateType::MainMenu, "MainMenu");
      std::string ip = menu->GetElement("IP")->GetText();
      PortNumber port = std::atoi(
         menu->GetElement("PORT")->GetText().c_str());
      std::string name = menu->GetElement("Nickname")->GetText();
      m_stateMgr->GetContext()->m_client->
         SetServerInformation(ip, port);
      m_stateMgr->GetContext()->m_client->SetPlayerName(name);
   }
   m_stateMgr->SwitchTo(StateType::Game);
}

void State_MainMenu::Disconnect(EventDetails* l_details){
   m_stateMgr->GetContext()->m_client->Disconnect();
}
```

The first check in the `Play` method is made to ensure the text field information is properly passed in to where it needs to go. Because we have the same button that's going to be pressed to both connect to the server and switch back to the game state once it exists, making sure the client instance's server and player name information is updated is important. We then switch to the game state, which could either mean that it has to be created, at which time the information we just passed in is used, or that it's simply brought back to being the dominant application state.

The disconnect button callback only invokes the client's Disconnect method, which in turn results to the game state terminating itself.

With that, we have a fully functional 2D multiplayer game where players can attack one another!

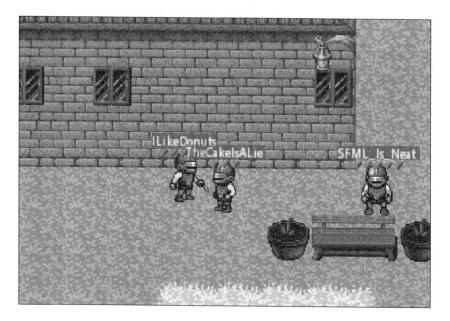

Summary

Congratulations! You have made it to the end! It has been quite a journey to take. With nothing more than some basic tools and concentrated effort, we have managed to create a small world. It may not have that much content in it, but that's where you come in. Just because you are done reading this book doesn't mean that either one of the three projects we covered is finished. In fact, this is only the beginning. Although we have covered a lot, there's still a plethora of features that you can implement on your own, such as different types of enemies, selectable player skins for the last project, magic and ranged attacks, animated map tiles, map transitions for the last project, a chat system, levels and experience for our RPG, and much more. Undoubtedly, you must have your own ideas and mechanics in mind that should instead be brought forth and realized in your games. Don't stop now; keep the flow going and get to coding!

Thank you so much for reading, and remember that ultimately whatever becomes of the world we created is in your hands, so make it a good one. Goodbye!

Index

E

ECS
  implementing 244-249
emulator 28
enemies
  adding 197-199
  loading, from map file 200
entities
  about 209
  animating 270-272
  entity manager, implementing 217-220
  managing 214-216
  used, for building characters 188, 189
entity component system
  about 209, 443
  bitmask 212-214
  client entity 482-484
  client network class, implementing 473-481
  combat, implementing 444-448
  component 210, 211
  expanding 466-470
  main class, adjusting 484-489
  main menu adjustments 489-491
  network class and interpolation 470-473
  position component 211, 212
  system management 482-484
entity events
  about 223
  event queue 224
entity manager
  factory pattern 220-222
  implementing 181-220
entity manager class
  defining 202-204
entity movement
  adding 255-258
  entity controller 268, 269
  movement system 258-264
  states, implementing 264
entity-on-tile collisions 174-179
entity storage and management 180, 181
entity types 166
event manager
  building 78-80
  defining 73-77
  expanding 340-345

  features 73
  implementing 80-86
Event Manager class
  improving 106-108
  integrating 86, 87
event queue 224
event types
  using 90

F

factory pattern 220-222
fixed time-step 32, 33
font management
  expanding 287

G

game class
  building 24, 25
  code, implementing 25, 26
game client
  developing 465
game framework
  building 20
game map 154, 155
game on pause
  defining 121-123
game server
  building 442, 443
  main server class 458, 459
  server action timing 448-450
  server entry point 464, 465
  server network system 450-452
  world class, implementing 459-464
game world
  building 156
  flyweight pattern 156, 157
  map class, designing 158-165
GUI element class
  defining 287-289
  implementing 289-295
GUI events
  defining 295, 296
GUI (Graphical User Interface)
  components 284
  defining 284
  GUI style 285

Thank you for buying
SFML Game Development By Example

About Packt Publishing

Packt, pronounced 'packed', published its first book, *Mastering phpMyAdmin for Effective MySQL Management*, in April 2004, and subsequently continued to specialize in publishing highly focused books on specific technologies and solutions.

Our books and publications share the experiences of your fellow IT professionals in adapting and customizing today's systems, applications, and frameworks. Our solution-based books give you the knowledge and power to customize the software and technologies you're using to get the job done. Packt books are more specific and less general than the IT books you have seen in the past. Our unique business model allows us to bring you more focused information, giving you more of what you need to know, and less of what you don't.

Packt is a modern yet unique publishing company that focuses on producing quality, cutting-edge books for communities of developers, administrators, and newbies alike. For more information, please visit our website at www.packtpub.com.

About Packt Open Source

In 2010, Packt launched two new brands, Packt Open Source and Packt Enterprise, in order to continue its focus on specialization. This book is part of the Packt Open Source brand, home to books published on software built around open source licenses, and offering information to anybody from advanced developers to budding web designers. The Open Source brand also runs Packt's Open Source Royalty Scheme, by which Packt gives a royalty to each open source project about whose software a book is sold.

Writing for Packt

We welcome all inquiries from people who are interested in authoring. Book proposals should be sent to author@packtpub.com. If your book idea is still at an early stage and you would like to discuss it first before writing a formal book proposal, then please contact us; one of our commissioning editors will get in touch with you.

We're not just looking for published authors; if you have strong technical skills but no writing experience, our experienced editors can help you develop a writing career, or simply get some additional reward for your expertise.

SFML Game Development

ISBN: 978-1-84969-684-5   Paperback: 296 pages

Learn how to use SFML 2.0 to develop your own feature-packed game

1. Develop a complete game throughout the book.

2. Learn how to use modern C++11 style to create a full featured game and support for all major operating systems.

3. Fully network your game for awesome multiplayer action.

4. Step-by-step guide to developing your game using C++ and SFML.

SFML Blueprints

ISBN: 978-1-78439-847-7   Paperback: 298 pages

Sharpen your game development skills and improve your C++ and SFML knowledge with five exciting projects

1. Master game components and their interaction by creating a hands-on multiplayer game.

2. Customize your game by adding sounds, animations, physics, and a nice user interface to create a unique game.

3. A project-based book starting with simpler projects and moving into increasingly complex projects to make you proficient in game development.

Please check **www.PacktPub.com** for information on our titles

SFML Essentials

ISBN: 978-1-78439-732-6   Paperback: 156 pages

A fast-paced, practical guide to building functionally enriched 2D games using the core concepts of SFML

1. Learn to utilize the features of SFML quickly to create interactive games.

2. Realize your game ideas by following practical tutorials based on the essential features of SFML.

3. Step-by-step guide describing the fundamental concepts of SFML with the help of plenty of examples.

Unity AI Programming Essentials

ISBN: 978-1-78355-355-6   Paperback: 162 pages

Use Unity3D, a popular game development ecosystem, to add realistic AI to your games quickly and effortlessly

1. Implement pathfinding, pathfollowing, and use navigation mesh generation to move your AI characters within the game environment.

2. Use behavior trees to design logic for your game characters and make them "think".

3. A practical guide that will not only cover the basics of AI frameworks but also will teach how to customize them.

Please check **www.PacktPub.com** for information on our titles

Printed in Great Britain
by Amazon

56288039R00289